GENERATIONS

Generations

An American Family

JOHN EGERTON

THE UNIVERSITY PRESS OF KENTUCKY

Publication of this volume was made possible in part by a grant
from the National Endowment for the Humanities.

Published by The University Press of Kentucky

Scholarly publisher for the Commonwealth,
serving Bellarmine University, Berea College, Centre
College of Kentucky, Eastern Kentucky University,
The Filson Historical Society, Georgetown College,
Kentucky Historical Society, Kentucky State University,
Morehead State University, Murray State University,
Northern Kentucky University, Transylvania University,
University of Kentucky, University of Louisville,
and Western Kentucky University.

Editorial and Sales Offices: The University Press of Kentucky
663 South Limestone Street, Lexington, Kentucky 40508-4008

Frontispiece: Homecoming, 1979. *Al Clayton*

07 06 05 04 03   5 4 3 2 1

Library of Congress Cataloging in Publication Data

Egerton, John.
  Generations: an American family.
  ISBN 0-8131-9059-2
  1. Ledford family. 2. United States—Social life
and customs. 3. United States—Social conditions.
  4. Family—United States. I. Title.
CT274.L43E38 1983
929′.2′0973   82-40465

This book is printed on acid-free recycled paper meeting the requirements of the
American National Standard for Permanence of Paper for Printed Library Materials.

Manufactured in the United States of America

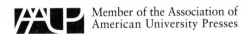 Member of the Association of
American University Presses

For Ann, who remembers:
If you keep a green bough in your heart,
the singing bird will come.

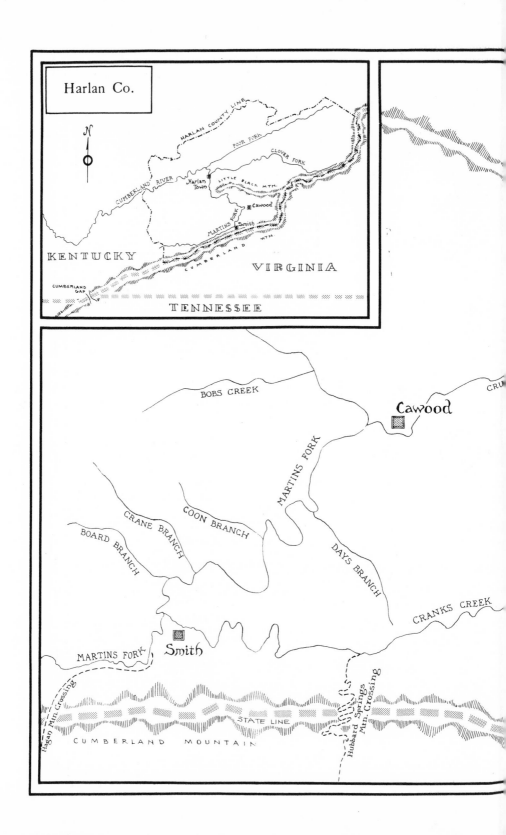

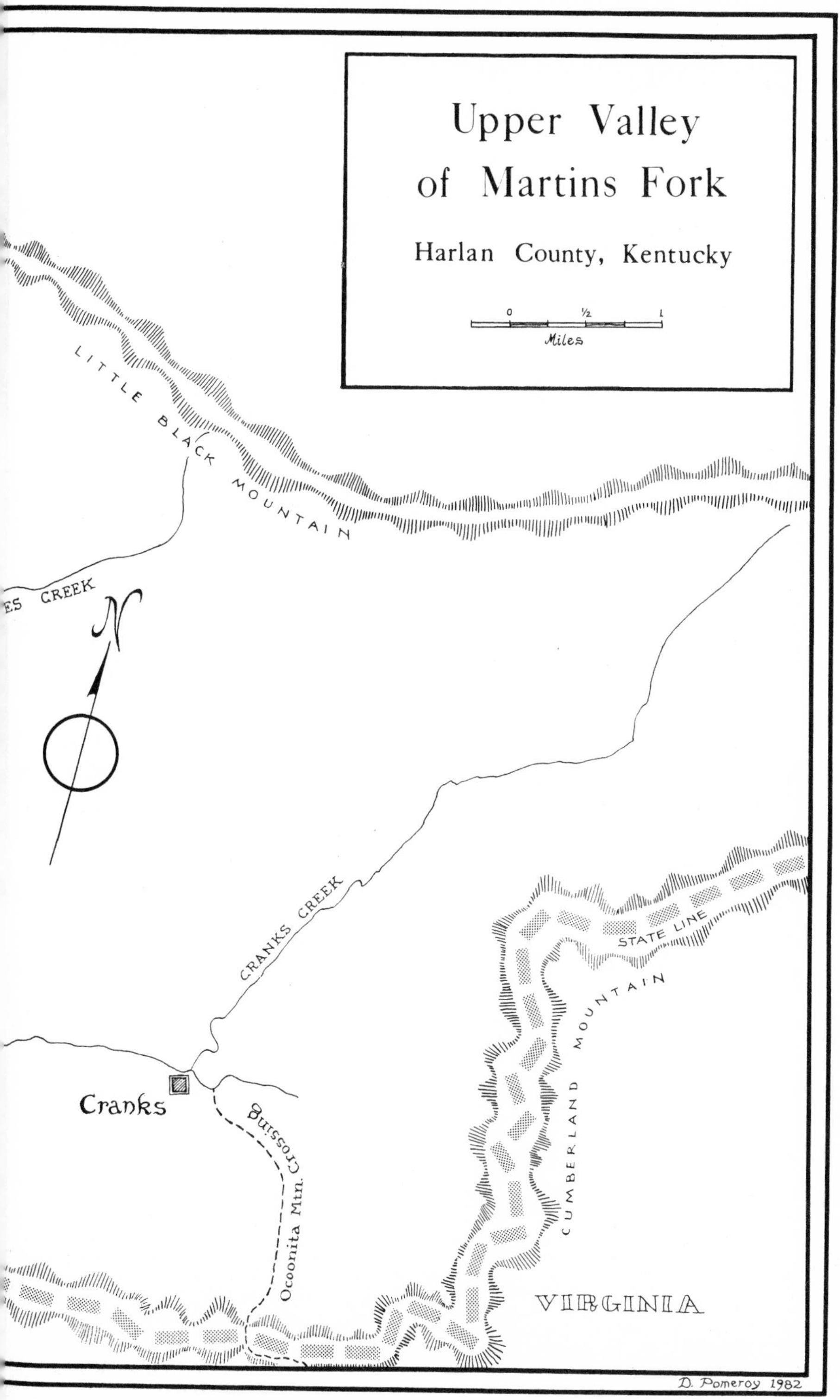

**Upper Valley
of Martins Fork**

Harlan County, Kentucky

0   ½   1
Miles

LITTLE BLACK MOUNTAIN

ES CREEK

N

CRANKS CREEK

STATE LINE

CUMBERLAND MOUNTAIN

Cranks

Crossing

Ocoonita Mtn.

VIRGINIA

D. Pomeroy 1982

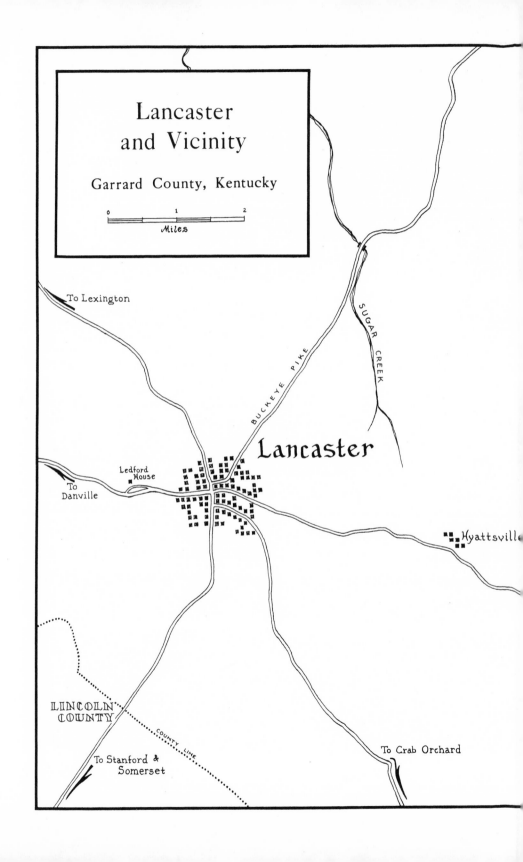

Lancaster
and Vicinity

Garrard County, Kentucky

0   1   2
Miles

To Lexington

SUGAR CREEK

BUCKEYE PIKE

Lancaster

Ledford
House

To
Danville

Hyattsville

LINCOLN
COUNTY

COUNTY LINE

To Stanford &
Somerset

To Crab Orchard

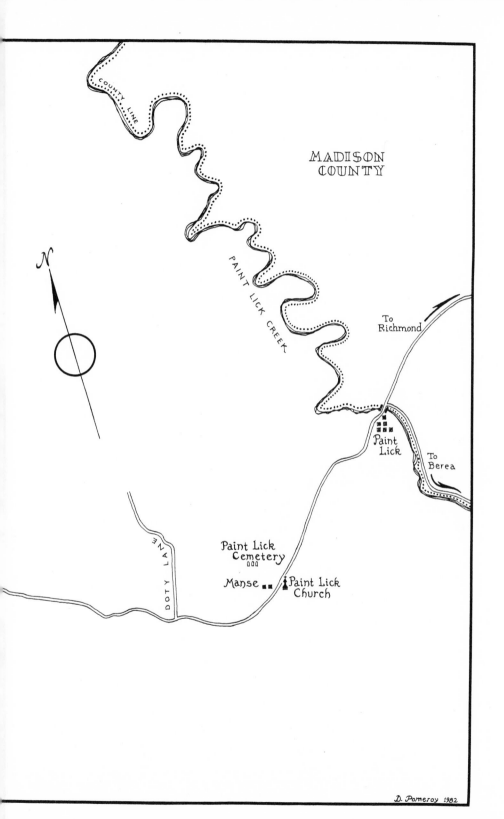

MADISON
COUNTY

N

PAINT LICK CREEK

COUNTY LINE

To
Richmond

Paint
Lick

To
Berea

DOTY LANE

Paint Lick
Cemetery

Manse ■ ■ ⚑ Paint Lick
Church

D. Pomeroy 1982

Contents

Photographs follow page 176

Acknowledgments

Six years passed between the conception of this book as an idea and its completion as a published work. That is a long gestation period. Had it not been for the help and encouragement of many people, I never would have been able to see it through. The dozens of Ledfords who welcomed me first as a stranger and then as a friend are due special thanks. I am also indebted to a number of very able and helpful librarians in Kentucky, Tennessee, North Carolina, and Virginia. In addition, more than a score of friends and associates and even chance acquaintances helped me with ideas, introductions, genealogical and historical research, manuscript criticism, photographs, maps, recollections, insights, professional judgment, moral support, and generous hospitality. For such gifts, I particularly want to express my gratitude to Sue Alston, David and Mary Britt, Charles F. Bryan Jr., Mavis Bryant, Will D. Campbell, Harry M. Caudill, Steven A. Channing, Kenneth Cherry, Joey Childers, Graham Egerton, Paul E. Fuller, Frye Gaillard, William C. Havard, Sharon Macpherson, J.A. McCauley, Father Isaac McDaniel, Bill Moyers, Gurney Norman, Bob and Jeanne Pitner, Helen and Henry Pope, O. Leonard Press, Frank Ritter, Dennis Smith, Randy Smith, Sam B. Smith, George Stoney, Lee Walker, Abner T. White, and Harmon Wray. If I have inadvertently overlooked anyone whose help sustained me, I sincerely apologize.

Finally and most especially, I want to acknowledge with deep appreciation the splendid photographs of Al Clayton, the excellent and indispensable maps of Dan E. Pomeroy, and the painstaking reproductions of old photographs by Leslie Pritikin.

One generation passes away, and another generation comes,
but the earth abides forever. The sun also rises,
and the sun goes down, and hastens to the place
where it rises. . . . What has been is what will be, and
what has been done is what will be done, and there is
nothing new under the sun. . . . There is no remembrance
of former things, nor will there be any remembrance
of later things yet to happen among those who come after.

—ECCLESIASTES

What was is no more. It is gone, changed
beyond recognition. But it lives and thrives
in the fecund soil of our remembrance.

Homecoming, 1978

By half past noon, the old man had finished his dinner and started through the house to the front porch. His narrow shoulders were hunched over an aluminum walker that he thrust ahead of him after each deliberate step. All about, people stood or sat in little clusters, talking, laughing. Their voices were a blended babble to his ears, their faces an unfocused blur to his watery blue eyes. They made way for him as he approached, and then watched in respectful silence as he shuffled through the living room and out the screen door.

He slumped down heavily in his accustomed chair, a painted wooden rocker, from which he could lean forward and spit tobacco juice into the grass. With a small pocket knife, he carved a dark chunk of Day's Work, his favorite plug, and stuck it between his toothless gums. The spring air was warm and humid, and no breeze stirred in the porch shade, but the old man seemed not to mind; neither the weather nor his labored walk through the house had brought sweat to his brow.

There was in his appearance a curiously contrasting show of forcefulness and vulnerability, a mingling of durable and fragile features. He was neatly dressed in a dark blue linen suit, a gold shirt that fit loosely about his thin neck, a multicolored nylon tie with a fist-sized knot, and a polished pair of wing-tip cordovan shoes. He clutched a tobacco-stained handkerchief in his gnarled hands. His hair—what remained of it—grew in a narrow fringe above his collar; it was as soft and fine as duck down, and its color matched the stark whiteness of his eyebrows. Warm sunshine had given his face and scalp a healthy looking touch of tan, and the veins in his temples stood out beneath his translucent skin with the blue-under-brown softness of a candled egg. His habitual smile often broke into laughter, and when he spoke, his voice was resonant with strength and good cheer.

"Well, I'm 102 years and two days old today, but I feel fifty years younger," he sang out, looking around into the hazy sea of faces. "You reckon I'll live another century?"

He was a centenarian wonder to his family and friends, a man stooped and bent but unbroken, a high-spirited elder whose mind resisted the toll of time even as his body yielded grudgingly to it. His guests came one or two at a time to sit within range of his sight and hearing and wish him a happy birthday, and at that distance he recognized almost all of them. He grasped the men's hands firmly in his own, kissed the women and girls, teased the children, charmed one and all.

"You're mighty pretty," he told one visitor, a matronly lady with tinted blue hair. "I thought you was some little girl."

"How many people do you think are here?" someone asked him.

"I don't know," he replied. "There's a whole bunch, though— so many I can't count them all. Children, grandchildren, great-grandchildren, nieces and nephews. It does me a lot of good to see them all. I'm mighty proud of every one of them." He paused a moment, and when he spoke again, his voice was softer:

"I was feeling pretty low yesterday. I got to thinking maybe it'd be best if I just died today, while everybody was here, so I could save them the trouble of coming back. But now, seeing them all, and having such a nice day, it's given me a new lease on life. I think I'll just live a while longer. I've always said if I live past March, I'll live the rest of the year. Now it's May, so I guess I'll stay around at least until winter." He laughed and squinted, and the lines at the corners of his eyes deepened and flared like wheel spokes.

While the old man talked, his wife sat erect and tranquil in a ladder-back oak chair a few feet behind and to the left of his rocker. Ignoring his cheerful banter, she chatted quietly with the relatives and friends who came one by one to bring her greetings and good wishes. She was wearing a striped silk dress, a light sweater, stockings, and soft black leather shoes. A single strand of pearls hung about her neck. Her silver hair was pulled up to the crown of her head and held there with a turtle-shell pin. She had high cheekbones, a prominent nose and chin, and no teeth. Her eyebrows, dark and thick, accentuated the gray-green clarity of her eyes, which seemed to bear a shadowy hint of sadness. Her expression was masked and unchanging, and her manner was as subdued as her husband's was outgoing. She could see and hear better than he, and it was her habit to watch and listen more—and to say less.

"I almost didn't know you with that mustache and all that hair, Eddie," she said softly to a grandson who stood before her, smiling shyly. "It's nice to have you here. I'm glad to see all of you with good jobs, or going to college." Others followed Eddie, and she called each of them by name. Her greetings were reserved, almost formal.

She had once been a large woman, but age had taken away some of the weight, leaving soft folds of wrinkled skin on her forearms and beneath her chin. Still, she bore her age well, and with a stoic strength, as if she had survived sorrow and outlived disappointment. Her handsome old face, her quick, knowing eyes, and the measured ration of her words made her seem hard to know— but all the more interesting.

When she was alone for a moment, she gazed out across the yard. "It looks like a playground," she said, touching a crooked forefinger to her lips. "There's enough children here to make a school."

Sunday, May 28, 1978, in Lancaster, Garrard County, Kentucky: As they had on almost every Memorial Day weekend since the Great Depression, Curtis Burnam Ledford and Addie King Ledford welcomed their family home for a celebration of the patriarch's birthday. To have all of their descendants present at once had long since become an impossibility, for the children and grandchildren, the wives and husbands and great-grandchildren, had grown in number well beyond a hundred and had fanned out from

Kentucky to Ohio and Florida and California, to a dozen states, even overseas. But more than half of them were there, and others were with them—nieces, nephews, cousins, neighbors, family friends—and they filled the six-room frame house and the front yard with laughter and conversation, with picnic coolers and covered dishes, with old acquaintance and mellow recollection and oft-told tales. The traditional American family homecoming—an institution as certain as sunrise, as perennial as political rallies, as enduring as church on Sunday—had become for the Ledfords an occasion of particular significance.

Burnam and Addie—Papa and Mama, Grandpa and Grandma—made it so. They had lived in the same modest house on the edge of Lancaster for five decades, lived in the same county as man and wife for nearly 75 years, lived in Kentucky for a century, more or less—he for all of his 102 years, she for all of her 93. They had produced thirteen children, and ten of them had survived to adulthood; in succeeding generations, they could count thirty-two grandchildren and thirty-nine great-grandchildren. With each passing year the longevity of the elders and the continued growth of the family made the celebration of their kinship more important to them. They were an uncommon union of four living generations, a single family bound together by blood and affinity across a century of continuity and change.

And more by blood than affinity. Not that they disliked one another, far from it; rather, they were simply *un*like one another, more diverse than uniform. In their many pursuits they resembled a broad cross-section of American life and work: merchant, salesman, engineer, nurse, homemaker, farmer, banker, secretary, student, chemist, bureaucrat, surveyor, clerk, lawyer, lineman, mechanic, teacher. They ranged in age from more than seventy in the second generation to less than one in the fourth. They came to the Memorial Day gathering in sedans and vans and station wagons, came in coats and ties, polyester pantsuits, bellbottom jeans. They were short and tall, stout and thin, plain and pretty, long-haired and bald-headed. They were outgoing and reserved, as close as brothers and sisters, as distant as strangers. They proudly displayed their kids and their cars and their cooking, talked about politics and the weather and the price of gasoline, argued about sports, laughed at good stories well told, and quietly discussed the health of the elders whose long lives held them all together.

Journalists and social analysts and poll-takers who roam the country in search of clues to the American character could have found a useful sample there. To be sure, it was not a fully representative sample; it included no one who was rich or poor, no racial or ethnic minorities, few Catholics or Jews or Democrats. But in one important respect—in the way they had evolved over a century as diverse and contrasting figures in the national mosaic—they were typically, quintessentially American, middle-class to the core, contributing members of the great central body of citizens whose favor has been courted by every politician since Andrew Jackson. Like the familiar characters in the modern American dream-myth—familiar because they are us—the Ledfords were an upwardly mobile, geographically dispersed, conservative-leaning, moderately religious family of job-holding, goods-buying, sports-loving, television-watching people, their place firmly fixed on the rounded crest of the bell curve that symbolizes the mainstream majority in the United States.

Seven of the nine surviving children of Burnam and Addie Ledford were present at the homecoming. There was C.B. Jr., known as Bill, a retired banker from Mt. Sterling, Kentucky, and at sixty-nine the eldest son; Carl, just retired from his laundromat business in Somerset, Kentucky; and Herbert, a Somerset banker who was beginning to give less time to his work and more to his farm and horses. Once these three had all been in the grocery business, they and their late brother, Bruce—and Bruce, a navy veteran and the only one of the children to become a Catholic, had also been the only son to move away from Kentucky. He had died in Toledo, Ohio, in 1969, at the age of fifty.

Four of their sisters were there: Dorothy Jackson, who worked in a Danville, Kentucky, department store; Jennie McLendon, a cashier for A&P in Lexington; Tillie King, who lived and worked in Indianapolis; and Gwen Gastineau, a farmer's wife, the only one of her generation to remain in Garrard County, and at age fifty the youngest of the Ledford children. The eldest, Eloise Beatty, seventy-one, was at her home in Boulder, Colorado. The only other daughter who was not present was Lucille Smith, who lived in Toledo.

The grandchildren were harder to trace. Bill's Billy, at forty-two the eldest, was on a golf course in Mt. Sterling with his two teenage sons. Carl's James, the youngest at nineteen, was at work in Somerset. Tillie's Gary was racing his car at a drag strip near Nicholasville, Kentucky, and Herb's Sarah was at a horse show in Danville. Bruce's John Bruce was in Lexington; Eloise's Mary Ellen was in Minnesota; Jennie's Bruce was in California; Lucille's David was in Germany. Others were scattered from Delaware to Florida to Colorado. Even among those who were present—Polly and Becky and Emily and Bobbie Jo, Richard and David and Stephen and Jerry and a half-dozen more—there was occasional confusion and uncertainty about who lived where, who did what, who belonged to whom. And the children of the grandchildren—the multitude of playing, giggling, crying, sleeping young—were too numerous to sort and count. About all of them, Burnam Ledford was proudly philosophical. "It's like planting seeds," he said. "They keep coming up. They're still going out all over, out in the world."

Cameras clicked, freezing scenes to be remembered in another year, another decade. Old photographs were brought out for review: an 1899 picture of Burnam as a young man with his brothers and sisters, gathered around Jesse and Vesta Ledford, their parents; and a memorable portrait, brown with age, of Burnam and Addie in 1904, the year after their marriage—he in a dark coat and tie, looking trim and stylish with his hair slicked down and curled in little half-moons on his forehead, she standing tall and pretty in a floor-length black taffeta dress with full sleeves and a high collar, her chestnut brown hair piled high and pinned up the way she would always wear it.

Except for the photographs, not much existed as a record of the Ledfords' lives. A fire that destroyed their house in 1913 took with it whatever written account there had been of the ancestors.

In the sixty-five years since, very little apparently had been pre-served—no family Bible, no diaries or journals, few letters. There was not much in the public record, either, for among all the members of the family from Burnam and Addie forward (or, for that matter, from Burnam and Addie back), there was no famous or infamous character, no figure of prominence or controversy, no politician or preacher or creative artist or notorious person who had been written up in the papers. Like the vast majority of Americans, past and present, they had been relatively anonymous people, just ordinary folks; they had not "made" history, in the customary usage of that term.

But they had seen history, and lived it, and participated, how-ever indirectly, in its shaping; inevitably, inescapably, they were both beneficiaries and victims of their nation's history. Without a single celebrity to draw attention to their lives, the Ledfords could claim a long and interesting past that was at once unique to them and common to millions of their fellow citizens, a past that stretched from eighteenth-century Europe to the modern United States.

The families whose successive unions had led to the marriage of Curtis Burnam Ledford and Addie King in Harlan County, Kentucky, in 1903 had followed the westward route of countless thousands of immigrants and pioneers and settlers. It had taken them the better part of a century to get from England to Tidewater Virginia, through the interior to the Blue Ridge Mountains and beyond, down the Great Valley of Virginia to the ancient gorge of the New River, south into the Piedmont hills of North Carolina, north-west across the corners of Virginia and Tennessee to the Cumberland Gap, through the gap to the heart of the Appalachians, and finally into the deep and distant hollows of Harlan County. When they arrived there early in the nineteenth century, the vast region of un-utterable beauty that lay behind them had been seized from its native inhabitants and made the new frontier of European immigration. Ahead lay more wilderness, and it too would be taken in time. But the ancestors of Burnam Ledford and Addie King chose not to con-tinue westward; instead, they settled in the Kentucky mountains, and there they put down roots that would grow a century deep,

four generations deep, so deep that the prior passage of their forebears from England to Virginia and North Carolina would become
obscured and finally be forgotten, lost beyond remembering. In
Harlan County, the Ledfords and their pathfinding kin and friends
would outlast every living thing, even the virgin timber; only the
coal and the rocks and the rivers would predate their tenure there.

As far back as Burnam Ledford and Addie King knew, their
ancestors had been Kentuckians, transplanted if not native Kentuckians; more than that, they had all been mountaineers, Harlan
Countians. But in 1889, almost a hundred years after the first
Ledford set foot there, another migration began. On a mild morning in December, the father of Burnam Ledford set out with his
family in ox-drawn covered wagons for Garrard County, 135 miles
to the northwest in the knobby foothills that separate the mountains from the fertile Bluegrass region of Kentucky. Seven years
later, after the family had lived on six different small farms in
Garrard County, Burnam Ledford went back to Harlan County to
teach school; by 1903, he had met and married Addie King there
and returned to Garrard County to stay.

For the young farmer and his bride, the relocation did not rep-
resent a radical severing of the ties that bind. Burnam's parents
were with them in Garrard County, but most of their kin remained
in the mountains; Addie's father was dead and her mother had remarried, but she too had scores of relatives in Harlan County. They
visited back and forth occasionally, maintaining the family connec-
tions, keeping the stories of their forebears fresh in their minds
through frequent retelling.

But time eroded and withered the roots; finally, nothing much
remained except the old stories, and almost no one was left to tell
them except Burnam and Addie. They still had a few cousins back
in the mountains, but no brothers and sisters, no aunts and uncles,
no close kin. No one but they could relate from personal recollection the tales that gave substance to their families' lives in a nineteenth-century mountain society.

Even after they had been gone from that society for three-quar-
ters of a century, there remained a sense in which Harlan County

was still "home" for Burnam and Addie Ledford. It mattered little that they no longer went there to visit—mattered not at all, in fact, for the Harlan County they had known was so vastly changed as to be almost unrecognizable to them, and all but a very few of the people they had known there were gone. What mattered was that the Harlan County of old, the isolated mountain precinct of their childhood and youth, was still vividly present in their thoughts and memories, and neither the multitude of physical changes nor the passage of more than seven decades could erase the images from their minds.

For the children of the elder Ledfords, however, the Harlan County of past and present held no personal significance, no attraction; to them, "going home" meant going to the house of their parents in Lancaster, or to one of the other Garrard County locations they had known when they were growing up. And for the generations after them, for the grandchildren and great-grandchildren of Burnam and Addie Ledford, home in the latter half of the twentieth century had come to mean towns and cities and suburban communities all over the United States. Increasingly, the descendants of the senior Ledfords had become pilgrims, seekers after greener fields and greater fortunes, just as their ancestors had been. Most of them knew no more of Harlan County, or even of Garrard County, than their mountain forebears had known of North Carolina and Virginia and England. Six of Burnam and Addie's children still lived in Kentucky, but none of them had ever lived in Harlan County, and only one had remained in Garrard. And when the Ledfords gathered for their reunion in 1978, more than thirty of the grandchildren and great-grandchildren could no longer call Kentucky home—if, indeed, they ever could.

LANCASTER WANTS INDUSTRY. FOLLOW THE KENTUCKY WILDCATS. EAT MORE BEEF. ENJOY SMOKING. GET RIGHT WITH GOD. Signs of the times around Garrard County in 1978. The main road through Lancaster, U.S. Highway 27, was a major north-south artery long before Interstate 75 was built parallel to it twenty miles to the east. Now, scenes along the old highway between Lexington and Lancaster told how typical—and how singular—this middle-American landscape was. Mobile home parks and subdivisions of brick and frame and stone houses were interspersed with fields of corn and tobacco, farmhouses and barns, and large old country estates, pillared mansions dating from the nineteenth-century golden age of the landed gentry. A drive-in theater near Nicholasville advertised a double feature: *Rape in the Suburbs* and *Teenage Passion*. Traffic crawled through the narrow streets of the old towns, past banks and churches and merchants' stores, past shady homes turned antique shops with jockey-boy statues on the lawn. On the outer fringes of the towns, shopping centers coaxed a thriving trade to their supermarkets and fast-food outlets.

South of Nicholasville, in the Camp Nelson National Cemetery, fallen soldiers of every American conflict since the Civil War lay in peace beneath the manicured and shaded sod. Beyond, a modern bridge crossed high above the Kentucky River, and in the gorge far below, where the old bridge still stretched between the limestone palisades, a bluegrass music festival was in holiday session. Across the river was Garrard County, an arrowhead-shaped, 236-square-mile jurisdiction of rolling hills, grassy meadows, streams and woodlands and furrowed fields and craggy outcroppings of stone.

It had been the home of three Kentucky governors, and it was named for a fourth: James Garrard, the state's second chief executive, who served in the final years of the eighteenth century. In 1970, the county population of about 9,500 was almost the same as it had been in 1810, thirteen years after its founding in the administration of Governor Garrard. There had been fluctuations in its population and in the size and nature of its farming operations in that long span of years, but Garrard County (its natives pronounced it "Garrid") remained essentially as it had always been: a small, rural, agricultural district, at the center of which was the county seat, Lancaster.

The town had grown up at the junction of two pioneer roads. East and west, the road connected Boonesborough and Harrodsburg, the oldest of Kentucky's frontier settlements; north and south, it linked Lexington with Crab Orchard and the famous Wilderness

Road. The intersection, formerly known as Wallace Crossroads, was given the name Lancaster when the county was formed in 1796, and a courthouse was built in the center of the square where the roads met. After the Civil War, the old courthouse was razed and a new one was erected on the southwest corner of the square; it stood there still in 1978, a two-story brick structure with Greek Revival columns and a domed clock tower topped by a weather vane.

History was no stranger to the Lancaster crossroads. Within a period of two centuries and a radius of forty miles had passed Daniel Boone, Abraham Lincoln's grandfather Abraham, Henry Clay, Cassius Marcellus Clay, Harriet Beecher Stowe, John Hunt Morgan, Carry Nation, lesser-known governors, congressmen, and judges, and innumerable heroes and villains, red, white, and black. Indian wars, the Revolutionary War, the Civil War had reached there. Speculators from Virginia had come early to grab the best land and to amass huge estates, but in time most of the estates were subdivided into smaller farms and sold to a new wave of settlers from the mountains, among them the father of Burnam Ledford. Another generation of speculators had passed through Lancaster on their way to Florida in the booming 1920s—and a decade later, many of them trudged back along the same route when the boom turned to bust and the Great Depression took its toll.

At Paint Lick in Garrard County, where the Ledfords lived when they first moved from the mountains, the Presbyterian Church in which Burnam worshipped as a young man had been founded in 1783, and Burnam could remember being there more than a century later, when the memory of war was still fresh: Republican Unionists sat on the right, Democrat Confederates on the left, and blacks in the balcony. In the cemetery nearby—one of the oldest known to exist west of the Allegheny Mountains—Ledfords had been laid to rest among soldiers, slaveowners, abolitionists, and former slaves. And when William O. Bradley of Lancaster was elected Kentucky's first Republican governor in 1895, nineteen-year-old Burnam Ledford had ridden on horseback from Paint Lick to stand atop a platform on the public square and hear Bradley address a cheering hometown crowd.

For the younger Ledfords who came to celebrate their patriarch's birthday in 1978, history was not a subject of overriding importance. They had heard the tales of pioneer migrations, of battles won and lost, of famous people's exploits, but they had remembered little; not even the stories of their own family's odyssey were altogether clear and complete in their minds. For most of them, history was a lifeless string of facts and dates, almost an abstraction; history was something that had happened to someone else.

For their elders in the old house in Lancaster, however, it was much more. In their reconstruction of it, history was a concrete and personal thing, a continuous story in which they and their forebears and their descendants were directly involved. In their eyes, it bound the past to the present, the distant to the near-at-hand; it made unknown people important, ordinary places extraordinary, common things significant. History gave meaning and continuity to their lives. From stories passed on to them by their elders, from their own witness and involvement and recollection, Burnam and Addie Ledford had become oral chroniclers of their time, and of a time before their time. From childhood, they had listened and remembered; now they were travelers from another age, the last survivors of a time and place that was almost lost and forgotten.

"I went to see my great-grandmother on Cranks Creek in Harlan County in 1881, when I was five years old," Burnam Ledford said to a visitor at his side. "She was born in 1791, when George Washington was president. She was Aley's Betsy, the widow of Aley Ledford, the man that brought our family name into Kentucky. We called her Blind Granny—she'd been blind for years—and I remember when they took me to see her she was sitting up in a big chair, and she called me to her, drew me up close and felt of my face and head to find out who in the family I resembled. Betsy Farmer she had been, daughter of Stephen and Nancy Farmer, and sister of Jim, old Surveyor Jim, who was Addie's great-grandfather. Granny was 101 years old when she died. I believe she's buried there in the old Wash Smith Cemetery on Cranks Creek."

The names and dates and incidents poured forth, washed over his listeners, and evaporated in the afternoon air. Burnam's knowledge was impressive, even awesome, and so was Addie's—but it was simply too much for anyone to assimilate. "Grandpa and Grandma remember everything," said one of the young men who stood nearby. "They know so many stories, and they keep telling them over and over—so they won't forget them, I guess."

History lived in them. In the year of Burnam Ledford's birth, the United States celebrated its first century as a nation, Alexander Graham Bell introduced the telephone, Mark Twain published *The Adventures of Tom Sawyer,* and General George Custer died at the Battle of Little Big Horn. When Addie King was born, there were thirty-eight states in the Union, Kentucky was among the nation's leaders in homicides (and little else), and Grover Cleveland, a Democrat and a bachelor, was about to become the twenty-second president of the United States.

They were old enough in the final years of the nineteenth century and the beginning of the twentieth to be lastingly impressed when the Spanish-American War started, when Carry Nation (born Carry Moore in Garrard County) launched her anti-saloon crusade, and when Theodore Roosevelt became the nation's youngest president. The Panama Canal was begun the same year they were wed, and Henry Ford built his first automobile that year, and Cassius Marcellus Clay, the fearless and controversial Kentucky abolitionist, died at the age of ninety-three. And on the day before Burnam and Addie were married, Orville and Wilbur Wright launched their fragile airplane at Kitty Hawk, North Carolina.

Coincidences, yes, but more than that: When Alexander Graham Bell's telephone was first introduced in the mountains of Eastern Kentucky (and after it, Thomas Edison's electric light), Burnam Ledford and Addie King looked upon it with an awe beyond forgetting, as if it had been invented there that very day. Later, when they were youthful teachers in the one-room schools of Harlan County, the fate of General Custer had become a part of the history they taught, and the works of Mark Twain a part of the literature. Burnam could remember supporting William McKinley, "a good Republican," in his presidential campaign against William Jennings Bryan—and he also recalled reading later in the Louisville *Courier-*

Journal, his main source of news, that McKinley had been assassinated.

But for illness, Burnam would have been a soldier in the Spanish-American War instead of a teacher in the Kentucky mountains. He was from the first an avid supporter of Teddy Roosevelt, and once he had the pleasure of shaking hands with the Bull Moose. He and Addie were never crusaders like Carry Nation, but they spoke out nonetheless for prohibition in Garrard County. Burnam proudly claimed a personal acquaintance—and even a distant kinship—with Cassius Marcellus Clay. And finally, the automobile was more than just a passing marvel in Burnam Ledford's memory, for in 1918, the greatest tragedy of his life resulted from the wreck of a Model T made by Henry Ford. History was not simply an abstraction to the Ledfords; it was central to their understanding of life, and they spoke of its prominent figures and pivotal events as if they had been personally acquainted with them.

"Fellow named Czolgosz shot McKinley," Addie Ledford said to one of her afternoon visitors. "C-z-o-l-g-o-s-z. A Russian. That was in 1901. I was sixteen years old. McKinley didn't die right away—he lived for several days. Just before he died, he said, 'God's will be done.' I read that somewhere."

"I don't see how you can remember all that, Grandma. How far back can you remember?"

"Oh, to about 1890, I guess—that's when I was five years old. My father died when I was ten, and I remember him real well. He was sheriff of Harlan County for two terms, and then Harrison made him a U.S. marshal, a revenue man."

"Who was Harrison?"

"Benjamin Harrison," she replied. "President Benjamin Harrison."

Their day had begun early, as usual: awake by six, up and stirring, then coffee, toast, and eggs for breakfast at the chrome and formica table in the kitchen, the ritual occasionally punctuated by high-decibel conversation about the food or the weather or someone in the family.

But this was no ordinary day; it was homecoming, the day to

celebrate the old man's long-ago birth, and they had awakened eager for it to begin. As soon as the dishes were cleared away, Burnam and Addie had taken turns bathing and dressing, using the tiny bathroom off the kitchen—a convenience that was a latter-day addition to the spare and simple farmhouse. Then she had swept the front porch, and he had sat by the front window in the bedroom to read awhile and make the time pass more quickly. Daughter Gwen came earlier than usual to help them, and Tillie was there from Indianapolis, and Dorothy drove over from Danville. The rest of the children followed. There was a flurry of last-minute cleaning and straightening, and soon the kitchen was crowded with people and their offerings of food and drink. By the stroke of twelve, family and friends were everywhere—not just a few or a dozen or a score of them, but a throng.

The old house creaked and sagged under so many feet. After a half-century as the family homeplace, it showed its age even more clearly than its two elderly residents showed theirs. The house was an anachronism, an unaltered throwback to the World War I decade of its construction. Like most modest old houses of its period, it seemed to face outward to the porch and the yard and the road, as if it were open to the world. It had no shutters at its windows, no air conditioning to close it off from summer breezes, no double locks on its glass-paned doors, no lack of chairs on its well-worn porch. It was a typically plain family farmhouse, an average-looking middle-class dwelling anchored at the geographical center of Kentucky—which was itself a middle-ground buffer zone and blending place between the South and the Midwest and the North. Neither the house nor the family it had sheltered for so long had ever been far from the center, where the beliefs and habits and practices of Americans are repeated so often that they are labeled "typical" or "common."

From a single nucleus, this family had spawned nearly three dozen of the more than 56 million family units in the United States. They were one and many, a confederacy of independent citizens united by a bond of allegiance to their elders.

"Well, if we stay here long enough, we'll get old, won't we?"

Burnam Ledford said. "That's something you can't stave off. I can still take care of myself—but I'm nearly a hundred years older than this boy here." He looked down at Casey Bryant, a snaggle-toothed three-year-old in blue jeans and a cowboy hat, who was climbing on his great-grandfather's aluminum walker, playing peek-a-boo with the old man. Someone took their picture. Casey eyed the thirty-five-millimeter camera expectantly.

"Show me the picture," he said. "Why won't it come out?" He waited in vain for a snapshot with his image on it to issue from the camera's underside. After a minute, he lost interest and returned to his game.

"Did you know your birthday is the same as John Wayne's, Papa?" one of Burnam's sons asked.

"John who?"

"John Wayne—you know, the big movie star."

"Uh-huh. How old is he?"

"About seventy-one, I think."

Burnam chuckled. "Just a young fellow. I never did go to the movies much, but I guess I've seen him on TV."

The porch talk turned to former President Richard Nixon, who the night before at his home in San Clemente, California, had entertained a group of American servicemen, former prisoners of war in Vietnam.

"I always felt like Nixon was a good president," Burnam said. "I voted for him three times. I've been reading *All the President's Men*. Nixon was a good man—but the men he had under him, they were the ones that got him in trouble. They wanted to break him. Some of them was Democrats, too." His listeners nodded in agreement.

"The whole government's in a mess," someone said, "and Jimmy Carter isn't helping it a bit. All they know how to do is throw away money. And starting tomorrow, a postage stamp will cost you fifteen cents."

"Yeah. Not so long ago, it was three cents—and the mail service was better then than it is now."

"I ran the post office in the store at Cawood eighty years ago,"

Burnam said. "The winter of 1898. I was just twenty-two years old. Back then, that was the only post office in the whole southern end of Harlan County. I had been teaching school there on Days Branch, and when school let out, this fellow that ran the store came to me and offered me a job. . . ."

All afternoon the conversations continued. The elder Ledfords never left their seats on the porch, and neither of them showed any signs of tiring. They sampled the birthday cake decorated with the numbers "102," but their main nourishment was talk.

By five o'clock, the guests had begun to leave, and the shadows of the shade trees had lengthened across the yard. The faint aroma of wild rose and honeysuckle on the fence row lent a sweet fragrance to the air.

"I bet you'll sleep good tonight, Mama," one of the daughters said.

Addie smiled ever so slightly. "Yes, but I'll be rising early, by half past six. Been used to it all my life."

The sun was a crimson circle on the edge of the horizon woods when the last visitors departed. "I hope I'll be here when you come back," Burnam said to one of them. "If I'm gone, you'll know they had to take me away in a box." He chuckled. "I'll try my best to stay around. Wouldn't want you to make the trip for nothing."

Back in the kitchen, they ate a little supper, and then they returned to the porch and sat quietly for an hour or so, letting the day and the dusk and the dark settle their thoughts. Lightning bugs flickered in the grass. Crickets and their insect kin commenced an evensong chorus. As if inspired by their example, Burnam began to sing one of his favorite hymns, and Addie soon joined in. Another Memorial Day was over. It was full dark when they went inside to bed.

ONE

The Last Ones Left

We were perfect strangers when we met, but I had been looking for Burnam and Addie Ledford for a long time.

The search had begun in my mind on a summer day in 1976. By chance, by sheer good fortune, I found myself sitting on the cabin porch of a 105-year-old woman in the marshy low country of South Carolina. At the beginning of the nation's third century, she could remember the start of the second—and in her vividly drawn impressions of nineteenth-century Carolina there was a sense of timelessness that could have belonged as well to the eighteenth-century birth of the nation. In the clarity of her recollections, in the specific detail of her observations, in the grace and eloquence of her language, the old woman was spellbinding; it was as if she had taken me on a personal tour of the past.

I came away from that experience with a heightened awareness of the treasures that waste away in the minds and memories of the elderly. The greatest gift they have to offer—their vision of the past—is too often unappreciated, neglected, ignored. The very old ones lived in a world unseen by the rest of us, a world long since vanished. Their memories evoke the sight and smell and feel of homespun clothes and handmade tools and candlelit cabins by the creek. And when they were young, they knew old people from a time when England claimed most of this continent and the United States was still a revolutionary dream. There remains a remnant of elderly Americans who have seen and heard every generation of citizens in the history of this nation. They are the last connecting link between our ancestors and ourselves. When their time is gone—

and it will not be long—there will be none who remember the nineteenth century.

From my encounter with the South Carolina centenarian, an idea evolved. It began, as a succession of questions: How accurate are the stories of the elderly? How typical? How complete? Can they be drawn out in conversation? Can they be verified? Are they consistent enough and lively enough to sustain interest? In the recent works of other writers—Alex Haley, Irving Howe, Theodore Rosengarten, Ernest Gaines, Studs Terkel, to name a few—I subsequently found both fiction and nonfiction that appeared to be inspired by the same kinds of questions. Looking beyond the power-wielders of history—the kings and presidents and generals—these writers had found among the uncelebrated masses, about whom history is seldom written, some portraits from the past that glowed with realism and authenticity.

Thinking of these efforts to explain us to ourselves, and thinking of the very old among us, I began to wonder whether a true story about continuity and change in four or five living generations of one family would add anything of value to our understanding and appreciation of our evolution as a people. Could I find a family whose collective life stories were sufficiently diverse to be typical or representative of the majority of Americans? Could I find an elderly couple with accurate and detailed recollections of their lives since the nineteenth century, and older stories passed on to them from an earlier time? Would there be enough people and enough variety in the couple's succeeding generations to form a complete picture? Could I gather and assemble this family biography in such a way that it could be seen as a social history of our national experience, a mirror of our times, a metaphor of America?

I became convinced that a careful search would turn up such a family, perhaps many such families—indeed, it seemed to me that almost any family would produce a representative portrait if its elders were old enough and clear-headed enough and if their descendants were numerous enough. The story of any large family, I thought, would give those who read it a glimpse of their own history, a better vision of themselves. One family could be a prism through which the shape and texture and resonance of American life could be transmitted—and the more carefully the family was chosen for its typicality, the more universally recognizable the resulting portrait would be.

The first step was to draw up a descriptive outline. I wanted to find a family that had been a part of the middle-class mainstream of national life for at least a century, a family securely anchored between the extremes of wealth and poverty. There must be a hundred or more people in at least four generations, beginning with elders born in or around the 1870s in a rural or small-town environment in the mid-American heartland. Ideally, the elders would still live in the same county—or at least the same state—in which they were born. Typical of the national majority, they would be white, Anglo-Saxon, mainstream Protestant, Democratic or Republican citizens—she a retired homemaker or perhaps a schoolteacher, he a retired farmer or teacher or preacher or merchant. They should be in good health, living at home rather than in a nursing home, and they should have lucid and detailed recollections of the past—and an untiring fondness for talking.

From such a couple, if they had produced a half-dozen or more children, would inevitably come succeeding generations progressively larger and more diverse than the first, until in the third or fourth generation they ranged across the spectrum of occupations, income levels, places of residence, political preferences, religious beliefs. Given sufficient numbers, they would have been almost everywhere, done almost everything; given even modest numbers say, a hundred past the age of eighteen or twenty—they would have been enough places and done enough things to tell a collective tale of the evolution of a nation. And in that story, I was confident there would be a true and accurate image that any American would recognize. In reading it, we could discover something of ourselves, and of how we came to be the way we are.

Every American family has within it the same general cast of characters: ancestors who journeyed to this continent from another land, people who moved and settled and moved again, generations of strivers who finally established an identity here. Every family has a homeplace somewhere, and names to recall of heroes and villains, and signs of the times to mark their passage. Every family, whatever its racial or ethnic or national origin, has faced war and peace, depression and prosperity, victory and defeat, life and death. I was eager to discover and record the chronicle of one such family from the middle-earth of our religious and philosophical beliefs, our labor and politics, and to hold it up as an imperfect mirror of our history.

In the fall of 1977, with the descriptive outline firmly fixed in my mind, I started looking for the elders who would give life to my idea. My inquiries reached from Virginia and West Virginia to Kansas and Missouri, from Kentucky to Mississippi. I found a Spanish-American War veteran in Arkansas, a couple in Tennessee who had been married for seventy years, a 106-year-old Kentucky man who still drove his own car. I found widows and widowers, childless couples, people whose physical or mental health was impaired. But for four months, I looked in vain for a vigorous and prolific old couple who had spawned a multigenerational throng and accumulated a storehouse of history and humor along the way. It seemed for a time that my idea would not even be tested, let alone proved.

But early in 1978, the mail brought a clipping from the Louisville *Courier-Journal* about a Lancaster, Kentucky, couple and their "gift of longevity, of life and memory." The story introduced me to Burnam and Addie Ledford.

"Could I come to visit them?" I asked their daughter, Gwen Gastineau, on the phone. She relayed to me the same answer her father had sent to the *Courier-Journal* reporter: "Better tell him to hurry up. At my age, I can't make any promises."

I knocked at their front door on a slate-gray afternoon in March, and Mr. Ledford, expecting me, shouted an invitation for me to come in. They were in their bedroom, the room on the right front corner of the house—a warm, snug space heated by a gas furnace in front of the sealed-off fireplace and cluttered with the necessities and diversions of their cold-weather confinement.

The room was about fifteen feet square. It had a high ceiling and single windows facing the side yard and the front porch. An electric clock, a calendar, and a few pictures hung about the walls on a muted rose pattern of aged wallpaper that was cracked and peeling in places. The entrance from the living room was on one side of the fireplace; on the other side was a closet door on and around which were hung lumpy heaps of winter clothes. Another door opened onto an enclosed porch that led back to the kitchen.

A hand-carved walnut double bed, its headboard reaching almost to the ceiling, dominated the back corner of the room. A matching marble-top dresser sat in the adjacent front corner, its mirror partially obscured by a high stack of boxes, books, and clothes. Potted plants clustered on a low table between the bed and the dresser received light through the curtained window. Beside the front window, a black and white portable television set rested on a metal stand, and on the floor around it were scattered piles of newspapers and magazines. A telephone sat on a small table behind the living room door. Above it was a display of presidential campaign buttons featuring every Republican candidate since William McKinley.

Mr. Ledford was sitting in a white vinyl upholstered chair near the front window. A bristle of pens and pencils sprouted from the breast pocket of his wool sport coat. He wore no tie, but his shirt was buttoned at the collar. On the linoleum floor beside his left foot was a crockery spittoon ringed by a dark stain of near misses. Mrs. Ledford was sitting in a wooden armchair near the center of the room. She wore a green cardigan sweater over her dress and apron. Between their two chairs was a low table on which a small radio vied for space with a bowl of fruit, a box of candy, and a stack of library books.

"Come in, come in, have a seat," the old man shouted, as if I were a member of the family or an old friend. He squinted for a good look at me. His wife watched me curiously, saying nothing.

I pulled a chair up close to them, and soon we were skimming smoothly through the customary topics of first acquaintance: I told them where I was from and how I had heard of them; they asked about my family; I asked about their health; we touched lightly on politics and sports and the weather. As the conversation proceeded, I was impressed by the clarity and detail and accuracy of their recollections—and surprised by their physical and mental well-being. The weight of the years had stooped his shoulders and etched deep lines in her face, and both of them had lost some sharpness of sight and hearing, but they were alert and quick-witted, clearly in full command of their faculties, and their independence and self-sufficiency were proudly displayed, like badges of honor.

Their children, I learned, had numbered thirteen in all, including two who died as infants. Their eldest son had died in 1918, their youngest in 1969, and all the others—three sons and six daughters—were still living, inheritors of the robust health of their parents. Three of them lived outside the state. The children had given their parents thirty-three grandchildren—and they, with their spouses and more than three dozen offspring of their own, were scattered all over the country.

"Tell me about your parents," I said at length to Mr. Ledford. Without a pause, he responded:

"My father was Jesse B. Ledford, born in Harlan County, Kentucky, on the twenty-fifth of April, 1855. He was twenty-one years, one month, and one day older than me. He married Vesta Jones. She was born in Tennessee, near Tazewell. She was about seventeen and he was eighteen when they got married. They had one child who died as a baby before I was born, and then I was next, born on May 26, 1876, in a log cabin on Coon Branch in Harlan County. There were seven of us children, not counting the one that died, and I'm the only one that's still living now. My parents are dead too, been dead over sixty years. I'm the last one—they're all gone but me. Mrs. Ledford is also the last one left in her family. We've outlived them all."

He went on to name his four grandparents and eight great-grandparents, giving dates of birth and marriage and death, names and numbers of children, details of life and work, death and burial. His wife in turn gave a similar account of her forebears, with the same wealth of detail. In two hours, they outlined the structure of an extended family that spanned two centuries and seven generations, from their great-grandparents to their great-grandchildren. They talked freely, continuously, indefatigably—and often simultaneously, as one added information to the narration of the other, or as fresh recollections came suddenly to mind. Far more than a dry recitation of genealogy, they told a rich, lively, complex, intricately connected story of a family's passage through time and space.

Surely this was the family I had been looking for, I thought. They had the age, the health, the numbers, the recollections. I knew nothing of them except what I had learned that day, but it was enough to convince me that I had come to the right place at last. To Gwen Gastineau, and later to her brother, Bill Ledford, I explained the project I wanted to pursue, the book I wanted to write. There were discussions back and forth, there were questions, and finally there was consent. "As long as it's okay with Papa and Mama, it's okay with me," Bill Ledford said. For their part, the elder Ledfords had no objection at all.

In the weeks before Mr. Ledford's 102nd birthday, I went four times to their house with my tape recorder. The conversations grew broader, deeper, more detailed. I listened and inquired and occasionally probed—and then I transcribed the tapes, reviewed the conversations, refined my questions, and went back for more interviews. At times, the volume and complexity and intricate detail of the material almost overwhelmed me. I began to realize that their story alone, without the addition of the later generations, would take repeated visits and many hours of tape to complete and countless hours for me to absorb and understand. It could be no hurried undertaking; it would require months, perhaps years, of concentrated effort.

More than once in those first few weeks of immersion, I wondered if I—and if the Ledfords—would have the time, the patience, the endurance to see it through. But the thought of turning back was never strong. Instead, a vague and inexpressible sense of urgency crept over me. There was so much to do, and so little time to get it done—or so it seemed.

It was the elder Ledfords who repeatedly shored up my confidence and reinforced my commitment to the task. They were willing and able, even eager, to work long hours with me. Time was for them both a lonely burden to be borne and a precious gift to be savored; they held back nothing, showing no concern for the hours and no fatigue from having spent them in taxing recollection and lengthy conversation. The warmth of the welcome they gave me increased with each visit. We became friends, comfortable together. Before the homecoming celebration and then after it, in visits throughout the summer and on into the fall and winter, our talks continued. The tapes and transcriptions and research notes grew steadily, and so did my understanding, and so too did the warmth of our friendship.

And gradually, over those weeks and months, a bond formed between us. More than a hope or a promise, it was a contract, an unwritten, unspoken agreement drawn up in our minds: They were the narrators, the historians, the deliverers of an ancient and contemporary human record; I was the conduit, the vessel for their story's survival and safekeeping.

For a very long time, I had searched for them along the back-country roads of almost a dozen states in the nation's interior. I had finally found them. And then, after we had spent many hours together, I made another discovery: I came slowly to the realization that they had also been looking for me, for someone with a notebook and a tape recorder and an interest in the story they had to tell.

It was as if they had been waiting patiently for me to come and write it all down.

TWO

Curtis Burnam Ledford

"I'll start this way. Aley was the first, the one who brought the Ledford name into Kentucky. He was still a boy when they came across the mountains in 1808, traveling in covered wagons from North Carolina, following the trail of Boone to the Bluegrass."

Thus did Burnam Ledford begin his tale. Winter was ending, and his spirits were rising like spring sap. He was counting off the days of March, waiting for the April signs of resurrection that would be his personal assurance of another year to live. He was eager, he said, to "stand barefoot in the grass," to sit on the porch and smell the flowers. "If I live 'til April," he told everyone who came to see him, "I'll live the rest of the year." Between our first meeting in March and his 102nd birthday in May, we spent most of our time together talking about the family's early history, before he and his wife were born. From stories handed down by their parents and grandparents, from a sparse but fully remembered written record, from a lifetime of listening and telling, the elder Ledfords had evolved their own intricately woven tale of the lives of their fore-bears. Their separate accounts were seldom in conflict or at variance with the truth, as far as it could be verified.

He began with his ancestors, as far back as he could trace them. The first, in every sense of the word, was his great-grandfather, Aley Ledford:

He was nineteen years old, and he had a new bride, Elizabeth Farmer—they called her Betsy. She was two years younger than him. Aley's parents were leading the way. I don't know what their names were, but I think his father might have been John Ledford. Anyway, there was three or four families of them in the wagon train—Ledfords, Farmers, Skidmores, Smiths, maybe six or seven wagons in all, including a family of slaves. They came from Randolph County, North Carolina, not far from Boone's Yadkin Valley, and they had heard the tales of meadows and fertile land in Kentucky, so they decided to go there and settle. I guess they figured they could make a better life in the West, where it wasn't so crowded and there was plenty of land for the taking.

So they had started out with all their belongings, them and the few slaves they owned and their livestock, and after many weeks of hard journeying over the mountains and across the rivers, they finally came to Cumberland Gap. It was in late winter or early spring—probably about this time of year, still cold at night—and when they made camp there at the gap, they built a fire at the base of a hollowed-out tree where many a family before them had cooked supper. Late that night, after they had finished eating and gone to bed, a big storm came up and blew that hollow tree down in the midst of them. The trunk of it fell right across the wagon that Aley's parents were in, and it crushed them to death.

It must have been a terrible shock to Aley, to all of them. They buried his parents there beside the trail, and after they had salvaged what goods they could from the wagon, it was time to move on. Some in the party still wanted to go on to the Bluegrass, and did, but Aley and Betsy and the slaves and maybe one or two of the other families decided to turn up toward Virginia, and up in there somewhere north and east of Cumberland Gap—probably at Pennington Gap—they cut across the mountain and came down into the valley of Cranks Creek, in what is now Harlan County, Kentucky. That's where Aley chose to settle, there in that big valley near the head of Cranks. He lived there all the rest of his life— another sixty-five years—and Aley's Betsy, the one we called Blind Granny, lived there more than eighty years. She was 101 years old when she died in 1892. Aley's buried up there near the head of Cranks somewhere, and Betsy's buried a little farther down the creek at the Wash Smith cemetery. Last time I was there—it's been over ten years, I guess—the log house that Aley built on Cranks Creek was still standing. It was a pretty big house for the time—two large rooms downstairs and two above them. They raised all their children there.

I heard the stories of those early times from the old ones, from my parents and grandparents and others who remembered. I learned a lot from an old man named Jim Botner, who had lived and worked on Aley's place as a boy. I visited Botner in Owsley County in 1928, and he told me all about Aley and them. Old Botner was 104 years old when I met him.

Aley Ledford was my great-grandfather. He and Betsy had thirteen children. The eleventh one was James Ledford, my grandfather, born in 1830. James had five children by his first wife, Polly Farley. One of them was my father, Jesse, who was born in 1855. Aley and Betsy's first child, John, born in 1809, was also my great-grandfather. His first wife was Martha Napier, and one of their daughters, Polly, married Samuel Jones and had a daughter named Vesta who was my mother. So I'm a Ledford both ways. My wife's family and mine are also connected. Her great-grandfather, Jim Farmer, was a brother to Betsy, my great-grandmother. I know it's confusing, but you see, the early settlers in the mountains intermarried a lot. They had to. The ones that homesteaded there around Harlan were hemmed in. They had no outlet except to walk across Cumberland Mountain to Virginia. No inlet or outlet, and not many people, and the same families living there for years and years, and they intertwined. After a time, they were kin so many ways you couldn't hardly tell what kin they were.

Anyhow, Aley was one of the earliest white men to settle there in what later became Harlan County. It was part of Knox County back then, and the county seat at Barbourville was a whole lot farther away from Aley and them than the seat of Lee County, Virginia, which was just across the mountain. Kentucky had been a state since 1792, but in the lower part of Knox County, there around Cranks Creek, there wasn't any towns or anything, and no government, so it was just the same as if it was still part of Virginia. Some of Aley and Betsy's children are listed as being born in Virginia, but

I think that's just where their births got recorded because they lived closer to that courthouse.

A fellow named Samuel Howard is listed as the first white settler in Harlan County in 1796, and pretty soon after him there was some Napiers and Hensleys—ancestors of mine, and Addie's too. When Aley and them got there in 1808, they claimed that a man named George Burkhart was living in a big hollow sycamore tree near the forks of Cranks Creek and Mill Creek, not more than a mile or so from where Aley built his house. Old Burkhart lived to be 115 years old before he died in about 1850. He was an old man when Aley and Betsy first saw him.

Aley and his slaves cleared land, set out crops, built homes. He not only farmed and raised stock—he was a miller, too, and he also ended up owning a lot of land in the mountains, in Harlan County and also over in Lee County, Virginia, on Stone Creek. He had horses, racehorses—some that they brought with them from North Carolina—and there in the valley below his house he built a racetrack. But that must have been later on. There wasn't time for that at first—too much work to be done. There was still some Indians around, too, but I think they must have been friendly, because I never heard of any battles between them.

Within ten years after they settled there, Aley and Betsy had seven children, and in the next fifteen years after that, they had six more. There was families scattered all along Cranks Creek by then, and in that valley where Cranks runs into Martins Fork, and along Martins clear to Mount Pleasant, where they established the county seat when Harlan County was formed in 1819. Three big creeks come together there—Martins Fork, Clover Fork, Poor Fork—to make the Cumberland River. It was a long time after that, even after I had moved away, before they changed the name of Mount Pleasant to Harlan Town, or Harlan Courthouse, or just plain Harlan. There were about two thousand people living in the county by 1820, but that still wasn't so many, considering how big it was: over three hundred thousand acres, and no roads to speak of, just mountains and streams and forests and a little cleared land wherever it was level enough to grow a crop. And if you counted all the people in ten or twelve families—all the Ledfords, Farmers, Skidmores, Smiths, Howards, Hensleys, Napiers, Turners, Noes, Ashers, Cawoods, Middletons—you'd have counted just about all the people there was living there. Harlan County didn't change much in those times.

Must have been along about the 1830s that Aley and his brother-in-law Jim Farmer and his son-in-law Noble Smith and his friend Johnny Skidmore made a big land survey there. Jim Farmer was Betsy's younger brother, and Noble Smith—they called him Nobe—was married to Aley and Betsy's daughter Nancy. Johnny Skidmore was the same age as Aley. He had a daughter that married one of Aley and Betsy's sons—and a son who later on became my wife's grandfather. Anyhow, those four men went together and surveyed a big boundary, and they ended up with a lot of land out of it.

They started on top of Cumberland Mountain, up above the Cranks Creek valley. Then they went south thirty miles, clear down across the corner of Virginia and into Tennessee, then west ten miles, then north thirty, and then east ten, back to where they had started from. Three hundred square miles, 192,000 acres. I could be mistaken about the exact size of it, but not by much. It was a very large boundary, and they kept everything inside of it that wasn't already claimed and homesteaded. They ended up owning a large part of the lower end of Harlan County, but I guess they couldn't hold their claim to the acres that fell in Virginia and Tennessee, because they didn't live there. But you could claim land back then just by surveying it and sending your plat in to the state to be certified, so Aley and them got to be big landholders. And that's how Jim Farmer got to be called Surveyor Jim—he was the main surveyor in the party, and a good one. Later on he served in the Kentucky legislature, and got to be a right well-known man in the state.

Getting back to Aley: By the time he was fifty years old, they claimed he had thirteen children, thirteen slaves, thousands of acres of land, and some of the finest racehorses thereabouts. Him and Betsy kept on living in their log house there on Cranks Creek, but he traveled around the mountains a right smart, went up to Owsley County and even up as far as Lexington to match his horses against the best there was. Jim Botner told me that Aley had a horse some said was the fastest in the world, and he raced him against horses owned by millionaires from New York. Old Jim said that horse was faster than a covey of quail. Aley trained two or three of his slaves to be jockeys—they was little bitty men, just young boys, I guess, and they was real good riders. Aley and his niggers took those horses everywhere and raced them, and they generally won.

Aley and another white man in Harlan County, old Bill Turner, owned more slaves than anybody around there—but it wasn't too many, really, because people in the mountains didn't have anywhere near as many slaves as the big plantation owners had. Aley handled his slaves different to what most people did. He treated them nicely—made his children respect the old ones, call them uncle and aunt. He never would break up a family, wouldn't sell a slave unless he caused a lot of trouble, and not many of them did. Most of Aley's niggers were nice—just like white people, you know. I heard tales about them from the time I was a little boy, and I can remember seeing some of the old ones that lived on Cranks Creek long after slavery ended.

When the Civil War came, two of Aley and Betsy's boys—James, my grandfather, and Stephen, his younger brother—went off to serve in the Union Army. My grandfather was stationed at Camp Nelson, right here in Garrard County. My other grandfather, Sam Jones, was a miller over near Tazewell, Tennessee, and they said he would grind cornmeal for Northerners one day and Southerners the next. He never took sides. But old Aley and his people were Republicans, and they were all for the Union, for Lincoln. As soon as Lincoln signed the Emancipation Proclamation, Aley gave all of his slaves their freedom. He also gave them a large boundary of land—several thousand acres—in the hollow at the head of Cranks Creek. It was heavily timbered with all kinds of oak, poplar, ash—virgin timber—and they prospered there, farming and cutting timber. They took Ledford for their last name, the way a lot of the slaves did. There was several other colored families besides them in that hollow. They built nice houses, had a store, a church, a school, and later on a post office called Ledford, Kentucky. Some white people lived up in there too, when I was a boy, but mostly it was colored people.

The oldest one of them I ever knew anything about was Sinclair Ledford. Some called him Sinkler, or just Sink. He was as old as my grandfather—probably born around 1830—and he was the head of that family of colored Ledfords. His son James—same name as my grandfather—became the postmaster at Ledford, Kentucky. There was several in that family—old Sink and James and George and the women—and some of them was very fair-skinned, could have passed for white. I remember James had a sister who taught school the same as I did and went to the same teacher training program that I did. She was the best-dressed girl there—wore a different outfit every day. Sat back to herself. I don't know where Sink's children went when they moved away from there after he died. I don't think any of them, not a single one, still lives on Cranks Creek.

But they lived there a long time, them and Aley and Betsy—and them after Aley and Betsy had died. Aley died in 1873, when he was eighty-four years old. He had given all of his children big boundaries of land, and what was left went to his youngest son, Steve, who looked after Betsy until she died in 1892. Two or three of their children moved away from Harlan County. My grandfather, James, sold out in about 1877 and moved to Powell County, up near the Red River gorge—and my father, Jesse, who was twenty-two years old and married, decided to go too. I was just two years old when we went up there. We stayed three years and came back, but my grandfather spent the rest of his life logging up there in Powell and Menifee County. He and my grandmother had got divorced in 1867. He married again, but she never did. She was Polly Farley—came from a long line of Farleys and Clays there in Harlan County. She lived in Virginia after they were divorced, and she didn't die until long after Addie and me were married, but we never saw much of her—or of my grandfather, who died in Powell County in about 1914.

James wasn't the only one of Aley and Betsy's boys to move to Powell County. His oldest brother John, who was also my great-grandfather, went there before James, and he stayed there most of the rest of his life. I only remember him coming back to Harlan one time. He was married twice—first to Martha Napier, my great-grandmother, and then to Malina Skidmore, who was Johnny Skidmore's daughter. William, another son of Aley and Betsy, also left Harlan County, I think, but Aley Jr. stayed, and so did his brother Steve, the youngest son, and so did all of their daughters, as far as I know. I think they all married and lived around there.

I don't know if it was before Aley died or after that most of the land him and Jim Farmer and Nobe Smith and Johnny Skidmore had surveyed was sold. Must have been after he died, because he gave most of it to his children, and I reckon they sold it. Anyhow, a New York company called the Kentenia Corporation bought up a lot of Harlan County land, including some of the old survey tracts. Kentenia was controlled by the Delanos, the family of Franklin D. Roosevelt's mother. They didn't actually buy the land, they bought the mineral rights and later on, they leased them to the coal mining companies and the L&N Railroad. That was when the coal boom came to Harlan in about 1912, but Kentenia had bought up the mineral rights long before that.

You see, it was like this: Aley and them was what you might call land poor—they had plenty of land with coal and timber on it, but without a railroad, they couldn't get much of it out, and after a while, they couldn't hardly afford to pay the taxes on the land. They hadn't paid much for it—some of it they got for practically nothing—and when they sold the mineral rights, they didn't get much for it either, though it must have seemed like a lot at the time. But the railroad and the coal interests that leased the land made plenty, and so did the Kentenia Corporation. They built the railroad and the roads, they got the coal, and they got rich.

So when Aley died, he didn't have much. He had either given it away to his children or his slaves, or sold it. Land was cheap back then, and people was very loose about deeds and titles. He had come there to the wilderness as a young boy, made a life for himself and his family, a good life—hard, but good—and when he died after nearly seventy years in Harlan County, a lot of things had changed, but a lot hadn't. In some ways, I guess it must have seemed about the same to him as it was the day he got there.

When my mother and father got married on Coon Branch of Martins Fork in 1873—the same year Aley died—most of their people lived right around there close to one another. My mother's parents had moved back from Tennessee and bought a farm—about five hundred acres, most of it hillside land—and my parents got married at their house. I remember that place real well from when I was a young boy. There was a lot of coal all around, a big coal bank right above the house, but nobody mined it back then. Didn't even burn it, because it didn't burn clean, and that ruined the ashes for making soap. My mother's father, Samuel Jones, was a miller as well as a farmer. I think his people were from Tennessee. I know their names, but I don't know much about them. My mother's mother was Polly Ledford Jones—she was John Ledford's and Martha Napier's daughter, and the oldest granddaughter of Aley and Betsy. Granny Polly lived to be ninety years old before she died in 1918. I went to Harlan to see her just before she died.

Not far from where Sam and Polly Jones lived on Coon Branch, my other grandfather, James Ledford, had a large tract of land. His house was just one valley and across a ridge away, right where Cranks Creek and Martins Fork join. He and my grandmother were divorced, and she was living in Virginia, and he was just before moving to Powell County. That grandmother's name was Polly too—Polly Farley. I already told you about her. Her mother was Lavinia Clay—they called her Vinie. She was a daughter of John Clay, who was some kin to Henry or Cassius one. I always heard that John and Cassius were brothers. You know, old Green Clay, Cash's father, made a big land survey down through Kentucky and Tennessee, had thousands of acres, and they said John settled on part of it there in Harlan County. When I was about six years old, Cassius Clay came to Harlan to see some of his kinfolks, and one night he stopped to visit my father and stayed all night at our house. He and my father stayed up past midnight, just sitting by the fire talking, and I wanted to stay up and listen to them, but I got so sleepy I couldn't keep my eyes open. He was an old man, then, Cash was—

but I met him twice more after that. John Clay was already dead when Cassius came to our house that time. He had been shot from ambush and killed by a fellow named Carr Clem, way back before the Civil War. They arrested Clem and hung him. I remember one of my grandfathers telling me that story.

Well, my parents were married up there in that valley of Martins Fork, in Coon Branch hollow, and they lived there in a log house on my Grandfather Jones's place for about five years, until we moved to Powell County to join my Grandfather Ledford in 1878. We came back to Coon Branch in 1881 and then moved up on Crane Branch, just above there, the following year. And that's where we stayed until 1889, when we moved here to Garrard County. So most of my growing up, until I was past thirteen, was along the branches in that big valley of Martins Fork, around the little village of Smith, Kentucky. It was nothing back then but a store and a schoolhouse, but that was the nearest I could come to saying where I was from—Coon Branch, Crane Branch, Martins Fork, Cranks Creek, and the village of Smith, Kentucky.

My father raised crops in the summer and logged in the winter—floated logs down Martins Fork all the way to Pineville. There wasn't any roads at all back then—just trails and paths through the woods, and the creekbeds was roads in the dry seasons. The houses we lived in were little log cabins beside the creeks—two rooms and a loft and a shed kitchen. My parents had their first child, a son, in 1874, but he died. Then I was born in the cabin on Coon Branch in the spring of 1876—delivered by a midwife, the same as all babies were back then. Our nearest neighbors lived about a quarter of a mile away, but everybody seemed close. We were connected by the streams. We helped one another. I plowed my first row of corn in the Martins Fork–Cranks Creek valley, and first went to school there at Smith. I knew every stream, every hill and hollow. It was twelve or fifteen miles to Harlan Town—Mount Pleasant—and the only way to get there was to walk or ride a horse. My father only went once or twice a year, and the rest of us didn't go at all. It was closer to walk across the mountain to Virginia, to Hagan or Hubbard Springs. Worlds of people lived down that way.

The U.S. Army Corps of Engineers is building a dam on Martins Fork now, down below that valley toward Harlan. They say it'll flood all of that bottomland at Smith. Where we lived on Crane Branch will be under water. I haven't been back up there in a long time. I'd sure like to go one more time, just to see it again. I wonder if I'd recognize anything.

THREE

Addie King Ledford

Addie Ledford had heard the narration countless times, but it never ceased to interest her. Whenever her husband began to talk, she sat motionless, her hands folded in her lap, her eyes averted from his face. As his narration lengthened, she occasionally buried her wrinkled face in her hands, as if overcome by grief—but then she would peek between her fingers, and her muffled laughter disclosed not grief but delight. She studied the thin gold band on the little finger of her left hand, then bent forward to peer out the window at the winter-brown grass, then stared at the pictures of her grandchildren displayed on the mantle. Her expression alternately registered amusement, agreement, boredom, disbelief—but always, she was listening. When she interjected a supporting bit of detail or a contradicting opinion, her voice sometimes rose to a shout, that being the only way she could make her husband hear and understand her. More often, her comments were expressed in a normal tone of voice, not for his benefit but for her own; she was simply trying to keep the record straight in her mind, to make the pieces of it fit into a logical and consistent and accurate whole.

At first, I tried to converse with both of them together, but the clash of voices was more than I could follow on the tapes. We tried taking turns, but their impaired hearing and their eagerness to make a point or relate a remembered incident often nullified the effort. Sometimes it was necessary for me to sit down with them separately and let them talk without interruption. Whatever the circumstances, Mrs. Ledford spoke in her turn with the studied detail and preciseness of a historian. She had a tendency to repeat stories

out of forgetfulness, but the stories themselves seldom differed in
substance from one account to the next. Taken together, they com-
prised a vivid summary of the lives of her forebears:

My mother's people were Skidmores and Farmers—the same
ones that came into Harlan County with Aley and Betsy Ledford.
Polly Skidmore was my mother, born in 1865 to Abraham Skidmore
and Margaret Farmer. Abram's father was John Skidmore. He might
have been from West Virginia or Pennsylvania, or his people might
have been, but he was the same age as Aley, and I always heard
they came together up through Cumberland Gap when they were
young boys.

John Skidmore—or Johnny, as most people called him—married Mary Polly Noe back in the early 1800s, and one of their children was my grandfather Abram. Old John was thirteen years older
than Mary Polly, but she died before he did, and in 1859, after she
had been dead for two years and he was seventy years old, he married a nineteen-year-old girl, Martha Stepp, and had four children
by her before he died at the age of eighty.

Margaret Farmer, my grandmother—they always called her
Peggy, or Peg—was Jim Farmer's daughter, old Surveyor Jim. Jim
was married to Margaret Asher, the daughter of a Revolutionary
War soldier named Dillon Asher. She was just eighteen years old
when she died giving birth to my grandmother. The baby was named
Margaret after her mother and was raised by her grandparents, old
Dillon Asher and his wife. Jim Farmer got married again—to Su-
san Skidmore, Abram's sister—and they had eleven children.

The Skidmores and Farmers lived mostly in the lower end of
Harlan County, around Cranks Creek and Martins Fork, where
the Ledfords and Smiths lived. They settled in that section when
they first came from North Carolina with Aley and them, and in a
hundred years they hardly moved at all. My Grandfather Skidmore
had the asthma, so he wasn't in the Civil War, but his brothers
were—old Henry was a captain in the Union Army, and the others
fought for the Union too. My grandfather had to hide out in the
mountains sometimes to get away from the Confederates—across

the mountain in Virginia, most everybody was on the Confederate side, and in Harlan County, most were for the Union. I remember my grandfather very well. He didn't die until after me and Burnam were married. My Grandma Peg died in 1895, when I was ten years old.

Most of my father's people, the Kings and Hensleys, lived in the upper end of Harlan County, across Little Black Mountain on Clover Fork. My father was Ewell Van King—signed his name E.V. King. His name might have been Ewell Vanderbilt—I know there was some people in Harlan County before him who had that name— but I don't know how they came to have it or whether he was kin to them.

My father was born on Britton Creek in 1858. Britton is a branch of Yocum Creek, and Yocum runs into Clover Fork there at Evans. His parents were Alva Byrd King and Rhoda Hensley, and both of their families lived on Britton, farmed there. I don't know much about the Hensleys, except that they had a big family, and they were scattered all up and down Clover Fork, and some even way up on Martins Fork. My grandmother's father was named Samuel Hensley and her mother was Martha Stanton. I think they came from North Carolina in the early 1800s and settled around Clover Fork, but that's about all I can tell of them.

I know more about the Kings. Byrd King came from North Carolina with his folks in the 1830s, when he was a little boy. I'd just as well tell you all of it: They always claimed that the Kings had Indian blood in them. Some of the children worried about it— my brother was ashamed of it—but it never did bother me. The Indians was as smart as anybody, if they had a chance to show it. I think Byrd's mother and father were both part Indian—Cherokee or what, I don't know. His name could have been Felix—Byrd had a brother by that name—but somebody else told me the old man's name was Woodard King, and his wife was Elizabeth Harris. I never knew either one of them, of course, or my Grandfather Byrd either—he died on Christmas Day of 1865—but I knew some of Byrd's brothers, my great-uncles, and they were all dark-complected. My father was sort of dark, too, and had real black hair. He was a good-looking man. Our son Bruce was dark like that. He took the best picture you ever saw.

They said Byrd wasn't in the Civil War because he had TB—what they used to call consumption—and he finally died of it when he was only thirty-seven years old. He was a Republican, and he was for Lincoln and the Union, and most of his brothers were in the Union Army. There was Sam, Woodard, Felix, Jefferson, and Chockley—that's an Indian name, I guess. If they called him Chocolate, that'd give him away, wouldn't it?

My Grandmother King—Rhoda—died when I was three years old. I can just barely remember her. She lived at the mouth of Britton Creek, owned a strip of land there about a mile long. Her oldest boy, Sam, was a good worker, knew how to make a living farming. He kept my father and the other ones busy. They'd go down to the river where the land was level and raise big crops. When my grandmother died, Sam got her farm, and he looked after the other boys until they were all grown and married.

My other grandparents, the Skidmores, I remember them real well. My Grandmother Peggy died in 1895, when I was ten. She was a craving woman—she wanted to have something, to make something, and she did. She had over a hundred bee gums, all with big stands of honey in them, and she made forty-seven of those coverlets, spreads woven of cotton or wool, all of them with real pretty designs, like you see on sale over at Berea College now for over a hundred dollars apiece. She was an industrious woman—a Farmer by birth, but a Skidmore by marriage, and a good one. They used to say, "You'll never hear of a Skidmore starving."

I think the Skidmores were Dutch. Some of them made money, and they held on to it, they were tight. They were Republicans too, like the Kings. My Grandfather Abram had the asthma real bad. He didn't go to the Civil War, but he was a Union man, and they said he hid out in the woods lots of times, afraid the Confederates would come across the mountain and kill him. His brother, Henry Skidmore, was married to one of old Aley Ledford's daughters. He was a captain in the Union Army, and once he was in command of about a hundred men at Camp Nelson, right here in Garrard County. He was in Washington when the war closed, though, and he had to ride clear across Virginia to get home. They said when he crossed over the mountain into Harlan County, a whole drove of Confederates was in hot pursuit of him, and they killed one of their own men shooting at him. One of old Henry's grandsons told me that story once when I was visiting back in Harlan.

My Skidmore grandparents had a farm on Cranks Creek—a nice place, two or three hundred acres. They grew crops along the creek, and had a good orchard on the slope, and they raised livestock too—killed about twenty hogs every winter. I remember going to their house, just below where old Aley and Betsy's house was. It was made of hewed logs—two rooms, side by side. That's where my mother, Polly Skidmore, was born in 1865, one of about a dozen children.

My father was the only one in his family to go off and get an education. He was real smart, good in his books, and when he was about seventeen he went across the mountain to a school at Rose Hill, Virginia. It was some kind of boarding school—they called it a college—and he went there for about two years. After that, he came back to Harlan County and taught school for a little while. Along about 1879, he went out to Washington state and worked in timber for four or five years—lived around Seattle, worked on Puget Sound. There was quite a few men from Harlan County who went West to work back then—Washington, Oregon, California. They was restless, I guess—wanted to get out and see the country. Besides, it was hard to make a living in the mountains, and the idea of going West appealed to lots of people.

My father liked it out there, but he must have got homesick, because he came back in the winter of 1884 to see his folks—and that's when he married my mother. On March first, 1884, they got married in the Skidmore house on Cranks Creek. He was twenty-five and she was eighteen. With the money he had saved up out West, he bought a five hundred–acre farm at Kildav, on Clover Fork just below Evarts. It had a good hewed log house on it, a two-room house, and they built on two more rooms—my father and a

carpenter from Virginia. That same carpenter made all of our furniture out of walnut. My father paid $1,200 for the farm.

All of Burnam's grandparents lived until he was grown, but
mine all died before I was twenty. My Grandfather Skidmore was
the last to die, in 1904, the year after me and Burnam were married. I was nineteen when he died. I suppose one of the reasons
Burnam knows more about some of his ancestors than I do mine is
that he learned a lot from his grandparents. I remember quite a bit,
though. I always was good at history.

I was born in that log house at Kildav on January 25, 1885. A
midwife named Polly Clay Thomas delivered me. She was closely
related to Cassius M. Clay—she might have been one of old John
Clay's daughters, I'm not sure. Children around there, I remember
they were afraid of old Polly. "I'd hate to get sick," one of them
said to me one time. "Old Polly might bring me a baby."

I remember the place where we lived ever so well. It was a good
farm and a real nice house. And the furniture, I remember every
piece of it—two beds, two dressers, tables and drawers, a big safe,
and all of it in walnut, hand-carved. I wish I had that safe now—
it'd be worth plenty. The house was on the off side of the river,
across from the road. It was hard to get to when the water was
high, but that was the only bad thing about it. My father bought
another farm a little farther down Clover Fork, at a place called
Bee Bottom, and he raised crops at both places. I grew up thinking
we were pretty well fixed.

It must have been about the time I was born, about 1885, that
my father was elected sheriff of Harlan County. He was a good
Republican, like most everybody else, and he was interested in politics. He served a two-year term, and then got reelected. People in
the county looked up to him and respected him. He was intelligent,
and he read a lot, and he was fair to everybody, and that made him
popular. I remember that he subscribed to the New York *Tribune*.
It came two or three times a week—depending on how often pack
horses brought the mail over the mountain from the train station in
Virginia.

Then after he had been sheriff, my father was appointed by

President Harrison to be a U.S. marshal, and that meant we had to move to Harlan Town—or Mount Pleasant, as they called it then. His job was to be the revenue man. He had to go around and get after people for making whiskey, tear up their stills. It was dangerous work, but he never got hurt. Never even got shot at, as far as I ever knew.

We stayed in Harlan about two years—I started to school there, learning words out of a McGuffey reader—and then when I was nearly eight, we moved back out to our farm on Clover Fork. It was only seven miles from Harlan, but it seemed like more than that. I loved that place. I went to school at Black Mountain Academy in Evarts. We had the best of teachers—they were Congregationals from New England. My father farmed and logged, and we lived a good life there. But then he got sick and wasn't able to work—and in 1895, he died of TB at the age of thirty-seven, just exactly the same as his father.

That was the beginning of hard times for the rest of us. My mother had had five children after me. Two of them had died of measles as infants, but there was still me and my three brothers, George and Logan and Willie. We lost both of the farms to pay off my father's debts, and we had to move over on Cranks Creek and live with my Skidmore grandparents—and that same year, my Grandmother Skidmore died too. I was just ten years old, but I remember it so well. It seemed like we had lost everything. Most of all, we had lost my father. That was a hard blow. I was real fond of my father.

FOUR

The Beginning: Aley and Betsy

"How in the world can you keep all of these names and dates and facts in your heads?" I asked them one day. Winter had passed. The gas furnace had been turned off, and a warm wind out of the south rattled the front window. It was almost porch season, almost birthday time, and I was struggling to sort out the lengthening cast of characters they had introduced to me.

Burnam Ledford laughed. "Well, we've just always had an interest, I guess always kept up with our families. And now, since we're the last ones, everybody else has to depend on us to tell them about the old times. There's some of it we don't know, and maybe even some we've got wrong, but we know most of it—and it's right, too."

I was amazed, not only by how much they knew but by the accuracy of it. In order to verify and clarify their recollections, I had begun to delve into whatever genealogical materials and recorded data I could find that might shed light on the story—birth and marriage and death records in courthouses, census information, old newspapers, books of history, family correspondence. Only a limited amount of such material apparently existed, but there was enough to give some reinforcement to what they had told me, and to help me formulate more specific questions that might lessen my confusion.

"I'm having trouble keeping everybody straight," I said. "There are so many names—even people with the same names." We were getting deeper and deeper into the early history of their families, concentrating on the oldest stories, prior to the time of their birth. What they knew of those years had been passed down to them by their elders. The stories spanned three generations and nearly a hundred years, beginning with Aley Ledford and Betsy Farmer in the last decade of the eighteenth century. As the chronology unfolded, I had to ask them time and time again to go back to the beginning, back to Aley and Betsy, and help me to get my bearings. They never hesitated; patiently, carefully, they went over everything once more, until at last I began to assimilate the complex pattern of relationships that made up the narrative.

Once in a while, the Ledfords would disagree on some point or other—on exactly when Aley and Betsy came to Kentucky, for example, or exactly who made the journey from North Carolina with them. Occasionally, rarely, my own research led me to a conclusion somewhat at variance with theirs. Whenever there was a conflict to be resolved, the three of us talked it out—sifting, comparing, reconsidering, weighing what we knew or believed against what we could prove, or at least against what seemed logical and consistent with the known. In the process, they were able to refine and sharpen the chronicle of their ancestors—and I was given a rare lesson in oral history.

To help me remember all the names and dates and events, I put together several abbreviated chronologies and charts of genealogy. One of these listed the names of Burnam and Addie's parents, grandparents, and great-grandparents, and the dates of birth and death if they were known. Fourteen marriages in three generations had led to their own births, and to their marriage, and to the succeeding generations of their family. When I had finished the chart, I reviewed each name and date with them.

"Yes, I think that's right," Mrs. Ledford said approvingly when I was finished. "To the best of my knowing, you've got it right. We don't know some of the dates, but I believe you've got everything as close as it can be got. Don't you think so, Burnam?"

"I believe so," he replied. "There's a woman up in Lee County, Virginia, who has put a lot of this down in a book about early

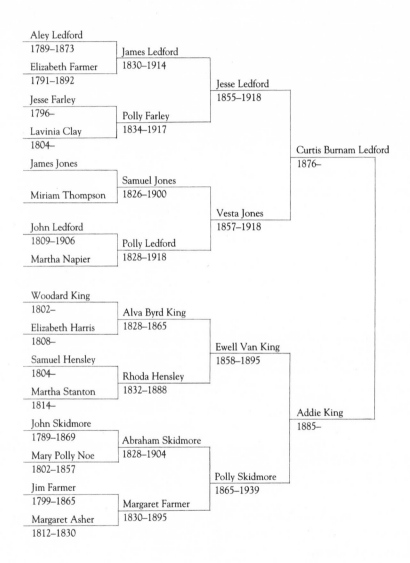

Aley Ledford
1789–1873
          James Ledford
Elizabeth Farmer   1830–1914
1791–1892
                              Jesse Ledford
Jesse Farley   1855–1918
1796–
          Polly Farley
Lavinia Clay   1834–1917
1804–
                                        Curtis Burnam Ledford
James Jones   1876–
          Samuel Jones
Miriam Thompson   1826–1900
                              Vesta Jones
John Ledford   1857–1918
1809–1906
          Polly Ledford
Martha Napier   1828–1918

Woodard King
1802–
          Alva Byrd King
Elizabeth Harris   1828–1865
1808–
                              Ewell Van King
Samuel Hensley   1858–1895
1804–
          Rhoda Hensley
Martha Stanton   1832–1888
1814–
                                        Addie King
John Skidmore   1885–
1789–1869
          Abraham Skidmore
Mary Polly Noe   1828–1904
1802–1857
                              Polly Skidmore
Jim Farmer   1865–1939
1799–1865
          Margaret Farmer
Margaret Asher   1830–1895
1812–1830

settlers of Lee and Harlan counties, and I've got a cousin by the name of Roy Ledford who's got some of it. Roy lives in Virginia too. He sent me some material he had written up, including a list of all the children of Aley and Betsy, and where they were born, and who they married, and when they died."

"Where did he get all that information?" I asked.

"He got a lot of it from me, and I reckon he got the rest from courthouse records and such. Roy says Harlan is the home of the Kentucky Ledfords, and Aley was the first—he was the granddaddy of us all."

In all my conversations with the elder Ledfords, I had been impressed with the prominence of Aley in their minds. Far more than any other ancestor, he loomed as a giant figure in the stories they told; he was, in fact, the central character, the legendary hero whose pioneering exploits seemed larger than life. I had found him, too, in the official records of Harlan County and in scattered other documents, listed variously as Aley, Aly, Alias, Elias. He had come to Kentucky early, raised a large family there, acquired a considerable amount of property. In Burnam Ledford's mind, he was more admired than any other relative, a dominating personality of the sort that comes along only once in every three or four generations, if then. More than a hundred years after his death, Aley Ledford still had the power to impress. The more I heard about him, the more I wanted to know—and to incorporate into the story we were compiling together.

"Old Aley, our Aley, the Aley of all the Aleys," said Mr. Ledford one day. "There's been a lot of others with that name since him, but there was only one Aley who's remembered: my great-grandfather. He was a good man—he did a lot. Him and Betsy started the Ledford family in Kentucky."

"Why do you suppose he stands out so much in your mind?" I asked. "You never saw him, and yet you talk about him almost as if you knew him."

Mr. Ledford pondered the question for a minute. "Well, there's a lot about his life and mine that's the same," he said. "His family moved across the mountains when he was a young boy—and so did mine. His parents were killed in an accident—and so were mine. He fathered thirteen children—and so did I. I've admired him all my life, and wished that I could hear him tell about all that happened to him. I'd love to have known him. He had only been dead about three years when I was born."

"Is there anything left that belonged to him—any diary, any letters, any personal belongings?"

"No, I guess not—not that I know of, anyhow. I sure wish he had written down his recollections and left them for us. It'd all be strange to us now—even though Harlan County didn't change very much from his time to mine. I can imagine him coming through the wilderness with his family, building his house on Cranks Creek, racing his horses, surveying big boundaries and such. I think about him a lot, and sometimes I can almost picture him, and hear him talking."

In the detailed stories of Aley Ledford and his times, in the scattered remnant of recorded information about him, in the retracing of his passage into the Kentucky mountains, and in the history of his generation in America, there was much upon which to build a speculative and conjectural account of his life as he might have recalled it in his last years. I suggested to Mr. Ledford that such a combination of verifiable fact and plausible imagination might help me to gain a better understanding of Aley Ledford and his generation.

"If you tell me everything you know," I said, "and I put it together with everything else I can find out, I could write Aley's story just as if it was in his own words. What would you think of that?"

He considered the prospect for a moment and then replied, "That would be just fine. I'd like to see that myself."

FIVE

Aley's Story, 1789–1873

May 5th, 1869

To my children and grandchildren—

I have promised you that in the idle time I have on my hands I will write down some of the stories I have told you and some of the things that happened to your mother and me when we was young. I mean to keep that promise while I am able, so you won't forget the old times.

Last Sunday I turned eighty, and my health ain't too good, and your mother is near blind. She is helping me remember the stories. We will do the best we can and hope the Lord lets us stay around long enough to finish.

The place to start is with my grandfather, John Ledford Sr. I can't go back much beyond him. He died in Randolph County, North Carolina, in 1799, when I was ten years old. He was seventy-five. I learned most of what I know about the early times from him and my father. He was born in the north of England, around a town called Lancaster, in 1724. His father farmed. They was right poor, the Ledfords was, so John and two of his brothers decided to make their way to America. There was a sea captain by the name of James Patton that sailed out of the ports there on the Irish Sea. He traded in slaves, and took convicts and such across the water for a price—a hard man he was, some said a pirate. Well, in 1738 he docked a ship called the *Walpoole* at a harbor there near where the Ledfords lived, and when he left out of there bound for Virginia, he had my grandfather and two of his older brothers aboard. John was just fourteen. His brother William was sixteen and his

49

brother Henry was eighteen. They had signed on to work for Patton seven years in return for free passage to America.

It must have been a hard trip—about two hundred people, men and a few women, crowded into the cargo hole of that little ship, with nothing much to eat but bread and water. They was more than four months getting to a port somewhere in the Tidewater region of Virginia. Patton and a fellow named John Lewis, some kin of his, had a big grant of land from the Virginia Colony. It was far inland, across a mountain range in a broad valley. Patton was taking these redemptioners, these contract laborers and slaves and convicts, to go there and settle in that boundary. So they went overland, Patton and Lewis and their cargo, and in what was called Augusta County they stopped and settled.

Old Patton was clever. He had the land, and he had the people to work it. He had everything he needed, and the Virginia Colony left him alone to build a kingdom. He was everything—the owner, the tax collector, the military leader. He even had the support of the King back in England. You might say Patton was a dictator. My grandfather and his brothers lived and worked there for seven years, just like slaves. They couldn't do else, for fear of what would happen to them. They just stayed on the right side of Patton and worked off their debt.

By the time they had done that, in 1745, Patton was settling more land farther on down the valley to the southwest. He got another boundary down there, and the Ledfords decided to buy a little piece of it and start their own homesteads. All three of them was married by then. So the three families moved down into the valley of the Roanoke River—a long way, but still in Augusta County—and in a few years they had bought about three hundred acres from Patton, and gone in debt to him for it. Later on, that section got to be called Montgomery County, Virginia. My grandfather used to talk about that valley on the West Fork of the Roanoke. It was the first place he could call his own, and even when he was an old man he could remember the lay of it, remember plowing the bottomland and hunting on the slopes.

Plenty of folks followed them in there to settle, and a few had even come before them, scouting on the New River and making homesteads in the bottoms. They claimed white men had been exploring in that Great Valley of Virginia for a century, and of course the Indians had been there forever, and it ain't hard to understand why. I rode up there once to see it, just to look around, and I can tell you for a fact, that's as pretty a place as I ever laid my eyes on. So John Ledford and them was not alone by any means. In a way, it must have got to seem right crowded to them.

They stayed about ten years. What caused them to leave was not too many settlers, though—it was too many Indians. Not so many lived around there, but they came from all over to hunt, and when they saw the white man building log cabins and clearing fields for planting, they must have got real angry. Trouble popped out all over, people being ambushed and scalped and shot. Old Patton organized a volunteer militia to give people protection, but the area was too big and the settlers too scattered. There wasn't any way to prevent the Indians from making attacks.

The worst of it came in the summer of 1755. Grandpa said one day Patton and some men rode up to their valley, took supplies and food from them, said he was taking from everybody that owed him money. Then Patton said one of the Ledfords—John or William or Henry—would have to saddle up and join the militia, even though it was crop time and every hand was needed on the farm. Henry, being the oldest—he was thirty-five then—said he would be the one, and he rode off with Patton and them toward Draper's Meadow, a settlement close to the New River that Patton's nephew and some other people had been building up for several years. They got to Draper's Meadow, all right, but they never left there. That evening, a party of Shawnee warriors caught them by surprise and killed them all but one—a woman that they took captive. Uncle Henry was among the ones that died there. So was James Patton.

Henry had a wife and seven children. Him and my grandfather and Uncle William had some of the best bottomland on the West Fork of the Roanoke. They were one for all and all for one, and they were getting ahead—but after Henry got killed, the rest of them never was able to feel safe. The Indian raids kept up, and more people died, and every week or two another family of settlers would pull up stakes and go back east or down into the Carolinas. Finally, John and William and their families and the widow and children of Uncle Henry decided they couldn't protect their valley no longer, so they packed up and headed south. They crossed back to the east side of the Blue Ridge Mountains and went on down to Rowan County, North Carolina. And there on a stream called Caraway Creek they started over.

They still owed for the land they had left back in Virginia, and even though Patton was dead, they kept paying some to his estate. But there was so much deserted settler land up in there that King George over in England reclaimed it and gave it away again to a new wave of settlers. After that, John and William never paid any more on it. They lived on in North Carolina for nearly forty more years before they died. When I went up to that Roanoke River valley years later, looking for their old homesteads, I found out that King George had given their land to some Wattersons—and they were still there living on it.

When they got old, my Grandfather John and old Uncle William claimed to be the start of the Ledfords in America. I wouldn't know about that, but I do know that all the Ledfords that settled around Rowan County in the 1750s and spread out west from there for the next fifty years was descended from John and William and Henry. They must have had close to thirty children among them, and most of those children had right many children too, so that by the end of the century there must have been at least two hundred Ledfords in North Carolina. Then some of us came on west, and now I have lived myself here in Harlan County for nearly seventy years. Me and Betsy can count close to a hundred grandchildren of our own, all in Kentucky, most here in Harlan County. No telling how many Ledfords there is in all by now. Must be thousands of us.

Clear on through the Revolutionary War and the start of the United States, Grandpa John and Uncle William and the next generation of Ledfords stayed right around there on Caraway Creek. That part of Rowan was called Randolph County by then. The

Ledfords was right prosperous—they owned farm land, livestock, even a few slaves. Grandpa John and Grandma Lucy had more than a dozen children. I can name at least ten of them myself. My father was one of the oldest. He was John Junior. He had been born in 1752 in that valley of the Roanoke River, back before they left there for Carolina. Him and some of his brothers, Peter and Joseph and Obediah and maybe another one or two, was all militia soldiers in the war, and I think Uncle Pete was in the battle of King's Mountain in 1780. My father never talked about it much. He wasn't one to say a lot about politics or religion or war. He just worked hard and smoked his pipe and looked after what was his.

My mother's people came from Virginia and North Carolina too, but not many of them lived around Caraway Creek. My mother was tall and heavy set, a big-boned woman, strong. Two of her brothers was killed fighting Tories and Indians, and she never had much use for the English or the red men after that. All she ever wanted was a place to keep house and raise her children.

Nobody around there was much interested in war—they was a lot more interested in land. Some of my uncles and some of Uncle William's boys got in with the Boones up around Yadkin valley and ended up going west. I remember James and Joseph and Philadelphia Ledford went to Kentucky before we did, and I guess some of their children and grandchildren are somewhere in this state now, but I never did know any of them. I think one of them went up in Illinois and started a settlement.

When I was born on Caraway Creek on the last day of April in 1789, my father and mother were up in their thirties and my Grandpa John and Uncle William were over sixty-five, and both their wives were dead. I was named for one of my father's brothers, Uncle Alexander. He was called Aley for short—sometimes Aly, Ely, Elias or Alias, but mostly Aley, and that's what I was called too. Everybody liked Uncle Aley. He was a real friendly man, never lost his temper. Later on he moved to South Carolina, and we never saw him after that.

Uncle William died in about 1798 and Grandpa John passed on the next year, and it seemed like the family was just cut off from the past. I was just a boy, but I could feel how hard everybody took their loss. So much had happened to them, and they told about it so well and so often that you couldn't forget. They had been born in England when America was a colony, and when they died it was a country. Their journey on that boat, and their time under old Patton, and their homesteads on the Roanoke, and their Indian troubles, and their move to Carolina—it all seemed like ancient history to me. We didn't have no luxury there, like wealthy people did, but we was warm and fed and safe, and we had something to show for hard work. We had gained so much that it must have seemed like luxury to Grandpa John and Uncle William. I can remember them saying the rest of us didn't know what hard times was.

Just the same as we was cut off from the past by their deaths, we was also kind of cut off from the future by staying where we lived. Seemed like the ones that had gone west with Daniel Boone was headed for the future. It was dangerous over beyond the mountains, but even with the hardships, men that came back for supplies and such talked about Kentucky like it was the Bible's Eden. They said as soon as they got shed of the Indians they would have a paradise, nothing but open land and woods and game enough to last forever. Some had also gone over into Tennessee, and settlers was flocking there too. Seemed like everybody was going west, everybody but us. My father held out til he was almost fifty. He had always stayed near his folks, said it was his duty to look after them, but after they had all died, he began to talk more and more about following the path of Boone to the Bluegrass of Kentucky.

You might say it was kind of late in life for my father and mother to be thinking of pulling up stakes and moving west. He was the head of the Ledfords by then, him and one or two of William and Henry's sons, and he felt a strong pull to stay in Randolph County. But him and Mama only had six children, and I was the youngest, the only one not grown up and married, and when they thought about leaving, it meant just the three of us—us and Sam's family, a family of slaves that had belonged to Grandpa John since I don't know when. Sam was younger than my father, had a wife and three little children.

I guess it was just the idea of striking out that my father couldn't get out of his head. He had come to North Carolina as a little boy, not hardly big enough to remember, and he had stayed there in the same place all his life. His father had left home at fourteen. Somehow the notion set in—get up and go while you still can. After a while, my father couldn't talk about nothing else but leaving.

We waited til the summer of 1801. Then Pa told us he wouldn't wait no longer, he was going. My sister Betty Smith and her husband decided they would go too, and that made me real happy. I liked her and Henry, and their oldest boy David was not only my first cousin but my best friend, even if he was a little bit younger than me. My Uncle Aley had stood up for Betty when she married Henry, and she was always my favorite sister.

So we got the wagons together, us and the Smiths and Sam. We yoked the oxen, loaded as many belongings as we could take, herded some of the cows and pigs. We was ready to go. Pa left the farm to my oldest brother Fred and his wife. They all gathered there the morning we left—Fred and Tom and Uncle Pete and Uncle Obediah and all their children, all the Ledfords around there. It was a July morning, hot and dry. I was excited the way a twelve-year-old boy would have to be on such a day.

"Which way you going?" Uncle Pete asked Pa. Pa told him, "Up through Yadkin to Surry County, through the low gap of the Blue Ridge, across the New River, down the Great Valley to Cumberland Gap."

"When you coming back?" Uncle Pete asked, and I'll never forget what Pa said. He said, "Never. This is the only move I've got in me. If you want to see us again, you'll have to come to Kentucky."

Me and David rode Pa's two best horses, a bay chestnut stallion named Star and a dark mare named Storm. I can still remember how big I felt, herding the stock along behind the wagons as we left the little valley of Caraway Creek.

But the journey was more than we bargained for. Two yoke of oxen pulling a wagon over rutted trails don't move fast, and the stock kept wandering, and the flies and mosquitoes was awful in the heat. We did good to make four or five miles a day. When one of the wagons broke an axle in the Yadkin valley, Ma and Pa got in a big fuss, and for a while I thought we might be turning back. Tell you the truth, I was near ready for it. They said it was about five hundred miles to the Bluegrass. At the pace we was making, it would have took us til winter to get there.

Pa knew of a man in Surry County, fellow named John Skidmore. Some of the others that went west before us had told of the Skidmores, said they was good folks, so when we got to their place we stopped a spell. John Skidmore was a big man, older than my father but strong as an ox. He had a son they called Abram, and Abram had a son named Johnny who was just my age. When we got there toward late August, it was plain to everybody that we wouldn't get to Kentucky before cold winter, and at night me and Johnny and David would lay awake in the loft listening to Pa and Ma and the Skidmores talking about what we ought to do. The trail was crowded with people going west, they said, and some of them was thieves and robbers. Indians was mentioned too. It was easy to get scared just thinking about it.

Abram Skidmore said he had been studying a move to Kentucky for a long time, him and his wife and kids, but he didn't want to leave Big John—that's what he called his daddy—there alone. "You go on," Big John said. "I'll be better off here than there. Maybe I'll come later, after you're settled." Abram was stout like his father, and we all wanted him with us. The Skidmores knew a family of Farmers, Stephen and Nancy Farmer, that had moved from New River down into the Clinch River valley, just across into Tennessee. We could go there, Abram said, and spend the winter, and next spring we could all go on together into Kentucky.

It was late September when we said goodbye to Big John and his wife and started for Stephen Farmer's place. Four wagons by then—ours, Henry and Betty's, Sam's, and Abram's. It took us about a month to find the Farmers living in a cabin on the Clinch, just south of the Virginia-Tennessee boundary. They had been gone from New River for nearly ten years, and Stephen Farmer had traveled over every trail leading to Cumberland Gap, been in and out of Kentucky several times. He said he had made a claim on a boundary of land up in there, and come spring he planned to take his family and settle on it. The Farmers had a baby boy named Jim and another older one named William, but the one I noticed was Elizabeth Anne, called Betsy. She was the oldest, just two years younger than me. I was big enough to notice she was right pretty. When my father and the others decided we would take shelter there and stay through the winter, that suited me just fine.

We put up lean-to shelters for sleeping and helped the Farmers with their chores. The women cooked for everybody, and there was plenty—deer, bear, fruits and vegetables in the cellar, fish from the river. We kept a big fire going in the house, and at night there was games by lamplight and stories by firelight. Me and Johnny and David and Betsy was as close as peas in a pod. That was a winter we all remembered a long time.

The grown-ups sat by the fire talking at night, but most of what they said didn't make sense to me. They talked about Thomas Jefferson of Virginia, who was the new president of the country, and about George Washington, the first president, who had died not long before that. That's about all I remember—just Washington and Jefferson and Virginia, how Virginia seemed to bring up leaders. I didn't pay no attention. I was too busy with my friends.

While we waited for spring, my sister made the younger ones of us use part of every day for learning to read and write. Ma couldn't read at all, or even sign her name, and Pa just barely could, but Betty had learned young from a woman on Caraway, and she said we all had to study while we was little and able to pick it up quick, cause older people couldn't hardly do it. We learned from a Bible that had belonged to my grandmother, and Betty gave us pieces of slate and chalk rocks to write with. She worked us hard, and me and Johnny hated it, but David and Betsy was just enough younger to mind better, and finally we all settled down to it. Sister Betty was sixteen years older than me—seemed more like a mother than a sister.

Mr. Farmer told the others all about Kentucky, made it sound so good they couldn't hardly wait for spring to come. The Farmers had already decided to go and settle on the land they claimed in

Knox County, not far beyond Cumberland Gap. He said they would go with us as far as the gap, then we could follow the others on the main trail on into the Bluegrass. I wondered was it really blue. Mr. Farmer said he hadn't been that far, but he had heard tell it was.

Soon as the first March wind shifted around from the north to the south and told us spring was coming, we was ready to go. The Farmers had already got another man and his wife to look after their cabin and bottomland, so all we had to do was load the wagons. We left out early of a morning, forded the Clinch right above the surveyors' line separating Tennessee and Virginia, and turned west along what Boone and them had been calling the Wilderness Road for thirty years. In a little more than a week, we had crossed the Powell River and come into a valley that had a north wall of solid rock—looked like it was a thousand feet high and running toward the southwest clear to the horizon.

Stone Mountain, Farmer said—some called it Cumberland Mountain, same as the gap and the river. For about thirty-five miles that mountain wall stayed on our right as we moved down the valley. One evening we stopped at a place called Martins Station, and Farmer told us a scout named Joseph Martin had come there before Boone to hunt and explore and trade with the Indians. "Over yonder," he said, pointing across the mountain, "there's a creek named for Martin, and below there is the land I'm going to." He said there was gaps along there where we could cross to the other side on foot, but they was too rough and narrow for wagons. This time, he said, he would try to take his wagon along the north ridge of Stone Mountain to Martins Fork. I couldn't understand what he meant, but it didn't matter, cause he kept assuring us we wouldn't have no trouble on our route to the Bluegrass. The other thing he said that made me feel better was that not many Indians was left, and they wouldn't bother nobody. I remember him saying, "I fear them less than I do some of the whites." That didn't make no sense at all to my mother—she hated Indians. But Farmer knew that country real well, and we could tell it, and all of us was glad to have him for our guide. I wished they was going on to the Bluegrass with us—specially Betsy.

On about the third or fourth day we were passing along that mountain wall, we began to see up ahead of us a place where the high ridge dropped off real sharp. Mr. Farmer said that was Cumberland Gap. As we got closer, we could see that several trails came together there and made one big path that cut right through the mountain. When we got near to the pass on a rainy afternoon around the first of April, there was families in wagon trains all along the side of the trails, so many people I thought they must be gathering for some kind of meeting. I remember thinking we was real lucky when we found an open spot level enough to gather all five of our wagons and corral our livestock. A long way back, before we got to Skidmores in Surry County, we had found out that there wasn't no way to keep all our stock from roaming. Only thing to do, Pa said, was to keep a sow and a boar, a bull and a cow, a few geese and chickens—and of course Star and Storm and the oxen—and let the rest go. So all the stock we had by the time we got to the gap was either pets that wouldn't wander or breeders that we kept tied up.

That was the year 1802, and I was just before turning thirteen. I remember it clear, like it was yesterday. Five families of us there together, and dozens more all around us, and it seemed like everybody but the Farmers was going to the Bluegrass. People was in good spirits, sitting around their campfires to get warm and dry after the rain, talking among themselves and with strangers they met there, like one big family. We built our fire in the hollow base of a big beech tree, a huge old tree with names and dates carved through the smooth bark of it. First night we was there the men stayed up late, talking. Nobody said it, but I thought they was dreading to see Steve Farmer and his family part company with us. I think that's the reason they all decided to stay a second night there at the gap—just to put off saying goodbye a little longer. Without Mr. Farmer, we wouldn't have no guide. We would be on our own.

Our second day there brought another warm southern wind, a hard blow that kept up steady right on into the evening. We all knew the next day would be parting time. Me and Johnny and

David teased Betsy about being alone there in the woods where they was going. We tried to scare her, but it was all just a way to keep her and us from being sad. The wind whistled around the wagons and fanned the blaze in that old beech tree. Ma and Pa sat by the fire with Steve and Nancy Farmer after the rest of us had gone to bed. I was sleeping in the rear wagon with Johnny and them. Ma and Pa's wagon was at the head of the line.

Once in the night I remember waking to the moaning of the wind. It was pushing so hard, seemed like it was going to lift the wagon up and blow it away. I must have fallen back to sleep, though, cause the next thing I knew, I heard a crash like heavy thunder, and then screaming and hollering, and it scared me wide awake. I looked out of the wagon and saw some men running past, heard them calling out something about a tree falling. The wind was still moaning like a grieving woman. I can still hear the wind.

It was early morning of a cloudy day, and first light was barely enough to see by. Henry came back to where I was sleeping and got me, didn't say a word, just took me to stand by Betty. Johnny and David and Betsy came too. We was kind of huddled together there, watching about twenty men with axes trying to cut away at that beech tree. It had split and crashed in the wind and fallen right across the wagon where Pa and Ma were sleeping, crushing them to death. I couldn't help crying, but I tried hard to act like a man. At least, I thought, they never knew what hit them.

We buried them there on a knoll above the gap, wrapped them up together in the wagon cover and laid them in a fresh hole under the leaves and moss. I threw the first little handful of dirt in on top of them, and I cried some more, me and Betty. I couldn't help thinking that she had Henry and her children, but I didn't have nobody. I was an orphan.

We couldn't go nowhere after that, because we had been following Pa to the Bluegrass, and with Pa and Ma dead, we didn't know who we was following. We soon found out, though. Only thing for us to do was stay with Stephen Farmer. At least he knew where he was going. He had made himself a map from his journeys there before, had measured the distance. He said it was about ten miles across the mountain ridge to the head of Martins Fork—hard going, maybe too hard for wagons. After that it would be rough for another five miles, and then we would have some fairly level land beside the creek for ten miles before we came to a big valley. On down below there was a waterfall where Steve wanted to settle and build a mill. "It's as pretty as any Bluegrass land," he said. "Only reason all these settlers have passed it by is because there ain't no trail." He said just about all the Indians that used to hunt there had cleared out, and we would be the first settlers, us and three or four others that had crossed over Stone Mountain on foot. We could have our pick of land to clear and plant.

It was decided. The next morning we left the gap and the graves, left the other travelers on the trail and turned east into the woods. I can still see that turning place. By the time we had gone fifty feet, we was so deep in the forest that it was like stepping into night. Even without leaves, the trees was so big and tall and thick that they almost hid the sky. Oak, poplar, chestnut, beech, all kinds of trees, some of them broader than two wagons side by side. We had to cut away the undergrowth with axes. It was steep, too, steeper than we had bargained for. The very first day we had to abandon the wagons, bind our belongings on the oxen and go ahead on foot. We didn't make a mile that day. I never had seen wilderness like that. It seemed like we had left the world. We heard bear and deer so big they sounded like boulders rolling through the under-brush, and panthers screaming at night. Everything in there was giant—the trees, the rocks, the animals. But no people, not a soul except us. The border between Kentucky and Virginia ran there along that mountain rim, but it was so hard to get there that no-body could have knowed which state they was in.

Finally we came to a stream that Steve said was the start of Martins Fork, and as we commenced to follow it I got my bearings for the first time since we left the trail. The stream got bigger, and after two or three days the bottomland got wider and the land around it seemed to open up just a little. I could see we was walking toward the rising sun in the morning. "We keep going this way, we'll be back in Surry County directly," Abram said one day, but

Mr. Farmer said, "Nope, when we get to that valley I told you about, the stream will turn north and then back to the west."

And sure enough, that's what it did. It took us nearly a month to get over that twenty-five-mile distance from Cumberland Gap to the valley, but we finally made it on a clear afternoon at the end of April—the same day I turned thirteen. Martins Fork was a big stream by then, rolling along through the woods between the hills. We came down a hill, me and Johnny Skidmore in the lead, and rounded a bend in the creek and cleared a rise, and there it was up ahead of us—a wide valley that opened to the north, blue sky above it and sunlight shining on the creek waters. I let out a whoop and a holler and we went running back to tell the others.

Everybody was glad, but we was too tired to celebrate. Betty had a sick baby, one of Sam's boys had broke his leg and had to be carried on an ox, the horses and stock was all hobbled, and Betsy's mother was so sick and weak she could hardly go at all. We made camp where another big creek ran into Martins Fork—Steve said it was called Thranks, or Cranks, after an old woodsman that had roamed there back in Joseph Martin's time. There was cane growing in thickets thirty feet high along the creeks, and hoof prints of big animals was sunk deep in the sandbars beside the water. We was out of the deep woods enough to where it almost seemed like a clearing, and when the men gathered by the fire that night to make plans, we could see stars shining up in the sky.

"This is Knox County, Kentucky," Steve Farmer said. "There to the east, in that Cranks valley, there's a good ten miles of bottomland and nobody on it. Up to the north, Martins Fork runs on for about fifteen miles, creeks joining it every mile or so, and finally it meets two more big forks and becomes a river that flows west. You can have all of it you want—except what I already claimed. I met a Howard feller up in here last year, Samuel Howard, and I guess he's still around here somewhere, and there might be another one or two, but that's about all. So we better pick our spots and get started clearing."

It was a long time after that day before I learned that Martins Fork was one of the branches that formed the Cumberland River, it and Clover Fork and Poor Fork. There wasn't no way for me to know that they come together down where Mount Pleasant is now, or that the river flows back to the west and crosses the Wilderness Trail just ten miles or so beyond Cumberland Gap. If we had stayed on the trail til it met the river and then followed the river, we would have come in to what is now the front door to Harlan County. But we didn't know that then. We had come in by the back door, and I was a grown man before I ever got far enough out of the valleys of Martins and Cranks to discover where I was.

That first night there beside the creek, me and Johnny and David and Betsy and some of the littler ones cut us some cane and made a shelter on the bank above a sand bar. I was feeling real good, just knowing that for the first time since we had left the Farmer cabin, we didn't have to rise the next morning and set out on a journey. Our journey was over. I thought about Pa and Ma, and wished they could have lived to get there with us. Henry and Betty had took over as my parents, and wherever they decided to build their house, I would be living with them. Probably right around here, I thought. Me and David could help, and Johnny and his folks would be close by, and maybe Betsy and her family too. Sam and them would stay with us, so we'd build them a house too. We had all been a long way together, a hard way. I was hoping we would stay together and not move again.

After we ate some supper and it was dark and quiet, a full moon came up over Cranks Creek and threw silver on the water. It seemed bigger and whiter than any moon I could remember. Sitting there by the fire, I thought how we was there together, alone together, in the middle of the wilderness. I felt safe—but sort of scared at the same time.

I can remember the first years we spent here just like they happened yesterday. This valley of Martins Fork and all the creeks that run into it clear down to Mount Pleasant was like the whole world, far as I knew. People was flowing through Cumberland Gap by the hundreds, but we never saw them. We was closed in here, surrounded by mountain walls, living off the land in these valleys, and the only people we saw was the few that came after us to settle.

Soon after we got here we split up to claim creeks of land, and then we came back together to help one another clear ground and build cabins and plant corn. Henry and Betty decided to live near the joining of Martins and Cranks, so that meant me and David and Sam had to work there first. The Farmers went on down Martins to the place Mr. Farmer had picked out, and Abram Skidmore brought his family up here to the Cranks valley. We was each about five or six miles apart, far enough so that all three families could claim several thousand acres, and once we got the cabins built and the crops set out, we didn't see much of one another. There was buffalo and Indian trails all through the woods and across the mountains, but there wasn't no buffalo or Indians to speak of. Farmers told of seeing that Howard feller, Sam Howard, and up on Cranks, Skidmores found a man named George Burkhart living with his wife in a big hollow sycamore. But that was all. I remember the first winter about six Indians came by our place one day, said they had been hunting. They was real friendly, and we was so glad to see any people that Henry asked them in to warm by the fire. They couldn't speak a lot of English, but they looked about like settler people to me, only darker.

The next spring and summer, a few more families crossed the mountains to settle. I don't recollect now who was first, but there was Napiers, Noes, Clays, Farleys, Hensleys. It wasn't like they was our neighbors, though—they spread out along every creek from Stone Mountain to Pine Mountain, over beyond Clover Fork and Poor Fork. In all of what is now Harlan County, I reckon there was not more than twenty families by 1805, and we was so scattered it still seemed like we was there alone. Up to the time me and Betsy got married in 1808, I can only remember leaving that valley twice— once to walk across Stone Mountain back into Virginia, and once to go through Cumberland Gap to the Knox courthouse at Barbourville. It was just a muddy little town, but it seemed like a big place to me.

The first cabin we built was small—two rooms, a loft, hewed logs chinked with mud, dirt floor, fireplace. We built another little cabin for Sam and his family, just one room. Me and David Smith, being the biggest children, got to sleep in the loft, and the littler ones stayed below. Sometimes on Sunday we would follow the creek to the Skidmores or the Farmers, or they would come to visit us. Most of the time, though, we stayed to ourselves and worked. There was always a lot to do—cut timber, raise corn and a little tobacco, make soap, make most everything we needed. Kill animals for food and hides, for lard and tallow and brushes. Betty was always cooking or preserving food or making clothes or having babies. Nobody was idle. We didn't have nothing to read, didn't have no school or nothing like that, and if it hadn't been for Betty, all of us children probably would have forgot how to read, or never knowed. Betty saw to it that we all knew our letters and numbers. She helped the Farmer and Skidmore children too. We was lucky. It would have been easy to grow up here and not know how to read or write, just because there wasn't much chance to learn it or practice it or be around people who did it all the time. Betty didn't let that happen to us.

In 1808, when I was nineteen, me and Betsy got married. She was seventeen. Seemed just as natural as anything for us to do it. She could have married Johnny or David, but other than that she didn't have much choice but me—and I didn't have no other choice at all, not to tell of. Good thing we liked each other. I guess I knew from the time I was fourteen or fifteen that I would marry Betsy, and she knew it too. When we finally did it one Sunday, Henry Smith served for the preacher and our families witnessed. Then me and Betsy rode old Star and Storm up through Cranks Gap and on to the courthouse at Glade Spring to register the marriage. Glade Spring is Jonesville now—Lee County, Virginia. It was a lot closer to where we lived than Barbourville was, so that's why our marriage—and some of you children's births—is recorded in Virginia instead of Kentucky.

After the marriage, we built our first little house right here on the same spot where this house sits. The Skidmores lived close by, but the next year was when Abram had to go back to North Carolina to see about his father, and he took his wife and little ones and left Johnny here in their house. Johnny was twenty that year, same as me. It wasn't as bad for him to have his parents go away as it was for me to lose mine, but he hated to see them go just the same. Then, before that year was gone, Betty Smith died in childbirth. It was one of the saddest days I can remember. All at once, Henry had lost his wife and David had lost his mother and I had lost my sister—and all of us had lost the one who looked after us. It took us a long time to get over our grief.

Johnny married Polly Noe after that, and it wasn't too many years until David married Sally Romaine. We wasn't children any more. Suddenly we was all grown and married and making babies of our own. But poor David had more grief ahead of him. He was helping his father look after his brothers and sisters when his own wife Sally had a baby boy they named Noble—but then Sally took sick and died, and David had that baby to raise by his self. It was right pitiful the way he loved little Nobe so much—might near spoiled him. When he got to be a lad, though, he was smart as a whip, real good at reading and writing and ciphering. It looked like they would be all right then, but there was more hurt to come. In 1820, Henry Smith died—so David had lost his mother and his father and his wife before he was thirty years old. And then, in the winter of 1828, David fell sick with a pox, and he never lived to see another spring. I felt like my own brother had died. Noble was about fifteen by then. I guess I ought not to brag on him too much, even if he did marry our Nancy later on. I just want to put it down here that his father and his grandfather was just like blood kin to me, and when they died, we looked after Nobe and saw to it that he didn't want for nothing.

Those years was filled with more deaths than I care to remember, and with plenty of marriages and births too. The first six of you children was born by the time me and Betsy had been married ten years—John, Nancy, William, Cameliza, Sally, Polly Ann. Babies come easy then. So did dying. Life come hard.

Slow but sure, people kept coming to Harlan County—not many, but some. Must have been about 1819 when Harlan was carved off from Knox and named for some general killed by Indians way back. They put a courthouse at the joining of Martins and Clover and

Poor Forks, and gave the name of Mount Pleasant to that place. I guess there was a thousand people in the county by then, but they was still scattered, and we was as cut off from the outside as ever. We got word of the big doings, heard about the battle of New Orleans and the coming of steamboats and the election of Andy Jackson, but not much news reached us. Up here at the head of Cranks and Martins, there wasn't no preachers or teachers, no law, no nothing. Didn't seem to need none, not at first. But when it started getting a little crowded, that's when our problems came. Me and Henry and Johnny went to Mount Pleasant to register our land at the new courthouse and come to find out that some other people was living on creeks we knew was ours, land we had stepped off and claimed long before. That was the start of trouble. That's when we commenced seeing lawyers coming around.

Wasn't no avoiding it, I guess. People had to depend on one another more and more. Had to have someplace to sell your crops and stock and timber, someplace to buy guns and salt and coffee. We couldn't all be farmers and loggers—somebody had to tend store, be sheriff, make law. We could have used a doctor, too, and some school teachers, but they was slow coming. Betsy's brother Jim become a surveyor, that was his main work, but he learned it from me and David and Johnny. He was a good one, and people called him Surveyor Jim, and they elected him to the Kentucky legislature—but the only reason he done more surveying than farming was just that times had changed.

Now and then we would hear tell of big farms up in the Bluegrass where white people might have a hundred niggers to do all their work. Wasn't like that here. Old Sam and his family belonged to me, that's true, and Bill Turner had a few slaves, and maybe there was one or two more. But Sam and his boy Jack worked with us in the fields just the same as anybody else, and Sam's Sadie worked alongside the other women, and we never had no trouble with them, nor they with us, to my knowing. I might have owned them, but it wasn't something we thought about. After Sam and Sadie died, Jack helped me look after my horses, and he got to be so good with them that he could beat anybody racing. He was a cripple, Jack was—he had fell and broke his leg as a boy way back when we was coming here from Cumberland Gap in 1802, and it never healed right. But that didn't stop him from riding a horse the best of anybody. We built us a track in about 1830, a straight track about a mile long, and Jack was the champion of it. I remember once in about 1840 me and him rode horses up into Owsley County to a track there at Travelers Rest. Jack rode against some jockeys from the Bluegrass. There was plenty of money bet against us, but we won every race. I made a right smart out of that, and had a big time too. I always wished I didn't have nothing else to do but race my horses.

Nancy Farmer died sometime after 1830, and Stephen died in about 1835, and that left me and Betsy and Johnny Skidmore the oldest ones of us that had come into the Martins Fork valley together in 1802. We had been here just over thirty years, but it seemed like a lot longer than that. All thirteen of you children had been born by then, and Johnny and Polly must have had at least ten. Me and Betsy was already grandparents, too, cause John had married Martha Napier and they had a little girl named Polly. We was blessed with good health—all our children living, didn't lose a one. Even if nobody else had moved in here but us, the Ledfords and Skidmores and Smiths and Farmers could have filled up the valley. We had claimed the land, cleared right much of it, farmed it and logged it, hunted on it, buried our dead under it. In just a little over thirty years, me and Betsy and Johnny had lived a lifetime here—and we was not much more than forty years old. We was the only ones in those four families that had a recollection of living anywhere else. We remembered North Carolina and Virginia and Tennessee, far off in our past. I guess remembering made us different from our children. All they could remember was Harlan County.

It might seem queer to you now, but me and your Ma can recall when they first brought window lights in here and made it so we could see outdoors from the house. And glasses you could drink out of, and plows made of iron, and food put up in tin cans. We wondered at all those things. I remember the first time I ever saw coffee beans, and how they smelled when they was ground up, and how good the brew tasted. The whiskey we made then was mighty good too, maybe better than now. Before there was a store hereabouts, peddlers would bring pack mules across from Virginia with goods to sell or trade, and we got to going more often across there ourselves, over to Glade Spring and all along the trail there—same Wilderness Trail we had followed to Cumberland Gap. It made me want to follow that road back to North Carolina sometime, back to see my kin, but I never went. I wrote a letter back to my brother Frederick one time, must have been about 1842, and he answered it. I told him what all had happened to us, and I remember it was a strange feeling to be telling him about our parents getting killed forty years before that. I told him about Betty and Henry, and about me and Betsy and our children. Fred wrote back and said some of them was still on Caraway Creek, but Ledfords had spread out all over, and lots of them had passed on. Uncle Pete had died in 1835, and Uncle Obediah had gone out to his barn one day in 1841 and hung himself with a bridle. He was eighty years old. A man brought me that letter from Mount Pleasant, from the post office. It was the first letter I ever remember getting.

They had camp meetings over in Virginia, at a big Methodist campground near Rose Hill and also in Glade Spring, and we went a few times. Then sometimes a preacher would ride through here and stop. Seemed to me like they was always trying to scare people into behaving. I never did care much for that. One of old Buckhart's boys made a preacher, but he was a pretty good feller just the same. He didn't tell people not to drink whiskey or play the fiddle or dance—just said don't overdo. I liked that about him.

I bought some land over in Virginia back in about 1830, and in 1843 me and my boy John and Johnny Skidmore and his boys and Nobe Smith and Surveyor Jim Farmer made a big land survey that got us all more land. We covered a big area—from the top of Cumberland Mountain down into Lee County, Virginia, then west to Cumberland Gap, then north to the Cumberland River, and then east along Little Black Mountain all the way to the upper valley of Martins Fork and across to where we had started. The whole thing covered nearly two hundred thousand acres, and we claimed every bit that wasn't fenced and deeded. When we finished, we had about a hundred thousand acres to claim. Four of us—Farmer, Ledford, Skidmore and Smith—divided it up. Jim Farmer got the most because he was the head surveyor, but each one of us got at least fifteen thousand acres. There was a lot of disputes over that land, and we lost some of it, but still we had a lot, and it didn't cost us much of nothing.

Your Ma and me had built our house over by then to make it big enough for all of us, and then the grown ones, John and then Nancy and William, had got married and moved out. Twenty years ago, around 1850, Mount Pleasant didn't have but about fifty people, and that was the only town in the county. Most of the people lived out, like us. There wasn't but two or three schools in all of Harlan County, and they didn't amount to much, and there wasn't one close to us. We had a Bible and a Webster dictionary I bought once off a peddler, and that was about all we had to read. We tried to teach every child we ever had to read and write, and most of you learned, but not good enough to suit me. We needed a school for that.

When I look around at all we have now, I can't hardly believe how different everything is from when we came here. In this house, there is a spinning wheel and loom, handmade furniture, feather beds, iron skillets, quilts, oil lamps, hand pistols and a Winchester rifle. There's geese in the yard, chickens, cattle and sheep and pigs fenced in, plenty of horses. We've got honey from our bee gums, tobacco to smoke or chew, whiskey to drink, a smokehouse full of ham and bacon and sausage. Back in the early days, about all we had was the bare little we could bring on oxback. We still work hard, but life is easier now.

It has changed another way too. There's more people now, over four thousand, and that means more fussing and fighting. People may be meaner than they was. I know for a fact they don't help one another as much. I see changes you wouldn't see—more meanness, more stealing, more shooting to settle differences. Seemed like it started back twenty or thirty years ago, back in the forties—people quarreling over land, politics, religion, slavery. The war made it worse, but it started way before that. You might say nothing has changed here, but it ain't so. Nobody stole your stock when I was young, just didn't do it. Nobody fought over the Bible til there was Baptists to fight Methodists. Nobody cared about politics til there was Whigs and Democrats. I've been a Henry Clay man from the first, so I am a Whig, a Republican, but I never wanted to fight about it. Before we ever got into that war I could see trouble coming. Ever since 1843, when we did that land survey, I've been feeling the wind shift. I was over fifty years old then, had come up to where I had a good life—but that was when the bad time commenced.

I saw that war coming, sure as rain. Slavery was a subject that made people mad, whichever side they was on. We heard about Abe Lincoln and Jeff Davis, two Kentuckians leaning different ways. When Lincoln got elected and the war started, I figured it would be a hard fight, and I was right. Across the mountain in Virginia, they was talking rebellion and secession, and so was the big slaveowners up in the Bluegrass. Harlan County was more for the Union, but there was some Rebs around here too. Cumberland Gap was still part of Harlan then, so both sides passed back and forth through here all during the war.

James and Stephen, our youngest sons, went off to fight for the Union, and me and Betsy was relieved when the war was over and everybody in the family was back home safe. In a way, though, it was more dangerous around here than it was where James and Stephen went. We had Rebs ambushing Yanks, and Yanks chasing Rebs, and marauders preying on one and all. Nothing but renegade outlaws and robbers is what they were, and they did more harm here than the unionists and seceders put together.

I was about slavery like I was about politics—I didn't want to fight over it. What seemed wrong to me was not owning slaves, but mistreating them. I had thirteen slaves when the war started, all of them in the households of George and Sinkler, sons of Jack, who died before the war. Sinkler's real name is Saint Clair, just because Jack wanted to call him that, but most people call him Sinclair, or Sinkler, or just Sink. In the fall of '62, old Abe declared that all slaves in the Rebel states would be set free come the next January. That didn't include Kentucky, cause it was not a Rebel state, but I was for Abe and the Union, so I knew what I was going to do. I went up the holler to see George and Sink. We stood out by the gate at Sink's cabin and talked. I said, "You fellers always stood by me, and I've tried to stand by you. Your father and grandfather, the same. The law said I owned you, but I never thought of it that way. Some people want to fight over it, but I ain't one of them. What you have in this holler is yours to keep." They said they was much obliged, and that was all there was for any of us to say. Nothing changed, hasn't changed to this day. But that day, I went home feeling better.

The end of slavery and war didn't end the bad times. I'm an old man now, I don't have no future, but I worry about the future for the rest of you. All I've got, I worked hard for. Now people crave it, and I have to guard it. It will all belong to you children, if it don't get stolen from me first. People are coming in here from New York and such far places, wanting to buy our land, or the minerals under it. They must think all the coal is worth something—but how they going to get it out? I can't see no way. They can't get a railroad up in these hollers. Some tells me to hold on, not to sell. Some says I should get shed of it. I don't know who is right, or who I can trust. I reckon Ledfords claim over twenty-five thousand acres of Harlan County land now. Me and John claim most of it. But the titles ain't clear, and there's lawyers trying to steal some of it, and there ain't no way to find out what it's worth. Used to be we didn't have no law, and didn't need none. Now we need law and law men to protect us from ourselves. And when the law men turn out to be outlaws too, that's when you know you got troubles. They used to say Kentucky was Eden. If it was, the snakes took it.

I can't hardly believe I have been here so long, or that I am so old. If I live two more years, I will be seventy years in Harlan County, and in all that time, I never did go far from here but twice. The first time was when me and Jack went to the horse races up in Owsley County. The other time was in 1846, when me and son James, a boy of sixteen, rode up to Montgomery County, Virginia, to see where my grandfather John Ledford and his brothers had settled a hundred years before that. We took two good horses and stayed gone over two weeks. Rode from Cranks up through Pennington Gap and on up the Great Valley of Virginia clear to Montgomery County, must be near on to two hundred miles. It was in the fall of the year, a real pretty time. I don't know why we went, except I just had a yearning to see where my grandfather had lived as a young man. I wanted to walk where he had hunted and plowed, just so I could connect up the place with the stories he had told me about it.

We stopped at the old Drapers Meadow settlement. That's where my grandfather said the Indians killed Uncle Henry and old James Patton, the man that brought Henry and John and William Ledford to America in 1738. Patton's nephew, William Preston, built a nice plantation house at Drapers Meadow later on, and it's still there. He had another nephew that claimed to be one of the early settlers of Louisville, right here in Kentucky. One died with an arrow through his heart, the other helped to start a city. You never can know how things will turn out.

The place where Grandpa and Uncle William and Uncle Henry built their first cabins in about 1750 was on the west fork of the Roanoke River. I remembered that from the stories—"where Bradshaws Creek empties into the Roanoke." It took us all one day to find Bradshaws Creek, but we finally located it about ten miles east of Blacksburg. The mountains there are not like our mountains. They rise up sharp and sudden, all right, but seems like there's fewer of them, or they are spread out more, cause the bottomland is flatter and wider than what we have here. All the way out there from Blacksburg is just one long valley between high mountains, prettiest valley I reckon I ever saw. Me and James studied it a long while. I could understand why Grandpa never forgot it.

At the mouth of Bradshaws we found a settlement of Wattersons, same family that had got the land after my grandfather and them left it. They never knew about any Ledfords being there before them. All they could tell was that the King of England made a thousand-acre land grant to Samuel Watterson in 1760, and four more generations of Wattersons had lived there since Samuel. Just a few years before, they had buried Joseph Watterson, the last son of Samuel.

Those people was real friendly to me and James. We stayed overnight with them. I laid awake thinking how it could have been Ledfords on that land for five generations, instead of Wattersons.

One of the Wattersons migrated to Tennessee and got elected to Congress. Now he's got a son named Henry that's the editor of a newspaper in Louisville. A Union man to boot. I'm glad to know that valley on the Roanoke was so fertile for the Wattersons. I wish it could have been for the Ledfords.

Me and James came back home from that trip feeling like we had been halfway around the world. I was glad to get home, but I never have forgotten the lay of that land. It made my grandfather's life seem very close to me. After that I wanted to go to North Carolina and see my own beginnings, but I kept putting it off, and now I guess I have waited too late. I am too old to make the trip. Everybody I knew there when I was a boy must be dead by now.

My home is here on Cranks Creek, not on Bradshaws or Caraway or in the Bluegrass. This is where I belong. I know every hill and holler of it, every creek from Martins and Cranks over to Clover Fork and Poor Fork. I know the woods and the wildlife, what there is left of it, and I know the weather, when it is best to plant and when to lay by. And I know the people. I have seen some things get better and some get worse and some stay just the same. And I know in my heart I belong here on this land with these people. The ones of us that came here first—Ledford, Farmer, Skidmore, Smith— is still here, and still close to one another, but all the old ones is gone except me and my Betsy. Old Johnny died just last year, right after me and him turned eighty. He had got married a second time when he was seventy, married a Stepp girl, and her just nineteen years old, and she bore him four children before he took sick and died. I miss Johnny more than a brother. We lost our Nancy too, our second born, the first one of you to die. She was married to Noble Smith, who we raised after his father died. David's bad luck followed Nobe, but now he is married again, and I hope his luck has changed.

Jim Farmer, Betsy's brother, is gone too. His daughter Peggy is married to Abram Skidmore, Johnny's son. I don't know if we are moving up or down or sideways. Sometimes I think we move in circles, and come back to where we started.

It was springtime when I started on these recollections. Now it is winter again. It has taken me and Betsy a long time to think of everything we had to tell. We are done now, and I have put down all I can. Maybe I left out some, and there was some dates I wasn't sure of, and some things I forgot, but I didn't make up none of it. What I have told is true as far as I know and remember. I can't go no further. Somebody else will have to finish it after me and Betsy are gone.

Aley Ledford
February 18, 1870

To the children, grandchildren, and great-grandchildren of Aley and Betsy Ledford:

I am Stephen Ledford, last son of Aley and Betsy. I am giving this statement to A.B. Cornet, clerk of Harlan County. He will write it down and give it to me so I can put it with what my father wrote and finish the story.

My father died on April 24, 1873, six days before his eighty-fourth birthday. He died a proud man, the same way he had lived. Consumption finally took him, and when he died he only weighed about a hundred pounds. We buried him on the hillside above the house on Cranks Creek. He had lived on Cranks since 1802, and that was where he wanted to die and be buried.

In the summer of 1870, three years before Papa died, a man named Edward M. Davis of Philadelphia, Pennsylvania sent some lawyers to Harlan County to buy the land my father and my brother and Noble Smith and others had surveyed in the 1840s. Nobody knew for sure just how much land was in the survey. They had covered a huge boundary of about two hundred thousand acres and claimed all the unoccupied and unfenced land, according to Kentucky law, but some of it was in Bell County and some was even in Virginia and Tennessee. The state of Kentucky finally gave the Ledford-Smith-Farmer-Skidmore surveyors a patent on eighty-six thousand acres of unclaimed land in Harlan County. My brother John claimed they paid the state five cents an acre for title to all of that. There was so many overlapping claims and conflicts and disputed titles and tax liens on the land that they never could tell exactly what they had.

The Philadelphia lawyers offered $86,000—one dollar an acre—and said they would pay the money whether there was clear title or not. They bought other land in the county the same way, and sometimes they even paid more than one claimant for the same piece of land. My father and them had paid less than $5,000 for their holdings, so the price sounded good to them. They couldn't use the land for much, or sell it for much, or keep clear title to it, so they were glad to sell it. They could not see how Edward Davis of Philadelphia was going to get his money back out of it. But now the railroad is just over the mountain. We understand now. I am glad Papa didn't live to see what he lost.

Before Papa died, he divided his money and belongings among us children. We got about $2,000 apiece. It was decided that Mama would come and live with me and my wife Sarah, and my brothers and sisters left it up to me to decide what to do with the old homeplace and the land around it there on Cranks Creek. Papa had told me to deed over some land to Sinkler and George Ledford, the colored people that live there. He had already deeded them two hundred acres. Since then I have given them eight hundred acres more. They now own most of the land at the head of Cranks Creek, except for a few acres around the old homeplace.

Harlan County has not changed much since Papa died. Noble Smith passed away about three years ago. My sister Nancy has been dead almost fifty years, and my brother William died ten years ago. The biggest families in the south end of Harlan County are still the Ledfords, Smiths, Skidmores, and Farmers. There's more people in the county—over six thousand in the 1890 census—but the roads are still very bad and it is very hard to go from here to anyplace else. Some do get out and go to places like California or Alaska, but most of them are never heard from again. The telephone and electric lights and the railroad and all those fine things we hear about have not got here yet, and the mail is not very dependable.

Almost everyone in Harlan County is still Republican, same as before. We helped put Benjamin Harrison in the White House, but we haven't been able to get a Republican governor in Kentucky yet. I have not figured out what we have in common with the Vanderbilts and all those other rich Republicans. There is not any rich people in Harlan County.

We have a little school on Cranks Creek now, and another one at Smith. Creed Smith, Noble's son, ran the store there until he moved to Virginia two years ago. The schools take up only three months a year. Me and Sarah cannot read or write, so we could not help our ten children to learn. Most of them have learned a little somehow, even though they have not been to school much.

The railroad has been built down through Pineville and Cumberland Gap and on up the Poor Valley of Virginia all the way to Norton, and we hear talk that there will be spurs of it built over into Harlan County so they can haul away the coal. The Louisville and Nashville Railroad and the big land companies have figured out some way to test under the ground to tell how thick the coal seams are and how far they run, so they are planning on digging a lot of coal. That will mean jobs for the men here, and the railroad will make it easier for us to get in and out of the county, so I am in favor of these changes. I am in favor of anything that will make life better for the people here. The family of Edward M. Davis of Philadelphia still owns the survey land and a lot more besides. They have never even been here to look at it. They pay a little bit of tax to the county. The land is just setting there. They must be waiting on the railroad.

The biggest change in Harlan County since my father died has been the increase of violence and the breakdown of law and order. Most any kind of an argument can lead to a killing, and sometimes it don't even take one. Two of my nephews, Aley Junior's boys, have been killed over nothing. We had a federal revenue agent, E.V. King, who was doing a good job against moonshine whiskey, but his health was poor, so he had to resign and go back to farming on Clover Fork. He made a good sheriff before that. But nobody wants these law jobs, for fear of getting killed. Law and order is a mess in Harlan County. Too many men are taking the law into their own hands and doing whatever they please. It is a shameful thing to be afraid for your life in your own community.

Some of this lawlessness has led to feuds between families, and the worst one of these right now is between the Turners and the Howards. They have been at war off and on since 1884, and two years ago the governor had to send the militia in here to break up a battle between them. As soon as the soldiers was gone, Leander Ledford, another one of my brother Aley's boys, and Jesse Ledford, one of my nephews, sold out their farms on Crane Branch and Board Branch and moved up to Garrard County, in the Bluegrass. Creed Smith lived close to Leeann and James, and he gave up and left about the same time they did, turned his land and store and mill over to his children and moved across the mountain to Rose Hill. The feuding and killing and destruction is driving decent people away from Harlan County, and the outlaws are getting the upper hand. I'm glad my father didn't live to see how bad it has gotten.

There is one thing I wish he had lived to see, though, and that's the Kentucky Derby in Louisville. It started about fifteen years ago, and now they say it's getting to be the biggest race in the state of Kentucky. If the Derby had been there when Papa and Jack was racing and winning, I believe they would have gone to Louisville and entered. I believe they would have won, too.

I never have been to Louisville myself, or even to Lexington. I have lived all of my life here in Harlan County. Three of my brothers have left here. John and James moved to Powell County and William to Owsley County. Me and Aley Junior have stayed, and all of my sisters married and settled here. We have lived the same way our parents did, but in some ways we have had it easier. Some ways maybe harder too.

I am sixty years old now. My health is poor because of asthma. After I finish with this statement, I am going to tell A.B. Cornet my last will and testament, so he can write that down for me too. The only land me and Sarah own is our farm on Cranks Creek, near the trail over Cranks Ridge. But I have enough to give each one of my eight daughters and two sons $1,000 apiece, and have some left for Sarah. We are not poor. We have done right good, thank the Lord.

Six months ago, my mother finally passed away at our house. She was completely blind, had been for years. She was exactly a hundred years old, had been born on the New River near the border of Virginia and North Carolina in 1791. Mama was a strong woman all her life. She suffered some toward the end, but she never did complain. She was the last person to die of all the ones that came together through Cumberland Gap in 1802. She talked about that a lot, about the old times, but I guess we had all heard it so much that we just didn't pay any attention to her. What she could remember seeing and doing was not something we could picture in our thoughts, because none of us ever got to see or do those things. She was what you might call the last real pioneer.

We buried Mama in the graveyard at the foot of Cranks Ridge, just about a mile below our house. From that little rise where the graveyard is, there is a good view of the whole upper valley of Cranks Creek. My sister Nancy is buried there. Me and Sarah will be buried there too. Maybe we should move Papa's grave down there too, so we can all be together.

And now I have come to the end of the story. Aley Ledford and Betsy Farmer Ledford was among the first settlers to come into Harlan County. They stayed all the rest of their lives. They was good people. They lived for others. I am proud I was their son.

Stephen Ledford
X (his mark)

Witness: Oliver Farmer
     John Napier X (his mark)
Attest: A.B. Cornet, Clerk

Harlan Court House
November 7, 1891

SIX

Goodbye, Harlan County

Burnam, 1876–1903

Burnam Ledford read the entire account carefully, holding each page close to his "reading eye," scanning every line. When he had finished, I explained to him again the technique I had used to dramatize and personalize the story.

"I had to make a few guesses, but not many," I said. "Almost everything is drawn from what you know or what I learned elsewhere. There are some names that can't be found and some dates we can't be certain of, but by and large it's a story with a very strong basis in fact, and I've tried to tell it in words that Aley himself might have used."

The oldest living descendant of Aley Ledford declared himself pleased and satisfied with the result. "You've done a good job," he said, "and I don't find much that's wrong. It sounds like Aley's story to me. Did you locate this statement of Stephen Ledford's somewhere?"

"No, but I did find his will in the Harlan County courthouse, and it was witnessed and dated and signed just like this shows. I needed some way to take Aley's story beyond his death to the death of Betsy, and since she died the same year Stephen did, I decided to put these last elements of the story into a statement that Stephen might have given when he made his will. He couldn't read or write, so he must have gotten the county clerk to write it down for him."

"Well," Mr. Ledford replied, "we can't be sure of every fact, but I've known about Aley all my life, and what you've put down here sounds very much like him to me. I always thought he was about nineteen and already married when they came to Kentucky, but I never was sure about it. There's one thing you said, though, that I'm pretty sure is wrong. You said that after Aley's parents got killed at Cumberland Gap, they turned up across the mountain there and followed Martins Fork into Harlan County. I think you're mistaken about that. You see, they were coming up through the corner of Tennessee. I think they approached Cumberland Gap from the south—and then, after the accident, they turned up the Poor Valley to Pennington Gap and crossed over into Harlan County there. That's what I always understood, anyway."

"You could be right," I conceded, "but I came to this other conclusion because of Stephen Farmer. He had been there before, and he knew the way. Of course, he could have known the way through Pennington Gap too. But the Martins Fork route was the most direct way from Cumberland Gap to where they were going. It was rugged, for sure—but every route was rugged. I think he led them the closest way."

"Well, we'll never know for sure, will we?" he said. Then, laughing, he added: "Your guess may not be as good as mine, but I won't quarrel with you about it."

We were deep into the porch season, the time of healing warmth. Burnam and Addie Ledford sat framed in a flowering vine that encircled the front porch, she with her broom nearby, he with his cedar staves and whittling knife and plug of tobacco. Extra rockers were in place, inviting company. With the ancestral preface to their story now finished, it was time for each of them in turn to begin remembering and relating the first years of their lives, the years prior to their marriage.

"I'd like to ask both of you to think about the time when you were young," I said, "starting with the first things you can remember and going forward to the time when you got married."

That was the beginning of the detailed personal remembrances, the autobiographical chronicles that would continue for weeks and months. The stories divided conveniently into four periods of

roughly equal length, one before marriage and three after. Gradu-
ally, the hours of tape converted to hundreds of pages of transcrip-
tion, and then to edited narratives. The first of these followed
Burnam to the age of twenty-seven and Addie to the age of eigh-
teen. Burnam's account was like a continuation of Aley's—which
in a sense it was, for he was the custodian of his great-grandfather's
story as well as his own. The unfolding narrative was richly de-
tailed, carefully organized, thoughtfully presented. Burnam Ledford
drew on a century of memories to reconstruct the years of his youth:

Aley died three years before I was born, but I heard so much about
him when I was growing up that it almost seemed like he was still
alive. He was not only my father's grandfather but also my mother's
great-grandfather, so I heard about him from both sides of my family. I knew most of his children, too, starting with John, the oldest,
who was past seventy when I was a little boy, and I told you about
going to see Blind Granny, Aley's Betsy, when I was five years old.

My mother's parents, Sam and Polly Jones, moved to Harlan
County from Tennessee after the Civil War and bought a hillside
farm of about five hundred acres on Coon Branch of Martins Fork.
Their daughter Vesta was my mother. She married Jesse Ledford,
my father, there on Coon Branch in 1873, and they lived in a little
cabin on that farm until we moved to Powell County in 1878. My
father's parents, James and Polly Ledford, had lived on a bigger
farm just a short distance away, right where Martins Fork and
Cranks Creek join, but they had separated by then, and right around
the time I was born my Grandfather Ledford sold that place and
moved up on Red River in Powell County, and we soon went to
join him.

I was born in that little Coon Branch cabin on May 26, 1876—
the second baby my parents had, but the first to live. I was named
for Curtis Burnam of Richmond, right over here in Madison County.
He was a well-known representative in the state legislature, a lawyer and a Union loyalist, a supporter of Clay and Lincoln, but I
think my parents especially liked him because he had got a state
law passed that if you had lived on your land for fifteen years, you

could have clear title to it. People from outside were coming into the mountains buying big blocks of land for the mineral rights, and all kinds of conflicts was arising between the local people and these outsiders. Curtis Burnam wanted to protect the rights of the little farmer. I'm proud of that.

My Grandfather Ledford had bought some land and gone into the logging business in Powell County, and he wanted my father to come there, so we moved, and my father and grandfather farmed together in the summer and logged the rest of the year. We lived just above the Red River gorge, and they floated timber down through the gorge to Clay City, where they sold it to the Norcross Milling Company. They were doing right well, but my father took typhoid fever and come very near dying, and when he finally got over it he decided we should go back to Harlan County.

I don't remember moving to Powell County or living there, but I have a clear recollection of returning to Harlan in September 1881. It took us three days to get there, with my little sister Polly riding in front of my father on one horse and me riding behind my mother on the other. We stopped in Clay City to buy some salt, and then we passed a little store where some people was gathered around a man playing a fiddle and two or three other men dancing to the music. We stayed and listened a little bit, and then I begged my mother and father to let me stay behind and overtake them later, but they wouldn't let me. Then we went on to Will Ledford's house to spend the night—he was my great-uncle, a son of Aley and Betsy.

When we got to Harlan, or Mount Pleasant, as they called it then, there wasn't any sidewalks, and the streets was all muddy, and hogs had rooted out holes under the hitch racks where people tied their horses. It was almost the same as being out in an open field—there just wasn't much to Harlan except the courthouse and the jail and a few stores and houses. George O. Barnes, the noted evangelist, was holding a meeting there, but the floor of the courthouse had fallen in the day before, and he had to move his meeting to a tent down near the river.

My sister and me went to every store in town trying to buy some candy, but there wasn't a piece of it to be found, so I bought me some brown sugar. As we started up Martins Fork toward my grandmother's I was eating that sugar, and I got it all over my hands and face. My mother was wearing a bonnet with a tail on it, so I used it for a handkerchief. When she saw what I was doing, she reached back and slapped me right good.

We stayed for about two months on Coon Branch, in the same cabin we had left in 1878, and then we moved down to Bill Day's place on Days Branch and stayed through the winter there. The next spring my father put out a crop there and another one on a little farm he had bought on Crane Branch, just one valley up from Coon Branch, and we moved into a little house on that place. It was really just one big room and a shed room, but my father hired a man to hew some logs and we added an ell to it. Before we left there to move up here to Paint Lick at the end of 1889, me and Polly had four brothers and sisters—Speed, Asher, Jim, and Sarah.

I was six years old the spring we settled on Crane Branch, and I was going on fourteen when we left there. In those years when I grew from a boy to a young man, I became familiar with every hill and holler along that big valley where Cranks and Martins join. The land was still nearly all in forest, and the roads was mostly in the creek beds, and it was hard work, steady work, to do the clearing and farming and logging that was necessary to make a living. As the oldest boy, it was my job to milk the cow, feed the stock, get in the firewood. We didn't have a stove, so my mother cooked over the open fire, and she weaved all the cloth for our clothing and blankets. We raised all our own food—didn't have fruit jars to preserve in, but dried our fruits or kept things like apples, potatoes, cabbages, and turnips in the cellar. I thought we lived pretty good. We had chickens and ducks and geese and turkeys, so that gave us meat and eggs. We made our own lye soap from ashes, made our buckets, churns, barrels, chairs. Didn't do much socializing with other families, but we kept so busy we didn't have time to get lonesome.

The virgin timber was being cut out of there fast in those days. When the big walnut timber was just about gone, my father commenced cutting poplar logs and taking them to market. He had some trees that were over seven feet in diameter. That was nothing compared to old Burkhart's sycamore on Cranks Creek, though. I saw the hollow stump of it when I was a boy, and stepped it off inside. Seems like it was fourteen steps across.

There was a little school at Smith, just a mile or so from our house, and we went three months a year. I started when I was seven. Didn't do much but reading and spelling. I was a good speller, and when we had matches on Saturday afternoons I nearly always won. My parents didn't have much schooling, but they could read and write. We had a Bible at home, and my father bought a book about the history of the land and sea, and I always enjoyed reading those books. There wasn't anything at Smith but the school when we first moved there, but Creed Smith opened a store and a grist mill in about 1885. The post office didn't come until after we had moved away. Noble Smith owned a lot of land around there. He's the one that married Aley's Nancy. His son Creed was about ten years older than my father.

I remember a right smart from the 1880s. Cassius M. Clay rode up to our house in a buckboard one day in 1882, looking for some of his kinfolks, and he ended up spending the night with us. We had a picture of President Garfield and Vice President Arthur up on our wall—that might have been after Garfield was assassinated in 1881. One time my father came back from Pineville, where he had floated some logs, and told us about seeing a woman talk to someone seven miles away on something called a telephone. We used to walk across the mountain to Hubbard Springs, Virginia, and watch men at work building the railroad with picks and shovels and mules, and we could hear the train whistling way down the valley, but we never saw it. Even as isolated as we were, we could still see and hear about things that was going on, and I remember a lot of them.

I went up to the head of Cranks Creek with my Grandmother Jones one time, and we stopped at old Sinkler Ledford's place to rest, and they gave us dinner. It was mostly colored people there then. Sinkler Ledford and his wife had several children. One of them was James—he went by Jeemes, just like my grandfather—

and later on he got to be the postmaster there on Cranks, at Ledford, Kentucky. After dinner, Sinkler's girls took me out and filled up my pockets with apples. They was all older than me. One of them later was a school teacher in Harlan County.

We might have stayed on in Harlan if it hadn't been for an outbreak of violence and lawlessness that caused my father to want to move. A feud had started in our end of the county in about 1884 when Charlie Cawood and John Day got into an argument and Cawood shot Day and killed him. Wilson Howard took up with the Day feudists and the Turner boys joined with the Cawoods, and their battles continued off and on for years. Several men got killed, and it got so bad that in 1889 the governor of Kentucky sent soldiers in there to arrest Wilse Howard and the other ringleaders. That slowed things down some, but Wilse got away, and everybody knew the feud would continue because the law wasn't strong enough to stop it. That's when my father decided he had had enough.

My father was bitterly opposed to the feud, wouldn't have anything to do with either side. Our neighbor and friend, Creed Smith, felt the same way. Noble Smith, his father, had died the year before, and Creed had inherited his land, but he wanted to leave. I remember him and my father talking. My father said, "Creed, the way this fighting keeps on, killing one another, it's a bad place to raise children. I believe the best thing we can do is get out of here." Creed turned over most of his property to his two oldest sons, Noble and Carlo—they were only about twenty years old—and moved with his wife and younger children over the mountain to Rose Hill, Virginia.

My father had a cousin by the name of Nathan Noe who had bought a farm here in Garrard County in about 1886. So my father and another cousin of his, Leander Ledford, contacted Nathan and made arrangements to buy a small place near him in the Paint Lick neighborhood. We sold our Crane Branch farm and Leeann Ledford sold his place, and the two families of us got ready to move right after Christmas of 1889.

I remember when my father came home and told us we were moving. We were all excited. I could just picture all this knee-high bluegrass, and I thought the land would all be level and there wouldn't be any blackberry briars. It sounded like paradise to me. None of us had ever been out of the mountains. We just didn't have any idea what it was going to be like to pull up stakes and go to a new place. But I think we had some idea of what we was giving up. I felt like I did, anyway.

In spite of the feudists, I liked the mountain valley where we lived. I knew every family that lived there, knew every creek and path and mountain ridge. I had family all around me—aunts and uncles, cousins, grandparents, even a great-grandmother. I had teamed to plow with a bull-tongue plow in that valley. I had learned to raise tobacco, tried to smoke it, taken up chewing it. Once an old man smoking a cob pipe in front of the fire offered me a puff or two, then a little bit more, and I commenced getting hot, moved back from the fire, finally went outside and laid down in the snow, then threw up everything, everything but my socks, and thought I was going to die, afraid I wouldn't. Every memory I had, good and bad, was from that place, that valley in the mountains. It wasn't an easy life we had there, but I thought it was a good life, and even with all the excitement of moving to a new place, I remember feeling a little bit sad that we had to go.

We left our home on Crane Branch on the twenty-eighth of December, 1889, and started toward Mount Pleasant. Each family—Leeann Ledford's and ours—had a covered wagon pulled by two yoke of oxen, and my mother and Leeann's wife rode on horses, sidesaddle, each one of them carrying a baby on her lap. It happened to be pretty warm weather for December, so the traveling wasn't too hard, but it took us three days to get about forty-five miles over to Pineville. We was driving our cattle and stock, and that slowed us some, and the road was so narrow in places that we feared the wagons would slide over the bank into the river. I remember one night we stayed in an old log schoolhouse. It had a dirt floor, and we spread pine brush around and put our feather bedding from the wagons on top of it, and we all slept very comfortably.

Our plan was to go to the train station at Wasiota, on the river right near Pineville, and put our livestock in a stock car for shipment to Stanford, up near Lancaster. One of us would travel with the stock, and the rest would go along in the wagons. When we got to Wasiota, we milked the cows, bought hay for them, and put them in the stockyard to wait for an empty stock car. They said it would be a three-day wait, so we decided to stay that night near the train station and get a head start toward Stanford the next morning.

That night while we was there a train came in to the station, and we all went to see it, because it was the first train we had ever seen. I was going to be brave, you know, and show the rest of them that I wasn't afraid, but that was the scariest looking thing I had ever put my eyes on. The big light was shining in the dark, and the smoke was puffing, and the bell was clanging, and the whistle blowing so loud that all the little ones started crying to be taken inside. I tried to stand my ground, but pretty soon I backed up a little bit, and finally I got over real close to my father. Leeann's dog was so scared that he ran away. We kept calling "Here, Sheppie! Here, Sheppie!" but we never did see Sheppie again.

The road from Pineville north was in better shape than the road from Harlan. It was the old Wilderness Road, Daniel Boone's first trail, and we could make about twenty miles a day on it. It took us four days to get to Stanford, but we still got there ahead of our livestock. When it finally came and we started up the road the last ten miles to Lancaster, some of the oxen got excited and wild and started running off. We had to get on the horses and steer those beasts into a hedge fence to stop them.

It was about noon when we got here to Lancaster, and as we drove the cattle out Richmond Street toward Paint Lick we let them stop and eat grass on the side of the road. The horses and oxen ate too, and we had some food for ourselves in the wagons, and I remember going in a store and buying a can of peaches and some cookies. We hadn't seen many canned goods before that. I had to get the storekeeper to open the can for me. Then we went on to Paint Lick and got there about sundown. That was January 4, 1890.

The place we had bought was a small farm with two houses on it—one for us and one for Leeann and his family—and the agreement between the two families was that we would divide the land evenly but work it together, the same as if it was still one place. We lived there for five years, and then it seemed like we moved to a different farm nearly every year until 1902, when my father bought a 138-acre farm on Sugar Creek, down below Lancaster.

The grass wasn't really blue and the land wasn't flat, but we liked it around Garrard County pretty much. Times were not easy for us, though. My sister Polly took the measles and died the same year we got here, and we heard from back home the next year that Blind Granny had died. We didn't have much money, and the farms we lived on those first few years didn't produce as much as we hoped they would. Young people were going west, the same as some had from Harlan, looking for a better life. It didn't take me long to figure out that Paint Lick wasn't paradise any more than Cranks Creek and Martins Fork had been. I decided there wasn't no such place as paradise, not on this earth.

Something else I discovered back then: The people that had built all these big mansions in the Bluegrass had wanted to live a life of ease, and they had relied on slaves to do their work. They raised their sons and daughters in that leisure society, never taught them to work, and they grew up thinking work was a disgrace. They had been taught how to be gentlemen, but the gentlemen didn't know how to swing an axe. You've heard the expression "a gentleman's mess"? Well, that's where it came from. And then when there wasn't any more slaves, there wasn't anyone to do all the hard work, and that's when the plantation society started coming apart. After the old people died, the young ones found themselves in debt and lacking the skills to work their way out of it, so they commenced selling off parcels of land just to pay the taxes and keep going. That's when people started coming down here out of the mountains, buying these farms that was being cut up from big places into small ones. That's how we bought our land. We knew about work. My great-grandfather had slaves, but he taught his children to work just the same as the slaves did. I worked from the time I was six years old. These rich people in the Bluegrass made a big mistake.

It wasn't too many years until mountain people owned a great many of the small farms around the Bluegrass. I don't know of any that got rich, but we knew how to get by—we had been raised to be self-sufficient people, hardworking and thrifty. When we killed a cow, for instance, we saved the hide to make leather, used the horn to make powderhorns and combs and buttons, made candles from the tallow—and that was the only light we had. We burned pine knots in the fireplace, made mattresses stuffed with goose feathers, and used river sand to scrub our poplar plank floors. You had to use everything, couldn't waste anything, couldn't go to a store and buy things already made. We grew up knowing what everything was worth, so when we got here where people wasted so much, it gave us an advantage to know how to make do. It was a big change, moving here was, but we made the best of it.

Not long after we moved here, I noticed a brick church on the road between Paint Lick and our farm, and one Sunday morning I decided to go there to Sunday school. Tried to get some of the others to go with me, but nobody would. It was the Associated Reform Presbyterians—the Seceders, the Southern church. I was dressed altogether different from the other children. All my clothes were homemade, even down to my shoes. The other boys wore knee pants and sailor collars. I went in and sat down on a seat behind a class about my size, my age, and pretty soon I saw they didn't know the lesson. So the teacher got to asking me questions, and I answered them. Directly she asked me, "Who are you? Where did you come from?" I told her I was from the mountains. She took me around and introduced me to everybody in the church, and they were real nice to me. The teacher gave me a Sunday school book and some papers and invited me to come back.

The next Sunday I had memorized the lesson perfectly, and before long they advanced me to an older class. Later on, the teacher asked me to teach her class one Sunday when she was going to be gone, and that day there was a young preacher there from South Carolina. He listened to me, and afterward he told some of the men, "This boy was teaching the class of young people, and I want to say there's not a man in this house who could have done it better." They wanted me to go off to school in South Carolina, go through college and theological seminary and be a preacher, but I was only fourteen then—and besides, my father had taken ill, and he depended on me so much that he said he couldn't get along without me. I had the ambition to be a home missionary—I wanted to go to college and then work all over the Appalachians organizing schools and churches and Sunday schools—but I saw that my parents needed me, so I sacrificed my education and the work I wanted to do for the sake of my family.

I did join that church, though, and my father joined right after me. We was baptized by sprinkling at the same service. My parents never had joined a church before, because we didn't have one where we lived in Harlan County. My mother went with Leander Ledford's family to the Mount Tabor Baptist Church at Paint Lick, and then my brothers and sisters started going to the Christian Church there. The church I joined didn't last, and when it went down in about 1902 I moved my membership to the Presbyterian Church in Lancaster, and after that to the Northern Presbyterian Church at Paint Lick. That's one of the oldest churches west of the Alleghenies, organized in about 1785. After the Civil War, the Union Republicans sat on one side, the Rebel Democrats sat on the other, and the colored folks sat in the balcony. A few colored people were still members when I went there.

The Civil War had been over for twenty-five years when we moved to this area, but there was still a lot of feeling for the South. A lot of men around here had served in the Union Army. They didn't believe in secession, but they believed in slavery, and after the war they became Democrats and strong Southern sympathizers. They stayed that way, too, them and their families, and they controlled this county and the other counties around here. All my people on my father's side had been strong for the Union, and old Aley had owned slaves, but he had freed them, and we were always taught to respect them: After we moved down here, though, I saw that the attitude was different, and I was influenced by it. Everybody here looked down on the niggers, wouldn't have anything to do with them or associate with them in any way except to work them. The people here were opposed to Berea College because they let niggers go to school there. Everybody said it was a disgrace to go to Berea College, and when I had a chance to go there, I wouldn't do it—the stigma kept me from going. I've always regretted that. When I moved here, I had a pretty good attitude toward colored people, but nobody here had an attitude like that, so I became like everybody else. I wouldn't mistreat them or anything—I never could stand to see one person run over another—but I just didn't consider them to be people I would associate with.

If I had been older, maybe I would have been influenced more by Cassius Clay. He lived at White Hall, outside of Richmond, not far from our farm, and he had given land to start Berea College for young people and poor people, white and black. I thought Clay was a great man—I liked him very much. He had stayed at our house in Harlan County when I was a small boy, and I always believed he was a brother to John Clay of Harlan County, whose daughter Lavinia was my great-grandmother. I never could prove that, though. Anyway, Cassius Clay was a Republican, and he was a slaveowner who favored abolition, and that kept him in plenty of trouble with all the people around him.

When I was about eighteen I went over to Berea to hear Clay give a speech. He gave the college the sword he had used in the Mexican War. After his speech, I went up on the platform and talked to him. He was about eighty-five years old then, and it was about then that he married a fifteen-year-old girl. Some of his family thought he was crazy. They sent the sheriff with a posse out to White Hall to get the girl, and old Cash loaded up his cannon with nails and scrap metal and drove them off with it. He didn't seem so old to me. Didn't seem crazy either.

Then in 1899, the year after Clay shot and killed two intruders at White Hall, I rode over there one day on my horse to see him. I found him sitting in a chair under a big tree in the front yard, had his shotgun propped up there, and over near it was his old cannon, pointed toward the gate. I left my horse grazing on the lawn while we sat and talked. He was real friendly, and seemed to appreciate me coming. I asked him about when he was minister to Russia, and about the duels he had fought. He was separated from that young girl then, I think, but his adopted son from Russia may have been living there with him—Launey was his name. I didn't see anybody there but old Cash. We didn't get to talk about a lot of things I wanted to ask him, but we had a very nice visit. He asked me to come back to see him and I said I would, but I never did. His health began to decline after that, and he died in 1903, a few months before Addie and me got married.

Clay reminded me a lot of Teddy Roosevelt. He was sort of a liberal Republican, what Teddy called a progressive. They were both wealthy, but they cared for poor people, and they looked after the colored people. They believed in freedom for all, and fought for the underdog. I always liked that about both of them.

It was in those years, in the 1890s, that I got interested in politics myself. In 1896, when William McKinley defeated William Jennings Bryan, I was just a few months too young to vote, but I voted for McKinley in 1900 when he beat Bryan the second time. It was a big shock the year after that when McKinley was assassinated, but I was already a big supporter of Teddy Roosevelt, and I was glad he was vice president so he could move up to the White House.

In 1895, Kentucky elected its first Republican governor, William O. Bradley, and he was from right here in Garrard County. They had a big rally for Bradley here in Lancaster, his hometown. At Paint Lick, we organized about a hundred horse riders to parade into town to the rally. Me and another boy led the way. I was riding a white horse and carrying a big flag. We rode past Bradley's house on Lexington Street and on up to the square, where they had set up a platform eight feet high. I got up there with Bradley and the other prominent people, and the biggest crowd I ever saw was filling the square and stretching out in all directions. That was a thrill for a nineteen-year-old boy—it's the biggest I ever felt in my life.

Bradley's opponent was a free silver Democrat named Wat Hardin. In those days, candidates often traveled together to campaign, stopping in the towns to debate. Bradley and Hardin were in the mountains around Prestonsburg one time, riding on horseback to one of those joint appearances, and they stopped at a big spring to rest their horses and have lunch. Hardin took a package out of his saddlebag, had something all wrapped up in a *Courier-Journal* newspaper, and Bradley watched him while he slowly unwrapped it. Finally, Hardin pulled out a quart of whiskey, and Bradley said to him, "Wat, that's the first good thing I ever saw come out of the *Courier-Journal* in my entire life."

The *Courier-Journal* was one of the benefits I got when we moved from the mountains to the Bluegrass. I had never read a regular newspaper until we came here. Henry Watterson was the editor of the *Courier,* and I admired him very much. I got to read a lot more after we moved here. I went to school some at Paint Lick, finished up the eighth grade work there, and since that was as far as the school went, I stayed on and helped the teacher and she gave me some high school lessons. I did that until I was nineteen years old. Then in 1896 I made plans to go to Lancaster and finish up my high school. I was still hoping I might get to go to college, so the first thing I had to do was get my high school diploma. But about that time I got a letter from one of my uncles in Harlan County asking me to come there and teach school. I liked teaching, and the idea of going back to Harlan appealed to me, so I decided to do it. My parents really needed me here to help them with the farm. My father's health was poor, and my mother had had a baby in 1894—that was Noble, my last brother—but they wanted me to be a school teacher, too, and they knew the schools in Harlan County needed teachers badly. So they encouraged me to go, and soon I had my bag packed and my ticket bought for the train ride to Hagan, Virginia, just across Cumberland Mountain from the valley of Martins Fork.

I taught first at the school on Days Branch, just below Coon Branch. It was a very plain little one-room schoolhouse, a hewed log building with board benches. I had a few worn-out books to use—readers, spellers, arithmetic books—and I had about thirty-five or forty students between the ages of six and my own age, twenty. It was all grades thrown together. The school year had been extended to five months by then—we took up in July and let out in

November. Best I recall, my salary was about thirty-five dollars a month. I took my room and board in the homes of some of my students, and I stayed there in the community for the whole school term and then returned to Garrard County to work on the farm the rest of the year. After that first year, I went back to the Days Branch school for a second term in 1897, and the next year I moved down the valley to a school on Bobs Creek because they had a better building and everything seemed to be in better shape. When the five months was over that year, they wanted me to stay on and teach several boys and girls from adjoining districts who were preparing to be teachers themselves. I did it for the extra money, but I also liked doing it very much.

Harlan County seemed a little different to me in those years when I went back there to teach. I had been gone over six years, and in that time they had built more schools, and there was more people. Still wasn't any good roads, though, and it was hard to move around from one community to another, let alone go outside the county. The isolation of people made everything harder to accomplish, whether it was schools or churches or law enforcement. There was still a lot of violence, a lot of killings. I guess it hadn't changed all that much.

Some of the young boys around there wanted to get away real bad, and a few of them headed for Alaska and the Klondike gold rush in 1896. Some more went away to fight in the Spanish-American War in 1898. I almost went myself, me and a cousin of mine named Peter Ledford. Peter did go, but I was ruptured, and I knew they wouldn't take me. I was twenty-two years old then, and me and Peter agreed to go and join the army, but he ended up going on without me. That was as close as I ever came to serving in the army. I was forty years old when World War I came along, and they didn't call me. That's something I never regretted. Being a soldier and fighting never was something I had a yearning to do.

The second year I taught on Days Branch, I came home when school was out, but then I went back for a visit right after Christmas, and I ended up staying through the winter. A fellow named Dave Hedrick had a store at the mouth of Days Branch, and him

and another fellow got to drinking there, and they went off to
Pineville, left the key with Dave's wife, and told her to ask me to
run the store until they got back. They stayed gone about a week,
and when they finally got back they hired me to run the store the
rest of the winter. After that they bought the store at Cawood and
moved Hedrick's stock of goods down there. The only post office
in that end of the county at the time was located in that store at
Cawood. They swore me in as assistant postmaster, and I ran the
store and the post office for the first six months of 1898. It wasn't
until several years later that post offices were set up at Smith and
Cranks and Ledford, Kentucky.

So by the time I was twenty-two I had been a farmer, a teacher,
a storekeeper, and a postmaster. I could have stayed there and kept
doing all those things, I reckon, but I knew I was not going to stay
in Harlan County. For one thing, my mother and father were up
here in Garrard County, and they were depending on me to come
back. For another thing, I didn't own any land in Harlan County,
and most of my kinfolks there didn't either. There wasn't much
good farmland anyway, not like in the Bluegrass. The railroad hadn't
reached Harlan then, and coal mining hadn't started, but the land
buyers from the North were buying up the mineral rights, and I
couldn't see any place for me there. I liked teaching, liked the people,
and I courted some around Days Branch and also across the mountain in Virginia, but I wasn't for marrying anyone, hadn't thought
of marrying, so when I finished that special class of new teachers at
Bobs Creek in the spring of 1899, I came on back to Garrard County
to the farm.

I taught a little in the school at Paint Lick after that, but mostly
I farmed with my father. My interest in politics was still strong, and
I was old enough to go to the polls for the first time in 1899 and
vote for William S. Taylor to succeed William O. Bradley as governor of Kentucky. It turned out to be the wildest election in the
state's history.

Taylor's opponent was Democrat William Goebel. I heard him
speak at Richmond. He declared, "I'm going to be governor!" and
I hollered back, "You'll never get there!" I worked hard for Taylor.

It was a vicious campaign, and a dangerous election—more than a dozen men got killed in fights that broke out at polling places across the state. The outcome was too close to call, and there was more trouble while everybody waited for a recount. Finally, Taylor was declared the winner by just a few hundred votes, and he was sworn into office in December, but Goebel challenged the election. By law, the legislature had to settle the issue, and since the Democrats controlled the legislature, it looked like they would give the victory to Goebel. There was charges of vote fraud, and Taylor called out the militia to keep order in Frankfort, and weeks went by while people got all agitated for one side or the other. Delegations from all over the state gathered at the capitol to try to influence the outcome. The L&N Railroad even sent a free train of Republicans from Harlan County to Frankfort to support Taylor.

All through January 1900, the legislature couldn't reach a decision. Then one morning someone shot Goebel from an office window as he was walking toward the capitol. He lived for about three days, during which the legislature declared him governor and swore him in, and as soon as he died of his wounds, the lieutenant governor, J.C.W. Beckham, was sworn in to replace him. Both parties made legal claims to the governor's office, and the whole big mess dragged on for several months before the courts finally upheld Beckham and the Democrats.

Several men were arrested and tried as parties to the Goebel killing, and some went to jail, but most people felt that the truth never came out. A fellow named Caleb Powers from Knox County was the Republican secretary of state, and he was tried and convicted of taking part in the conspiracy to murder Goebel, but he was pardoned—and later on, he was elected to Congress. I have heard it claimed by people who knew the participants that the murder was planned by Caleb Powers. According to the story, Powers had three men draw straws to see which one would do the shooting. One was Jim Howard from Clay County, another was a Skidmore from Harlan County—he was a cousin to Addie—and the third was Henry Youtsey from northern Kentucky. Youtsey drew the short straw. The morning of the shooting, Powers left on the train for Louisville. Youtsey fired the shot from Powers's office window, then locked himself in and handed the gun out through the transom to Skidmore in the hall. He got away with the gun, escaped and went back to Harlan County. Youtsey and Howard— and later Powers—all got arrested, but Skidmore never did. They never did know who he was, or how the gun disappeared.

Now that's the story I always heard, but I couldn't prove it. Skidmore sold that rifle to another cousin of Addie's, George Eager, and he still had it when he moved to Lancaster later on. I've seen the gun many times, even fired it a time or two. Eager finally moved to New Mexico. I guess he took the gun with him. Skidmore turned out to be a fine man, highly respected in Harlan County. Me and him used to be chums when we was little. I didn't hear this story about the Goebel assassination from him. I heard it from George Eager, who said Skidmore told it to him.

There was a lot of hard feeling toward mountain people after the Goebel killing. So many mountain Republicans had opposed him, and everybody seemed to feel it was a sharpshooter from the mountains that shot him. All the newspapers, the *Courier-Journal* and all, was calling the mountaineers bloodthirsty cutthroats and murderers and everything of the kind. I remember former Governor Bradley coming back to Lancaster after that and making a speech in defense of mountain people. I appreciated that a lot, because I was from the mountains, and I thought it was very unfair to brand everyone from that region as mean people and killers and all. Seems like it's always been that way, though. You always hear about the moonshiners and the hillbillies, but you don't hear about the hard-working people, the law-abiding citizens.

I turned twenty-four that year. It was the start of a new century, and it was an eventful year in a lot of ways. The Goebel assassination was the worst of it, I reckon. We've had Watergate in this age, but it was nothing like as bad as the Goebel mess. There was more rascality among higher-ups then than anything I've ever seen since, and both parties was to blame for it. Violence was a common happening all over Kentucky in those years. Ever since the Civil War, Kentucky had been just about the easiest state in the nation to get killed in.

It was an eventful year in our family, too. My Grandfather Jones, who had been living with us for several years, passed away. He was the first one of my grandparents to die. Then my father bought a little farm on Broaddus Branch in Garrard County, and we moved for the sixth time in ten years. The house on the new place had burned down, so we had to build a new one. We cut the timber for it right there on the place, and had a sawmill come in and saw it up. The next year, after we was settled in our new house and had put out our crops, I left my father and brothers to run the farm and took a job operating a sawmill at East Bernstadt in Laurel County. It was hard work and didn't pay too good, and it got tiresome pretty fast. When fall came, I decided that since I was already fairly close to Harlan County I'd just go on up there for a visit.

Most of my friends and relatives lived along the branches of Martins Fork, and that's where I went. I especially wanted to see Vinie Howard. She had been one of my students when I taught on Bobs Creek, and her brother John was my best friend. Also, me and John had been in the habit of going over to Evarts to see some girls. The one I was interested in was named Nan Farley.

They was having a political speaking at my old school on Days Branch, and I stopped there on my way to Vinie and John's house. I saw several of the girls who had gone to school to me, and they introduced me to a new girl in the neighborhood. Her name was Addie King. I thought she was a pretty fine girl. We talked along, and pretty soon she told me there was going to be an all-day meeting at Turkey Creek on Saturday, dinner on the ground, and I said, "I'll be there."

When I got to the Howards' house, first thing John said to me was, "When we going to Evarts?" I said, "Well, I was hoping we could go tomorrow," but I was already starting to worry that I had too many girls I wanted to see. I spent the night there at John's house, several of us there, and I gave all my attention to Vinie. She was in love with me, I could tell, but I never did say a word to her about it. Then the next morning, when me and John started to leave, I put my arms around Vinie and kissed her, and she kissed me back, and she laid her head on my shoulder and said, "Don't leave me. How can I live without you?" I didn't know what to say, so I just stood there holding her, and finally I said, "I'll be back."

Well, John and me walked over to Evarts, and we got there just as school was turning out. As we stood there at the gate talking to some people we knew, I saw Nan Farley with a young man coming down the walk toward us. When she saw me she ran up and hugged and kissed me, and then the young man came on up, and I shook hands with him. He was carrying her books, and she just reached over and took them from him and said, "Bye"—and then she took me by the arm and we walked off. Right away I knew I had made a big mistake going back there. I'd have given anything in the world if I hadn't done it. I was getting deeper and deeper in trouble.

Later on, me and John walked back across the mountain, and I stopped at my aunt's house on Turtle Creek and he went on home. When we was eating supper that night my aunt and uncle asked me who all I had seen, and I told them about Vinie Howard and Nan Farley, and then I told them about Addie King, how pretty she was and all. My aunt looked surprised. She said, "John Howard has been squiring her around ever since she moved up here, and everybody thought that would be a match."

I had told John about meeting Addie, but he hadn't let on that she was his girl. I had even told him I was going to have a date with her on Saturday. All of a sudden I realized what I had done. "My God," I thought, "the best friend I ever had—to think that I butted in there and stole his girl from him."

The next day was the big meeting, and there wasn't any way I could get out of going, so I made up my mind I would go down there and give all my attention to Vinie. I didn't want Addie King any more—John could have her.

But John and Vinie didn't come. They knew I had promised to be with Addie, and I reckon both of them was hurt by that, so they just stayed home. Addie was there waiting for me, though, and we went on together to where the crowd was gathering for the singing. As we started in, Addie saw a teacher she had met at a camp over in Virginia, and she led me over to introduce me to him.

"Would you know this boy?" she asked the man.

He looked me over real close. "That wouldn't be Burnam would it?"

I said, "That's me."

He was William Snodgrass. I had gone to school to him at Smith years before, when I was about eleven, and he had boarded at our house. "I've thought of you many a time, Burnam," he said, and he went on telling me how much he thought of my mother and father and what a good student I was. The singing had started, and it was time for us to go in, but old Snodgrass took Addie by the arm and said, "Wait a minute. I always admired you, Addie, and I told you I was going to give you one of my boys. Well, I take great pleasure in giving you this one, the best I ever had. I wish you both all the happiness in the world, and I hope you'll have a long and pleasant married life."

After that, we went on up to where they was singing, and directly this lady come over and sat down by Addie, and they commenced whispering. When the lady left I said, "Who was that?"

Addie said, "That's my mother."

I laughed and said, "How come her to be so much better looking than you are?" I knew who Addie's father was, remembered when he was sheriff of Harlan County, but he was dead by then. Her mother was about to get married again. Addie wasn't but sixteen, and I was twenty-five, but she had been off to school at Williamsburg, and she was starting to teach at Cranks Creek. She was smart and pretty, and I couldn't get her off my mind, even though I had Vinie Howard and Nan Farley to worry about too. I didn't know what in the world I was going to do.

When the meeting and dinner was over, we went back to my aunt's house, me and Addie and two or three more couples, and all of us spent the night there with my aunt and uncle. The next day there was another big political speaking to be held at Harlan, and we all walked down there, stopping several times along the way to visit or eat with kinfolks of one or another of us. Me and Addie said goodbye after that, and I left her and started back across the mountain to catch the train home. I stopped at Vinie and John's one more time, but John was gone, and I could see that Vinie was hurt, and I didn't have much to say to explain why I had treated her the way I had.

It was a long walk on up to Smith and across the mountain to Hagan, and it seemed even longer because I was thinking of the mess I was in. I had hurt too many people, people who had loved me so good, and all I wanted to do was get away. At the top of the mountain, I stopped and looked back down into that valley, and I said out loud, "Goodbye, Harlan County, I hope to God I never set foot on you again."

But I couldn't get out of it as easy as that. I stayed busy on the farm and teaching a little, but I found time to write letters to all three girls in Harlan County, and each one of them wrote me back, fussing at me for writing to the others. Then all three of them—Vinie, Nan, and Addie—ended up going to the same Presbyterian school in Harlan Town, and I knew my three-timing days was over. I wrote each one of them a short letter saying I was leaving right away for Texas, and would write again as soon as I got located. It was a lie, of course, but it was the only way I could see to get out of the whole mess.

That was the end of my courting of Vinie and Nan. I never did hear from either one of them again. I didn't hear from Addie, either, and I put my mind on my work. My father bought another farm, 138 acres on Sugar Creek, three miles out the Buckeye Pike from Lancaster, and I kept on teaching at Paint Lick and working on the farm. The winter passed, and another whole year went by. Then one day in the early part of 1903, one of my students went to Berea College on a weekend visit, and she came back telling me about meeting a girl from Harlan County who said she knew me. Her name was Addie King. Right quick I called over there and got her on the phone, and made a date to go see her. And that's how me and Addie got back together again.

She stayed at Berea until spring, and I went over there to see her several times, and she came to visit me and stayed at my aunt's house. We'd take rides in the buggy. When the time came for her to go back to Harlan, we didn't want to part. She was going home to teach school, and I had taken a job at Cartersville, here in Garrard County, where I was going to work in a store.

One day we was out in the buggy and I said, "When are we going to get married?"

"I don't know," she said. "When would it suit you?"

"Well," I said, "school will be out the first part of December. How about Christmas?"

"That would be all right with me," she said. So that was all there was to it—I had proposed, and she had accepted, and we were engaged.

As soon as school was out on the thirteenth of December, I got ready to go to Harlan. The train was late several days in a row, and I finally had to go to Lancaster and stay in the hotel so I could catch the early morning train. When I got off at Hagan, they told me at the livery stable that I couldn't ride across the mountain because the Kentucky side was covered with a solid sheet of ice.

So I set out walking. It was about six miles across to Addie's mother's house, and it was slow going. Just as I was nearly there, I saw Addie and her mother coming toward me. Her mother stopped and turned around, never said a word, and Addie came on and met me, and we went on down to her Aunt Jerusha Pope's house and spent the night. The next day, we rode horseback into Harlan Town to get married. Jerusha's son George, Addie's first cousin, went with us. He was our only witness.

It was the eighteenth of December, 1903. I was twenty-seven and Addie was almost nineteen. Randall Browning, a Baptist preacher, married us at his house in Harlan Town. George Pope and the preacher's wife stood up with us. I remember George pulled out a quart of moonshine whiskey before the ceremony, wanted us all to take a drink. The preacher took one, his wife did, George did, Addie did. She passed it to me.

"No, no," I said.

"Anybody can take a drink to celebrate their marriage," George said.

"Not me," I said. "I wouldn't touch it," and I didn't.

After that, we went and bought us some dinner at Sam Howard's hotel, and then we rode back up to Jerusha and Curl Pope's house to spend the night. The next morning we started walking up to

Addie's mother's house, me carrying two bags and Addie one, and before we got there it commenced to rain. It had been very cold, so cold that Martins Fork was full of ice, but then it warmed up and rained. Seems like it took us two or three days walking in the rain and mud to get back across the mountain to Hagan. All the ice was melting, and it was hard going. Finally we got there, stayed all night there at a boarding house, and the next morning we rode the train to Lancaster and then walked on to my mother and father's house on Sugar Creek. And the next Monday, I hooked up a team and went to farming.

SEVEN

A Craving Woman

Addie, 1885–1903

"That Nan Farley, the girl Burnam was telling you about, she married a Kelly," Addie Ledford said. "Bismarck Kelly. I believe they moved to Oklahoma. Vinie Howard married Henry Ball there in Harlan—had two pretty daughters. I used to see them a lot. Vinie died of cancer."

"Did you get along all right with those girls when you were in school with them?" I asked.

"Oh, yes. We never got mad at one another—but we were all mad at Burnam for having so many girls, and we all quit writing to him. I quit for over a year. Then he came to see me at Berea. I liked Nan and Vinie just fine. Nan was always disappointed she didn't get Burnam." She paused for a moment, chuckling, and added, "I wish she had."

"Mr. Burnam, did you kiss Miss Addie when you were courting her that time back in Harlan County?" I asked.

"I don't know."

"You'd remember that, wouldn't you?"

"I guess I did."

"What about that, Miss Addie?"

"I don't remember."

Burnam laughed. "She knows I did. She remembers."

"I'll tell you one thing," Addie said emphatically, "I never was too fast with the boys. I was kind of shy. But I'll tell you another thing, and it's the honest truth: I never was slighted. I was always one they made over, at the parties and all. I didn't think I was pretty, I really didn't—but I made a good picture. You can ask Burnam."

"Well, I guess she's right about that," he said.

"She was a pretty girl, though, wasn't she?" I asked him.

"Fair."

"What did you like most about her?"

He smiled. "I don't know. I never did know. It was just one of those things that happens. I never did know how it happened."

Both of them burst into laughter.

After nearly seventy-five years of marriage, they seemed both puzzled and amused by their longevity, and by the durability of their relationship. It had hardly been one long, unbroken honeymoon; there had been hardships and grief, tears and anger, even thoughts of separation. Yet here they were, married longer than most people live. They spent their days and nights in constant proximity; they still slept together in the same bed; they remembered the same history in more or less the same versions. Occasionally they argued over some resurrected memory, some bitter thought best left buried. Much more frequently, they saw a humorous side to their lengthening past and their limited present and their precarious future.

Their health was astonishing, as marvelous as their memories. They could not picture themselves as old people. They took quiet pride in their independence from doctors and drugs and debts; they resisted all thought of living with one of their children, or in a nursing home. Only their own home, battered as it was by age and wear, would do. The only place for them was here, together. They were resigned, accustomed, attuned to each other. More than they liked to show, more than they may have known, each considered the other, depended upon the other, cared for the other. They had come too far and seen too much and endured for too long to live any other way except together, here.

Addie Ledford was less demonstrative than her husband. There was a somber, stoic side to her that served as her defense against pain and hurt, against loss. It seemed to say: "I won't break." That hardness and the humor in her were in a constant struggle for domi-

nance, but there was no clear winner. When she thought of the first nineteen years of her life, she thought with satisfaction of what was—and with longing for what might have been:

Up until my father died, I always thought we lived a good life. He owned that five-hundred-acre farm there at Kildav where we lived, and another three hundred acres just below there on Clover Fork, and he was a well-respected man in the county because he had been sheriff and marshal.

There wasn't anything at Kildav, not even a store, but there was a store about a mile up the creek at Evarts, and Harlan Town was only seven or eight miles below us. My father had eight yoke of oxen for logging, and he made good at farming, and after we moved back from Harlan Town he hired a carpenter to add on to our house and build us some furniture. We even had a solid walnut organ, a tall organ my father bought in Cincinnati, and my mother took lessons so she could play it. Yes, we had a good life. We was pretty well fixed.

I wouldn't go with every boy that came along. I had a reputation for acting right. I was invited to all the pie suppers and socials and infares—that's what they called wedding dinners—and I always had a good time. I had the asthma when I was a girl, and had to take good care of myself, but I had a real good time.

I went to good schools, too. I started to regular school in Harlan when my father was marshal, then went one year to a country school close to our house at Kildav, and after that I mostly went to schools run by the Congregational Church. The American Missionary Association, which was the Congregationals from up North, sent some teachers in there in about 1890 to start a school at Evarts—Black Mountain Academy, they called it—and I went there from about 1894 until I finished the eighth grade in 1899. We had the finest teachers at that school, people from Massachusetts who had graduated from Harvard and all. J.W. Jewett was one of them, him and his wife—and their widowed daughter, Mary M. Pond, was the best teacher I ever had. Another one from New England was Sarah Endicott Ober. The Endicotts are a famous family up there, you know. Some of our teachers had studied under the same men that wrote the grammar books we studied from.

The Congregationals and Presbyterians was starting lots of mission schools in the mountains at that time, but our school was actually started by local people. A preacher who worked for the Kentucky Lumber Company organized people to start the school, and the Congregationals came and joined in with them. We had students from surrounding counties and even from Virginia who boarded in the community. The school went through the eighth grade. Part of its aim was to train teachers.

I went to their Sunday school and church, too, and later I joined that church and got baptised in Clover Fork by a Congregational preacher. So I had a good church and a good school to go to, and we had a nice house and some land, and my mother had a cookstove and a sewing machine and an organ. Harlan County was an out-of-the-way place, but I never did notice. Seemed to me like we had about everything we needed.

My father got along well, too—that's how come him to be sheriff and marshal. That Turner-Howard feud Burnam was telling you about, that was going on when my father was sheriff. He was the only man that ever arrested Wilse Howard—not during the feud, but once before that. Wilse was a mean man—they couldn't hardly do nothing with him. He got away from Harlan, went west and committed some bad crimes, killed some Indians and robbed people. Finally he got caught by a detective named Imboden, a famous detective, and Wilse was hanged in St. Louis. Somebody sent us a newspaper story about it.

My father's health was bad when he quit being marshal. He drank some—too much, sometimes—and then he got TB and couldn't work, and he died a young man, just thirty-seven years old. At one time, every bit of the land he owned was all paid for, and it had good timber on it, coal too. But he was too good-hearted, too lenient with people—just like Burnam. He got careless, loaned too much money, went on people's notes and such as that, and he lost a lot that way. By the time he died, he was in debt. Me and my mother and my three younger brothers tried to hold on. We put out a crop by ourselves one year, and we kept cows, and I did the milking and helped Mama tend the little ones—but finally we lost the land.

That was in 1899. I was fourteen, had just finished eighth grade at Black Mountain Academy. Mama deeded away the Bee Bottom land to cover debts, but it wasn't enough, so she had to let the Kildav land go. She didn't end up with anything from it, not a dime. Some company got the land. They knew the railroad was coming. Later, they built a company town for miners right there on our farm.

It's hard to have that much and then lose out. I never did think of us as being poor, but I guess we were. If it hadn't been for my grandfather, Abram Skidmore, and my Uncle Asher Skidmore, we would have been poor sure enough. We moved over on Cranks Creek to live with them. My Grandmother Skidmore had died the same year as my father, but the family was still there at the old homeplace. The Skidmores kept us from being poor. They believed in working—and keeping their money. I've been careful with my money ever since then. I just fear losing everything like my father did. They say a burnt child dreads the fire.

The next year I went off to a Congregational boarding school at Williamsburg, Kentucky, and after that I stayed away at school or teaching most of the time. I went to Williamsburg Academy one year, and to a Presbyterian school in Harlan the next. In about 1901, my mother got married again—married George Napier, a farmer—and they lived on Martins Fork near Cawood. I stayed there with them some, but not much. I went to Lincoln Memorial University down near Cumberland Gap for a year, and then to Berea, and then I got married.

Before me and Burnam got married I had taught three years in Harlan County, and then I went back there and taught one year after we was married. See, you could teach school in the late summer and fall—five months of school—and then go away to college five months in the winter and spring. The two didn't overlap. I was just about on my own, out seeing things and learning things, reading poems by Longfellow and Poe, getting an education. I saw electric lights for the first time when I went to Williamsburg, and soon after that I saw a telephone, and I saw my first train at Cumberland Gap. And then I met Burnam, and went to Berea, and got married—and I was still only eighteen years old. I've always wished I could have finished college and made a career of school teaching.

A few years before I went to Lincoln Memorial, they had a big boom there at Middlesboro and Cumberland Gap. It was all tied in to the railroad coming through. English people and rich people come in there and bought, and they built big expensive buildings. One was the Four Seasons Hotel. They said it had as many rooms as there was days in a year. They was expecting the whole world to come in there and see the mountains. It was going to be a big resort. But then times turned bad, and pretty soon nobody came. They finally had to tear that hotel down. By the time I got there the boom was all over, but Lincoln Memorial had bought up some of the resort land. A man named Oliver Otis Howard started the school. He had been an officer in the Union Army, had lost an arm at Gettysburg. I remember one day in chapel he told us about the night Lincoln was shot at Ford's Theatre in Washington. Seems to me Howard said he was there when it happened. Lincoln Memorial was a real good school.

So was Berea. The American Missionary Association had a part in it, too, just like they did in the other schools I went to. Old Cassius Clay gave the first land for it back before the Civil War. People from the North ran it, and they allowed colored people to go there right from the start. The white people around here was mostly for slavery, and they didn't like that. They got after John Fee and his white teachers at Berea, and the colored students, and tried to run them off. The school was shut down during the war, but it opened up again after that, and it kept on serving young people from the mountains and colored people from all over.

To tell you the truth, people where we lived on Clover Fork in Harlan County taught their children to beware of niggers, said they might take you off somewhere or harm you in some way. That's what I grew up thinking: to look out for niggers, and look down on them. There wasn't hardly any of them living around there where I grew up. The only one I remember well was an old man named Pres Turner. He was a carpenter and a good cook, baked cakes and pies for everybody's weddings and all. He had been a slave of old Bill Turner, and after that he had drawn a pension because he had gone to the war. Old Pres wanted to stand in with the best people, you know, and he never bothered nobody.

So I had been taught to look down on colored people, but nothing that ever happened to me had made me be afraid of them, and when I came to Berea I didn't mind going to school with them. The ones I met was all nice. Burnam missed the boat by not going to Berea. He could have got a lot more education if he had. I wish I could have stayed there and finished.

A lot of the money that was put into Berea by Northern people was from abolitionists, and they specified that it was for white and colored alike. In about 1904, Kentucky passed a law saying colored people couldn't go there with whites any more, so some of the Northern people pulled their money out. They opened up Lincoln Institute for colored people over near Frankfort soon after that, and Berea helped to get that school started. Berea has always done a lot of good work. Our daughter Eloise went there. She was just nineteen when she graduated—the youngest graduate in the history of the college.

Where I missed out was by getting married and not having a chance to go on and finish college. I had had the best of teachers everywhere I had gone, and I had learned a lot and made good grades. I got a ninety-six in history on the last examination I took. Only missed two—one was a question about Cotton Mather. The other was about George Bancroft, a writer from Massachusetts back before the Civil War. I wanted to go on and be a teacher, but after I got married and taught one more year in Harlan County, I had to quit. I was too busy.

My Skidmore grandparents always lived on Cranks Creek, and Burnam's Jones grandparents lived near the joining of Cranks Creek and Martins Fork. They was right across the mountain from one another—about six miles, if you took the near way—but I lived way across another mountain on Clover Fork, and I never did see

Burnam until I was fifteen years old. I don't remember who introduced us, but I met him at a political speaking at a school where he used to teach, and right after that there was a big Baptist association meeting close to where his aunt lived on Turtle Creek of Martins Fork, and I went down there and he came and met me. He was a right nice looking fellow, looked pretty good.

That was in 1900. I was fifteen and Burnam was twenty-four. I was living with my mother and brothers at my Uncle Asher Skidmore's house on Cranks Creek, just getting ready to go to school in Harlan Town that year. Burnam was back in Harlan County for a visit when I met him.

It was at that association meeting that we saw old Mr. Snodgrass, and he told me he was giving Burnam to me. I had met Snodgrass over at a big camp meeting in Virginia. Me and his wife was some kind of kin. People came there to that Methodist camp meeting from all over the mountains, and I saw more finely dressed people there than any place I ever went. Burnam had been to school to Snodgrass. We both liked him a lot, and when he presented us to each other that day at the meeting, it was sort of like we was engaged.

After Burnam left and came back up here to Garrard County we corresponded, but he was also writing to Nan Farley and Vinie Howard, and when the three of us ended up at the same school together and found out what he was doing, I quit writing him. I kept some of his letters, though. Ewell, our oldest son, used to get them out and read them. He'd die laughing.

Burnam was bad about leading girls along. Why, he went back on a dozen of them before we was married. He'd get them to like him, you know, and he really didn't give a hoot about them. I never did believe in such as that.

We was out of touch for over a year—more like two. I went to school, and taught, and then when I was at Berea, that's when we saw each other again. My mother had remarried by then. I hated to see her do it—and she didn't want me to get married either. We didn't get along too well. Didn't fuss or anything, but we wasn't real close. She didn't want me to get married at all—not to Burnam or anybody. I've thought about it lots of times. Maybe I ought to have stayed on and helped her with the children, and kept on going to school.

Anyhow, I went home that summer of 1903 and taught school. We had decided to get married in December, as soon as school was out. I had saved a little money, so I had me some dresses made. Good material just cost a few cents a yard, and the woman who made my dresses charged sixty cents apiece. They'd probably cost five or ten dollars now, at least. Everything was a whole lot cheaper then.

I was ready to leave Harlan County. We had lost our land, didn't get a dime for it, and my mother was remarried and starting a new family. All my grandparents was dead but Grandpa Skidmore, and he died the year after we married. There was talk of the railroad coming, and people from up north was coming in to buy up land, and there was lots of boundary disputes and people claiming they was being fooled out of their land or forced off of it. Our teachers at Black Mountain Academy had always told us the railroad was coming, be prepared, but not many people was prepared when it came. I had some distant cousins, the Ashers, that did get in on it, but I wasn't close to them. Old T.J. Asher owned big boundaries of land and had lumber mills at Pineville, and later on he built the first railroad from Pineville up toward Harlan, and then sold out to the L&N. He made a mint of money. But nobody that was close family to me was getting rich, and none ever did. I couldn't see nothing to hold me in Harlan County, and when me and Burnam decided to get married, I was glad we would be moving to live in another place.

The way it all turned out, I never was sorry I left. My brother George left too, moved out to the state of Washington and got into timber, stayed there all his life, and did right well. I went out there to visit him one time. My other brothers, Logan and Willie, both died of TB when they was young men. After my mother remarried she had three girls, and all three of them ended up going west too. They're still out there, my three half-sisters. They lived with me and Burnam off and on, and we've always been close to them. My mother come and stayed with us some, and then she died in the hospital in Lexington in 1939.

I still remember a lot about Harlan County, but I haven't been back there in a long time. After I had been gone from there just a few years, all of my close kin was gone too, either died or moved away, so there wasn't any reason for me to go back.

Well, when Burnam came to Harlan for us to get married, it was a frosty morning, a sunshiny day. It had been cold, bitter cold, and Martins Fork was froze over in places. I didn't know for sure when he was coming. My mother was living on Coon Branch then. Burnam walked across the mountain from Hagan to Smith and then turned down toward Coon Branch, and just as he did he saw me and my mother coming down toward him. When my mother saw him, she turned back. She wouldn't go to the wedding.

We walked on down to my Aunt Jerusha Pope's, a mile or so above Cawood. She was my mother's sister, and my favorite aunt. Her husband was Moses Lemuel Pope, but nobody called him that— they called him Curl, because he had curly hair. We spent the night there at Aunt Jerusha's that night, me sleeping upstairs and Burnam down, and the next morning we borrowed two black horses from them and rode on in to Harlan Town to get married. Curl and Jerusha's son George, my first cousin, went with us. He was married and had a farm of his own up on Martins Fork.

It was a pretty day for the eighteenth of December, still frosty but not as cold as it had been. Burnam had on a black suit and an overcoat and a felt hat. I was wearing a teal blue wool dress with a long train on it, the way the dressmakers liked to make them back then, and I had on a big wide-brimmed hat with feathers in it. We rode to the preacher's house—Randall Browning was his name, a friend of Burnam's, a Baptist—and him and his wife and George Pope was the only ones there with us. Burnam likes to tell that George passed around a bottle of whiskey and everybody took a drink except him, but I don't remember that. It was about two o'clock in the afternoon when we had the ceremony. After that, we went over to the hotel and ate dinner, and then we rode back up to Aunt Jerusha's to spend the night. Their house was a weatherboard frame, two stories, had six rooms. That night, Burnam and me stayed upstairs.

Most of my belongings was in a big trunk that I left there for the Popes to send across the mountain and put on the train later. We had three small suitcases to carry, and we had to walk across the mountain with them. When morning came, the weather was threatening, and it got worse it came a big rain. We got as far as George Pope's house and had to stop and spend the night. The next day we made it to my mother's house, not far from Smith. It turned warmer then, but it kept raining, and it was hard to get across the creeks. Finally the next day we walked the last four or five miles across the mountain to Hagan, and we stayed that night at Crouse's boarding house next to the train station. It had taken us four days to get from Harlan to Hagan—less than twenty miles. It was a hard journey, but we didn't mind it so much. We sure couldn't make it now.

And then we rode the train up to Lancaster the next day and came to live in the house with Burnam's parents. That was the start of a new life for me. I went back and taught school in Harlan County the next summer after that, but it was the last time I ever taught. I was saving all I could, and I knew how to dress well, and we didn't waste anything. That picture of Burnam and me—you've seen it, our wedding picture—it was made over at Berea in 1904, not too long after we were married. I had on a black taffeta dress trimmed in silk medallions. It was a real pretty dress. I was very happy then. We were just starting out, and Burnam knew how to manage—he had farmed and tended store and all—and I was sure we had a chance to make something. That suited me fine. I was a craving woman, just like my Grandma Skidmore. We had us a nice place to start, here on the edge of the Bluegrass, and I was glad of it. I put Harlan County behind me.

EIGHT

Tracing the Path of Aley

We had inched over into the twentieth century. All that had preceded Burnam Ledford's and Addie King's marriage and their departure from Harlan County, Kentucky, in 1903—all that made up
their longest remembrances, their early history—had been summoned, discussed, examined, recorded. We had reached a resting
place in the long journey from the past to the present. It was time
to pause and take stock, to reassess and clarify and confirm, before
we moved on.

"Have you ever been back over this trail, Mr. Burnam?" I asked
one afternoon. "Ever tried to retrace Aley's steps, to see where he
came from?"

"Only once," he replied. "Years ago, my son Bruce took me on
a trip up through Cumberland Gap and over into North Carolina.
We asked about Ledfords around Asheville, even met a few, but
they didn't know a thing about the family, hadn't heard of Aley, so
they couldn't give us any help. I always wanted to go back and try
again, but I never did."

"I never was in North Carolina," said Mrs. Ledford, "or anywhere in Virginia except Lee County."

"I'm planning to go and cover some of that ground," I told
them. "I've already seen most of it, but I want to take another look,
a closer look, to see if I can find any people or any records or any
clues that might be helpful to us."

"That ought to be a nice trip," Mr. Ledford said. He gazed out
the window. "I'd love to go with you."

"Well, I'd love for you to go. Do you want to?"

"I want to, but I doubt if I could do it. I feel well enough and all, but I couldn't leave Addie here alone."

"We can all three go," I said.

He was hesitant. "I better not say right now. I just don't know."

I offered an alternative. "Maybe in the fall, when the weather is cooler, we could make a trip to Harlan."

"That would suit me fine," he said. "I haven't been in over ten years. I'd like to go back one more time, just to see if I recognized anybody or anything."

"I've been a few times," I said, "but this time I want to pay attention to what it's like now, and how it got that way, and what traces I can find, if any, of Aley and Betsy and their descendants."

"I expect you'll find a right smart," Addie said. "When are you going?"

"I'm not sure. First, I'm going to Virginia and North Carolina."

When it was formed in 1738, Augusta County, Virginia, embraced all of the vast region claimed by the Virginia colony west of the Blue Ridge Mountains. All of present-day West Virginia, western Pennsylvania, and certain "lands on the waters of the Ohio and Mississippi Rivers" were included in the claim. The Six Nations of the Iroquois Confederacy had asserted a proprietary claim to much of the same territory for centuries, and regularly came to hunt there. French and British interests also coveted the land, and various exploring Germans and Dutchmen had also set their sights upon it.

The governing council of Virginia—and, by extension, the British crown—was determined to secure its claim by means of what had become a conventional colonial technique: populating the wilderness with adventurers, indentured servants, convicts, African slaves. One of the men to whom this task was entrusted was James Patton, a forty-five-year-old slave trader and land speculator, a onetime sea captain of ill fame, an opportunist born of Scotch Presbyterian parents in Northern Ireland. In 1737, Patton and John Lewis, a fugitive from justice in Ireland, formed a partnership with William Beverley, a resident politician of Virginia and the possessor of a 118,000-acre colonial land grant in the Shenandoah Valley west of the Blue Ridge. In return for generous boundaries of land for themselves, Patton and Lewis agreed to recruit and transport large numbers of people to that valley beyond the mountains. With his family, a crew of ten, and an undetermined number of indentures, Patton left England in a leased vessel, the *Walpoole,* in the spring of 1738. From Belhaven, a Virginia port on the Potomac River, he went overland with his party to meet John Lewis in the Shenandoah Valley and begin the settlement of "Beverley's Manor."

Within four years, James Patton had established himself as the most powerful man in Augusta County. He was the landlord, the tax collector, the king's agent, the prince; he traded in horses and humans with the same hard-eyed devotion to profit. Though he expressed a public loyalty to the crown, he was in fact faithful to no power—not his king, his church, his colony. Only the pursuit of land and wealth and power held his unqualified devotion and commitment.

With a 100,000-acre land grant of his own, Patton extended his influence southwest into the heart of Virginia's mountain-bordered Great Valley early in the 1740s. The wagon road he ordered laid out there followed a route roughly traced today by Interstate Highway 81, and a few intersecting cross trails were hacked between the Blue Ridge and the Allegheny chain. On November 19, 1746, the administrative court of Augusta County ordered that such a trail be cut along a ridge dividing the New River from the Roanoke River. Several men, presumably residents of the area, were named to build and maintain the road. Among them were "all the Ledfords."

In Staunton, the county seat of the greatly diminished jurisdiction still known as Augusta County, the musty record books of the eighteenth century are safely preserved in the courthouse. Deed Books 4 and 6, covering property transactions of the early 1750s, record three instances in which James Patton conveyed small tracts of land to Henry, William, and John Ledford. All of the parcels were on the West Fork (later called the North Fork) of the Roanoke River; one tract was further identified as "crossing Bradshaw's Creek."

Bradshaw Creek still trickles into the Roanoke in a tranquil valley of Montgomery County, ten miles east of the town of Blacksburg. Two and a quarter centuries after the Ledfords made their brief imprint in that wilderness valley, the fertile river bottom soil brimmed with row crops, lush and symmetrical. The densely wooded mountain slopes rose abruptly from the valley floor. A Norfolk and Western Railway trestle crossed the creek just above its mouth, and out of sight, trucks crossing the mountain on Interstate 81 bounced echoes into the river bottom.

I met Louise Watterson Spangler at her mobile home a short distance from where the creek meets the river. On a hillside above her residence, she showed me a tiny graveyard, honeysuckle-choked and bordered by a rusty iron fence. The oldest tombstone there was for Joseph Watterson, 1770–1842.

"This valley has been in my family since 1760," Mrs. Spangler said. "That's when King George made a thousand-acre land grant to the first Watterson that came here. There was three Watterson brothers, so I've been told, and one of them settled this land. He must have been the father of this Joseph. One of the other brothers went on to Tennessee. Did you ever hear of a famous Kentucky newspaper editor named Henry Watterson? He came out of that Tennessee branch of the family." Mrs. Spangler did not know that another family of Englishmen had preceded her Anglo-Saxon ancestors on the land. She had never heard of the Ledfords.

The Augusta County court record does not indicate how long the ancestors of Burnam Ledford remained to clear and till the land in that Virginia valley, but the names of William and John Ledford showed up in the record books of Rowan County, North Carolina, in 1759, just five years after their last purchase on the Roanoke. In 1763, the Augusta clerk noted that "John Ledford of Carolina, late of Virginia," had assigned to one Isaac Taylor his power of attorney "to convey his 142 acres of land in Augusta County, Virginia"— the same 142 acres he had purchased from James Patton in 1751.

In Asheboro, North Carolina, the seat of Randolph County (once part of Rowan), records indicate the presence of two Ledford families—William's and John's—on Caraway Creek in 1760. Thirty years later, in the census of 1790, thirteen Ledford households were counted in western North Carolina. Ledfords showed up in the records as jurors, constables, buyers and sellers of land, owners of slaves, litigants in court, recipients of pensions, and finally as deceased citizens. With each new fragment of information, the shape and quality of their lives came more sharply into focus. Still, no record of Aley Ledford's birth could be found, no positive identification of his parents could be made—and thus the exact location of his birthplace, the names of his brothers and sisters, and all other particulars of his life in North Carolina remained a mystery.

Inquiries in a dozen other counties of the state yielded little more. Courthouse fires and Civil War hostilities had destroyed the records of several jurisdictions. The Ledford name appeared in many places and circumstances—an Absolom declared a lunatic by a court, an Obediah found hanging in his barn, a Peter drawing $79.56 a year for his services in the Revolution, an elderly William leaving a large estate to a son named John—but nowhere could I find positive identification of the elusive Aley. (An Aley Ledford did witness the marriage of his niece Betty to Henry Smith in South Carolina in 1792, but the Aley who later went to Harlan was only three years old in that year.)

The 1978 Asheboro telephone directory listed not a single Ledford, but there were fifty in Charlotte, an equal number in lightly populated Haywood County far to the west, and nearly twice that many in Asheville-Buncombe County. Even a casual canvass revealed them to be a mixed lot—rich and middle class and poor, young and middle aged and elderly, white and black and Indian. Random phone calls to a few brought responses of amusement, curiosity, puzzlement, and total lack of interest—but uncovered no new clues. (Later, I found the Ledford name in phone books from Boston and New York to Chicago and Los Angeles; there were a dozen or more in Miami, Houston, Birmingham, Detroit, Indianapolis, Louisville—and well over a hundred in Atlanta.)

Other names that figured in the Ledford chronicle in Kentucky also appeared in the North Carolina record, among them John and Abram Skidmore, Stephen Farmer, and Woodard King. Likewise, the record showed that there were Ledfords in North Carolina and Virginia before 1700, and the Kentucky census of 1800 showed three Ledford men—James, Joseph, and Philadelphia—living in the Bluegrass region. But, the recorded facts were too sparse and unconnected to lend any continuity at all to the Ledford story.

I turned north again into Virginia, crossed the Blue Ridge, and headed west along the approximate route of the Wilderness Road. At Richlands, deep in the mountains of southwest Virginia, I stopped to see Roy Ledford, a distant cousin of Burnam's. A seventy-four-year-old retired coal miner disabled by black lung disease, he spent his time reading and writing letters, pursuing the history of his ancestors.

"Aley's youngest son, Stephen, was my great-grandfather," Roy Ledford said. "I've been to Augusta County and found the Ledford brothers in the deed books, and I'm pretty sure the John Ledford that's named there is Aley's grandfather, but I can't prove it. I've got it down in my notes that Aley was born near Asheboro, North Carolina, in 1789. He migrated to Harlan County, Kentucky, as a young man, and married Betsy Farmer, and had thirteen children, all born in Harlan County. I found out that much on my own. And then, several years ago, I heard about Curtis Burnam Ledford over in Kentucky. We struck up a correspondence. He told me that story about Aley's parents being killed in their wagon at Cumberland Gap. It all connects up, I know it does, and I'm hoping to prove it. Sometimes it's frustrating, downright disgusting, to need a few more facts and not be able to find them. But I enjoy looking, I really do. It sure as heck beats digging coal. Only problem for me is, I just got started fifty years late."

At Pennington Gap on the Virginia-Kentucky border, eighty-seven-year-old Anne Laningham, a great-granddaughter of Aley Ledford Jr., had compiled and published a genealogical study of early Lee and Harlan County settlers, including the Ledfords, Farmers, Skidmores, and Smiths. It was a labor of love, incomplete in many particulars but nonetheless far more comprehensive than any previous effort. Mrs. Laningham had wanted to pursue Aley Ledford's ancestors into North Carolina and beyond, but failing health had stayed her. "I believe his father's name was John," she told me, "but I can't be absolutely certain of it. I've heard the story that Aley's parents were killed at Cumberland Gap, but I can't verify that, either—I'm not even sure where I first heard it. Unless I can do more research, I won't be able to add anything to what I have already written."

Another of Aley's descendants, Charles Edward Ledford of Harrodsburg, Kentucky, remembered hearing from his grandfather the story of the Cumberland Gap tragedy. When I met Charles, the tale as he told it was strikingly similar to Burnam Ledford's version—yet the two men had never met or talked.

Charles had always been interested in his ancestors, but not until he was sixty-three years old did he finally get around to compiling some of the genealogical information that eventually led him to make contact with his aged Cousin Burnam. In 1978, he composed "an incomplete cross section of different descendants of Aley Ledford of Harlan County, Kentucky (1789–1873), the original Kentucky Ledford." Charles Edward traced his own line of descent through his great-grandfather, John Ledford, the eldest son of Aley and Betsy. He also generalized that the Ledfords of his acquaintance were "innovative, conservative, ambitious, patriotic people who possess a thirst for knowledge . . . with somewhat more than an average inclination to be opinionated, with an extra dash of stubbornness (few are flexible enough, or deceitful, if you will, to be politicians). . . ." A few, he went on, were "seemingly lacking in ambition or initiative." They were not known as "outlaws and jail-birds," he said, but simply as people who "did not contribute much to their community." By far the largest number of Ledfords, he hastened to add, were hardworking, law-abiding landowners who "are not well known over a very large area, most desiring a low profile."

Charles Ledford also recorded his recollections of his grandfather, Henry Clay Ledford, a proud, hot-tempered, fearless and deeply conservative native of Harlan County. Though he was "blessed with very little or no formal education," he was a shrewd and successful businessman who acquired a large amount of valuable property and died a rich man at the age of eighty-seven because "spending money was not one of his vices." And Charles also wrote with obvious pride and fascination of one of his grandfather's brothers, Noble Skidmore Ledford, a lawyer who traveled through the West as a young man, who "made and lost several fortunes" and died in Harlan County while researching the land titles in the Ledford-Skidmore-Smith-Farmer survey that supposedly contained eighty-six thousand acres.

The story, as Charles remembered hearing it, was that John Ledford, the son of Aley and the father of Henry and Noble, owned one-third of the land in the survey, but when he sold his share, his wife refused to sign the deed. Under Kentucky law, she thus retained a claim to one-third of his one-third interest (in round numbers, about ten thousand acres). Noble was researching the titles in order to claim his mother's unsigned dower interest, but he died suddenly, and rumor had it that he was a victim of foul play. "I will win by honest and legal means," he told a friend before his death—but in the end, no Ledford retained any portion of the eighty-six thousand acres.

Beneath the approximately ten thousand acres claimed by the mother of Henry and Noble Ledford there was buried, by Charles Ledford's rough estimate, a deposit of 250 million to 500 million tons of coal. "That is more money, at $20 a ton, than the five richest families in the U.S. are worth combined," he concluded. "Well, so legends are made of such tales."

It was Henry Clay Ledford, the grandfather of Charles Edward, who passed that legend down to his son and grandson—and it was the same Henry Clay who also told his descendants the story of the death of Aley Ledford's parents at Cumberland Gap. As Charles remembered hearing it, the family was camped at the gap on its journey to the Bluegrass when a tree fell across their wagon in a storm and killed the parents. They had two surviving sons, small boys, who were taken by other families. One ended up in southern Illinois, and there eventually started a town that bore the Ledford name. The other stayed in the Kentucky mountains, in Harlan County. His name was Aley.

When Charles Edward Ledford and Curtis Burnam Ledford finally met for the first time in 1978, they shared their slightly different versions of that story with the calm certitude of true believers, knowers of the truth.

But Charles Ledford was not on my journey through North Carolina and Virginia; I met him later, in the Bluegrass. My search along the creeks—Bradshaw, then Caraway, then on toward Cranks—took me beyond Pennington Gap into the Poor Valley, where Joseph Martin's pioneer station and the later railroad whistle stops of Hagan and Hubbard Springs and Ocoonita were separated from Smith and Cranks Creek and Martins Fork by the stony barrier of Cumberland Mountain. At Ocoonita, I found Millard Ledford, a retired farmer. After I had described my mission to him, he brought out a photograph of a somber-looking man wearing a coat and vest, a black hat, and a long gray beard.

"That's my grandfather, Stephen Ledford, the youngest son of Aley and Betsy," he told me. "He lived in the Cranks Creek valley, right across this mountain. He died before I was born. I've lived all of my seventy-three years on this side of the mountain, but I've walked across there to Cranks many a time. The trail is just up the road, beside the Noe Cemetery. It's about four miles across—two up, two down. I guess it's been twenty years since I walked it."

I found the trail's beginning, and it tempted me—but it was late in the day, too late for me to walk it. After pausing there for a few minutes, I turned again toward Cumberland Gap.

Driving westward along the last Virginia section of the Wilderness Road, I could see no break in the mountain, no place where the rocky face could be scaled and the other side attained. There were such access points, I knew—first found by buffalo and deer, then by Indians in pursuit of them, and finally by exploring backwoodsmen like Stephen Farmer—but from the perspective of the valley road, only the impenetrable wall could be seen.

For almost forty miles the mountain loomed there, far above the highway. When the gap came into view at last, it appeared in the distance as an interruption in the ridge line, a slight indentation in the earth. But as the miles fell away, the cut deepened, and its craggy face became an imposing presence. Around each succeeding bend in the road, the stony promontory towered ever more dramatically. The gap seemed more than a mountain passageway carved by nature; it was a deep slash through the rock, an astonishing cleft. The rock wall fell away suddenly, like the edge of a table. The land parted as decisively as if it were the final precipice at the end of the world.

Around the next turn, the road began a winding ascension that led directly into the cleft. As it left the valley floor it became a shelf, a slender path around the curved base of the mountain wall. On the right, the wall rose to its crest almost directly overhead; on the left, the ledge fell away into a deep and narrow valley. Then, a short distance farther on, the interrupted mountain ridge seemed to reemerge suddenly on the left, and I realized that I was standing directly in the gap. The massive and prodigious and seemingly endless walls of forest-crowned stone reduced me to a fly-speck figure in the gap that separated them.

Here was the principal path between the East and the West for the aboriginal inhabitants of the North American continent, long before the land mass was given a European name. Here was the saddle, the pass, the needle's eye, the doorway through which migrating thousands of colonial Americans found their way to the continent's heartland. Here had passed more than three hundred thousand people in the last quarter of the eighteenth century—predecessors of Aley, among them many who would become founders and architects of the new nation's principal communities and institutions. Cumberland Gap was as important to American history as St. Louis or Ellis Island; it was a gateway to the land beyond. For several minutes I stood there in the stone threshold, ignoring the passing traffic, listening instead to echoes from another age. The hoofbeats were faint, almost beyond imagining.

Civilization intruded. On the approaches of the highway through the gap, the trail was studded with motels and gas stations and fast-food restaurants. The contemporary boundaries of Kentucky, Virginia, and Tennessee converged near there. On the Tennessee side was the village of Harrogate, where Union Army veterans and

Congregational Church missionaries had built a school in memory of Abraham Lincoln. As a young girl in her teens, Addie King of Harlan County had gone there at the beginning of the twentieth century, when the school was in its infancy. She remembered its bearded, white-haired benefactor, Oliver Otis Howard, his missing right arm a testament to his war sacrifice at Gettysburg, standing proudly before the assembled students in chapel to praise the martyred Great Emancipator.

Along Virginia's approach to the gap was the Poor Valley, once the main route of the railroad to the East and the closest connection between the upper valley of Martins Fork and the outside world; now, in the silent twilight of the railroad age, the once-busy villages there were as deserted and forgotten as Smith, their cross-mountain sister village.

And on the Kentucky side of the gap was the city of Middlesboro, where men who had controlled the land and the coal and the railroads had dreamed of creating a sprawling mountain paradise, only to see it crumble and fall in the panic of 1893. The town had survived, and in time it had become a small city, but little remained as visual evidence of its brief bid for glory.

Between Harrogate and Middlesboro, Cumberland Gap and the long ridge of Cumberland Mountain had been placed in the stewardship of the National Park Service. The history of the region was preserved there in trail markers and museum exhibits and collected artifacts that told of the long stream of migrants through the gap.

But the Park Service had come much too late to record the passage of the first settlers of Harlan County. Somewhere there on the mountain slope near the gap, the father and mother of Aley Ledford had been laid to rest in 1802. No stone remained to mark their placement in the soft forest humus. They had been returned to the mother earth and left there, forgotten in the long march of the years, and finally no one was left who could remember that unmarked spot. Late in the twentieth century, a hundred and eighty years after their passing, no amount of searching could ever deliver the proof of their former presence there.

For a dozen miles, the Wilderness Road beyond Cumberland Gap curved northward through a broad valley to its meeting with the Cumberland River. That was the route the vast majority of early settlers had taken. But just north of the gap itself, as the road descended to its valley path, a narrow cut extended from it and wound back toward the east, following the northern base of the long mountain ridge. A few pioneers, a mere handful, had gone this way. Stephen Farmer and the Ledfords and Smiths and Skidmores who followed his lead must have been first among them. The evidence strongly suggested that they had chosen this more arduous and dangerous and uncertain trail, and on it they had gone not beyond the mountains but deep into them, confident of finding the valley of their dreams.

The departure of the side trail from the Wilderness Road was so hidden, so inconspicuous, that only the most seasoned woodsman's eye would have noticed it. The trail was not heavily traveled, far from it; narrow and twisting, it lay so deep in the shadows of the mountains and the forest that only the position of the morning sun gave reassuring confirmation of the traveler's easterly direction. From every fold in the mountain wall, a thin trickle of spring water descended to join the west-running creek in the bottom of the hollow. For ten miles or more, the trail looped and twisted beside the creek but never wandered far from it.

Somewhere there on the northern slope of the extended mountain wall, Stephen Farmer had found the headwater of Martins Fork, an east-flowing creek, but that source was well hidden. Almost twenty miles deep into the forest, the westbound creek seemed to disappear; then, a little farther on, out of a tangle of rhododendron and mountain laurel, there was Martins Fork, running friskily toward the east. Almost imperceptibly, the trail had begun its descent beside the creek, and the one followed the other on a crooked course for several miles.

The creek bottom widened gradually as it sloped eastward. Finally, the trail opened upon a broad valley ringed by mountains. Martins Fork snaked across the valley, picking up several smaller streams as it went, including Cranks Creek from the right and Crane Branch from the left. The direction of the main stream shifted from east to north, and the descent continued. Several miles beyond the valley, Martins Fork would converge with Clover Fork and Poor Fork to form the Cumberland River—and still farther along its way, the Cumberland would cross the Wilderness Trail in the valley north of Cumberland Gap, and wind on westward for nearly seven hundred miles to its meeting with the Ohio.

But it was that first high valley of Martins Fork that attracted Stephen Farmer and his companions, and it was there that they stopped and stayed. The north slope route must have been Farmer's way into what would later be known as Harlan County; no other passage seemed plausible. There had been no route up the Cumberland River from the Wilderness Road at the start of the nineteenth century, and even if there had been, it would not have continued all the way to the headwater of Martins Fork. As for the over-mountain routes into the valley from the Virginia side of the stony wall, they had all been bypassed as impractical when the Ledfords and their companions made their way to Cumberland Gap. No, there was a better way, and Stephen Farmer knew it, for he had traveled it—not from Cumberland Gap to the Martins Fork valley, but from the valley to the gap.

He had first entered the valley by walking across the stony southern ridge on one of the buffalo paths, and thus had found Martins Fork. Then he had followed the stream westward to its source, crossed one short ridge beyond there, picked up a west-flowing creek, and pursued it to the Wilderness Road near the Cumberland Gap. Stephen Farmer thus found the way *out* of the Martins Fork valley; it would have been a simple matter for him then to reverse the direction and lead his land-seeking companions *into* that remote place.

On my own journey into that mountain region, I could more easily imagine the wilderness appearance of the route from Cumberland Gap to the Martins Fork valley as it must have been in 1802 than I could summon a mental vision of the Wilderness Trail to the Bluegrass in the days of Daniel Boone. The Wilderness

Trail had been transformed as thoroughly as any American highway, and bore no resemblance to its original form—but the country road to Martins Fork followed the same winding contours and passed the same rural streams and woodlands as before. A scattered few mobile homes and four-wheel-drive vehicles had taken the place of log cabins and oxcarts along the narrow road, and strip-mine scars were a telling sign of modern technology's intrusion, but the road itself had never been much more than a trail, and it remained that: a rough, slender, primitively constructed and sparsely traveled route across a short and rugged section of the Appalachian Mountains.

Long after the arrival of Stephen Farmer and his companions, the mountain village of Smith had come into being there in the high valley, but now it was gone. The houses and barns were gone too. A wall of concrete had been thrown up across the narrow neck of the valley on its northern end, and soon the waters of Martins Fork and the creeks that fed it would be trapped behind that wall and held there until the valley was inundated, drowned in its own life-giving fluid. Already, the wilderness appearance of the valley had been stripped away by the dam-builders and timber-cutters and coal-diggers. Only in the most distant hollows along the trail could any semblance of the virgin wilderness of young Aley Ledford's day be glimpsed, or even imagined. He had seen it first as a thirteen-year-old boy, and in the seventy years he remained in the valley, it had lost little of its original appearance. Even his great-grandson, Burnam Ledford, could share a similar remembrance of the place, for it had hardly changed when he was born or when he left it at the age of thirteen. It was not until the twentieth century that permanent and irrevocable change was imposed upon that high valley of Martins Fork.

Smith, Kentucky, could hardly have been called a village on the December morning in 1889 when Jesse Ledford and his wife and children took leave of it. It did not even have a name in any formal sense, there being no post office to give it one. It was called Smith because Creed Smith owned the largest portion of the valley and the surrounding slopes and hollows, and because he had a store and grist mill there; the only other structure at the confluence of Cranks Creek and Martins Fork was a one-room log schoolhouse. Smith embraced a network of creeks and branches and hollows in a narrow valley thirteen hundred feet above sea level. On the south, Cumberland Mountain loomed another fifteen hundred feet, impeding the passage into Virginia. To the west, from whence Martins Fork came, the twenty-five-mile trail to Cumberland Gap was almost as much an empty wilderness as Aley Ledford had found in 1802. Cranks Creek rushed in from the east to join Martins and twist on northward, gathering others to form the Cumberland at Harlan Town.

It was in that valley of Martins Fork that Burnam Ledford learned to plow a straight furrow, as his father and grandfather and great-grandfather had learned before him. He mastered the creeks and hollows as completely as any streetwise city boy could know the avenues and alleys and neighborhoods of his environment—knew their names in sequence, their length, their distance from home, their residents, their lore and reputation. Beginning at the mouth of Cranks Creek, he could navigate a creekbed-and-ridgetop route to Harlan Town, and every tributary along the way was indelibly branded in his memory and his imagination.

Then Creed Smith, son of Noble, grandson of David, great-grandson of Henry, left his land in the care of his sons and crossed the mountain into Virginia; Leander Ledford, the one they called Leeann, fourth-born of Aley Ledford Jr. and a grandson of old Aley, sold his land and left for the Bluegrass; and Jesse Ledford, another of Aley's grandsons, son of James, father of Burnam, sold out too, and took his family with Leeann's out of the mountains. With hardly an exception since Aley Ledford and David Smith had entered Harlan County as youngsters, their descendants in three generations had remained with them on Martins Fork and its tributaries. The departure of Creed Smith and Leander Ledford and Jesse Ledford marked the acceleration of an exodus that would become more a new rule than an exception.

When he came back to Harlan County to teach school seven years after he had left there with his parents, Burnam Ledford could see some changes in the valley of his birth. There was a post office called Smith by then, and people stopped in frequently on their way to or from the train in Virginia's Poor Valley, across the mountain. Smiths still predominated, and many Ledfords and Skidmores and Farmers also remained. But the changes Burnam saw were slight and insubstantial, not transforming, not radical. Harlan County remained a mountain-bound district cut off from the currents of social and cultural and economic change in Kentucky and the nation, and the valley of Martins Fork was a remote subdistrict of the county. The high valley was still very much the same woodland wilderness it had been in Aley's day; only the greater number of cabins and patches of plowed ground made it different. Harlan's twentieth-century metamorphosis was yet to come.

It began in 1911, when the railroad finally reached the mother lode of Harlan County coal. Farsighted men had known for fifty years that the coal was there; it was only a matter of time until they brought the trains to it. The Louisville and Nashville Railroad completed a line from Lexington to Pineville in 1888, and three years later a connecting link was made through Cumberland Gap and up the Poor Valley all the way to the Norfolk and Western Railway's terminus in Norton, Virginia. Almost immediately, tributary lines were started along the route. One of the most important was T.J. Asher's Wasioto and Black Mountain Railroad, a line that ran from near Pineville to the vicinity of Harlan. Between the time it was begun in 1908 and the time it reached Harlan Town in 1911, the L&N bought controlling interest in the line from Asher. Further extensions followed the creeks: Poor Fork, Clover Fork, Martins Fork, and their principal tributaries. Finally, in 1930, a rail tunnel through Cumberland Mountain near Smith allowed coal trains from the Martins Fork valley to reach Hagan and the main line in Virginia. The valley would never be the same.

In 1911, the year the railroad first reached Harlan County's coalfields, twenty-five thousand tons of coal were moved to market. Within three years, more than four million tons were shipped from the county. By 1928, the annual yield exceeded fifteen million tons.

The patience of Edward M. Davis of Philadelphia had been richly rewarded. Assured by geologists that hundreds of millions of tons of high-quality coal were buried in thick seams beneath the surface of Harlan County, he had sent agents there in 1870 to buy mineral rights. Their first and largest purchase was the eighty-six-thousand-acre Ledford-Skidmore-Smith-Farmer survey. Much timber had been cut from the land since Aley Ledford and his partners had surveyed it in the 1840s, and numerous overlapping and conflicting claims had prevented them from gaining clear titles to the property. None of that concerned Davis. His agents simply offered a dollar an acre—less in some cases—for the right to extract whatever minerals lay underground. They bought everything they could get, and if more than one party claimed ownership of a given parcel, they cheerfully paid every claimant the same per-acre price. The Ledfords and their partners took the money and kept the use of the land, thinking they had received something for nothing, a bonanza for underground minerals that could never be moved.

Edward M. Davis held on to his collection of deeds and waited. The years passed. His son succeeded to ownership of the properties, and then his grandson. In 1901, the grandson, Charles H. Davis, helped to underwrite a more extensive geological survey by federal and state geologists. It confirmed what he already knew: "practically an inexhaustible supply" of high-grade bituminous coal—billions of tons of it—waited to be mined in Harlan County.

Charles Davis and his business associates, one of whom was Warren Delano Jr., an uncle of Franklin Delano Roosevelt, moved quickly to clear away all remaining legal obstacles to the land. They formed the Kentenia Corporation, a holding company, to manage the property, and made preparations to lease large tracts of it to major national coal-mining companies as soon as the railroad was in operation. And that, too, was a matter over which the Kentenia officials had some control, for Warren Delano was also a director of the L&N.

On April 10, 1908, three months before T.J. Asher formally organized his Wasioto and Black Mountain Railroad with L&N backing, a special newspaper supplement advertising the formidable combination of coal, trains, and the Kentenia Corporation was distributed in Harlan County. It announced the corporation's offer to pay fifty dollars an acre for clear title to mineral rights on additional Harlan lands. The sum was payable in corporation stock, not cash, and the offer was made for one month only, after which the price would drop to forty dollars. If sufficient lands were not made available, the statement implied, railroad and mining operations would be delayed, perhaps even canceled. Harlan Countians rushed to accept the offer. One who thus became a small stockholder in Kentenia was a nephew of Surveyor Jim Farmer; another was a grandson of Noble Smith; Ledfords and Skidmores may also have traded their holdings for stock.

Two months after the purchase offer, Warren Delano and his nephew, Franklin Delano Roosevelt, went to Harlan County to have a firsthand look at the Kentenia holdings. They left the train at Hagan, crossed Cumberland Mountain on horseback, rode upstream on Martins Fork toward Cumberland Gap for a few miles, and then crossed Black Mountain to Cartons Creek and the house of Henry Smith (a brother of Creed), whom Roosevelt described in a letter to his wife Eleanor as "about the most prosperous farmer of the county." He also wrote that Harlan County from the top of Cumberland Mountain offered "one of the most magnificent views I have ever seen," and later he described a ride up Martins Fork from Harlan Town as a journey through "the most beautiful country we have seen yet—the sides of the valley going up 2,000 feet, heavily wooded with great poplars, chestnuts and a dozen or two other deciduous trees and every mile or so a fertile bottom with fine crops and a stream of splendid water."

He had seen Aley's Harlan, Creed Smith's Harlan, the Harlan of Burnam Ledford's youthful remembrance. It would not long remain in that state of unspoiled beauty. Seventy years after Roosevelt's visit, more than a quarter of a billion tons of coal had been extracted from the Kentenia lands alone, and the Harlan County tax books still showed twenty-three thousand acres of land belonging to the Kentenia Corporation—land for which the company paid an annual county property tax of only twenty-one cents an acre. As

surely as coal extraction had enriched Kentenia, it had impover-
ished Harlan County.

Burnam Ledford never saw that Harlan, the Harlan of the coal
age. He had been gone for five years when the future president of
the United States came to call, gone for eight years when the railroad came to stay, gone for twenty years when the corporations
and the mine operators and even the state of Kentucky used force
to prevent union organization by the men who dug the coal. The
conflict between miners and owners erupted into such bitter and
protracted strife in the 1930s that the county came to be called
"Bloody Harlan."

Burnam missed all of that. He went back for an occasional
visit, but he never returned to live. Considering how many Ledfords
had been there in about 1870, when Aley and Betsy had thirteen
children and more than a hundred grandchildren, the number still
living in Harlan in the turbulent early years of the coal age was
surprisingly small. Most of them had gone—and once gone, they
seldom returned.

One of the exceptional few was Lee Ledford, a grandson of the
Leander—Leeann—who had moved from the valley of Martins Fork
to Garrard County with his cousin Jesse, Burnam's father, in 1889.
Leeann had a son named Lee, born in Garrard in 1892, who went
to Berea College and there met and married Mary Smith of Lee
County, Virginia, a granddaughter of Creed Smith. In 1918, Lee
Ledford went off to serve in World War I; his wife went to live with
relatives on Board Branch of Martins Fork near Smith, Kentucky,
where she gave birth to a son, Lee Jr.

The young Lee grew up dividing his time between Paint Lick in
Garrard County, where one side of his family had put down new
roots, and the valley of Martins Fork in Harlan County, where
both sides of his family had kept a presence for more than a century. He graduated from high school in Harlan, went to the United
States Military Academy at West Point, served as an officer in World
War II, and then graduated from Harvard University Law School
in 1950.

The following year, Lee Ledford built a seventeen-room house at the mouth of Board Branch, on land he had inherited from the estate of Creed Smith. His mother and father lived in the house for two decades, and when his father died, Lee left his law career in New York and went home to live with his mother. Three years later, in 1976, the United States Army Corps of Engineers exercised its power of eminent domain to force Lee Ledford and his mother from their home so that the land could be cleared for a flood-control dam and recreation lake.

Ledford fought back in court, hoping to save his house, but he lost, and in time the house was razed and the land cleared and the dam built. Back in New York, involved again in corporate law, Lee lived in an apartment on Park Avenue with his eighty-three-year-old mother. He returned once more to see the denuded valley of his birth, the finger-thin hollows and the creeks and the vanished community of Smith, before they were inundated by the backed-up waters of Martins Fork. Lee Ledford saw what was happening, and he was bitter.

"I know the story about how Aley Ledford and David Smith and the others came in here in 1802," he said. "I'm a Ledford and a Smith, and I've heard the legends all my life, from both sides of my family. This valley means a lot to me. I never have given up fighting to keep my little piece of it, and I don't intend to give up. I still have hope I'll win in court and get to build another house here. When Aley and Noble's heirs sold that big land title to the Kentenia Corporation, they sold it for a song—and they sang it themselves. They didn't have any kick coming when it was over, because they chose to deal. But look at me: I don't want to sell. I'm trying to hold on to a little piece of the valley of my ancestors. I don't want to sell it at any price. The government is forcing me against my will to give it up. For a small, puny dam that'll only cover three or four thousand acres, the Corps of Engineers bought five or six times as much land as it needed, spent over $16 million, evicted a number of families—Smith, Ledford, Burkhart, all old names in Harlan County. Worst of all, they don't even know if the dam will do what they claim, which is to prevent floods on lower Martins Fork around the town of Harlan. And for that, they drove me out."

Lee Ledford sat for a moment in brooding silence. "One way or another," he said finally, "the Ledfords have lost just about everything they ever had in Harlan County—their land, their wealth, their identity. It's all gone but a little bit—and the water will cover what's left."

HARLAN, POP. 3,318. In a seventy-year cycle of coalfield boom and bust, Harlan had known flush times and desperate times in predictable alternation, if not in equal measure. It had ridden the whiplash of union-busting by the coal companies and retaliatory violence by miners. It had suffered grievous loss of life in dark and dangerous underground mines and devastating loss of land and water in the ravaging bite of strip-mine shovels. It had endured fire and flood, railroad rule and absentee ownership, courthouse gangs and government intervention. It had known frontier law, gun-barrel justice. Harlan was a tough town, tempered to a steely hardness by its history.

The thirty-mile highway route from Pineville, following the weaving path of the Cumberland River, was from early in the nineteenth century the main entrance to Harlan from the outside, but not until late in the twentieth century was it made a safe entrance. Modern highway improvements had made the way not straight but at least no longer narrow—and strong enough to bear the weight of hulking, eighteen-wheel coal trucks. The better roads notwithstanding, snail's-pace traffic still crept through the narrow, crooked streets of the town, and rush-hour jams were worthy of a metropolis.

Harlan in the late 1970s had a hospital, a country club, three schools, five small hotels and motels, a dozen churches, and about fifteen insurance agencies. A plague of lawyers encircled the courthouse—some two dozen in private practice, most of them specializing in matters of land and coal. The railroad was a continuing, dominating presence; it and the trucks hauled away more than fifteen million tons of coal a year from about 160 Harlan County mines. Flat land was at a premium, and newly cleared sites were quickly filled with shopping centers and subdivisions and mobile home parks. Signs told a story of their own: Kentucky Fried Chicken.

Pizza Hut. Dairy Queen. Cadillac. Datsun. Toyota. Jeep. No Parking. One Way. Food Stamps. Saturday Night Fever. Jesus Is Coming Soon.

The Harlan County telephone directory, with approximately 7,500 residential entries, listed 140 Smiths, 32 Skidmores, 32 Farmers, and only 11 Ledfords. In the public library, a few census documents from the 1800s yielded little beyond a confusion of names (Aley, Aly, Elias) and a small amount of supporting information, including this 1880 listing: Sink Ledford (elsewhere Sinkler, Sinclare), colored, age fifty, wife Darkes, children America, James, Edison, Rebecca, Mary, Alabama.

Deed books in the courthouse contained many listings of property transactions involving Aley Ledford, his son John, and other of his children. Between 1820 and 1860, they held in excess of twenty thousand acres of land, most of it acquired in the mid-1840s, when the Ledfords and their Smith, Skidmore, and Farmer partners made their extensive survey. The deed books showed Noble Smith to have fifteen thousand acres, Jim Farmer thirty-six thousand and Johnny Skidmore eleven thousand. The books also showed transfers of about a thousand acres on Cranks Creek from Aley Ledford and his heirs to Sinkler Ledford and his heirs.

More elusive was the record of E.V. King's tenure as sheriff of Harlan County. He served two terms in the 1880s, and after that he was a U.S. marshal, and then he had gone back to his Clover Fork farm at Kildav, near Evarts. Sick with tuberculosis, he had died there in 1895, leaving his wife and his ten-year-old daughter Addie and his three small sons with the farm and a large debt. They had sold the land to cover the debt, and a coal company had come after them, building plank shacks for miners on the land. Now, frail cottages still crowded the narrow strip of level earth between creek and hillside where Kildav had been. No one there had ever heard of any prior resident named King. Nor was Ewell Van King a familiar name in Evarts, a short distance upstream, and the Black Mountain Academy of Addie's childhood was also gone. From Smith to Harlan to Kildav to Evarts, far less remained to mark the prior passage of Burnam and Addie Ledford and their forebears than the venerable couple held in their own collective store of passed-down accounts and personal recollections.

Back through Harlan and then south and east along Martins Fork, the road led past Farmers Mill and Chevrolet and Lenarue to a larger community, the creekside and railside village of Cawood. As a young man, Burnam had briefly tended the store and post office there—Steve Cawood's old store—and he and Addie had ridden on horseback from near Cawood to Harlan Town to get married. Then, Martins Fork had been a swollen river, ice-choked and log laden; now it was almost dry, a trickling stream in a rocky, trash-littered bed.

The road divided at Cawood, one prong continuing to Smith and the upper valley of Martins Fork, the other crossing Cranks Ridge and descending into a long valley sheltering the headwaters of Cranks Creek. The latter route passed through the community of Cranks and continued eastward to Pennington Gap, Virginia.

Near the bottom of Cranks Ridge, the Wash Smith Cemetery lay in a clearing on a gently sloping hillside facing up the valley. Just below the cemetery, a narrow blacktop road turned to follow Cranks Creek toward its meeting with Martins Fork at Smith. Along the entire southern flank of the valley, Cumberland Mountain paralleled the creek; it and Little Black Mountain, the northern rampart, were the towering ridges that defined the Cranks Creek valley. The railroad had never penetrated there; the only passages in and out were the Harlan-to-Pennington Gap highway and the slender country road to Smith. The original path of entry and exit—the mountain trail between Cranks and Ocoonita—had long since been abandoned, it having been too rough and precipitous for any traffic except hardy pedestrians and sure-footed pack animals.

In place of the ancient woods that once had grown thick and tall at the base of Cranks Ridge, smaller cedars and dogwoods and maples now provided the cemetery shade. Part of the fenced graveyard had been cleared and mowed, but in the upper section, the older section, tombstones were hidden beneath heavy underbrush.

The familiar names were there: Ledford, Smith, Skidmore,

Farmer. Stephen Ledford, 1831–1892, last-born son of Aley and Betsy. Nancy Ledford Smith, 1813–1844, Stephen's oldest sister, first wife of Noble Smith. George Washington "Wash" Smith, son of Noble and Nancy, the one for whom the cemetery was named. Betsy Farmer Ledford, Blind Granny, the wife of Aley, was buried there too, in the same year as her son and caretaker Stephen—or so it was believed—but no stone marker could be found for her in the thick and tangled undergrowth.

The valley stretched green and flat toward the eastern mountains. Old Aley had built his racetrack there, according to the legend, and he and the black jockeys who rode for him had taken their victorious mounts to compete elsewhere—at Lexington, perhaps, and at Travellers Rest in Owsley County. (It might have been simply a myth, a romantic tale without any basis in fact; there was, after all, nothing in the extensive and voluminous recorded history of horse racing in Kentucky to indicate that racetracks had ever existed in Owsley or Harlan County. But then there was eighty-year-old Dewey Botner of Travellers Rest: he remembered that his grandfather, a child in the 1830s, had moved with his family to Owsley from Harlan County. And yes, Dewey Botner firmly asserted, there was a racetrack at Travellers Rest, a mile-and-a-half oval. "I know," he said. "It was on my farm, the farm that was passed on to me by my father. I remember the track. I've still got a board from the fence that went around it.")

Day's Store served as the post office for Cranks, and Cranks itself was not so much a village as a scattering of houses and trailers along the valley highway and in the hollows extending from it. Behind the store counter, Mrs. Mabel Day presided. "Ledfords?" she asked, repeating the name. "There's a few left, mostly around Cawood. The last Ledfords to live around here was all colored, lived just up the road and to the left, up toward the head of Cranks Creek. Ledfords and Turners, most of them were. Mrs. Anna Turner moved to Lexington about a year ago; she was the last one. All the colored people are gone now, died out or moved away, and whites bought up the property. Then when that tide come last year, that flood, it washed away the village of Ledford, Kentucky. Wasn't no

post office left there or nothing—just a little community—and that
tide just washed it away."

On the highway near the turnoff to the head of Cranks Creek,
Howard Skidmore lived in a mobile home. He had lived on Cranks
Creek all his life, had known Ledfords white and black. "Most of
the people up that holler there, they was colored people," he said,
pointing. "Turner, Ledford, Stout, Howard, Pope—nice people. Like
old Parrish Pope—he was a good feller, but buddy, nobody fooled
with him, white or colored." Howard Skidmore had heard of Aley
Ledford, and he remembered where a log house had stood that
some said had been the home of Aley and Betsy. He did not know
what ties bound the Ledfords of his acquaintance to the Aley of
old. He simply shrugged: "You track it down far enough, buddy,
you'll find everybody in the world's kin."

Wade Madden knew more. He lived in a white frame house on
a neatly manicured hillside two miles up the gravel road that led to
the end of the Cranks Creek hollow. Madden had been born in
Evarts in 1900, had been a coal miner for forty-one years, had
lived since 1957 in the same house, he and his wife. The Ledfords
he had known there in that last hollow of Cranks Creek included
no whites at all.

"First colored man I ever saw in my life was at Evarts, when I
was eight years old," he said. "Might near scared me to death. It
was Jeemes Ledford. I can almost see that man now. He wasn't real
dark. Had kinky hair, steel gray, and he wore leather leggings. His
father was old Sinkler Ledford—and Jeemes had a son named Sinkler
too. Jeemes was the postmaster of Ledford, Kentucky, which was
right here. See that concrete foundation down there?" He pointed
toward the road's edge. "That's where the post office was, and I'm
living now in Jeemes's house. It was just a two-room log cabin
then—it's been added to. The Ledfords were good folks, and Jeemes
was honored by all who knew him. I remember in 1914, a fellow
named John A. Ward was running for county judge, and he got me
to drive him around the county in a buggy so he could campaign.
We come up here into this holler, and Ward got drunk, stayed drunk
several days, and it was Jeemes Ledford and his wife that looked

after us, fed us and gave us a place to sleep until we could get Ward sobered up.

"I don't know for sure when Jeemes died, but it must have been sometime around 1915 or 1920, and I reckon the post office closed about then too. Jeemes is buried here on Cranks Creek, but I'm not sure exactly where."

Wade Madden remembered fifteen or twenty black families living on the creek "until they died off or were bought off by the coal companies." He mentioned one of the last, "Bradley Turner, a preacher, who died in an accident a couple of years ago. His church was just down the road a way. Colored and white both went to it. I think Turner's son lives in Harlan now."

I located him on the phone. James L. "Jake" Turner, a janitor at the Harlan post office, remembered living on Cranks Creek until about 1947, when he moved as a young man into Harlan to work. "That holler is just ruint now," he said. "Peabody Coal Company took it all. Them poor people didn't know what they was doing, didn't know what the coal or the timber was worth. My father and them didn't get much of nothing for their land when they sold it."

Jake Turner said he "used to know some white Ledfords up around Cawood and Smith," but he had been better acquainted with Sink Ledford, the only son of Jeemes. Sink had died childless. "That line has played out," he said. "Jeemes had one daughter, Ollie, and she would be the only one still living that comes straight down out of that line of old Sinkler, going all the way back to the first Ledfords, white and colored."

It took me a while to find Ollie Ledford Morrison. She was living in Detroit, and her four children lived there too. Age had slowed her, but she still remembered Harlan, and on the phone I could still hear a touch of the mountains in her voice. "I was born on Cranks Creek," she said, "at Ledford, Kentucky. My father was James Ledford. People called him Jeemes. He was the postmaster there. I remember when my grandfather, Sinkler Ledford, lived with us. His wife's name was Darkes. They were born in slavery. My father may have been too, but he was just a little baby when freedom came. Whites and blacks both lived on Cranks Creek way back. My Grandfather Sinkler was light-skinned, had long curly hair. I guess his father was white, but I don't know who it was. It's been a long time since I was back in Harlan County, and I've forgotten a lot. I'm ninety-two years old now. Ninety-two years is a long time."

The last road, the road to the head of Cranks Creek, had been left in ruin by the daily pounding of coal trucks and the devastation of a flash flood in the fall of 1977. This was Aley's hollow; his log house had stood near the lower end of it for more than 150 years, and he and Betsy had spent seventy years together on the creekside land. Johnny Skidmore's homeplace had also been nearby, and Johnny's Abram, the grandfather of Addie Ledford, had succeeded him on the land, and George Burkhart's sycamore tree had spread its shade at the mouth of the hollow. For more than a century after Aley's death, numerous families had come and gone in this farthest hollow of Cranks Creek, tilling the narrow bottomland plots, living hard and simple lives, burying their dead in hillside graveyards above their houses. Throughout all the long decades, the creek was their lifeline—their water supply, their irrigation canal, their roadbed in dry seasons, their log run in the times of rain. It was their only avenue to Smith, to Harlan, to the towns beyond. The hollow was their shield and protection, but the creek was more; the creek was everything.

   And then there was the coal. Even as it created work and wealth and warmth, it destroyed land and life. Coal was the hope of the hard-pressed people of Cranks Creek—and finally, coal and the creek were their despair.

   The rutted, broken, washed-out road passed the site of Aley's old house and wound its way toward the head of the hollow. Near the creek, coal spilled from a conveyor belt onto a glistening black pyramid. The creek was a mere trickle, almost soundless, and in its stony bed was strewn the awesome detritus of floodtide: uprooted trees, rusted automobile bodies, even the splintered shells of houses. High upon the flanking ridges that closed in on the road, stripmine spoil banks and slag heaps, the afterbirth of coal, smothered the vegetation and dumped mud and boulders into the hollow. Past the Reverend Bradley Turner's deserted frame church, past Wade Madden's incongruously neat and attractive home, past the concrete foundation of the Ledford, Kentucky, post office, past abandoned coal tipples and empty houses, the broken road led on. A sign on the door of one house said STOP STRIP MINING AND SAVE OUR HOMES. There were no people about. In the stillness, I heard birds singing. Two miles, three miles, four. The hollow was deep and narrow, like a knife blade. The spoil banks seemed to be almost directly overhead, the walls of mud and rock and splintered wood almost vertical.

Suddenly, the road ended. The scarred and shattered face of Little Black Mountain loomed above the debris, and at its base, muddy water seeped like tears from the source of Cranks Creek.

A house stood there, surrounded, silent. Its survival seemed miraculous. A young woman came to the doorway. She regarded my presence cautiously, and at first gave no answer to my question, but then her sense of loss overcame her silence. "The flood was awful," she said. "There was nothing up there to hold the water, so it just came on down." Her eyes swept over the ravaged mountain.

"They're supposed to put it back the way it was," she said finally, "but there ain't no way they can do that. This place can't ever be put back the way it was."

Burnam and Addie Ledford remembered the way it was when virgin timber grew there, and canebrakes lined the creek, and the bottomland was cleared and planted, rich and fertile. They remembered the house that Aley built, and the house of Johnny Skidmore that Abram had occupied. They remembered the wild turkeys, the deer, the black bears and panthers. They remembered Sinkler and the others, and Burkhart's sycamore, and the graveyards. They remembered the sparkling creek, the life-giving stream. But what they remembered was gone, and it could never be put back the way it was.

Aley was there somewhere. They had buried him on a hillside plot above the house—on which side of the creek, no one could remember. When his body was returned to the dark earth, ageless chestnuts and poplars were still rooted there, and Cranks Creek was a stream that roared and whispered with the seasons. Now his grave was lost—buried deeper, perhaps, by the muddy overburden of a strip mine. There was no trace left of Aley.

NINE

At Home in Garrard County

Addie, 1903–1928

"I couldn't find the graves, Burnam—not Aley's or Betsy's either."

The old man pondered my report for a minute. He asked me several questions, and when he was finally satisfied that I had looked in all the right places, he was silent again. "I guess it's too late," he said finally. "It's been over a hundred years since he died."

We sat in the shade of the porch, facing the road. Addie had brought iced cola from the kitchen, making two trips to deliver the glasses. She shunned help, saying simply, "It's good for me to be up walking—keeps my knees from getting stiff." As we sipped our drinks, I told them what I had discovered and what had eluded me on the trail of the Ledfords from Virginia to North Carolina to Harlan County. There were still a few gaps that I might be able to fill if I could keep looking, I said, but for the most part I had covered the early history.

Burnam, too, seemed to sense that it was time for us to move on. "If we get to go to Harlan in the fall, maybe we'll find some more then," he said. "You've got most of it, though, and I believe you've got it right." After an interval of silence, he turned his thoughts away from the stories that had been passed down to him and concentrated on his own experiences as a young man:

"The day I walked across the mountain from Hagan to Coon Branch, going to meet Addie so we could get married, that was the very same day that Orville and Wilbur Wright first flew their airplane over on the coast of North Carolina. We didn't know about it at the time, of course—didn't hear about it until much later. I got to be very interested in airplanes, but I never did even see one for years—it must have been after World War I, when a fellow over at Crab Orchard was taking people up for rides. I wouldn't go, though. I never have been on a plane myself, and I don't reckon I ever will be. But I still think about the Wright brothers, because this December will be the seventy-fifth anniversary of their first flight—and it'll be me and Addie's seventy-fifth wedding anniversary. We've been married as long as man has been flying. Now they've gone around the world and clear to the moon—and we've stayed right here on the ground, in this same old house."

The thought amused Burnam enough to make him chuckle.

"That was a big year, 1903," Addie interjected. "I've read up on it, and I remember a lot about it, too. That's when Henry Ford built his first automobile, but we didn't see one of them for a long time either."

"First one I saw," said Burnam, "was down at Paint Lick. I don't remember the year, but I remember the car. Some drummer was driving it."

"And Teddy Roosevelt started the Panama Canal," Addie went on. "People talked about Panama quite a bit. And that's the year old Cash Clay died. And do you remember Helen Keller? A book came out about her life, and everybody was interested in that."

"The first World Series was played in 1903," Burnam said. "I've been a big baseball fan might-near all my life. But speaking of Teddy Roosevelt—I saw him once over at Berea when he was running for president. Must have been 1904. He was supposed to make a speech there, but his train was late. There was thousands of people gathered, and I was right up front, standing close to the platform, when the train came in. He came out on the step, looked over the crowd and said, 'Upon my honor, I wish I could talk to these fine people.' The train slowed down, but it never stopped. When he came past me, I reached up and he shook my hand. I trotted along beside the track holding to his hand until the train speeded up, and then I let go, and they rolled away. I always supported Teddy. In fact, the only time I didn't vote for a Republican for president was in 1912, when Roosevelt left the party and opposed President Taft—and both of them lost to Woodrow Wilson. I remember bringing the ballots to Lancaster from Paint Lick that night after the election. There came a report that New York had gone Republican by 151,000 votes. Looked like the Republicans was sweeping the nation, but something told me it was too soon to crow, so I stayed quiet and waited. Good thing I did."

Burnam had belonged to a minority within a minority: a small group of Roosevelt backers among Taft Republicans in predominantly Democratic Garrard County. Denied representation in the Garrard delegation to the state Republican convention, the Roosevelt faction had gone to Louisville to fight for credentials and a voice—and been denied again. It was Burnam's only defection in a lifetime in the party.

"I've voted for Democrats a few times in local races for county office," he said, "but except for that one time, I've always supported Republicans in national elections. I didn't vote for Wilson or Franklin Roosevelt or Truman—even though I liked Truman. I never did care much for Franklin Roosevelt."

"I liked his wife," Addie said. "She was popular—and smart, too. I looked on her as a straightforward woman. If she had run, I might have voted for her."

"She was smart, but she wasn't pretty," Burnam responded. "One night she was eating at a restaurant, and a man at the next table leaned over and said, 'Lady, excuse me, but you're the ugliest woman I ever saw in my life.' She said, 'And you're the drunkest man I ever saw.' And the man said, 'Yes, but I'll get over it.'"

"Oh, hush, Burnam," Addie hissed. "She wasn't any uglier than Franklin—and Teddy looked like a walrus. They called him the Bull Moose, you know."

"Have you always voted Republican too, Miss Addie?" I asked.

"Yes, but I never did take much interest in politics. My father was a politician. To tell you the truth, I wasn't too much in favor of letting women vote at first. Elections were so rough back then, I thought it was kind of indecent for women to have to go to election day. I voted in 1920, the first time women were allowed, but I wasn't very proud of it. I got used to it, though, and I've never failed to vote since then."

"Before that," Burnam explained, "women and children never got out on the street on election day—they stayed home. Even the schools closed. I guess it was because there was always trouble— men drinking, getting into fights, everything. Elections were dangerous in those days. But I was in favor of letting women vote. You hear the same arguments now against women preaching. I'm for that, too."

Politics had played an important part in their lives, and in the lives of their children and grandchildren. For all of the twentieth century, they had been active participants—not as candidates (though Burnam did make an unsuccessful bid for county office in the 1930s) but as campaign workers, contributors, and voters. And throughout the family history, no characteristic of their lives had been as consistent as their loyalty to the Republican Party. For most of the Ledfords, politics—Republican politics—was thicker than blood.

The first quarter of the twentieth century was a time of such political ferment in the United States that only the most disengaged citizens could stand apart from party strife, and none could escape the consequences of it. Politics permeated the nation's life, as even the most general listing of prominent personalities and dominant issues of the time clearly indicates. It was the age of McKinley and Teddy Roosevelt and William Howard Taft, of William Jennings Bryan and Eugene V. Debs and Robert M. LaFollette, of Wilson and Harding and Coolidge; it was a period of multiple parties: Democrat, Republican, Progressive, Populist, Socialist; it was a time of emotional and divisive issues: world war, prohibition, suffrage, racial segregation, immigration, robber barons, gold and silver. And in Kentucky, where politics long had been thought of as a periodic exercise in legalized bloodletting, the century had opened with the stunning murder of Democrat William Goebel, the only American governor ever to die in office as a result of assassination.

In those turbulent times, with the actions of politicians receiving such extensive public notice and having such profound effect, young people such as Burnam and Addie Ledford often saw politics as a dominating presence in their lives. It was not surprising, then, that their remembrance of so much that happened to them in those years should be pegged to the political reference posts of the period. "That fire was the same year Taft beat Bryan," one of them would say, or "The Titanic sank the year Wilson was first elected," or "That baby was born right after Harding died."

But the constant reference to politics had a certain distorting effect, obscuring numerous other influences that had helped to shape their lives and the lives of millions of other Americans. There were the obvious technological influences—the automobile, the airplane, the telephone, the radio—and there were countless personal and human influences as well. For all its prominence in their recollections, politics mattered less than birth and baptism, marriage and divorce, work and idleness, life and death—the simple joys and shattering sorrows of ordinary people coping with a complex world.

Addie gazed pensively in the direction of the mailbox and the road beyond. Her long gray hair was twisted in a rope and piled atop her head, pinned there just as she always wore it, as she had worn it on that day in 1904 when she and Burnam had sat for their first portrait together. Her eyesight was failing now, the process hastened by cataracts that had all but eliminated her ability to read. Her placid expression masked the discomfort and pain she felt from a variety of minor ailments. She seldom discussed her health, except in terse response to direct questions. As the afternoon's conversation turned to politics, she had gradually given up interest and finally fallen silent, lost in thought.

I was ready to begin recording her recollections of the early years of her life as a new bride in a new community in a new century. As soon as Burnam had turned his attention to the afternoon paper—holding it close to his one good eye, reading slowly and with strained effort, but eagerly—I moved with Addie to the corner of the porch. The faintest hint of a breeze stirred there. When we were settled in the rockers and I had reminded her of the point at which our previous conversation had ended, she concentrated for a few moments on the life she had entered in rural Garrard County in the closing days of 1903, and then she began to describe that life to me:

I'll tell you what was always my ambition: I wanted to make something of myself. Because my father died broke, I was always ashamed of being poor. I didn't want to run over anybody or make any rascally deals or anything like that—but I wanted to forge ahead.

We came here to Garrard after we married and lived for a year with Burnam's parents on their farm on Sugar Creek. It was close enough to Lancaster that you could hear the courthouse clock strike in the still of the evening. That first year, 1904, should have got us off to a good start. Burnam farmed with his father, and he taught school at Cartersville, and worked in the store down there, and in the summer I went back to Harlan County to teach. We had a good place to live, and Burnam and his father was building us a house there on the place, and we was working hard. But then Burnam took sick with typhoid fever that fall, got real sick, and he wasn't able to work any more until after we moved into our house in December.

Burnam bought thirty-eight acres of that Sugar Creek farm from his father, and we lived there in our new house for about a year. It was a very small, plain house—two rooms and a shed kitchen. Our first child was born there on July 1, 1905. It was a boy, and we named him Jesse Ewell, for Burnam's father and mine. Dr. J.B. Kinnaird delivered the baby. He was our family doctor, and he delivered several of our children. They were all born at home—wasn't any hospitals around here back then.

It was about that time, about 1905, that Burnam's parents sold their farm and moved to a rented place near Paint Lick, and the next year they bought a farm just beyond Paint Lick in Madison County. That's where they lived the rest of their lives. I liked them a lot. Burnam's mother was a woman who loved to have company, and people loved to go there. She'd cook big dinners for everybody—we used to go every Sunday for dinner, and all of Burnam's brothers and sisters would be there. She was a real good manager—

and he was a good farmer, too, a hard worker. They depended a lot on Burnam because he was the oldest.

After Ewell was born and Burnam's parents had moved, we sold our little place and went just across the hill to another farm, a place owned by Guy Davidson. It was a pretty nice place, 180 acres, and the house was especially fine—a big six-room hewed log house, with pear trees in the yard, just loaded with sugar pears. We felt like we was getting into wealth when we moved there. Mr. Davidson and his tenant had put out a crop, but the tenant got to mistreating the colored people that worked on the place, so Burnam was asked to take over. We lived there and ran that farm for five years.

Our next two children were born there in that house: Marian Eloise, on April 4, 1907, and Curtis Burnam Ledford Jr.—Bill, everybody called him—on April 27, 1909. Dr. Kinnaird delivered Eloise, but he was out of town when Bill's time came, and Burnam called for every doctor in town before he finally got one—and then the baby came before he could get there. I had help, though. An old woman we called Aunt Sook was staying with us. She was from Harlan County, and she was some kin to me and Burnam both. She had closer relatives than us around here, but she just liked to come to our place—and she'd stay until she got ready to leave.

We lived pretty well in those years. Burnam had given up teaching, and of course I couldn't teach any more, but we had that farm to work, and I raised about two hundred chickens at a time and kept a Jersey cow that gave four and a half gallons of milk a day. She was the best milk cow we ever had. We bought her for ten dollars when she was a year-old heifer calf. I could take a hundred baby chicks and not lose over four or five. We had plenty of eggs to sell, and some milk too, and things didn't cost much back then, so we were able to save. You could buy good cloth for dresses and such for a few cents a yard, and hire somebody to sew for practically nothing. I had a woman who helped me do the washing and ironing—a colored woman named Mandy Turner—and Aunt Sook would come, and another woman from Harlan named Em Irving lived with us off and on and helped cook and take care of the children, and later on my half-sisters from Harlan came. I was seldom alone with the children. One time Burnam was gone overnight, took his tobacco to market, and I was out milking in the evening, and one of the little ones stayed close by me, finally said, "Mama, we're not afraid, are we?" He wasn't used to being there alone.

Our house was a busy place. We did a lot of canning and baking, made pies and cobblers all the time. One year I put up fifteen gallons of blackberry jam. Seemed like the house was always full of people. We were lucky to keep good health, though. When Bill was a baby—just four days after he was born—I went up to where Burnam was weeding the tobacco bed and weeded with him until dinner. I've always had good health, except for having asthma when I was a child. I've always taken good care of myself, never smoked or drank or took much medicine—and I was strong, and didn't get tired easy. You'd have to be strong to have thirteen children.

In 1910 we moved to Manse, about two miles from Paint Lick, and bought the store there. We lived in a house behind the store, and Burnam had a little bit of land to grow tobacco on. Our fourth child, Edwin Carl, was born there on Thanksgiving Day, not long after we moved in. Dr. Nelson Mays delivered him. He was married to Governor Bradley's sister, and he had been through the Civil War as a Confederate doctor and then turned over to be a Republican after the war. The next child, Vesta Lucille, was also born at Manse. Old Dr. Kinnaird delivered her on October 24, 1912. That gave us five children.

When they got old enough, they went with Burnam to that historic old church at Manse, the Paint Lick Presbyterian Church. I never did go much. I generally stayed home and cooked dinner. There was always so many people to feed, always somebody besides us—and more of us all the time.

When Burnam took over that store at Manse, that was a big change for us, and I liked it. I worked in the store some, helping with the ordering and such. I just loved that—and I was good at it, too. I think I would have made an extra good businesswoman, but I couldn't do it all the time because I had to be at home. We did a lot of trade there. Burnam had kept stores before, and he knew how to manage. We had a telephone in the store, and people traded there from all around the neighborhood. We kept a few horses, and Burnam had a colored man, Arch Kavanaugh, who helped him farm, and our oldest children, Ewell and Eloise, started to school there. Seemed like we were getting along real well, but then our luck turned bad.

One day in 1913, I was in the store and Burnam was outside working somewhere. All of a sudden, the children came running and hollering: "The house is on fire!" For a minute, I thought Lucille, the baby, was inside, but she wasn't—nobody was. We never did know how it started, but it burned down fast, and we lost everything we had except the clothes on our backs. It was a pitiful shame, but there wasn't a thing we could do but stand there and watch it burn.

I've thought many a time about all the things we lost—furniture, my sewing machine, a twenty-volume encyclopedia set, a lot of books and letters and family things. It was November, and winter was coming, and we didn't have any place to live except there in an old schoolhouse. After the first of the year Burnam sold out the store, and we bought a house and an acre of land on his father's farm over in Madison County, about five miles from Manse. We lived there a year, and while we were there our next child was born— Dorothy Eleanor, delivered by a Dr. Treadway on November 27, 1914. She was another Thanksgiving baby. I guess we did have a lot to give thanks for—at least we were alive. But it seemed like just when we was stepping into prosperity, along came that fire and set us back.

On the first of January, 1915, we went back to Garrard County and bought another farm—sixty-six acres and a house on Doty Lane, about a mile from Manse. Burnam built on an extra room and a front porch, and we settled down and stayed there for the next five years.

That neighborhood around Manse and Paint Lick had been the domain of old Thomas Kennedy many years before, and some of his descendants still lived around there when we did. Kennedy had been a general in the Revolutionary War, and he got a big land grant in this county, thousands of acres. He built up a big estate and kept hundreds of slaves. I remember the old house very well—in fact, the night our house burned I took the children and went to stay with the family that was living there. It was a great big house—had a basement big enough to turn around a wagon and team in, and there was a prison down under there where they kept slaves that disobeyed. It was a scary place. And that's the house that Harriet Beecher Stowe visited in about 1850 and got the material for her book, *Uncle Tom's Cabin*.

Old Kennedy had died before then, but his son Thomas owned it. He drank a lot, and they said he used to light his pipe with five-dollar bills. Harriet Beecher Stowe lived in Cincinnati, and she came down here with a friend to visit at Dr. Charles Spillman's house. They went to the Kennedy place to see someone, and that's where she saw the cabin and met the slaves she wrote about in her book. One of the slaves escaped later and went to New England, and she saw him again up there. I remember asking Mrs. Kavanaugh, a great-granddaughter of old Kennedy, if Harriet Beecher Stowe really did visit there. She said, "Yes indeed, yes indeed."

The old cabin that the slave Tom lived in was still there on the plantation when we lived at Manse. I've seen it many a time, been in it. And old Kennedy's grave is still there in the Manse cemetery. They covered it with a big flat stone, and lightning struck it three times, cracked it clear across. What do you suppose that means? They claimed he was a very cruel man, mean to his slaves, and killed lots of people.

Somebody else that was born in this county back in about 1850 was Carry Nation, the woman that busted up saloons with her axe. She didn't live here very long, though. They said her father was a drunkard, and that's how come her to be so opposed to whiskey.

Nobody famous lived around Manse when we were there. It was just a nice country neighborhood. We lived right around there for fifteen years, all told—from 1910 to 1925. At the farm on Doty Lane, we had two more children: Herbert Raymond, born on April 11, 1917, and Bruce Barton, born on April 26, 1919. Both of them was delivered by Dr. Harmon Smith from Paint Lick. Bruce was named for a famous magazine writer named Bruce Barton, whose father was William E. Barton, a Congregational preacher from Boston that me and Burnam met several times over at Berea. He gave us a Bible once. It burned up in our house.

It was while we were living on Doty Lane that my half-sisters from Harlan started coming to stay with us a lot. My brother George had moved out west by then and gone to work in the timber business in Washington state, and my two younger brothers had died. Delora and Martha, the two oldest girls, stayed with us most of the time when they weren't in school. Ethyl, the younger sister, stayed with somebody else. You see, my mother wasn't well. She came for a visit a time or two, and she got to imagining things, and she wandered—got out and went as far as Richmond once, and old Dr. Mays picked her up on the road and brought her back to our house. Finally, we had to take her to the hospital in Lexington, and she stayed there the rest of her life. I felt sorry for her, but there wasn't anything we could do to help except look after her daughters, and we did that.

Me and Burnam was both real fond of Delora and Martha, and they felt close to us. They were just teenagers, and they'd come and stay all summer with us until it was time to go back to school. They always felt indebted to us for that, but I told them I didn't want them to feel that way. We had plenty to share, and they were older than my children, so they helped out a lot. But they never forgot. They both live out west now, and almost every year they come to see us. I guess we were almost like parents to them.

It was right around the time my mother went to the hospital that we had that bad winter, the winter of 1917–18. I can't remember a worse winter than that. Burnam had stock out in that weather, had to get out and feed them, and he lost some to the snow and cold. Once the mailman's horse got stuck in a snowdrift, and he never would have made it if Burnam hadn't helped him get out. He was a preacher, and afterwards he was so glad to be safe that he said he would pay Burnam back by preaching his funeral for free. Burnam was forty-two years old and almost bald-headed by then, so I guess the fellow though he'd be called on to pay the debt soon enough. He never got the chance, though—he's been dead for years.

The children never stopped going to school that winter—Burnam took them there on a sled. But just about everything else came to a stop, and it was so hard on some people that they didn't make it through. If we could have known what a terrible year 1918 was going to be for us, we might not have made it either.

The war was going on in Europe, and we knew several boys that went away to fight. One of them was Jesse Calico, a neighbor boy that we was real fond of. He come home on furlough at Christmas, and walked to our house in a snowstorm to pay Burnam some money he owed him. Right after that he was sent across, and we never did see him again. You know, I've always thought it was sad to send boys from this country to fight in all them foreign places, like Vietnam.

Burnam's youngest brother, Noble, got called to the service, but he never had to go overseas. Burnam was too old to serve, and Ewell, our oldest boy, was too young—just thirteen—so the war didn't affect us personally the way it did a lot of families. There was a real bad flu epidemic that same year, and thousands of people died all over the country, but we all stayed pretty healthy. I thought we were going to be lucky all around, but then our luck ran out.

Burnam's parents had lived for over ten years on their farm in Madison County. They were up in their sixties by then, but their health was good. They had bought a brand new Model T Ford—first car in the family—and they was real proud of it. One day in June, just before Noble was supposed to leave for the army, Burnam's parents and Noble and his sister Marian got in the car to drive over to brother Jim's so Noble could tell him goodbye. It was early in the evening, about dusk, when they come to the railroad crossing just below Paint Lick. Noble was driving, and Marian was in the front with him, and their parents was in the back seat. As they started over the crossing, they heard the whistle of the L&N train.

It struck the car right at the back wheels. Marian was thrown out and Noble was pinned inside, and both of them was hurt, but not bad. The worst of it was on Burnam's parents—it killed them instantly.

It was an awful blow for the whole family. I still remember

what a sad funeral that was. They were buried in that cemetery near the Presbyterian Church at Manse. And then, just three months later, we had to go back to the cemetery again.

That September, Ewell was out on his horse, driving some cattle for his father, and he didn't have his saddle on tight or something, because he slipped off, fell and twisted his back, and it paralyzed him. He laid in bed for about two weeks, and the doctors couldn't find out what was the matter with him. They was going to take him to Lexington for some X rays, but he just kept getting worse, getting weaker, and finally he died. It seemed like that paralysis just slowly cut off his breath. He was thirteen years old, the oldest one of our seven children. The shock of it hit me mighty hard, and Burnam too, but there's times when you can't do nothing but just stand and take it. That was one of those times.

Later on that fall, Burnam's sister Marian took sick and died in Louisville. I don't know if it had anything to do with her being hurt in that train crash or not, but she never was strong after that. So the fourth member of the family was buried there at Manse inside of five months.

Not long after that, Burnam got to thinking about his grand-mother, Polly Jones, who was living with a daughter back in Harlan County. Polly was John Ledford's daughter, the oldest granddaughter of Aley and Betsy, and she was the only one of Burnam's grandparents still living. He got to thinking about her being the last and all, and finally he got on the train and went to see her. He come back feeling glad he had gone—and it was a good thing he did go, because just a short time after that, before 1918 was over, old Polly died too. It took us a long time to get over that year.

Bruce was born the next year, so we had seven children again. Then in 1920 we bought a half interest in the old store at Manse and bought a house and farm right across the road from it—about 110 acres. I was really glad to be getting back into the store business, and I also liked our new house, a big house. It was the seventh place we had lived since we got married. If somebody had told me then that we would move three more times in the 1920s and then not move again for over fifty years, I never would have believed it.

We stayed that last time at Manse from 1920 until we moved to Lancaster in January 1925. Burnam had tied up all our money in the farm and store, but it looked like an extra good opportunity, and we stood to gain more than we ever had before. Our children were coming right along—Eloise was almost thirteen—and Delora and Martha stayed with us a lot, and others was always coming and going, so I had enough help that I could spend some time working in the store. I liked it just as much as I had the first time.

In 1921, we had another little girl. Dr. Smith delivered her. We were going to call her Myrtle. But she was poorly right from the start, and finally the doctor had to give up—he couldn't do nothing to save her. She only lived five days. A year later, on November 22, 1922, our tenth child was born, and we named her Jennie Slaven, after a close friend of mine. Dr. Virgil Kinnaird delivered her. He was the son of old Dr. J.B., who was dead by then. And then Tillie was the last one to be born at Manse. She was delivered by Dr. Smith on the eighth of April, 1924, and we named her Matilda Elizabeth.

I kept hoping that we would do well with the store and farm, but it turned out to be a bad time to make a gamble like we did. Burnam just had too many irons in the fire. He was on the school board, the tax board, the loose-leaf tobacco warehouse board, and he was also involved in politics, and he had the store and the farm and his family to look after. It was just too much—and besides, Burnam was too good-hearted, too easy. He let just anybody buy from him on credit, and lots of times they didn't pay their accounts. We had a big mortgage on the farm, owed I don't know how much on it—and then the bottom fell out of the tobacco market, and the people that owed us money couldn't pay, and we couldn't pay the ones that held our mortgage. They foreclosed in 1924, and we found ourselves with no place to live and no way to make a living.

It was a mean time. I felt like we had been cheated—but part of it was Burnam's fault for being too easy, for letting people have too much credit. I told you about my father having such a nice place in Harlan County and us ending up losing everything—well, that made it even harder for me when we lost our farm at Manse. The old men that held our mortgage on the farm, J.B. and Ernest Woods, they didn't treat us right, and there wasn't a thing we could do about it. Their luck turned bad too after that, but it didn't make me feel any better. We had already lost, and there wasn't no way to get it back. I was upset to think that after twenty years of hard work, we would have to start all over again.

People thought it would worry me to death, and it did bother me plenty, but I took it as well as I could. On the first of January, 1925, we moved in to Lancaster, and Burnam went to work selling grain and feed and coal for Hudson and Farnau. It was the first time since the early years of our marriage that he had worked for anybody but himself and his family—and by then he was almost fifty years old.

We rented a house and a few acres on Danville Street. Eloise had been away at school, but she came home that summer, and so did Delora and Martha—and that was the year I went with the two of them on the train out to Washington state to see my brother, George King. I hadn't seen him in twenty years. The girls convinced me that Eloise and the other bigger children could help Burnam take care of the little ones, and finally I agreed to go.

It was a grand trip. I had never been out of Kentucky before, except to the corner of Virginia and to Lincoln Memorial University in Tennessee, close to Harlan. My ticket to South Bend, Washington, and back cost $104. We went through St. Louis. It was so exciting—and then after we got there, they showed us such a good time that I almost forgot about all our troubles. My brother had a new Buick, and he took us everywhere—Portland, Seattle, Mount Ranier, all the important places. I didn't come back home for two months, and Delora and Martha didn't come at all—they stayed out there to live. My brother and his wife tried to persuade me to come home and get Burnam and the children and move out there, but I didn't want to. When I left to come home, George gave me money for a sleeping berth and gave me a thousand dollars besides—he had just made a big timber deal, and he had plenty of money. Instead of getting a berth, I sat up all the way home—five days and nights—and I kept every cent of that money, and when I got back I put it on interest at the bank. I had made up my mind I wouldn't get caught empty-handed again.

I didn't know it at the time we left here, but I was pregnant again, and that fall after I got back home I had another baby. We named him George King. He was sickly—had a weak heart, and he couldn't cry. I never could understand what the matter was, but I knew something was wrong right from the start. He lived two months.

Burnam was working, but he didn't earn enough for us to make a good show on, not compared to what we had before. He stayed with Hudson and Farnau three years and then went to work for the Conn brothers in the hardware business. We stayed one year in that house on Danville Street, and then we rented a house on Stanford Street and stayed there for over two years. That's where our last child, Gwendolyn, was born on February 3, 1928. Dr. Virgil Kinnaird delivered the last two. I was forty-three years old then, and Burnam was almost fifty-two. Gwen was our thirteenth child. Eloise was twenty-one by then, had graduated from Berea and started teaching school, and Bill and Carl was up in their teens. We had lost everything on the farm, but in a way, it was the making of our older children. They learned young to make their own way. It was hard, but maybe it was a blessing.

Burnam found this tract of land where we live now, this house and about twelve acres, and we bought it in 1928. He rented out the land for crops, made a few payments on the note, and then I decided to take that money my brother had given me and pay off the rest of it. I wanted us to own the place, so nobody could take it away from us. Eloise and Bill gave us a little help, and we put together all the money we could get and paid off the note in full. I think it was about $3,000. The house was about twenty years old then, and had six rooms, just like it does now. It had been wired for electricity, but it wasn't hooked up, and it didn't have running water. We got the electricity right away, but we didn't have a bathroom put in until about ten or fifteen years ago, sometime in the 1960s.

It's a good thing we bought this place. It's served us well for fifty years. Burnam grew a little tobacco, rented out a few acres, and we got two good Jersey cows and some chickens, sold cream and eggs, and we kept a big garden. When the Depression hit in the 1930s, Burnam was working, and we raised most of our food, and the house and land belonged to us. We got by a lot easier than most folks did.

When we celebrated our twenty-fifth anniversary in this house on December 18, 1928—fifty years ago come this December—we had lived in ten different houses. Most of those other places have either gone to rack and ruin or been completely torn down. An awful lot happened to us in those years, seems like, but I guess we made out pretty well. We lost Burnam's parents, and we lost Ewell and the two babies, but the rest of us stayed healthy. Burnam had a job, and Bill and Carl did too, and Eloise had graduated from Berea College at the age of nineteen—younger than any graduate before her time. I still thought about the farm and the store at Manse, about all we had lost—but when I look back on everything now, I realize we've been fortunate to come out as well as we have.

"Did you ever wear glasses, Addie?" I asked.

"Not much—but to tell you the truth, I need them bad now. Jennie took me to see a specialist over at Lexington, and he said I was allergic to something. I've noticed for years that my eye trouble always comes on me in the summertime. When I was about fifty I started wearing glasses some, but then I quit. Now they tell me I've got cataracts. Can you tell it by looking at me? I can see you all right, but I need glasses to look close at things. I can't see to read at all. I can see off at a distance pretty well—but Burnam says sometimes I imagine things."

"Like what?"

"Well, two or three times I've been sitting at the kitchen table, looking out over the back field, and I've seen a neighbor man cutting our hay, putting it on a wagon and hauling it to his barn. He took it to sell, I guess, and probably made good money on it, and that bothered me. I hollered at him when he was cutting it, and that made Burnam mad."

"What did he say?"

"He said there wasn't anybody out there, said I didn't see anybody, I was just imagining it. But I did see them—the horses, the men, the wagons. I was in the right. You can go over there yet and see where they cut it. Carl and Herb went over there, but they said they couldn't tell where anybody had cut the hay. I guess they was just siding with Burnam. I don't fuss at Burnam. It wouldn't do no good. I have, but it didn't help. He's just too good-hearted, always was. He can be talked into anything. I guess he just decided to let the man have the hay."

"Have you had any other health problems besides your eyes?"

"When I was younger, back about fifty years ago, I got too heavy, weighed over two hundred pounds. I fell off, though. Then in 1949, when I was sixty-four years old, I was operated on for gall stones, and a year or two later I went to the hospital when I got down in my back. I never did let anything bother me much, though. My knee is out of place now—has been for years and if I fall, I can't get up by myself. A couple of times I've been outside and fallen, and had to holler for help. Once I fell out there under the apple tree. I could get a-hold of a limb, but some way or other I couldn't pull myself up. But Gwen was here, and she came out and helped me."

"What about your teeth—when did you lose your teeth?"

"Oh, I had good teeth until somebody stole my pocketbook. Took everything I had, including my money and that good set of teeth. Burnam's had teeth too, but he finally quit wearing them. They're in there in a drawer somewhere."

"No, what I mean is, when did you have all your teeth pulled?"

"Oh, that was about thirty or forty years ago, I guess. I never did get used to wearing the ones I had made. They didn't do me much good. I'm just as well off without them. It'd probably cost me $200 to have a new set made now."

"Well, I think you're in mighty good shape for a ninety-three-year-old. You've got a lot of stamina. Do you ever get tired?"

"Once in a while—but not much. I've always watched after my health, always eaten good and slept good and stayed away from medicine as much as I could."

"*Do you think it's a blessing to live to be old?*"

"*Not for everybody. Some people stay sick when they get old, have to go to an old folks home, and they get lonely there. To tell you the truth, I never did think I was old until recently. I've had a very pleasant life, everything considered. It hasn't always been easy, but there's been a lot to be thankful for. As long as me and Burnam have got our house and can stay in it, I'll go on thinking we're lucky to be here. The house is not in the best of shape, but it suits us, and that's the main thing. We don't owe money to anybody—I never did like to have debts—and we've both got a little bit put away. I always could look after my money. Yes, if you can be old the way we are, I'd say it's a blessing.*"

It was nearly suppertime. Addie stood up slowly, got her balance, and then moved toward the door. Halfway there, she stopped and turned.

"*Listen,*" she said. "*Did I tell you Dr. Smith was the one that delivered Bruce? I was mistaken. It was Dr. Montgomery.*"

TEN

Irons in the Fire

Burnam, 1903–1928

"I never did know any of that North Carolina and Virginia history before now," Burnam Ledford said, "except for those Augusta County records my cousin Roy found. You've helped me a lot. I'm glad you made that trip back up through there."

It was early on a summer morning. A warm wind rustled the east window curtain, and sunlight brightened the room. "You knew about Harlan, though," I said, "and just about everything you remember is accurate, as far as I've been able to tell. You and Addie don't make many mistakes."

"Well, there's some that we don't know, and I'm sure there's some we've got wrong—but we go back, so far, there's nobody left to contradict us."

Addie was in the kitchen. She and I had talked at length about her early years in Garrard County, up to the time of their last move in 1928; I was eager now to begin hearing Burnam's account of the same years. He seemed in good spirits, ready for a morning of conversation.

"Maybe today would be a good time for us to start talking about the first part of this century," I said, "the years when you and Addie were farming and keeping store and raising your family."

"All right," he replied. Then, after some reflection, he struggled to his feet, leaning on his walker. "Let's go out on the porch," he said. "I'd like to sit in the sun a while."

We were entering a new phase, a period of time remembered by others besides Burnam and Addie, a period more thoroughly docu-

mented in newspapers and other written records. The recollections of their nine surviving children would now be added to theirs, and in the various remembrances there would inevitably be some conflicting accounts, some disagreements. As we moved from the distant past toward the present and from the lives of departed others to personal histories of the living, the stories of triumph and tragedy would be more sharply drawn, more specific, more emotional.

Burnam made the transition without any noticeable adjustment. In all of his narrative monologues, there were elements of both involvement and detachment. At times he seemed to stand in the midst of his stories, playing a leading role in them; then again, he appeared to be standing on the outside looking in, interpreting and evaluating the acts of his characters—including himself. As always, he treated history as an inseparable extension of his own life.

He began his Garrard County chronicle with a descriptive remembrance of its turn-of-the-century character:

I've seen Lancaster grow from a dusty little crossroads village with nothing but a courthouse and a jail to a modern town with good schools and churches and a hospital and more than three thousand people. It's changed a lot. When we first came here in 1890, Garrard County was already nearly a hundred years old, and it was dominated by old families of Democrats that had been for the South—either that or they was Republicans that had favored slavery and opposed Lincoln. They owned big plantations, like the Kennedy place at Paint Lick, and they tried to live in a grand manner, with servants and private tutors for their children and such as that.

That small upper-class group had raised up plenty of prominent men earlier on, men like Governor Letcher and Governor Owsley and several congressmen, but the kind of privileged life they had wasn't possible any more after the war was over and slavery had ended. Still, some of them tried to keep up that life, didn't want to let it go, and for a long time this county just sort of slid downhill. The same thing happened all over Kentucky. Kentucky had been a right prosperous state before the war, but by 1900 it was behind in just about everything—income, education, growth, everything. Seemed like violence was all it had the most of.

Just to give you one example of the problems here back then: Garrard County wasn't nearly so isolated as Harlan County, and it had a lot more educated people and rich people—but it was just as badly messed up by whiskey and violence as Harlan was, and its schools was just as bad, if not worse. What few schools was in this county before about 1890 was mainly academies and institutes for the children of the upper class. If the public schools had been what they should have been, I would have finished up my eighth grade work the first year we were here and been clear through high school by 1894. As it was, I hadn't even finished high school when I went back to Harlan to teach in 1896—and I never did get to finish. When we came here, there was Baptist and Presbyterian churches in this county that had been here over a hundred years, and there was a newspaper, and the roads was excellent compared to Harlan's—but the lawlessness was about the same.

My family was one of the earliest mountain families to move to Garrard County, and as the others came later on, I began as a boy of about seventeen to come to the courthouse at Lancaster and check on the deeds and legal papers for them. That's how I first became acquainted with the lawyers and county officers around here. I was very interested in politics even then, and I was ambitious to get ahead, and those trips to the courthouse helped me to learn who ran the county and how everything was set up and operated.

That's also when I discovered that politics was a rough game. It was a whole lot meaner and rougher then than it is now. I never ran for office but once—in 1932—but I always took part in some way or other. For nearly fifty years, starting when I was twenty-one, I served as a county election officer, and I was always active in the county Republican Party. But it was dangerous business to be partial toward almost any candidate, because there was so much vote-buying and gambling and violence connected with it.

I met a lot of important Kentucky politicians of that day, like William O. Bradley, the governor from Lancaster—he later was a

U.S. senator—and J.C.W. Beckham, who took over as governor after William Goebel was assassinated in 1900. Beckham was a Presbyterian, and a pretty fair governor, even if he was a Democrat—but he never could control all the killing and violence that was going on all over the state in those days.

There was reform parties then, too, like the Populists and the Socialists. I never cared much for them. I was for reforms, but they was too radical for me. The reforms I wanted was giving women the right to vote and outlawing the sale of whiskey. I figured if women got involved in politics, the men would have to behave better. An election precinct just wasn't a safe place for a woman to be.

Something else: There was some states that didn't allow colored people to vote, but in Kentucky, one side or the other generally made them vote—gave them money or whiskey or threatened them, and used their votes to raise the count for their candidate. I've known people in this county to pay colored people to vote a certain way—I've been involved in that myself. I never was a party to threats and violence, though. I remember once when a big bunch of colored people was herded into a bend of the Dix River and held there under armed guard to keep them from voting, but I wouldn't have nothing to do with that. One time when I was an election officer, this colored man started in to vote and a close neighbor of mine grabbed him by the collar and said, "You black son of a bitch, stand your ground!" The colored man started backing away, and I said to him, "Hold on, Dave." I took him by the arm and led him back up there to the polls, and I said out loud, "Go in there and vote—I just want to see anybody try to stop you." He voted, and my neighbor who had threatened him came up later and apologized.

I had learned long before then that colored people was treated more harshly in Garrard County than they was in Harlan, and the longer I lived here, I guess the more I believed in segregation, in separation of the races. When the legislature passed a law in 1904 to stop whites and coloreds from going to school together—the law was aimed at Berea College, which had always declared it was open to both races—I thought it was a good law. I didn't take an active part in preventing whites and blacks from attending the same schools, but I didn't approve of it. At that time, I thought I was right—but now, it would be wrong. Times have changed. I guess I have changed too. I can see now that segregation wasn't fair to the colored people. I still think, though, that sometimes they've gone to extremes to change it, and they've pushed too far too fast.

So I was for segregation, like practically all the white people around here—I just didn't think it was right to be mean to the colored people. It was common, though. I remember one incident that happened on a farm right across the hill from us when we was living on Sugar Creek in 1905.

The man that owned that farm, Guy Davidson, lived in what he called the big house, and his father lived just across the creek, and he had a tenant that also lived on the place. His father got sick, so Davidson and his wife had to go over there and look after him, and they let the tenant move into the big house. Davidson had a crop there, and he had hired some niggers to work it for him, but this tenant man wouldn't let them come in to the cistern to get water. There was a beech woods there alongside the field where the people was working, and old Parker, the tenant, he had a Winchester rifle, and he'd get in there behind them trees and peep around, pointing that rifle, and he just about scared them niggers to death. They went and told Mr. Davidson about it, and he got after Parker real strong, and they had a big row. So then Davidson come to me and asked me to buy Parker's crop out and tell him to move, and if I did I could live in the big house and put my cattle in the pasture, and it wouldn't cost me a cent. So that's what I did. We moved in to that house in August of 1905 and stayed there until January 1910, and we never had any trouble with the colored people around there.

Those early years of this century was also when the Night Riders was active in Kentucky, but we never got mixed up in that. Most of the Night Riders was tobacco farmers in western Kentucky who tried to break up the monopoly that was holding down prices. They organized, just like the Ku Klux Klan, and they notified big farmers to cut down on their crop or face the consequences. They rode like vigilantes, went around destroying plant beds and burning barns. I was opposed to that business—it was just more violence, and we already had too much. I was also opposed to the men that tried to organize a farmers' union. Nobody ever bothered my tobacco—but one time I started a rumor that the Night Riders had threatened me with a switching, and it took me about a week to get that cleared up. I was just making a joke out of it, but people took it real serious.

I never did like to make trouble. I believed in minding my own business, and keeping my nose out of other people's. If everybody did that, we wouldn't have so much trouble—and everybody would be better off.

That Davidson place we moved to in 1905 was the third house me and Addie lived in after we were married. We stayed first in the house with my father and mother on Sugar Creek, and then we built a little house of our own on that farm, and then we moved to the Davidson place.

As the years went by, we sort of lost touch with the mountains. I could refresh my memory by reading the novels of John Fox— *The Trail of the Lonesome Pine* and *The Little Shepherd of Kingdom Come*—but I didn't go back there very often. We had a good farm on Sugar Creek—it wasn't mine, but I was doing well with the crops and the stock—and we lived in that nice big house, had a telephone and all, went to the Presbyterian Church in Lancaster, and by then we had three children. We had prospered. But I wasn't satisfied—I wanted a place of my own—so in the fall of 1910 I bought a country store and a small farm at Manse, about three miles from Paint Lick. I decided that was a good opportunity for us to move up.

It was just a little general store when we went there, but I built it up—handled groceries, hardware, clothing, farm machinery, just about anything. We did a right good business, and I reckon we would have stayed on there if it hadn't been for the fire that burned our house down in 1913. The house was right behind the store. Somehow it caught on fire and burned clear to the ground. It was a discouraging setback for us, but we felt lucky that nobody was hurt or killed.

My father and mother were living then at their place in Madison County, just beyond Paint Lick, and a man next to their farm had a house and one acre for sale, so I sold out the store and we moved there. I farmed with my father for a year, and we built two barns to house our tobacco in, and then at the start of 1915 I came back to Manse and bought a sixty-six-acre farm on Doty Lane. We lived there until 1920.

All of my immediate family lived right around there in Garrard County, or Madison. My brothers, Speed and Asher and Jim, and my sister Sarah were all married, and the younger ones, Marian and Noble, lived at home with my parents. Later on, Speed and Ash moved away, but the rest of them never left here. Now they're all dead.

Me and Addie had a large family of our own by then. Herbert, our seventh child, was born on Doty Lane in 1917, coming after Ewell, Eloise, Bill, Carl, Lucille, and Dorothy. The house was big enough for all of us and more besides, but sometimes two or three of the smallest children had to sleep together. Seemed like we always had somebody there staying with us—Aunt Sook or Em Irving from Harlan County, or Addie's half-sisters, Delora and Martha—and everybody helped with the chores. It didn't take much paddling or anything like that to make the children mind. They respected me and obeyed me, and never was much trouble. We raised our own meat and vegetables, and Addie had a cookstove and a sewing machine, and we even made our own electricity with a generator. We got along pretty well in those years.

I was very active in the Presbyterian Church at Manse, that old church that's been there for nearly two hundred years. In fact, I stayed in that church from 1910 until we moved to Lancaster in 1925, and was superintendent of the Sunday school for several years. Addie didn't go to church very much, but the children went with me, and I used to read Bible stories to them at home in the evenings. We built a school there at Manse, too—I was the one that got it started— and after that I was a member of the county school board.

Outside of my farm and my family and the church, my main

activity was still politics. Democrats controlled the county, and the Republicans just tagged along with them until 1912, when some of the younger ones of us in the party led a rebellion for Teddy Roosevelt against the Taft regulars. The party met in Lancaster that fall to pick delegates to the district convention, and the old man who was the party chairman tried to cheat us out of representation in the delegation. By our own count we knew that we had a four-to-one majority for Roosevelt, but the chairman gave the credentials to the Taft people, so we decided to go to the convention at Shelbyville and challenge them. Me and Brutus Clay, old Cash's son, stayed together in that, and we raised a ruckus, but the credentials committee turned us down.

So we went to the state convention in Louisville and tried again. We stayed up until two o'clock in the morning waiting to be heard, and when they tried to pass over us again, we pushed our way in. I remember Ed Morrow from Somerset, a Taft man, offered to compromise with us—later on, Morrow was elected governor—but we turned down the offer of half the delegation seats. Finally, when it looked like we was going to lead a bolt from the convention, they decided to let us all in. We had to fight all the way, even threatened to take the challenge to the national convention in Chicago, but they finally seated us.

Taft got the nomination anyway, of course, but we stayed with Teddy, and that was the start of a reform in the Garrard County Republican Party. The next year we elected a new county chairman, and then I was head of the party for several years. While I was a strong Republican, I was respected by the Democrats because I had a reputation for being honest. I always stood for a square deal, and I wanted both parties to have their due. Even the boss and dictator of the county Democrats always said I could be counted on to deal fair and square with everybody. I worked for my party, though, and I guess it rubbed off, even on my children. One time when Eloise was a little girl, she was in the store there at Manse listening to people talk about candidates and all, and she piped up and said, "Vote the Republican ticket and you'll always get the best man!"

A man had a lot better chance of getting ahead in Garrard County than in Harlan, whether he was a farmer or a merchant or a politician. Long before we came here, there was roads and trains to get in and out on, and that kept us from being so isolated. By about 1917, cars got to be a right common sight on the roads, and even if you didn't drive—like me—you could go to Lexington and Louisville and Cincinnati on the train. My father bought a brand new Model T Ford in 1918, and my youngest brother, Noble, who was twenty-two, was the main driver of it.

The first roads were made by farmers, and they'd have toll gates every few miles along the way. The farmers would haul big rocks, take sledgehammers and break them up, and then they'd have a man go with a small hammer and beat up them rocks into little pieces and spread them in the roadbed. They'd pay the man so much a rock for breaking them up, and after the buggies had run over them awhile it would make a good road. When they could get river sand and gravel, they'd put that on top and make it real smooth for a horse and buggy. Then the cars came along, and they made potholes in those roads. By then the county had taken over road maintenance from the farmers, but the roads got in bad shape. I was on the school board then, and I remember some of us called a meeting in Lancaster to see if the people would favor turning the roads over to the state. There was a big disagreement over it, but we finally got approval to call a referendum, and the people voted by a big margin for state roads. That must have been in about 1920.

We had some other good reforms in those years. One of the most important was a tax equalization program that required the biggest landowners to pay their fair share of property taxes. I was proud to serve on that board and have a hand in taking an unfair burden off the small farmers.

Those years when we lived on Doty Lane were a busy time for us, and a good time—up until 1918. I remember 1918 as the saddest year of my life.

It started out bitter cold, the worst winter I could ever remember. I went to Menifee County with my father late in the fall of

1917, and before we could get back the snow was blowing in drifts waist deep. It hardly left the ground all winter long. I remember one day going out to the barn where we had been stripping tobacco, had Ewell and Eloise and Bill with me, and a blizzard came up suddenly. We stayed in there waiting for it to ease off, and finally about dark we started for the house, not more than a quarter of a mile across the field. The wind blew our lantern out, and we couldn't see where to go, got all turned around and confused, and we like to have never made it home. I had the children all huddled up around me, just struggling along against the wind and snow, and it really scared me. I was afraid for our lives, afraid we'd get lost out there and freeze to death, but I never let the children know how scared I was.

The war was going on in Europe that winter, and there was so many sad stories about young men dying that people just seemed to be half expecting bad news everywhere they looked. Me and Ash and Jim was all up over thirty and didn't get called to serve, but Noble did, and when the time drew close for him to leave, I could tell my father was really worried about him.

I always managed to go see my parents about once a week, and on a Friday in June just before Nobe was supposed to leave, I went down to their farm and me and my father took a walk out across the field. He was up past sixty by then, and that day he seemed older than that. He told me Mama had had a spell with her heart that had him worried, and said he depended on her so much that he didn't see how he could ever live without her. Then he got to talking about Nobe going to war in a few days, and Papa sounded so sad I finally said to him, "You wouldn't want Nobe not to go, would you?" He said, "No, no, I wouldn't have him be a slacker for anything. I want him to do his duty—but his going is as far as I can see for me in this world."

It must have been some kind of vision he had, some kind of premonition. On Sunday, a big lot of people came to their house to tell Nobe goodbye, and Mama cooked a huge dinner as usual, and there was plenty. And then the next day, Nobe decided to drive the Model T over to brother Jim's house, to see Jim before he left, and sister Marian was going too, and at the last minute they persuaded my father and mother to go with them. Nobe intended for Papa to get in the front seat with him, but somehow it turned out that Papa and Mama got in the back and Marian rode up front.

It was after sundown, about dusk. About half a mile from Paint Lick, they had to drive up over a bank and cross the track. The L&N came through there every night, but the schedule had just been changed and the train was coming an hour earlier than usual. Papa and them had forgot all about it. He was the most careful man I ever knew in my life, but that one time, he forgot. They turned up the bank and drove onto the track—and just as they did, my sister looked up and saw the train. She heard the whistle blow once, and then they were hit.

The weekly Lancaster paper reported the accident three days later. A yellowed clipping of the story gave the details. At about eight-thirty in the evening on Monday, June 24, 1918, an L&N train struck a Model T Ford at Francis Crossing, a half-mile east of Paint Lick. Noble Ledford was driving, his sister Marian was with him in the front seat. The car apparently stalled in the center of the crossing, its rear wheels in the center of the track. Engineer P.H. Rice blew the train's whistle in vain. Marian jumped from the car, screaming, "her screams being heard above the noise of the on-rushing train." Noble escaped serious injury. Mrs. Ledford was killed instantly; her head was horribly mangled. Mr. Ledford died minutes later, his head cradled in Noble's lap.

The train struck right at the back wheel, where my parents were sitting. Marian was thrown from the car and off to the side of the track. The car was knocked sixty feet through the air, and Noble was still holding to the steering wheel when it landed. He was stunned, but not hurt bad. When he come to his senses, he turned and saw our mother was dead, killed immediately by the impact. Then he turned to our father, took his head in his hands, and Papa just kind of gasped, and then he was gone.

Somebody called me up to tell me there had been an accident, and I went rushing down there and saw it, saw the wreck and the bodies—they hadn't moved them or nothing, you know, they was still laying there—and the awful sight made my blood freeze in my veins. I couldn't move, I couldn't do nothing.

We buried them in one grave in the cemetery there at Manse. It was just heartbreaking, just the saddest thing that had ever happened to me. I was stricken with grief—and then, before we had time to get over it, a tragedy struck our oldest son, Ewell.

It was in September. We had had an auction to settle my parents' estate, and afterward I sent Ewell to deliver the cattle to the man who had bought them. Ewell was thirteen years old, an unusually bright boy, good in his books, and I yearned for him to have all the educational advantages that I had missed. That day, he was driving the cattle along the road when they turned all of a sudden, and he swung his horse back to head them off, and the horse jerked to a stop and threw him to the ground. He got up and finished driving the cattle, but that night when he got home he complained of pain in his back, like maybe he had tore something loose in there.

He never did get any better. The doctors come and examined him, couldn't find out what was the trouble, and Ewell just kept getting weaker and weaker, started getting paralyzed in his legs, and finally he couldn't walk at all. After about two weeks, the doctors still couldn't help him, so they decided to take him up to Lexington for some X rays.

The night before the trip, we were all there at home together, and Ewell was propped up in the bed, talking just like he always did, his mind as good as ever. After a while, everybody went to bed but me and Ewell, and I was sitting there by him, telling him we would soon find out what was wrong and he would get better. Directly he said to me, "Papa, I'm just getting so sleepy. Ain't you getting sleepy?" I said, "No, not yet, but you go ahead and get a good night's rest, son, and we'll get you X-rayed tomorrow, and pretty soon you'll be all right."

I just sat there looking at him, and directly his head kind of fell over, and I stood up and took his face in my hands, just cradled it, and in a minute or so his breathing got shorter and fainter. His countenance never changed, but his breath just quit coming. It was like he had gone off to sleep. He didn't gasp or anything—he just stopped breathing. I guess when that paralysis hit his lungs, you know, and hit his heart, it just took him away. So I was standing there holding his face in my hands when he died.

Then it wasn't two months after that when my sister Marian got sick in Louisville and died suddenly. She never did get over being in that train wreck, but that may not have had anything to do with her dying. I think some disease killed her. But whatever the cause, I had lost four loved ones in the space of just five months, buried four of my dearest relatives there at Manse. I tried to keep busy after that, tried to keep my mind off of it so I wouldn't go crazy—and then one day out in the field I got to studying about my ninety-year-old grandmother, Polly Ledford Jones, who was living with one of her daughters back in Harlan County. She was the only one of my grandparents still living, and I hadn't seen her in years. Her husband had been living with my parents when he died, and after that she had gone to live with Lydia Browning, her daughter, in the same house on Cranks Creek where Blind Granny had spent her last years.

I couldn't get Grandma Jones off my mind. Finally, one warm and sunny day near the end of November, I came to the house and said, "Addie, do the best you can—I'm going to see my grandmother." Addie fixed up a suitcase of gowns and things for me to take to her, and pretty soon I walked across the field to a flag station and flagged the train down, and the next morning I got off at Hubbard Springs, Virginia.

I saw some people I knew there, but whoever they was waiting for didn't come in on the train, so they offered me their extra horse to ride across the mountain. I made some excuse, though, because I wanted to be alone, and I waited until they got far enough ahead of me that I wouldn't overtake them, and then I started out walking, carrying the suitcase.

I can't remember anything about going up the Virginia side of the mountain, but halfway down on the Kentucky side I stopped

Garrard County, 1899. Front: Miriam, Noble, Jesse, and Vesta; back: Jim, Speed, Sarah, Burnam, and Asher.

Burnam and Addie Ledford in 1904, soon after their wedding day.

May 1946. Front: Herbert Ledford and Bruce Mills (age four) with Burnam and Addie; back: Bruce, Carl, Eloise, Lucille, Jennie, Tillie, Dorothy, Bill, and Gwen.

May 1982. Burnam and Addie with Herb, Carl, Eloise, Lucille, Jennie, Tillie, Dorothy, Bill, and Gwen. *John Egerton*

Addie Ledford, 1982. *John Egerton*

Burnam Ledford, 1979. *John Egerton*

Garrard County Tobacco Festival parade, 1982. Burnam (front),
Tillie, and Addie. *John Egerton*

Burnam and Addie Ledford, 1979. *John Egerton*

Burnam and Addie on their seventy-ninth anniversary, December 18, 1982. *John Egerton*

and set my suitcase down and just stood there looking up at the cliffs all around me. I realized I had been talking out loud, and when I came to myself I said, "Well, we think we're important—we think if we stop, everything stops. But we're just an atom, just a drop—when we're gone we're soon forgotten, and the world moves on just as though we had never been here. God made us from nothing, and nothing is what we end up returning to."

I stood there for a long time, almost like I was in a trance. I felt like I was alone with God, just talking with God, like Moses at the burning bush. Finally I walked on the last two miles or so to where my grandmother lived, and when I went inside I found her propped up in bed. They always claimed I was her favorite grandchild. I put my arms around her and hugged her, and I said, "Grandmother, do you know me?" She looked at me real close, her eyes just as bright and sparkly as they could be, and then she said, "Oh, yes, I know you, Burnam, bless your heart, and I love you so very much." She talked just a little bit. She said Jess and Vestie—that was my father and mother—"are waiting for me over yonder," and she said everything looked so bright and beautiful over there that she was anxious to go on and join them. She was living more in that life than this, and I could tell that she was at peace and ready to die.

That completely satisfied me, not only about my grandmother but about all the loved ones I had lost. I believed what my grandmother said about another life over yonder, and I went home feeling at peace for the first time in five months. About two weeks later, they sent word to me that Grandmother had died, and they buried her there in the Wash Smith cemetery on Cranks Creek.

If I remember correctly, it was the next year after that when we had another crisis in the family. That time, it was Addie's mother. She came to visit us, and she wasn't well, and one day she wandered off. She got to imagining her children had been kidnapped. Dr. Mays, our family doctor, found her on the street over in Richmond and took her home with him, and the next day he put her on the train back to Paint Lick. I had started out to meet her there when I saw her coming toward our house with some school children. I tried to get her in the buggy with me, but she kept walking, so I drove along beside her. She told me she had died and been to heaven, and had come back to evangelize the world. I said, "Charity begins at home, so come home and start with Addie." She got in the buggy, but then she wanted out, and when I wouldn't stop, she jumped out and ran. I finally had to get the sheriff to help me find her, and after a lot of talking back and forth and worrying about what to do, we all decided the only thing to do was to take her to the asylum in Lexington. That was a hard thing to do. They had to keep her locked up there. We went to see her regularly as long as she lived—and that was a long time. She died twenty years later, in 1939.

Another big change came for us in 1920, when G.C. Cox, the man I had sold the Manse store to, offered to sell me back half interest in it. I had inherited about $3,000 from my parents, so with that and other money we had saved I bought into the store, and then sold the farm on Doty Lane and bought another one, a 110-acre place right across the road from the store. Bill and Carl, my oldest boys, were not hardly big enough to help me much, but Arch Kavanaugh, a colored man and his family, lived on the place, and Arch looked after the farm while I worked in the store. Arch was a good man, an honest man. He took care of my horses and stock. I could always depend on him.

Eloise finished school at Manse that year, and we sent her off to the school over in Asheville where Delora and Martha went. Addie lost a baby not long after that, but even with Ewell and that baby gone and with Eloise away at school, we still had six children at home.

We built up a good trade in that store, me and Cox, and Addie helped us some. We had a wide assortment of merchandise, and we stayed plenty busy. Somehow or another, that car of my parents wasn't ruined in the wreck, so when it came out of the garage I took it, and that's when I started to drive. About a year later I bought a Ford truck, and after that I bought a Chevrolet car— what they called a big Chevrolet, a Baby Grand. It wasn't long before Bill was driving the truck.

The store was the center of the community. Everybody in that end of the county traded there. I liked storekeeping. We never had much trouble. I kept a gun, but I never had to use it. I can only remember two times when we had serious problems. Once was when a fellow broke in at night and stole some clothes. Me and another man chased him clear over into another county, finally caught him and brought him back to stand trial. The other time was when some drunks was hanging around the store, and we come to find out they had a moonshine still down in the woods. Had to get the law to break it up—and I helped the marshal do it.

I was involved in so many things then that I had a hard time getting everything done. I was active in the church, I belonged to the Odd Fellows lodge, I served on the school board and the tax board, I was an organizer of the loose-leaf-tobacco warehouse in Lancaster—and most of all, I was what you might call the dictator of the county Republican Party. I just had too many irons in the fire.

After a couple of years, G.C. Cox sold out his half of the store to Burdette Ramsey, and Ramsey had a drinking problem, so we didn't get along. Then Ramsey sold out to Tom Little, and there was a big disagreement over the settlement, and we all ended up in court. It was a nasty mess.

To make matters worse, a bad tobacco depression had set in, and money was very hard to get, and people couldn't pay their bills. Tobacco had gone up to about a dollar a pound one year and fallen to seventeen cents the next, and people who had bought on credit got into deep trouble. I remember one farmer had a poem printed up on a piece of paper. I memorized it:

Hayseed farmer, settin' on a fence,
Hoein' his tobacco for 17 cents,
When tobacco went down to 7 cents,
He shit in his pants and fell off the fence,
And there he lays, flat in the ditch,
The poor deluded son-of-a-bitch.

It was a good thing we could laugh about it—there wasn't anything else to do. We had that squabble over the property settlement in the store, and people owed us money, and I owed $15,000 to the men I had bought the farm from. J.B. and E.L. Woods had sold me the place in 1920, and two years later I had tried to pay off the note, but they wouldn't take the money. Then the next year, when they saw that my creditors couldn't pay me what they owed me, and saw I didn't have any cash, they come and told me they wanted me to settle up my debt with them by the first of 1924. There wasn't any way I could do it. I told Jim Woods, "Nobody could have made me believe you and your brother would treat me this way." But they did—and then the tobacco warehouse failed, and I found my-self broke and in debt. When they foreclosed on me, I had to turn the farm back to them, and I had to sell my share of the store inventory for a fraction of its value. It left me almost penniless.

Several businessmen in the country tried to get me to hold on, said I could get loan money and pull out of it, but I said there was no way. I had eight children then, and they all had to be educated, and that meant more to me than anything else. I couldn't take any more risks that might jeopardize their future.

So when 1924 came, I lost everything—the farm, the store, ev-erything but our personal belongings. I lost about $65,000 worth of assets. You might say we was about six years early experiencing the Great Depression.

We managed to stay in the country through that year before we had to vacate the farm, and then Banks Hudson offered me a job at Hudson and Farnau in Lancaster—a hay, grain, feed, and coal busi-ness. I had worked for myself from the time me and Addie had married, but I couldn't do it any more. I took the job, and we moved to Lancaster at the beginning of 1925 and rented a house on Danville Street, and I became a traveling salesman in eastern Kentucky for Hudson and Farnau.

It was a hard change to make. I had never been rich or poor, never looked up to anyone or down on anyone—but then I had to swallow my pride and start over, two years before I turned fifty. Eloise finished school at Asheville and came home, but she was too young to teach, so she went to Berea, where she could have a job and graduate from college. She graduated in 1926 when she was nineteen. She asked me for advice. I told her if she was just out for the money, that was one thing, but if she wanted to help people, help make the world a better place, she should be a teacher—and that's what she did. Bill and Carl were up in their teens, in high school, and the others were in school too. Addie went out west to see her brother in 1925, and then she lost another baby, and we moved again in 1926 to a house on Stanford Street. We couldn't do nothing but just struggle along, making ends meet. When I was fifty years old in 1926, we were poor. That's the only honest way to say it.

I worked for Hudson and Farnau for three years, and then I went to work for the Conn brothers, Jim and John Conn, in the hardware business. That same year, 1928, we scraped together enough money to buy this house and twelve acres. Our last child, Gwen, was born that same year, just before we moved out here, and in December, me and Addie had our twenty-fifth anniversary.

In some ways, it didn't seem like we had much to celebrate. We didn't own much, and I didn't make a big salary, and times was getting hard all over, soon to get worse: But I couldn't dwell on the problems. We had a garden and a cow, a roof over our heads, clothes to wear, and good health—and we were all together. That was a lot. Me and Addie had children to raise, and I had a living to make. We had to keep going.

Burnam carved off a small cube of dark, sweet-smelling to-bacco, gummed it for a few minutes, and then sent an amber jet of juice into the grass at the edge of the porch. The air was still and humid, but he showed no fatigue or discomfort, even though we had been talking for a long time.

"How long have you been chewing?" I asked him.

"Oh, I'd say . . . about . . . ninety-four years," he calculated with a laugh. "Started when I was about eight. Chewing relaxes me. I used to chew nothing but homemade plugs, but it got to where they was putting so much chemical on it that it burned my mouth, and I was afraid it'd kill me. This stuff is milder." He held the cake up close, examined it, sniffed it, and stuck it back in his pocket.

"Did you ever drink whiskey?"

"*I never drank but very little. I felt like it was wrong. I thought drinking whiskey and playing cards was two of the worst habits a person could have.*"

"*Has your health always been good?*"

"*Yes, I'd say very good. I never was really sick but once in my life, and that was when I took typhoid fever in 1904. Other than that, I've had a mild case or two of pneumonia—and oh, yeah, back in 1911 I had to be operated on for a strangulated hernia. Bris Conn owned one of the first cars in Lancaster, and he took me to the hospital in it, and old Dr. Kinnaird operated on me. I wore a truss for a long time after that, but the hernia came back on me in 1922, and finally I just learned to live with it.*"

"*How about medicine—do you take any medicine?*"

"*Never. Oh, sometimes I'll take a Rolaid or something like that when my stomach gets sour, and I've taken a few aspirin, but generally I don't take any medicine. I think I'd have been dead a long time ago if I'd gotten into that.*"

"*Did you ever wear glasses?*"

"*Yeah, about forty years ago I had a blood clot on my left eye, and when I was being treated for it I discovered that I was very nearsighted in my right eye. I had glasses made and wore them for about a year, but finally I got accustomed to not using them. My eyes don't focus at the same distance, so I just use one for close up and the other for far off. Neither one of them works very well now, but I still manage to read all day, just by holding things up close.*"

"*When was the last time you went to a doctor?*"

"*I don't remember—it's been six or seven years, I guess.*"

"*Do you have a family doctor?*"

"*No, I don't. Dr. Kinnaird's dead, Dr. Montgomery's dead—I guess I don't have one. I stopped one time to have my lungs checked at one of those machines on the street, and the nurse asked me who my doctor was, and I told her, 'I ain't got one—they're all dead.'*"

He was laughing heartily when Addie came to join us on the porch. "You know," Burnam went on, in high good humor, "everything Kentucky is famous for—coal, whiskey, tobacco, horses—can either make you rich or kill you."

"*You left out women,*" *Addie chuckled.* "*And some are trying to get marijuana in there too. You know, they used to grow a lot of hemp around here, and they say that's the same thing as marijuana. People didn't smoke it much then—they made rope and coarse cloth out of it. They're claiming it ought to be salable now, for medicine. What's it good for? I never did know.*"

"*I never fooled with any of that stuff,*" *Burnam said.* "*Nothing but chewing tobacco. I've lived to be old by avoiding too many vices—and by minding my own business. That's my advice on how to grow old. That and this: Stay away from doctors and medicine and hospitals.*"

"*Doctors cost too much,*" *Addie put in.* "*When they take you to a hospital, it runs up on you, maybe as much as $500 a week. I'm glad we don't have to do that. We've got a little money, so we can stay here. Some of these old people around here, they didn't have a great deal when they broke up housekeeping, and now they're on the outside, and they have to depend on the state. You can live at home a lot cheaper than you can board out—or stay in the hospital either one.*"

"*It's not a question of the money,*" *said Burnam.* "*I just don't want to go to no hospital. I'd rather stay here and die at home. Neither one of us wants to go to a nursing home. We want to stay home and take care of ourselves as long as we can.*"

Neither of them spoke for a few moments. Then Burnam said, chuckling, "*They have a place here in town where they feed dinner to old people. I went up there and ate when I was a hundred years old. One of them said to me, 'What are you doing here?' I laughed and said, 'I just came to see how old people act, so if I ever get old I'll know what to do.' They had a dinner for me, and a birthday cake, and I got my picture made with the president of the women's club kissing me. I had a big time.*"

"*But I don't want to live in a home, or with any of my children. We want to live by ourselves as long as we can get away with it. I hope neither one of us leaves here until we go to the cemetery. We've got a place waiting for us out there at Manse, where my parents and Addie's mother and our son Ewell are buried. There's money in the bank to care for that plot as long as time lasts. We've talked about it, Addie and me, and we've decided we want to stay here in this house just as long as we possibly can."*

ELEVEN

A Nice Place for Old People

Early August, early morning: Burnam Ledford was hunched down in his imitation leather easy chair, reading a book. His short-sleeved blue shirt was buttoned at the collar, and his checkered slacks were tightly hitched about his waist. A day's growth of snow-white whiskers accentuated the thinness of his tanned face. When he recognized me, he put down his book and told me the news. An accumulation of minor ailments had resulted in Addie's hospitalization.

"When did she go?" I asked.

"Day before yesterday. Wednesday."

"Do you think she's very sick?"

"I'm hoping it's not too serious. She says it's nothing but her eyes and her knee. I talked to her on the phone a while ago—told her she'll be all right pretty soon. She wants to come home pretty bad."

"Have you stayed here by yourself the past two nights?"

"Just the first night, then Tillie came. I was only here alone one night."

"Did you mind doing that?"

"Oh no, I don't mind at all. I made out just fine. I can do everything except make up the bed and wash the dishes. This morning I got up and bathed—didn't shave, but I did yesterday. It would have tickled you to see me getting breakfast yesterday morning. I put my coffee on to perk and an egg on to cook, and then I realized I couldn't carry my coffee from the stove to the table without spilling it. Walking with this walker, you see, I just can't carry anything that'll spill.

185

So I stood there and studied the situation a while, and then I had a good idea. I went over and got a big serving bowl and set it down on the floor beside the stove. Then I poured my coffee and put the cup down in the serving bowl, and then I pushed it along with my foot until I got it over to the table. I sat down then and had myself a real nice breakfast."

With buoyant humor, the old man was resolutely transforming an unexpected and unsettling turn of events into an amusing adventure story. The reassuring news that his wife's condition was not serious had lifted his spirits; his discovery that he still possessed the ability to fend for himself had sent them soaring. Far from being discouraged or frightened or helpless, as some of his children feared he might be, Burnam was breezing along with casual self-confidence.

I was both amazed and amused. "So you don't mind staying here alone?" I repeated.

"Oh no, um-um. Gwen's been here, and Tillie came in from Indianapolis—she's uptown right now—and the neighbors come over, and everybody's been awfully good to me. I'm perfectly safe. The last one to leave at night locks the doors when they go out, so all I have to do is just lay down and go to sleep."

"I guess you've missed Addie, haven't you?"

"Yeah, I have. I'm like old King David in the Bible. When he got to be an old man he couldn't stay warm in bed, so they brought a woman to lie with him and keep him warm. Me and Addie are used to keeping each other warm. The first night she was gone, I sat up listening to the ball game, the way I usually do. Pete Rose just had his hitting streak broken after forty-four games, you know, and I was helping him get a new streak started. Anyway, Addie generally goes to bed before me, and when it gets along late in the game, she'll always say, 'When you gonna quit? What time you coming to bed?' Well, I was sitting here all by myself, and suddenly I caught myself saying, 'Wait a minute til the Reds bat—I'll be there in a few minutes!' I'm so accustomed to answering her, you know, that I just imagined she had hollered at me. And then when I finally did turn off the light and go to bed, I crawled in over here on her side, and I got so turned around and confused that I didn't hardly know where I was at. After a few minutes, I had to get up and go around to my side and start over."

"Did you sleep well, Burnam?"

"Just fine. I preached a sermon to myself, sang a few hymns, and went right off to sleep, slept good all night. A few years ago I had a vision about heaven—it came to me while I was sitting out on the porch—and every night when I go to bed I think about that vision, go over it in my mind. I feel pretty well acquainted with heaven now. I think I'll know my way around there pretty good. I'm not afraid to die, because that'll be a better place." He thought a minute and added, laughing, "I'll probably have to quit chewing tobacco, though."

His mood was shifting, becoming more reflective, more philosophical. "Everybody has to die sometime," he said. "I don't dread it. When the body dies, it returns to dust. This 'born again' business, I don't believe in that. The body won't ever be born again. But the soul never dies. So man is both mortal and immortal. Plenty of people claim they've got religion, but not enough of them have got faith. You've got to have faith. We are saved by grace through faith. You can't earn it—it's a gift. God said, 'Love thy neighbor, love them that despise you.' And who is my neighbor? It's everybody—rich and poor, white and black, Republican and Democrat, American and foreigner. God is a spirit—infinite, eternal, unchangeable. God is merciful. God is love."

He paused for a moment, thinking. Then he remembered a poem:

Love is something so divine,
Description would make it less,
It's what I know but can't define,
What I feel but can't express.

"I memorized that ninety-two years ago," he said.

Presently we got up and moved out to the porch, where a warm breeze stirred faintly. "I'm going over to the hospital to see Miss Addie," I said. "Would you like to go?"

"Not right now. Tillie or Gwen one is going to take me later. I told Addie I was coming. They've got a nursing home that's attached to the hospital, a place for old people to stay, and we probably know most of the ones that's living in it. I'd like to go visit with some of them."

"Is it a nice place?"

"Yeah, it's pretty nice. The people seem to like it."

"Are you thinking that you and Addie might want to go there and live sometime—just move over there?"

"Well, if I ever get to where I can't help myself, I'd be willing to go. When I can't take care of myself any more, somebody can call the ambulance to come and get me. I've already got them paid to carry me to the hospital, or the old folks home, or the funeral home. I'll give up then—but I'm not giving up until I have to. I'm just this way: I'll do for myself as long as I can, and when I can't do no more, I'll give up. I've done it before. I used to drive a car, but then I had trouble with my eyes, so I just quit driving. Then I worked, you know, until I was past seventy-five, and when I found out I couldn't keep it up, I quit. Me and Addie gave up our cow when we couldn't milk her, and we gave up our garden about two years ago when it got to be too much for us. We know how to surrender when we have to—but we're not ready to give up our home, not yet. I don't want anybody to make that decision for me. I'll make my own decision. When the time comes, I'll know it."

Addie emerged slowly from her room. Her slippered feet scraped softly along the polished floor. She wore a flowered robe over a starched white hospital gown. I watched her move a short distance down the long, quiet, antiseptic hallway. When I approached her and called her name, she looked up alertly.

"Listen!" she whispered, in the conspiratorial tone that she often used. "I've got to get out of here! This place is full of old people!" This time, there was an edge of urgency in her voice, but her handshake was firm and steady. She looked more vigorous and self-sufficient than any of the patients I had seen in the sitting room.

"How are you feeling, Miss Addie?" I asked.

"Fine, just fine. There's not much wrong with me. They say I've got cataracts, but I already knew that. I can't see to read. I just need some glasses. The only other problem is my knee—it's got water on it. They don't want me to get up and walk around much—but walking keeps me in shape to travel. I've got to be ready to go."

The plastic bracelet fastened around her wrist gave her identification as a patient in the extended care wing of the Garrard County Memorial Hospital:

```
Ledford, Addie    8/2/78         E-17A
Dr. Yash P. Verma
44290      Age: 93      Presbyterian
```

The extended care unit was flanked on one side by the main hospital and on the other by the nursing home. It was well equipped and orderly and clean. Everything had its place and its label: Examination Room. Treatment Room. Physical Therapy. Men's Bath. Women's Bath. Clean Linen. Soiled Linen. It was a sanctuary for the halt, the lame, the blind, the aged, the infirm. Nurses and aides moved about with quiet efficiency. A faint, mingled odor of medicine, bodies, and cleaning solution was in the air. A woman's cry, frail and anguished, echoed down the hall.

"I tried to get them to take me home yesterday," Addie said. "The woman in the room with me hollered half the night, and they keep the lights on all the time, all over. It's never dark. I didn't sleep too well. The food's not much good, either. I need to go home and see about Burnam."

"Have you missed him?"

"Yes. He's coming to see me this afternoon. I'm thinking about going home with him. Being here makes you realize you're old. I never did know I was old until I got here. They sent a psychiatrist to see me. I told him my mother lost her mind, but I don't have any notion of going crazy."

She laughed. "They'll keep me here as long as they can, because they know I'll pay my bill. But I may fool them. I'll pay, but I may not stay."

We walked past the nurses' station and entered a large, simply furnished sitting room where several elderly patients from the extended care unit and the nursing home sat quietly. There was about them a look of resignation and defeat, or so it seemed; they seldom smiled or spoke, and the flicker of interest they showed when someone appeared at the door lasted only long enough for the hope to die that whoever stood there had brought release or amusement or even a nod of recognition to them. Addie searched their stolid faces, looked into their dull and lifeless eyes, listened to the interminable emptiness of their silence. Her own face was anything but lifeless; she looked around the room with an expression suggesting anger, defiance, disgust, and profound sadness.

"These old people are a pitiful sight," she said finally. "This is no place for a healthy person."

I sought to divert her thoughts from the other patients and from her own predicament. "I bet you'll be out of here in no time, Addie," I said. "As soon as they get through checking you over and finish the tests they're making, they'll probably let you go right on home."

"I don't need to wait any longer," she replied. "They've already checked me enough. I'm ready to leave now."

I tried again: "Burnam said Tillie is here. Maybe she'll be able to stay with you all for a while."

"That would be nice, but I doubt it. Tillie's got a good job in Indianapolis. She'll have to get back to work."

In preparation for my interviews with the children and grandchildren of the elder Ledfords, I had been working on a chart of names, dates, marriages, and other basic information (the finished chart begins on page 354). I had brought it along for Addie to check, and now I took it out, hoping that it would turn her thoughts from the hospital and its elderly patients to her younger and healthier family.

"I've been meaning to ask you about the marriages of all your children and the names of all your grandchildren," I said. "Would you like to talk about that? Can you remember all the names?"

She put a finger to her lips and thought for a minute. "I can remember most of them," she began. "Starting with the first—after Ewell, who died—there was Eloise. She married Fred Beatty. They had one daughter, Mary Ellen, and a son who died when he was a baby. Then Bill, he married Joan Enoch. They have four children—Billy, Polly, Sally, and John. Then Carl has the biggest family of all, eleven children. He married Geraldine Dutton. There's Eddie, Sue, Richard, Jerry, Judy, Becky—that's six. I can't name the others right now. Then there's Lucille—she was divorced once, and then she married Harry Smith, and they had one son, David. Dorothy's next. She married twice, had no children. Her last husband died. And Herb, he's married to Hazel Perkins. They have four girls. One of them is Emily—she's a lawyer. I'll think of the others in a minute. Bruce was next. He and his wife Anita had a boy and a girl, John Bruce and Dolly. Then Jennie, she was married to Revis Mills first, had three children—Bruce, Nancy, Arletta—and after that, Jennie married three more times. Tillie's been married four times, too—twice to the same man. She's got a son, Gary, and a daughter, Bobbie Jo. And then the last one is Gwen. She's married to Russell Gastineau, and they live here in Garrard County. He's a farmer. Their four children are Carole, David, Richard, and Becky."

As she talked, I followed on my chart. Her memory was flawless as far as it went—and it went most of the way through her thirty-three grandchildren. The last five of Carl's children—Michael, Charlie Bob, David, Stephen, and James—returned to her mind momentarily, and so did Herb's other three daughters—Jane, Alice, and Sarah. She could not have given the dates and places of their birth, as she could those of her own children, but later she would name most of her grandchildren's children for me—and they numbered about forty.

"You've got a spectacular memory, Addie," I said admiringly. "You remember the names, the dates, the marriages, the births, even the divorces."

She laughed. "I was always good at memorizing facts. I did extra well in history when I was in school."

After she had named everyone, I showed her my chart, and then I read each entry to her.

"Are you sure I have all the information right?" I asked, when I had gone over the chart carefully with her.

"I think you've got every bit of it right. Where did you get all of your facts and dates?"

"I got most of them from your children. And Polly helped me a lot."

"Polly did? She's a worker, isn't she? She's our oldest grand-daughter."

We had passed a pleasant hour together. Addie had talked intently, forgetting for the time being where she was. When a pause came in the conversation, she remembered. She gazed around the room at a dozen expressionless faces staring passively back at her.

"What time is it?" she asked, after a long silence. "I wonder how soon Burnam will get here."

Addie was standing in the hallway waiting impatiently when Burnam came through the door. Tillie King and Gwen Gastineau, their two youngest daughters, were with him. Burnam smiled broadly, but Addie's expression was serious.

"You've got to get me out of here, Burnam," she said. "Listen—I'm going home tonight."

He appeared not to detect her state of anxiety. "How are you feeling, Addie?" he exclaimed heartily. "You're looking good. I've missed you. You should have seen me getting my breakfast the other morning." He told her about getting his coffee to the table.

"Why didn't you let me fix some food for you before I left?" Addie said. "Have you got enough to eat? Did you stay by yourself last night?"

"No, Tillie was there. Did I tell you I started talking to you while I was listening to the ball game? I just forgot all about you being gone. And then I got in on the front side of the bed instead of the back, got all turned around, and I had to get out and go around to my side and start over."

"Did you fall?"

"No, I got there all right. I'd have been in a bad fix if I had fallen."

They sat down on a bench in the hall and continued their conversation. Tillie and Gwen watched the reunion with smiles, but concern was apparent in their voices. They had talked at length about the possible consequences of their mother's hospitalization, and they had also been on the phone with some of their brothers and sisters, but no conclusions had been reached.

Tillie Ledford King was fifty-four years old. She worked as an interviewer for a market research agency in Indianapolis, where she had lived most of the time since the early 1950s. Divorced now, she lived alone there, but she came back to central Kentucky frequently to see her parents and her two married children.

Gwen Ledford Gastineau, Tillie's younger sister, was fifty. She had spent all her life in Garrard County. She and her husband, Russell, lived on a farm about ten miles from the home of her parents. Three of their four children were married, and lived nearby. Gwen had gradually given more time and attention to the needs of her parents in recent years.

"I'm really worried about them," Tillie said as she watched her mother and father in animated conversation. "There's no telling how long she might have to stay here, and Papa can't be left at home alone. And even if she went home tomorrow, I don't think they're able to look after themselves any more. We're either going to have to find somebody to move in with them, or they're going to have to move over here to the nursing home. I just don't know what we ought to do. I'm all torn up about it."

"Then you know how I've felt for the past six months or so," Gwen said. "I'm worried to death about them. It may be that we won't have any choice but to move them here—but right now, the nurse told me there's not even a vacant room. They couldn't get in today even if they wanted to."

As the sisters talked, their parents were the center of the resi-

dents' attention: Their advanced age, their obvious vitality, and
their closeness to each other caused them to be watched with awe
and envy, and soon a small group of people had gathered around
them.

"You look pretty good for your age," one man in his seventies
said to Burnam. "You must be getting along right well."

"He *is* well," Addie cut in. "He eats hearty."

"Hello, Mr. Ledford," another man said. "How are you getting along?"

"Why, Mr. Parrent," Burnam exclaimed in astonishment, "you
look like an old man!"

Addie laughed. "Hush, Burnam! Don't let him say that to you,
Mr. Parrent. You look young to me."

"This is a nice place you've got here," Burnam rambled on.
"It's nice to have something like this to come to when you can't
look after yourself any more."

"You'd better come up here and live with us," Mr. Parrent said.
"It's comfortable—cool in the summer, warm in the winter—and
they've got plenty of help to look after everybody."

"Well, that's fine," Burnam replied. "I can't see how I could
leave home right now, though."

Another of the patients greeted the couple and exchanged a
few words with them. When he had gone on, Burnam looked at his
wife and said, "What are you thinking, Addie?"

She put her hand to her mouth and said, "I sold that man's wife
a pair of shoes about fifty-five years ago, and they never did pay
for them." Burnam laughed knowingly at the sudden remembrance.
Addie frowned.

The daughters wanted their parents to see the full range of fa-
cilities and services in the nursing home unit, so they would know
what to expect when and if they should have to move there. One of
the nurses arranged for a tour by wheelchair, but Addie declined.
"I'll just stay out here," she said. "I've already been back there. I've
seen it all."

With Gwen and a nurse at his side, Burnam proudly wheeled
his borrowed chair down the hallway, stopping and starting, speed-

ing up and slowing down, getting the feel of it. Addie watched with some amusement as he rounded a corner and disappeared.

"He's just like a little boy with a plaything, like Casey on his stick horse," she said. "If he had that thing at home, pretty soon he'd be out in the road with it."

Tillie and another nurse sat with Addie while she waited. She said little to them. She was in no mood for small talk; she had something else on her mind. "I'm going home tonight," she said firmly to no one in particular. The determination was fixed in her mind, and on her face. Her words were no idle remark, not a wish or a boast or a question; they were a resolution, a declaration. "I'm going home tonight," she repeated.

Tillie and the nurse exchanged a quick glance. "I hope you'll be able to go home soon, Mrs. Ledford," the nurse said kindly. "We need for you to stay a few more days, though. The doctor is making some tests to see why your eyes have been bothering you. We want you to feel your best, so you can take care of yourself when you go home. If you'll stay with us just a few more days . . ."

"I've *been* here a few days already," Addie interrupted angrily, and then quickly regained control of herself. "I'm feeling okay now," she went on in a softer voice. "There's no use for me to stay any longer."

"We do want to get the test results back, though," the nurse responded soothingly. "That won't take long, and then I'm sure you'll be able to go home after that."

"I don't know," Addie muttered, shaking her head. "I just don't know. I'll think about it."

The nurse and Tillie got up and strolled over near the door. They talked in whispers. "You probably don't need my advice or want it," the nurse said. "You've got to make the decision yourselves, and it's going to be tough, no matter what you do. But I'll tell you what I think: If it was my parents, I wouldn't put them in here. They're too healthy. As nursing homes go, this is a very good one, but nursing homes are not for the strong—they're for the helpless, for people who have to be looked after. Even in the best nursing homes, patients lose their identity, their independence, their privacy—and if they have any health when they come, they lose that too. If you bring any of those qualities in with you, you lose them fast. Your parents have got all of that now. If I were you, I'd do everything I could to help them keep what they've got."

Tillie's distress was noticeable, but she managed to control it in much the same manner as her mother. Her eyes blinked behind her gold-rimmed glasses, and a slight frown creased her smooth forehead. She kept her voice low. Still, the anguish and uncertainty were there. "What are we going to do?" she lamented, and then provided the only answer she had: "I don't know. None of us know what to do."

On his tour, Burnam paid close attention to everything he was shown and told, and he declared himself impressed with the facility. "It's a nice place," he said more than once. "I guess for a day or two it'd be all right. I'd come in a minute if I felt like I couldn't handle myself."

"See, Papa," Gwen said, "you can get up and move around whenever you want to, and there's always plenty of people around whenever you want to talk. You can have your own radio and TV, too. You can even chew tobacco."

"Well," he replied, "if someone would look after our house, maybe we could come for a few days. I'd be willing to make the sacrifice—if we just stayed for a few days."

He saw some people he recognized as he passed them in the hall, and his garrulous nature prompted him to stop and talk with anyone who showed the slightest interest in him. With one elderly but apparently healthy woman he had this exchange:

"They treat you good here?"

"Depends on what you call good."

"How long you been here?"

"Three years."

"Must be like home now."

"No. It won't ever be like that."

When he finally returned to where Addie waited, Burnam had lost his cheerfulness. He sat quietly in the wheelchair, saying nothing.

"Listen, Burnam," Addie said to him. "I want to go home tonight. It puts me in misery to see all these old people. I didn't know there was this many in the whole county. I've got better things to do with my money than spend it here. It'd make me miserable if I had to live around these old people—I'd pity them so much. Everybody is encouraging us to come here to this senior citizens place and live. I hear them—they know how to talk real smooth. But I couldn't stay here, Burnam. I want to go home."

Burnam made no reply. After a few minutes, Addie rose slowly from her seat and started walking down the hall.

"Where are you going?" Burnam called.

"To get my dress," she answered. "I'm going home."

Gwen and Tillie seemed near tears. Burnam shook his head. "She's stubborn," he muttered. "I understand why she can't go home for a day or two, but they'd better let her loose pretty soon. She seems all right to me—just the same as always." After a short silence, he looked up at his daughters and said, "I guess you'd better take me on out to the car."

They held back for a moment, hesitant and uncertain—and then, with great reluctance, they wheeled him through the door. It took several minutes for him to transfer his stooped frame from the chair to the car seat. When he was finally settled, Gwen and Tillie joined him in the car and they drove away.

Just as they left the parking lot, Addie rounded the corner, returning from her room. She still wore the white hospital gown beneath her robe, and she was empty-handed. Her gray eyes swept deliberately around the entrance hall. I stood up and walked over to her, but she went past me to the bench near the door and sat down.

"They went on home, Miss Addie," I said lamely, stating the obvious.

When she responded, her voice was calm and composed, as if she had known all along exactly what would happen. Her face was a perfect mask, like sculpted granite.

"I knew they'd slip off," she said. "But that's all right. I'm okay."

TWELVE

Children of Burnam and Addie

A week after she had entered the Garrard County Memorial Hospital, Addie was rocking contentedly once again in the shade of her front porch. When I drove into the yard and got out of my car, her shouted greeting was a triumphant boast:

"I got away! I let myself out!"

Her escape had lightened her heart and filled her with cheer. Burnam, too, was in good spirits, obviously delighted to have her back.

"How did you persuade the doctor to let you come home?" I asked.

"I just told him I had to leave," she replied, laughing. "I released myself. Just got up and walked out."

"No, it wasn't like that," Burnam cut in. "She kept wanting to come home, so finally I went up there to see what I could do. The doctor said she had some infection in her kidneys—he wanted to keep her three or four more days. I was prepared to stay with her that long, so Jennie and Tillie took me up there, and they talked to the doctor and the nurses, and then the doctor talked to me and Addie together. He insisted that we come up there and go in the old folks home, just stay there and live. I said I couldn't do that. He said, 'You'd do it for her, wouldn't you?' I said, 'Yeah, if it'd help her I would—I'd make the sacrifice.' So I turned to Addie and said, 'Addie, would you be satisfied for us to come up here and live in the old folks home?' She said, 'No, we wouldn't have nothing to come back home to.' So I told the doctor, 'That settles it. I'm not leaving home. We're staying home while we can.' The doctor couldn't keep us against our will, so we sat there and waited while he talked some more with Jennie and Tillie, and directly they came and got us, said we were going to take their mother home. So we came right on, and she was perfectly happy to get here, rested good that night, and we have been doing fine ever since."

"I wasn't sick," Addie explained. "I didn't need to stay. Nothing's wrong with me but minor things. I showed the nurse my hand—she said I've got arthritis. Then my shoulder got to hurting too, but I said it wasn't nothing—just a sign that bad company's coming." She chuckled. "That's an old saying: A pain in the shoulder means bad company."

"If she'll take her medicine like the doctor told her to," Burnam went on, "I'm sure she'll be all right. He told her she's been on her feet too much, too, aggravating that knee. But she wanted to come home so bad I just couldn't take it, so Jennie and Tillie signed the papers to get her released."

"I'm taking my medicine," Addie said. "I don't mind going to let him examine me—but I'm coming right back home."

"We've got a woman that's coming in now to cook and clean, and she's very pleasant," said Burnam. "Dorothy will be coming over from Danville while she's on vacation next week, and Gwen comes every day, and Jennie drives down from Lexington quite a bit, and Tillie will be back. We've got plenty of help. We're a whole lot better off staying here."

"Better keep your home while you've got it," Addie declared. "Besides, it would take everything we've got to live over there. How much did they say it would be a month, Burnam?"

"About $900 for both of us. When they told me that, I said there's no place like home."

"Two can live cheaper than one at home," said Addie. "You've got to look out for yourself. That's the way we've always done. This was the first time we've been separated overnight in a long time—so long I can't remember when the last time was. I reckon it was way back when Burnam worked at the hardware store and had to go to the city to buy goods."

Over the next several weeks, all of the Ledford children came on visits that ranged from a few hours to several days. They experimented with a variety of temporary arrangements for the care of their parents, but no permanent solution presented itself. On two points, there was general agreement: first, that Burnam and Addie would not be moved to a nursing home unless or until one or both of them became incapacitated, and second, that it was no longer prudent for them to live alone. But who could move in with them and provide the daily care they would need increasingly in the months ahead? No one could be found. For their part, the elders continued to insist that they were perfectly capable of taking care of themselves.

Finally, just before Labor Day, Tillie Ledford King pulled into the driveway on one of her frequent trips from Indianapolis—and this time, her car was loaded to the roof. "I've come to stay, for as long as I'm needed," she told three of her sisters. "I've quit my job and given up my apartment. There's just not any other way. I've been having dreams about Mama and Papa. Nightmares. I had to come."

Soon thereafter, at a gathering of the children, Tillie's voluntary decision was adopted as the formal solution to the problem: She was "retained"—in her word, "drafted"—to stay through the winter. "We all want Mama and Papa to be taken care of," she told me later, "so I just decided I wanted to do it myself. They cared for us all these years—now it's our turn to look after them. I hope I've got the strength to do it. I've prayed to God to help me do what's right. Now I know this is what's right—and I can do it, as long as the others all stand behind me."

Addie's unexpected hospitalization and the long-term implications of it had brought Tillie and all the other Ledford children back to the homeplace just as my conversations with their parents were reaching a turning point of their own. They had told me of the first twenty-five years of their marriage; the youngest of their children, Gwen, had just been born, and the eldest, Eloise, had finished college and begun her career as a school teacher. I would, of course, continue the interviews with Burnam and Addie—they had fifty more years to tell me about—but the time was at hand for me to move to the next phase and begin to record the stories of the Ledford children and grandchildren and great-grandchildren. My intention all along had been to construct a representative American social history from the patterns of change and continuity that emerged in the generations of a single family. Burnam and Addie had given me a detailed picture of their generation, and of the three generations preceding theirs; now it was time for me to start sketching profiles of the people who made up the three generations after them.

Throughout the remainder of the summer and fall, as members of the family came to Lancaster for visits or as I went out to meet them where they lived, I added nearly fifty new interviews to the Ledford chronicle. I talked to the nine surviving children, almost all of the thirty-two grandchildren, the older teenagers among the great-grandchildren, and several of those whose membership in the family was through marriage. There was no way for me to know at the time how I could arrange these biographies with those of Burnam and Addie and their forebears into a single continuous story. It would take months of effort for me to accomplish that—if, in fact, I could do it at all. But one thing was certain: I could never find out how well the story held together or how typical it was of the American experience until I had finished the interviews and the research and assembled the material.

Having no blueprint to follow, I could only proceed on instinct, and on what I felt was a logical course. From the mass of new tapes and transcripts, I first put together a collection of short profiles of Burnam and Addie's children, moving in chronological order from the eldest to the youngest:

ELOISE LEDFORD BEATTY was born on Sugar Creek in Garrard County in 1907 and grew up around her father's country store at Manse. She was only four when she followed her brother Ewell to the one-room schoolhouse there, five when she went with her mother on a long journey to a strange place called Harlan, and six when a fire burned their house to the ground and destroyed, among other priceless things, a little girl's brand new blue velvet coat.

Sixty years after the fact, she remembered vividly the shock and grief of Ewell's death, and the accident that killed her grandparents. Those were the saddest memories; most of the rest were pleasant. She was the oldest child after Ewell, and her parents looked to her for help with the other children, and the children in turn looked to her as a sort of assistant mother. Her mother's half-sisters, Delora and Martha, spent their summers with the Ledfords; they were not much older than Eloise, and she was very fond of them. In 1920, she went with them to Asheville Normal School in North Carolina, a boarding institution that combined the upper years of high school with teacher training and the first years of college. When she graduated at the top of her class in 1923, she was only sixteen—considered too young to get a teaching job—so she entered Berea College in Kentucky and worked her way to a diploma in 1926. At nineteen, she was thought to be Berea's youngest graduate ever.

It was in the midst of her Berea years that a mortgage foreclosure and too many debtors cost her parents their farm and their store and their house. Her father took a job in Lancaster, and the family moved into a rented house in town, and Eloise remembered especially how hard her mother took the loss. That first summer in Lancaster, Mama went to the state of Washington with Delora and Martha to see her brother, and Eloise helped Papa take care of the children. Her mother came back in better spirits, but she was soon grieved again by the loss of the child she had been carrying.

Eloise borrowed the money to finish her last year at Berea, and then, with her father's help, she got a teaching job in the one-room school at Buckeye in Garrard County. The pay wasn't great, but there was nowhere to spend money, and after three years she had saved a little. Part of it she contributed to the family's purchase of a house and a few acres on the edge of Lancaster—the house her parents would stay in for more than fifty years. Then, in 1929, she moved to a new teaching job in Fremont, Missouri. The $150-a-month salary seemed like a small fortune.

From Missouri, Eloise went to a small farming community in western Kentucky and taught for a few years, returning to Lancaster in 1932 to contribute time and money to her father's unsuccessful campaign for county clerk. From 1936 to 1938, she lived in Lancaster and taught in the high school there, and while taking summer courses for her master's degree at the University of Kentucky she met a young engineering professor named Fred Beatty. He was from Illinois, a widower with no children. A few months after he left to join the faculty of Colorado State University, he came back to Garrard County to marry the trim and pretty thirty-one-year-old school teacher he had left waiting there.

For the next ten years they were at three universities in Colorado and Missouri, having in the midst of that time a daughter, Mary Ellen, in 1944, and Eloise gave up teaching for homemaking. Then, in 1948, they settled at the University of Colorado in Boulder, and built a house there in the shadow of the Rocky Mountains in 1951. For more than twenty-five years, that would remain Eloise's home.

She had another child in 1954, when she was forty-seven—a son named James Burnam Beatty. He was a joy and a heartbreak; he was retarded. Eloise found "resources I didn't know I had— some inner strength that came, I suppose, from my mother and father"—and she and her husband strived to do their best for the child, who died, mercifully, after three very difficult years.

In 1959, Fred Beatty developed heart trouble and pneumonia and died after a short time, and his wife and daughter were thrown back on their own resources. Eloise went to work at the university. Mary Ellen finished high school and went for her freshman year to the University of Kentucky, in part because she wanted to meet some of her cousins and other members of the family and get to know them. She returned to the University of Colorado after a year and finished her bachelor's and master's degrees there, and in 1967 she married a fellow student, Hobart M. Corning III, and went with him to the University of Minnesota to work on her doctorate in English.

From that time on, Eloise Beatty was alone in Boulder. She retired from the administrative staff of the university's graduate school in 1973. The oldest Ledford, she had also gone farthest in school and farthest from home. Her experiences had been so different from those of her brothers and sisters that she seemed the one among them most unlike the others—and yet there was in her appearance and in her personality a clear resemblance to each of them, and to her parents. Her life had changed in many ways, but once a year she came back to Lancaster to be with her family and to remember a time of harder but simpler and more innocent pleasures.

Curtis Burnam Ledford Jr.—nicknamed Bill early in his boyhood— followed after Ewell and Eloise in 1909 on the Sugar Creek farm and spent his youth in the Manse community. He was nine when Ewell died of paralysis and the train struck and killed his grandparents. He remembered seeing the horses pull Ewell's hearse to the cemetery, and remembered hearing the long, steady wail of the train whistle after the family car had been hit.

But tragedies aside, life in the country around Manse and Paint Lick was very much to Bill Ledford's liking. His father's store had everything imaginable in it, including a telephone. The school and the baseball diamond and the horse pasture and the swimming hole and the candy counter were all right there, close by, and it was no small privilege to be one of the storekeeper's kids.

Bill thought of his father as a storekeeper, not a farmer, because he wore white shirts and bow ties and suspenders rather than overalls and brogans. He was on the school board, too, and a director of the tobacco warehouse, and an active Republican Party leader. In Bill's eyes, he was an important man, and he was no hypocrite: he practiced what he preached, whether it was temperance or honesty or hard work.

Bill's mother worked hard too. They were both ambitious to get ahead—but they were, as Bill remembered it, "in the wrong business at the right time to go broke." They argued about giving too much credit to customers or having too many outside involvements, but probably nothing could have saved them from the tobacco depression that forced them to give up their farm and store in 1924. Bill remembered going from being well off in the country to being poor in town, and he felt the shame of poverty at school and at church.

But he and his sister Eloise and his brother Carl had learned early how to work, and by the time he graduated from high school in 1929, he had earned enough from his job in a grocery store to help his parents pay for their house in Lancaster. The day he graduated, he moved to Lexington to take a new job in an A&P store, and before the year was out he was a store manager, making almost twice as much as his father. Just as the Depression was taking hold, Bill was moving up the ladder.

He had his mother's innate business sense, his father's winning way with customers, and his own keen ambition to succeed. A&P moved him from Lexington to Mount Sterling and back to Lexington, and each time he turned a money-losing store into a money-maker. He was earning seventy-five dollars a week—splendid wages for a twenty-one-year-old bachelor—and he had a convertible roadster and a wardrobe full of new clothes.

Then, in 1932, Bill had a falling out with his boss at A&P, and he found himself out of work. After a short stay with his family in Lancaster, he got a job with Kroger in nearby Stanford, and though the salary was only one-third what he had been making, he felt lucky to find any work at all. He had a steady girlfriend, Joan Enoch, in Mount Sterling. In 1934, after Kroger had sent him to Somerset to manage a store there, he and Joan got married; the following year, Bill quit working for chain groceries and opened a store of his own.

He had driven his new bride to the Chicago World's Fair in a brand new $740 Dodge coupe, stayed in the bridal suite at the Palmer House for $5.50 a day, and come home broke to a new house he had built for $1,900 on a one-acre lot he had bought from County Judge John Sherman Cooper. Bill didn't mind spending all the money he had, because he was confident that he was going to make plenty more.

The younger Ledford boys, Carl and Herb and Bruce, all worked for Bill at one time or another. Carl went on to manage other stores for Kroger and Bruce went into the service and Herb moved into a bank job before World War II started, but Bill kept his grocery and prospered until 1944.

He was thirty-five years old then, had a wife and three children at home and eighteen people working for him in his store, and the draft board sent him greetings. He sold his store and entered the navy, spending the better part of two years aboard a ship in the vicinity of the Panama Canal Zone. Back home, Herb had started a new Ledford's Market with first Carl and then Bruce in partnership, but Bill didn't see a place for him in that, and soon after he was discharged in 1946, he bought a farm near Bowling Green. Less than a year later, Bill and Joan moved again to Mount Sterling, and Bill went into the glove manufacturing business with Joan's father.

Mount Sterling became their permanent address. When their fourth child, John, was born there in 1948, Billy Jack was twelve and Polly was nine and Sally was four. Joan's father died, and Bill and Joan sold the business and built a new house on a two hundred–acre farm in the country, where they raised purebred Angus cattle and tobacco. Bill bought into a bank, too, and served as president of it for several years. By 1975, when all their children were married and had children of their own, Bill and Joan moved back into Mount Sterling.

Retired from business and banking and farming, Bill Ledford approached his seventieth birthday as a man of leisure. From an early age, he had been a hardworking and successful businessman. He had made good investments, and acquired some wealth. He had served on the local and state boards of education, had belonged to Rotary and Kiwanis, had been a solid citizen of Montgomery County for more than thirty years. Unlike his father, he had not been active in church or in politics; like his father and most of the other Ledfords, he was an avid sports fan and a devoted follower of the University of Kentucky Wildcats.

He and Joan liked to travel. They had toured the Civil War battlefields from Gettysburg to New Orleans, and cruised the Caribbean, and been to New York, and they were planning tours overseas. Once or twice, Bill had been to Harlan, but he didn't know much about the place except what he remembered from the stories of his father and mother. The thought of taking them on a trip there appealed to him. Maybe his son Billy and Billy's son Mark would like to go too; they were the oldest of the third and fourth generations of Burnam and Addie Ledford's family. Bill was himself the oldest son, as his father had also been. If they went to Harlan together, they would be four generations of first sons, returned to the land where three generations before them had put down Ledford roots.

EDWIN CARL LEDFORD was a year and a half younger than Bill, having been born in the house behind the store at Manse in November 1910, a few months after the family moved there. He barely remembered the house fire, and his mother's momentary panic at the thought that he or his baby sister, Lucille, might be inside.

He was eight when Ewell died, and that remained, six decades later, the saddest memory of his life. Carl kept thinking every night that his big brother would be all right the next morning, but he overheard the doctors' worried whispers, and he saw the helplessness of his parents; finally, he watched Ewell's casket being carried from the Presbyterian Church to the horse-drawn hearse, and the little brother cried uncontrollably—and remembered the hurt forever.

The death of his grandparents just before that had also hit him hard, for he had spent his summers on their farm and thrived on their easygoing ways. They and his parents had also raised him and his brothers and sisters to do their share of milking and gardening and other chores, and Carl took those duties in stride as a small price to pay for the privileges of a well-fixed country life. But then, when he was fourteen and a freshman in high school, the bubble burst; almost overnight, the Ledfords fell from the pinnacle of a small community to the pavement of a larger one. Carl thought it might be the end of the world.

He and Bill went to work to earn their own money and take a load off their father. Carl worked after school and in the summers at McRoberts Drugstore on the square in Lancaster. In 1928, when he had finished his junior year of high school and the family had moved (for the last time, as it turned out), he left his father to take care of the corn and tobacco and headed west with some of his friends to work in a Montana sugar beet factory.

After a productive summer in sugar beets and wheat, Carl and one of his friends returned to Lancaster, but the next year, without finishing high school, he went back to Montana and eventually on to Washington to work in his Uncle George King's Niagara Logging Company. From there he made it into a business college in Centralia, Washington, working for his room and board, and a year later he was out looking for a job just as the Depression took hold.

He hired on as a timekeeper for a road-building company, living with three other men in a furnished summer cottage that cost each of them only ten dollars a month. They had a cookstove, and they could buy two-foot-long salmon for a nickel. Carl was living on pennies and piling up savings in the bank—and when the banks got shaky, he took his money out. But the construction company soon had troubles of its own, and Carl moved on to a short stint in the apple orchards and then on to Seattle, where he saw able-bodied men waiting in mile-long breadlines. One man, he recalled, turned his empty pocket inside out and called it "Hoover's flag."

All the while, Burnam Ledford was writing weekly letters to his son, admonishing him to "be honest and associate with good people." But Carl was meeting few "worthwhile people," and jobs were virtually nonexistent. When his father wrote and told him that Bill was running a Kroger store in Somerset, he decided to head for Kentucky again.

From a start with Bill, Carl went on to manage a half-dozen Kroger stores in eastern and central Kentucky, including one in Harlan. He stayed with the company through the remainder of the 1930s, but recurring bouts with asthma drove him to an outside job. The respiratory problems also kept him out of the army. In 1940 he married Geraldine Dutton of Somerset, and in the mid-forties they bought a three-bedroom house on Ohio Street and Carl left his job as a route manager for a laundry and went into the grocery business with his brother Herb. Bruce came in later, and then both of the brothers left, and Carl ran the store alone until 1959, when he went into the laundromat business.

In the little house on Ohio Street, Carl and Gerry raised eleven children, and saw every one of them through high school and most of them through college. They were a close-knit family, industrious and frugal; they knew how to work together, how to share the load. Gerry ran things at home, and Carl, though his income was not great, managed to be the breadwinner for thirteen people. He also managed to fight—and win—a battle with alcohol, and that victory was an inspiration to all who knew him.

When he sold out his laundromat business in the late 1970s and retired, he thought of his life as not having changed very much. They went to the Christian Church instead of the Presbyterian, and he watched ball games on television instead of listening on the radio—but he still voted Republican, and the kids still came often to visit (bringing a dozen grandchildren with them), and he still went to Lancaster every few weeks to see about his parents, who still seemed old to him, just as they had when he was a teenager in the 1920s.

Carl didn't see much of his brothers and sisters—not even of Herb, who lived just across town. Since the breakup of their grocery partnership after the war, he had worked alone and socialized little, giving most of his spare time to his own growing family. Only at the annual Memorial Day homecoming in honor of his father's birthday did he take time to catch up with the comings and goings of his siblings and their children. He was not a loner—he was, in fact, an easygoing and good-humored man—but he was responsible for an unusually large family, and in his quiet and deliberate way, he gave most of his time to them.

LUCILLE LEDFORD SMITH was named Vesta Lucille—for her Grandmother Ledford—when she was born at Manse in 1912. She remembered almost nothing of her grandparents, and all that she could recall of her brother Ewell was that he wore thick glasses, like hers.

She was a sickly child, afflicted with asthma, and sometimes the other children taunted her. The house seemed perpetually crowded with its residents and its transients and its hired help—

Em Irving and Aunt Sook from Harlan, and Martha and Delora, and Mandy Turner, and Arch Kavanaugh and his wife and three children. The adults whispered a lot, seldom shouted, and when there was stress they tried hard to show no emotion, and Lucille didn't understand that, for she was inclined to show her feelings openly.

Her mother worked most of the time in the store, and seemed to like it very much. But as stoic as she was, she couldn't hide her hurt when, for reasons the little ones failed to understand, men came and padlocked the building and forbade anyone to enter. They moved to Lancaster, and Lucille began to notice how crowded they were. Eloise took command when their mother went out west on the train, and the smaller children, Jennie and Bruce, were delegated to Lucille's care. She didn't dare protest; Eloise was her idol, a smart and attractive young lady.

As soon as she graduated from high school in 1931, Lucille impulsively married "a nice guy" from Danville named Lee Bell. It was a mistake remedied by divorce six months later. She went back home to live with her parents, got a clerical job in a government relief agency, and spent the next six years in what she remembered as "a good relationship with my family." One of her friends told her candidly that she needed to get out on her own, but she was afraid to.

Finally, a high school classmate living in Toledo wrote and invited her to come and meet "the rich man we've picked out for you." She packed one suitcase and left on the bus. Forty years later, she was still in Toledo.

Her friend introduced her to Harry Smith, a middle-aged businessman who had started with a single carload of peppers and quickly developed one of the busiest wholesale produce businesses in the Midwest. Lucille went to work as his office manager and bookkeeper. A year later, in 1939, they were married.

Harry was fifteen years her senior. She recognized in him a brilliant mind, a natural gift for making money, and a deep sense of pride, but she knew nothing about his family or his past. They loved each other very much. Gradually, painfully, he told her his history. He had been born Herschel Pasternak, son of an East European Jew and his second wife, in New York City in 1897. His father's two sets of children didn't get along, so when his father died in 1911 or thereabouts, Herschel left home and wandered through the South. A woman somewhere in Georgia gave him a home, and he spoke of her as the only real mother he ever had.

Somehow, twenty years later, Herschel Pasternak had become Harry Smith, a merchant in Toledo—and a few years after that, when he was well established in business, he married a country girl from Lancaster, Kentucky.

It was two or three years before Lucille found the nerve to take her Jewish husband home to meet her parents. The initial encounter was a little strained, as she recalled it, but in a short time the doubts had faded and Harry was once more in the bosom of a Southern family.

In 1948, when Lucille was thirty-five and Harry was past fifty, they had a child, a son named David. Harry was by then the pepper king of the Midwest; he could afford the best for his son, and he was determined to provide it. Having thought of himself as a man with no family of his own, no blood relations, he looked upon David as a gift from God. From some deep inner stirring, he concluded that the child must be given, along with every other treasure, a priceless gift: his Jewish heritage. Though he allowed himself no personal involvement in Judaism, Harry sent his son to the Orthodox temple for his religious training and his education, and he supported the synagogue with generous gifts.

Harry's feelings about his own religious and cultural and personal heritage remained deeply divided. Lucille remembered that once a chauffeured limousine had pulled up in front of Harry's business, and the backseat rider, a relative of his, had sent the driver inside to beckon him, but Harry had refused to go out. She also remembered that the only time she ever saw him cry was in a theater, as he watched a movie newsreel about the Holocaust. Until the day he died in 1962, he thought of himself as a former Jew, but his feelings about David were not ambivalent at all; he wanted David to be kosher.

David graduated from a public high school two years after his father died. In his own mind he was Jewish, at least on one side of his family. But on the other side he was Kentucky Protestant, and that too was a wonder and a mystery to him. To gain a better understanding of it, he drove to Lancaster that summer and took his grandfather on a journey to Harlan, a memorable journey for the old man—and the young one.

He started to college, then joined the army and ended up in Vietnam, and that was the beginning of Lucille Smith's Toledo solitude. With Harry dead and David gone, her only family contacts were occasional visits from one of her sisters or a call from Bruce, her younger brother who lived in Toledo but was then too burdened with personal problems to be of any comfort to her. In the 1970s, after Bruce had died and David had come home safely and married and moved away, Lucille reestablished the once-close ties she had had with her parents, and at least once a year she went to see them.

But Toledo had been her home for so long that she couldn't imagine leaving. She had her house there, her friends, her church (the United Church of Christ, the same denomination that had started the missionary schools her mother had gone to in the mountains). She worried about her parents living alone, worried about the inevitable phone call that would bring bad news, but she was grateful for the full life they had had. She thought of her own life as a good one too. In it were blended country and town and city, South and North, hard times and flush times, Christianity and Judaism. It was an unusual combination. Lucille was comfortable with the memory of it.

DOROTHY LEDFORD JACKSON was born on her grandparents' farm near Paint Lick in 1914, the year after the house fire at Manse. All she remembered of the 1918 deaths in the family were hearses pulled by black horses. Of her maternal grandmother, she held an equally vivid but limited recollection: a beautiful and very quiet woman in a large hospital in Lexington, talking softly about seeing serpents on the ground.

With three brothers and two sisters ahead of her, Dorothy was not soon pressed into service around the house. The older ones did the chores, and other helpers usually were around, and that left time for the childhood pleasures of country life. If things were a little crowded, no one seemed to mind. Dorothy thought nothing of kids sleeping three and four to a bed. Their lives revolved around the school and the church, the house and the store, and that was more than enough to keep them busy and happy.

The loss of the farm and store and the move to Lancaster were developments that Dorothy couldn't understand. She was thrilled at the prospect of moving, seeing the town through her child's eyes as a big and important place. But she sensed that her mother was very upset, and her father was also acting a little strange, and she suspected that they argued after the children were in bed or before they got up. With all the family's troubles, though, Dorothy never thought of them as poor; in fact, she shared with most of her brothers and sisters a feeling that they actually were rather privileged. All of them knew families worse off than they.

In 1932, Dorothy went to Asheville Normal School, as Eloise had done before her, but when she came home two years later there were no teaching jobs to be had. She found other work in Lancaster and lived with her parents until 1939, when she married Ed Siegel of Danville and moved with him to Louisville, where he had bought a liquor store. The fact that his father was Jewish—and Siegel himself was "mixed up" about religion—bothered Dorothy's father less than the fact that his daughter, trained to be a school teacher, was going to sell liquor instead. To make matters worse, Siegel also had a drinking problem—and he was a Democrat.

The marriage ended in divorce in 1950. Dorothy went back home and lived a short time, then went to Toledo to be with Lucille when her child was small; she stayed in Toledo and worked for three years. When she moved back to Lancaster, she got a job in a department store in Danville, ten miles away. Both the store and the town became permanent fixtures in her life.

She was married again in 1962 to Henry Jackson, who was a store manager in Lancaster. He was a Georgian, a Southern Democrat, an inactive Presbyterian, a divorcé with two teenage children. Dorothy had remained active in the Presbyterian Church and she was still a Republican, but their differences were minor. For more than ten years, they enjoyed a happy life together. Then Henry found out he had cancer, and Dorothy took care of him at home for the last year of his life. They lived on a shady side street just off the main avenue in Danville. Dorothy had her job, and they had their friends, and Henry's good disposition made him a better patient than most; with the doctor's support, they were able to maintain a reasonably normal life at home until the week before he died.

Through it all and after, Dorothy stayed close to her family, and particularly to her parents. She went to see them every week, and she thought of their relationship as one of unchanging mutual affection down through the years. She fondly remembered the letters her father had written her every week when she was away at school, and she credited her mother with "giving us all more than we realized." As a widow with no children, Dorothy was in a position to give back to her parents some of the support and affection they had given to her, and she did so with quiet pleasure.

HERBERT RAYMOND LEDFORD came seventh in the line of Burnam and Addie's children, being born on the Doty Lane farm near Manse in 1917. His recollection of the country store was that his father sold just about everything there, including Willys Overland automobiles, and it was considered a real advantage to belong to the storekeeper's family.

The loss of all that when Herb was eight didn't make a deep impression on him, but he remembered that it took a lot out of his mother, and that his father, though he never looked back and never begrudged anybody anything, was hard-pressed to make ends meet on his $125-a-month salary.

Herb started working at the A&P after school and on Saturdays when he was about ten. Before he graduated from high school in 1935, he and another boy had a thriving laundry and dry cleaning agency, launched in part with a bank note signed by Burnam and Eloise. He was thirteen before he ever got as far away from home as Lexington, but he found plenty of opportunities around Lancaster to show that he could earn his own way.

The Depression-era roads around central Kentucky were mostly gravel and dirt, but the transition from buggies to automobiles was in progress. One sign of the change was the paving of the road to Danville that passed right in front of the Ledford house, and Herb watched that great feat with pride and satisfaction. Lucille and Dorothy were back at home then, but Eloise and Bill and Carl had moved on, and for a few years Herb was looked to for special help by his parents.

As soon as he finished high school, he headed for Somerset to work in the grocery with Bill. At one time or another, Carl and Bruce did the same, and the four brothers were all Somerset grocerymen. None of them remained in that business, but Herb remained in Somerset, never again living in another town.

He went from grocering to bookkeeping in a bank, and he was doing that when World War II started. A few days before he was to be called for the draft, he joined the marines, but he was sent home from Parris Island, South Carolina, twenty-two days later with a medical discharge. A combination of physical ailments ranging from dental problems to pneumonia subsequently kept him out of the air corps and the army as well. Classified 4-F, he finally returned to his job in the bank.

It was there that he met Hazel Perkins, a daughter of one of the bank directors; they were married in 1943, after Herb had started a new job selling cigarettes and tobacco for Liggett & Myers in a ten-county area around Somerset. When Bill sold his grocery and went into the service in 1944, Herb started a market of his own. Carl soon bought half-interest in it, and two years later Herb sold his half to Bruce and tried his hand at farming. A few months after that, he found another partner and started a wholesale grocery business, and for the next twenty-five years that remained Herb's main line of work.

All along, he and Hazel raised cattle and horses and a little tobacco on a farm that belonged to her father. By the time Herb sold his grocery company and became a bank vice president in the

early 1970s, the farm belonged to them, and they had enough as-
sets to assure them a comfortable life.

They raised four daughters in their house a block from Somerset
High School, and spent much of their time in support of the girls
and their various school and church activities. They were civic boost-
ers, Methodists, Republicans. They put Jane and Alice and Emily
and Sarah through college. They traveled more frequently and more
broadly as the years passed, from the Gulf Coast to Canada, from
the West Coast to Europe.

Herb could see enormous changes in their lives. They were more
affluent, they moved at a faster pace, they had more opportunities
and more worries. Somewhere in the basement, he still had the first
television set he had ever bought—just twenty years before. At the
bank, computers did work that Herb had once done by hand. He
remembered when the first Burroughs adding machine with a hand
crank was brought in—and the president told them not to use it
too much because they might wear it out. And the air travel that
Herb had come to take for granted was something he never experienced until he was fifty years old.

Lancaster was barely more than forty miles up U.S. Highway
27 from Somerset. There, Herb's parents lived much as they had a
half-century before, when their seventh-born child was starting his
first job as a delivery boy at the A&P. Computers and jet planes
and even color television were foreign to their experience. Herb
looked upon them as if they had been there forever, almost as if
they were permanent and unchanging, yet he knew they could not
remain for many more years. His life was much different from theirs,
and their early lives in Harlan and Garrard counties were not part
of his experience, but the years they had shared between 1917 and
1935 bound them securely to each other. Herb's frequent trips to
his parents' room in the Lancaster house were his way of making
sure that the bond between them never broke.

BRUCE BARTON LEDFORD was the only one of Burnam and Addie's
adult sons and daughters who could not render a personal recollection of his childhood and youth; he had died in 1969 at the age of

fifty. The others remembered him fondly as a handsome, cheerful, outgoing boy—and remembered him sadly as a brooding, erratic, deeply troubled man after the war. He had left school early, joined the army at sixteen, served at Schofield Barracks in Hawaii in the mid-1930s. When he was twenty and out of the service, he had married a Catholic girl, Anita Wahle, a Somerset physician's daughter, and gone to work for Bill at Ledford's Market there. Things went well enough for a while, but when the war started, Bruce was restless, and after months of indecisiveness, he volunteered for the service again.

Bruce and Anita had one child when he joined the navy in 1943, and they were expecting another when he was sent to the Pacific the following year. When he came home in 1946 he had become a Catholic, but he was a wounded soul, scarred by his war experiences. He worked off and on with his brothers, but his behavior was unpredictable. He had an alcohol problem, and soon his marriage was foundering. No one seemed able to reach him. He and Anita were divorced in 1949. The following year, he joined the navy again and went to Korea.

After that third military hitch, Bruce lived in Toledo with his sister Lucille and her husband, working in their produce business. For a time, it seemed that he had regained his balance; his drinking appeared to be under control, and he worked productively in the small family circle where his presence was welcomed and appreciated. But by the time Harry Smith died in 1962, Bruce's mental and physical health had begun to deteriorate. Lucille and various other members of the family tried repeatedly to help him out of his downward spiral, but every effort failed. Bruce became a loner, a drifter. He was in and out of hospitals and treatment centers. Finally, in July of 1969, he was found dead on a Toledo slum sidewalk, a victim of alcoholism and pneumonia. In one of his pockets, the police found a scrap of paper with Lucille's and Herb's phone numbers written on it. In another pocket, they found a rosary.

Bill Ledford remembered his brother in those last years: "He had done pretty well for quite a while, but then he got back on liquor again, and we never did see much of him after that. He drank all day long, just went to the dogs—and finally, whiskey killed him. Mama and Papa worried about him a lot, but there was nothing they could do, nothing anybody could do. My son Billy went up there once to see him, found him in a low-class place in the roughest part of town, skid row. Billy offered to help him, but Bruce said he didn't need anything. Not long after that, he died."

Anita Wahle Ledford remembered too: "When he came back from the war, he was a different man. The ship he was on had been torpedoed, and he was thrown overboard into blazing oil on the water. By some miracle he lived through it, but the war scarred him, and I knew something was wrong right after he came home. He was belligerent and abusive. It was hard, so hard—and finally I couldn't take it, couldn't bring up the children that way. I still loved him, but it was just impossible to live with him. Everybody had loved Bruce before that—he was a fun-loving, happy-go-lucky man—but the war changed him, and he never was the same again. When I finally divorced him, just about everyone in the family was kind and understanding toward me. I divorced Bruce, but I didn't divorce his family. We all grieved for him when he died. His death was a great sorrow to his parents, especially his mother. She took his loss hard. He was her baby boy."

And finally, Lucille Ledford Smith remembered, for she had been closer to him than anyone else during the last fifteen years of his life: "I practically raised him when he was a baby, carried him around like I was his mother, and he idolized me. I think that's why he came to Toledo in the early 1950s, after he had been in Korea. He lived with us for almost ten years—and then, after Harry died and David and I moved to a smaller place, he got a job and a room elsewhere, and we didn't see much of him. By that time he was having a lot of trouble, and I just couldn't handle it. Until Harry died, I always felt like there was hope for Bruce, but finally I had to admit I couldn't get him straightened out. No one could.

"It wasn't that he was mean or dangerous, far from it. He was always kind, not loud or aggressive. He was so good-hearted—gave money away to kids in the street, never met a stranger. He was just an outwardly cheerful, polite, kind person, even when he was drinking. But inside, he was like a wounded animal—he just wanted to crawl in a hole. I don't think he could help himself, any more than he could fly, and he wouldn't accept help from others. I tried to tell him I still believed in him—I just couldn't let him down—but it was no use.

"The day they called me from the hospital and told me he had been found dead on the street, I called Dorothy and asked her to pass the news on, and I talked to Bruce's son, John Bruce, in Lexington. John Bruce asked me, 'Do you reckon somebody knocked him in the head?' I said, 'No, honey. He killed himself. He's been dead for ten years.'"

Bruce Barton Ledford came home from Toledo in a coffin. All the family gathered for his funeral, and then they took him to the old cemetery near the Paint Lick Presbyterian Church at Manse, and left him at last to rest in peace.

JENNIE LEDFORD MCLENDON was just two years old when the family moved to Lancaster, so she had no recollection of living in the country. During most of her childhood years, she was the middle one of five children at home—younger than Herb and Bruce, older than Owen and Tillie. She thought of her father as a steady workhorse, never bothered by bad luck, and of her mother as strong and kind but sad, a woman whose modest dreams never came true. Jennie was especially fond of her mother, and indebted to her for countless gifts of support and faith.

Two months out of high school in 1941, Jennie married Revis Mills of Danville, a journalist three years older than she, and went with him to Harlan, where he had been assigned as a correspondent by the Louisville *Courier-Journal*. The mountains awakened in her an interest in the family roots of her parents, but she never got far into the subject, because she and Revis were quickly preoccupied with personal conflicts—the opening salvos in a stormy ten-year marriage.

On several occasions, Jennie returned to Lancaster and lived with her mother and father—because, she said, "that seemed like a safe place for me to be." In the summer of 1942, she gave birth to a son there in her parents' own bed, and named him Bruce Burnam for her brother and father, "the two most important people to me at that time." Two years later, she had a daughter, Nancy, in the same bed, and a year after that, another daughter, Arletta, was born in a Danville hospital. It was as if making babies was the only thing Jennie and Revis could do right. She remembered those years bitterly as "an ungodly time for me."

Finally, in 1951, she got a divorce and moved to Indianapolis, where she stayed for ten years. She found a good job as a checker at the A&P, and worked her way up to head bookkeeper. Her sister Tillie was married and living there during part of that time, so Jennie and her children kept a family connection through her. Jennie also got married again, to a Louisvillian named Charles Thornberry, but it was, in her remembrance, "another bad marriage for me," and it ended in divorce nine years later.

Once more, she went back to Kentucky, back to her safe harbor in Lancaster. In 1961, she married Morris Toomey, who was in the construction business in Harrodsburg. She worked in his office, and they built a house, and they went to the Presbyterian Church, where Jennie remembered praying for stability and order and peace in her life. Instead, in 1969, she got another divorce.

Working again for the A&P in Lexington a year or so later, she met Alex McLendon, who was also in the food business. He had four grown children by a previous marriage, and Jennie saw him as "a kind and decent man, a fine person, nice to my mother and father, good to me." She married him in 1971, convinced that after three failures, she finally had a marriage that would work.

Seven years later, she still worked for the A&P, and she and Alex lived in a comfortable Lexington apartment that was a far cry from "that old house in Lancaster, where we didn't even have a bathroom when I was growing up." But she remembered "that old house" as a place where things more important than material comforts were present, and sometimes she wished for the sense of happiness and security she had known there as a child. Her children were grown and scattered from the Cincinnati area to Colorado and California, and she spoke of them and of her grandchildren with pride, but she seldom saw them. All three of her children had spent a large part of their early years living in Lancaster with her parents, and Jennie often reflected on "how fortunate it was for them that they had such grandparents to influence them."

She reflected, too, on the many positive ways her parents had influenced her—and yet, in spite of her father's stern admonitions against whiskey, she had fallen victim to it more than once. "Bruce was not the only one of us to have trouble with alcohol," she said ruefully. "Just the unluckiest."

Jennie McLendon's admiration for her mother and father had grown stronger through the years. They had been through so much together, had suffered heartbreak and heavy loss, and yet their marriage had survived every stress and strain. Such perseverance and durability was especially impressive to Jennie; she thought of her parents as being "closer together now than they have been in years, maybe ever," and she prayed that nothing would separate them: "After all these years, after all they've been through together there, it would be just terrible if they couldn't stay right on through to the end."

MATILDA LEDFORD KING—Tillie—was the last of the country-born Ledfords, a babe in arms when the family moved to town. She grew up adoring her father, "the most wonderful person in the world, a neat, good-looking man, kind and sweet, very honest and up-standing," but disliking her mother, whom she saw as aloof, unaffectionate, uninterested in her children, and deeply embittered by the family's misfortunes.

Right after she turned sixteen in 1940, Tillie quit school and "broke out" of Lancaster, moving with a girlfriend to Cincinnati, where she went to work as a clerk in a Woolworth's store. Later she moved to Toledo, and in 1943 she married Lawrence Edward Woods, an Alabama man who had just gotten out of the army and was working in a factory. They had a son, Gary, in 1945, but the marriage was on shaky ground by then, and Tillie soon took her baby and went back to Lancaster. Her mother went to court with her and helped her get a divorce.

She stayed with her parents until 1948, when she married Robert Hammon. He was older than she, and Tillie saw in him some of the good traits of her father. They had a daughter, Bobbie Jo, the following year. Bob Hammon traveled with a pipeline company, and Tillie went with him as much as she could until the early 1950s, when they settled in Indianapolis and put the children in school. They stayed there twelve years—long enough for Gary to finish high school—and then Tillie left her husband and took Bobbie Jo with her to Lancaster once again. Gary liked his stepfather so much that when he was eighteen he went into court and had his name changed from Woods to Hammon. But Tillie and Bob Hammon weren't able to maintain such affection for each other, and in 1969, as soon as Bobbie Jo finished high school and got married, Tillie got a divorce.

Soon after that she moved back to Indianapolis, and in short order she met and married Charlie King, a skilled craftsman recently retired from General Motors. He offered Tillie financial security and "a good, clean, honest, religious life," and she accepted. No one in her family was very pleased about that, but she thought once more that she was seeing some of her father's best qualities. Much later, when she could "look back and laugh about it," she described the marriage as "the second biggest mistake of my life." The biggest mistake was in 1974 when, a year after she had divorced Charlie King, she married him a second time. In 1976, she received her fourth divorce.

Somehow, through all the changes of name and address, Tillie seemed to remain the same cheerful, humorous, outgoing person she had been from the first. She had what one of her sisters called "bounce-back"—a capacity for overcoming trouble. Through all of the unstable years when her children were small and her parents were so supportive of her, she managed to moderate her feelings about them, coming at last to understand that she had "held my father too high and my mother too low." Their strength and their constancy were sometimes Tillie's only security; just thinking about them, she said, "has brought me through some pretty dark periods."

After her last divorce, she stayed on in Indianapolis, sharing a house in the western suburbs with another woman and working as an interviewer with a market research company. Gary and Bobbie Jo were both married and had children, and they had settled in central Kentucky. Tillie didn't see much of them or of her parents, and the only time she saw most of her brothers and sisters was when she made the annual Memorial Day pilgrimage to Lancaster for the family homecoming and the celebration of her father's birthday.

But then her mother was hospitalized, and she came for one visit, and another, and finally she came to stay. They had helped her through too many tight spots for her to overlook their own time of need. "I'm glad to have the chance to show Mama and Papa that I appreciate all they've done for me," she said. "I've gotten over the confused feelings I had about Mama, and I feel pretty good about myself right now, too. Coming back to Kentucky, I can see more of my children and my grandchildren, I can be closer to my brothers and sisters—and most of all, I can give back to these two great old people a little bit of what they've given to me and my children and all the rest of us down through the years. I don't want to ever see them have to go to a nursing home. If I can keep that from happening, there's nothing better I could be doing with my time."

GWENDOLYN LEDFORD GASTINEAU, the thirteenth and last of Burnam and Addie's children, was born on Stanford Street in Lancaster in 1928, a few months before the family's last move to the house on the edge of town. Burnam was past fifty then, and Addie was forty-three; in the earliest memory of their youngest child, they were already old.

Until she was about ten, Gwen saw a good bit of half a dozen of her brothers and sisters, but when she was a teenager during the war, she and her parents were often at home alone. Then, Jennie came back and had two of her children there, and Tillie and her baby boy returned, and the house seemed to fill up again. She remembered it as being like a hotel, a boarding house.

Burnam was "Pappy Ledford" to the town. He worked at

Thompson and Morrow's hardware store on Stanford Street—
walked in to work every morning and walked home every afternoon, reading the paper as he went. Addie stayed at home, where
there was a garden and a cow and flowers to look after. Gwen saw
them as independent, hardworking people.

When she went to school, she was known as "Little Ledford,"
there having been so many before her. She graduated from the high
school in Lancaster in 1947, and soon thereafter she married Russell
Gastineau, a Garrard County farmer's son. When she first started
dating him in 1944, her father had noted disapprovingly that the
Gastineaus were Democrats, but he came to like Russell in spite of
that. The Gastineaus—French Huguenots by way of Canada—had
been in the county for three generations. They had always been
farmers, and the land was passed down, and it would eventually be
Russell's. There on the family farm in the Bryantsville community,
they raised four children—Carole, David, Richard, and Rebecca.
Gwen stayed a Republican and Russell a Democrat, but they com-
promised on religion, joining the Forks of Dix River Baptist Church,
a congregation first formed in 1782 by Virginians who followed
the Wilderness Road to the Bluegrass.

Gwen had been married for more than twenty years and the
oldest of her children was soon to marry herself when Bruce died in
Toledo in 1969. (In the previous half-century, the only deaths in the
family had been those of Addie's mother and two of Addie's infant
children.) Burnam was then ninety-three years old, and Addie was
eighty-four. From that point on, Gwen gradually assumed greater
responsibility for them, though they were by no means dependent
on her; they kept a milk cow until he was ninety-eight, and a garden until his centennial year.

Long after all of her brothers and sisters were gone from Garrard
County, Gwen Gastineau remained. She was not only the last of
the Ledford children—she was also the only one who never moved
away, and she had no regrets about it: "I've stayed right here in the
same county with my parents all my life, and I've never been sorry.
They always left us free to choose our own way, never tried to live
our lives for us, and this was my choice. This is a nice community,

and I just never was interested in going someplace else to live. My brother Herbert asked me once why I never moved away. I told him, 'Because a Coca-Cola tastes a little bit better at McRoberts Drug Store than it does anyplace else in the world.' His wife said that was silly, said a Coca-Cola is a Coca-Cola, they're all the same. But Herbert knew what I was talking about. He said, 'You're right, Gwen—they do taste better at McRoberts.' It wasn't the Coke, of course—it was the familiar place, the friendly spot where everybody gathered to gossip and have fun. That's what you remember. They sold that drugstore just the other day. It's shut down now. Lancaster will never be the same."

They were alike—and different. Their lives were a combination of new departures and old repetitions, of lessons learned and labors lost. They had advanced and retreated and marked time, and I had recorded brief segments of that movement, like frames on a roll of film. I had hoped to discover in their collective histories some clues to the rhythm of a larger history, but I had found nothing as profound as that. I saw the ways in which they followed the patterns of their predecessors in temperament, manner, health, politics, appearance, and I also saw how their life experiences had given them different religious beliefs and occupations and levels of education and income. But those were general and predictable observations; the deeper causes and effects of continuity and change were still a mystery to me.

And they would remain so. As I slowly became acquainted with the extended family, of Burnam and Addie Ledford, meeting and talking to upwards of eighty blood relatives and forty spouses, I reached two paradoxical conclusions. The first was that I had come to know more about the family as a whole than any individual member of it knew. The second was that I could never know them well enough to grasp the full story of generational evolution that I had set out to tell.

I knew them better than they knew themselves simply because I alone had made a point of knowing; I had sought them all out, and listened to their elders, and studied whatever written records I could

find of their past. But the reasons for my inability to fully understand their history and to tell it all with clarity and candor were
more numerous and complex.

In the first place, there were so many of them that I couldn't
possibly make as detailed a study of their lives as I had made of
their elders. That would take more time and produce more material than I needed for the book I was preparing. Furthermore, such
detail inevitably would result in too much repetition of stories and
experiences, and that would tend to overshadow the variety in their
lives and make them seem more alike than they actually were.

And in any event, I couldn't get to know the children and grandchildren and great-grandchildren as well as I had gotten to know
Burnam and Addie. The elders were far enough from their active
past to look upon it with some detachment, almost as if they were
observing the lives of others and not their own; time and distance
had given them a deeper perspective, better understanding, and more
candor. The later generations, on the other hand, were still in the
midst of their productive years. The advantage of hindsight was
less available to them; they were more private and more protective,
less frank and less philosophical than their elders. And even if they
told me every intimate detail of their lives, it seemed likely that I
would be ethically or legally bound not to repeat some of the things
I had heard.

Like an artist painting a portrait or a photographer shooting a
picture, I was searching for the optimum distance between myself
and my subject. I wanted to be close enough to capture details in
sharp focus, yet distant enough to see the whole picture in its larger
context. It occurred to me that I might be too close to Burnam and
Addie and not close enough to the others, and that could produce
distortions in the finished picture that would diminish its authenticity.

But those risks were inherent in the project itself, and could not
be avoided. I had known from the first that a true story would
place more limitations on me than a fictional one, yet I was determined to find and tell just such a real tale. No other approach, I
was convinced, could more securely connect the past to the present,

or better reflect the essential realities of everyday life in the United States. I was thus bound by the facts as they were gradually unfolded before me—but I was also confident that the truth could be presented without romanticizing the past or camouflaging the present.

I had begun with an idea, and the idea had led me eventually to Burnam and Addie, and my early acquaintance with them had persuaded me that the history of their family was just the sort of story I wanted to tell. Now that I was well along into that story, I realized with new and greater understanding how vital the elders were to it. The children and grandchildren and great-grandchildren were important, and so were the ancestors, but the living elders were essential. The story hinged on their lives; only they could see three generations backward and three forward from their own—and it was that long view, that perspective, that made the Ledford chronicle both an original tale and a universal one. Even though I might not be able to fully understand its deepest causes and effects or to interpret their meaning, I could at least listen to the voices and let the words speak for themselves.

THIRTEEN

A Quieter Time

Burnam and Addie, 1928–1953

When fall came, two more doctors examined Addie's eyes and advised against surgery to remove her cataracts, saying the slim chance of improving her sight was not worth the risk to her general health. She had steadily regained her strength, and was in remarkably sound and stable condition. One day she fell in the bedroom, but when she had been helped up and the excitement had subsided, she dismissed the fall as a minor accident. "I think my knee just gave out temporarily," she explained. "I wasn't dizzy or anything—I didn't black out. It's just my limbs, that's the only trouble—my limbs and my eyes."

Shortly she announced that she had quit taking her medicine. "I don't think I need it any more," she said. "I couldn't tell that it was doing me any good, and I feel just as well without it." No amount of pleading from Burnam and Tillie could change her mind; Burnam, in fact, seemed almost to agree with her. Both of them were tired of talking about hospitals and doctors and medicine, so they simply changed the subject. Occasionally, Addie seemed as if she were a little confused, and Burnam too had his days of shaky fragility, but for the most part they manifested the health and humor and mental clarity of a couple thirty years younger.

"We've always been told that our bed is a Lincoln bed," Addie said one afternoon, giving me the history of the massive, hand-carved walnut headboard and frame that made up the bed she and Burnam had slept in for more than a half-century. "It's over a hundred years old, and they say it's just like the one in the White House. It was bought new by a young couple around here back in the last century, and then I bought it at an auction. Actually, Bill and Carl paid for it with their money. You see, they had bought a heifer, and she had a calf, and when they sold the calf they bought the bed with the money. So it rightfully belongs to Bill and Carl. Owen is the only one of our children to be born in that bed. She was born in it over on Stanford Street, just before we moved to this house in 1928. But two of the grandchildren were also born in it—Bruce and Nancy, two of Jennie's children. We helped to raise them back during World War II."

Burnam interrupted with a laugh. "I remember one morning I was sick, and Nancy was laying there in the bed with me—just a little baby, laying there while Addie was at the barn milking. I guess Jennie was at work. Anyway, Dr. Kinnaird came to the house to see me, just came on in, and when he got in here he pulled back the covers to examine me and saw that baby laying there. He jumped back, threw up his hands and said, 'Is that what's the matter with you? You had a baby?' He acted real startled, you know, and we both got a big laugh out of that."

"I can barely remember sleeping in any other bed but that one," Addie said. "Seems like we've had it forever. I've always liked it. When I was in the hospital, trying to sleep in a strange bed, I stayed awake half the night. When you get used to something like that, it's hard to change."

The Lincoln bed had come into the Ledford household at the end of Addie's child-bearing years, and it had remained; it was as much a part of their children's remembrance as any piece of furniture, almost as much as the house itself. The youngest sons and daughters had grown to maturity there, and each in turn had left along a separate path, just as their brothers and sisters before them had done. Whenever they returned, they were reminded of how much they had changed, how different they were from their parents and from one another. But somehow, in spite of the mounting years, their parents seemed to stay almost the same—older and a little less active, but essentially the same, like the Lincoln bed and the drafty old house.

They had moved into the house in time to celebrate the twenty-fifth anniversary of their marriage. The Great Depression was coming, but Burnam and Addie had already suffered a depression of their own. It had cost them their farm, their business, their economic security, their country roots, their peace of mind; now they were starting over in a six-room house on a twelve-acre plot of ground a mile or so from the Lancaster crossroads. The house had no electricity at first, and it would have no running water for years. They had bought the place for less than $5,000, and they were determined to own it outright as quickly as possible, fearing from bitter experience that whatever was not paid for could easily be taken from them.

This was the Ledford's tenth move in a quarter-century of married life, and it would prove to be their last. When they arrived, the road in front of the house—Route 52, the New Danville Road—was still unpaved, but it had effectively replaced the Old Danville Road nearby. The old road was one of the most ancient in all of Kentucky, it having been an Indian trace, a longhunters' trail, a path of pioneers, a wagon road; the new road was a turnpike, a toll road, and it soon would be given a macadamized hard surface. Eventually, the curve on which the Ledfords lived would itself be bypassed in favor of a straighter route across the way, and the "old" New Danville Road would become simply a narrow side street serving the half-dozen homes that faced it.

But in 1928 it was the main route, and the presence of the Ledfords beside it was in a sense a symbol of their strong ambition to regain a modest foothold near the center of economic and civic life in Garrard County. They had suffered heavy losses, but by the time the national depression arrived they had recovered enough to avoid a repetition of their personal disaster. Burnam had a steady job in town. He and Addie had a garden and a milk cow and patches of corn and tobacco. Their oldest children were either gone or soon to be gone from home—gone to school, to work, to marriage. In Burnam's recollection years later, the decade of the

1930s seemed less devastating for him and his family than it was for many others:

I spent three years traveling through eastern Kentucky as a salesman for Hudson and Farnau, and then I started to work for the Conn brothers, Jim and John Conn, in their hardware store here in Lancaster the same year we bought this house. When the Depression hit, I was making twenty-five dollars a week, but not long after that I agreed to take a salary cut of five dollars a week. We didn't have much money, but it didn't seem so bad, because a dollar would go a long way—and besides, everybody was hurting, and some people were a lot worse off than we were. Even President Hoover volunteered to take a salary cut, if I remember correctly. Millions of people were unemployed, and a lot of the banks had closed. If you had a steady income of one or two thousand dollars a year, you were considered fortunate. We grew most of our own food, too, and that helped a lot.

By 1930, Eloise was teaching school and Bill and Carl had gone off to work. Lucille and Dorothy got out of school pretty soon after that, but both of them lived with us part of the time in the 1930s, and so did Eloise. This was a busy house. Herbert and Bruce had jobs after school and on the weekends, and it wasn't long before they were gone too. Everybody worked. We didn't get ruined in those lean years like we had in the tobacco depression a few years earlier, and the main reason was that we didn't have a lot to lose, and every one of us was carrying part of the load. I guess we were pretty lucky.

We hadn't been living in Lancaster very long, but I had a good reputation in town. I had served on the school board and the tobacco warehouse board, and of course I had been a big Republican. I had also been in on the tax equalization program that helped to make the property tax fair for small farmers. So people knew me and trusted me. We had moved to town without any money, but I don't think anybody looked down on us like they did when we moved here from the mountains. Nobody held poverty against you in the Depression, because everybody was poor.

All through the thirties I stayed a strong Republican, the same as I had been before—and have been ever since. I never did care much for President Roosevelt, Franklin Roosevelt. I didn't approve of the way he wanted to give everything away. People ought to work for what they get, if they're able to work. When you go to paying people not to do things, they'll just keep their hand out—and when you can't give them all they want, then they're your worst enemies. They get to where they think the government owes them a living, and if they don't get it, they might turn desperate and start robbing and stealing. I've always believed people ought to work as long as they possibly can, and take help from the government only when that's the only thing they can do. Roosevelt got us out of the Depression, but I didn't like the way he did it—and we've been paying for it ever since.

I didn't vote for Democrats, but I can remember one or two that I liked. Alben Barkley was one man I always admired, and if he had ever run for president, I might have voted for him. And Happy Chandler, I always liked Happy. He served two different times as governor, and he did a good job. He made a good commissioner of baseball, too. I met Happy several times. Kentucky has had some Democrats I could admire, even if I wouldn't vote for them. On the national scene, I liked Harry Truman pretty well, and John Kennedy too.

But I stuck with my party, even though the Democrats dominated Kentucky politics up until John Sherman Cooper came along in the 1940s. Now there was a good man. You never heard of anything crooked with John Sherman Cooper when he was in public office. He was one of the best politicians I ever knew. He was a statesman. He would even cross over and support the Democrats if he thought his party was wrong.

In 1932, the same year Roosevelt got elected, I ran for county clerk of Garrard County. That was the only time I ever ran for public office, and I lost. I was running against the incumbent, a Democrat, and he had all the advantages. He could give out money when there wasn't any jobs, and he had paid campaign workers at every precinct in the county. I couldn't afford to buy votes, and I didn't believe in it anyway, had no patience with it. One night before the election we had a party meeting up at the courthouse, and everybody wanted money. It was clear the Democrats were going to buy the election, and somebody said he wished he had enough money to out-buy them. I said I wished I had enough to get me a machine gun and kill every vote-buying son-of-a-bitch in the whole business. By the time it was over, I was glad I got defeated. It was just too crooked. Politics has been cleaned up a lot around here since then. It may be worse than ever in higher up places, but it's not nearly as bad here as it used to be. Both parties have made a lot of improvements.

I slacked off from politics after that. When Roosevelt got reelected in 1936, I was sixty years old. It was along about then that I got the blood clot in my eye—couldn't see well enough to drive the car, so I had to give it up. From then on, I generally walked to work, and walked home in the evenings. I never did drive a car again after that.

Those years when the nation was coming out of the Depression, I didn't do much of anything except work about ten hours a day at the store and go to church on Sunday. I still liked to read a lot, and I kept up with what was happening in the country, and we had the radio then. Will Rogers was one of the most popular national people—it was a big shock when he got killed in an airplane crash. Prohibition had been repealed in the country, but not around here—most of Kentucky was dry. At least, that's what the law said—but moonshining and bootlegging was still a big problem. The papers was full of John Dillinger, the big bank robber—he got shot by some G-men in Chicago. And Billy Sunday was the best-known evangelist. I always liked him. I read about all those people, and we talked about them in the store, and talked about the New Deal, and I remember the 1937 flood that did so much damage in Louisville. But I wasn't involved in anything much outside of working and raising a family. It took us a pretty long time to get over the big losses we had in the twenties.

In the last part of the thirties, our children was spreading out. Eloise got married and moved to Colorado. Bill was married, had his own grocery store in Somerset. Carl had been out West, then worked for Bill, and he was a store manager for Kroger. Lucille went off to Toledo and got married, and Dorothy was married and living in Louisville. Both of them married Jews. Herbert worked for Bill some, and then went to work for a bank in Somerset. Bruce quit school and joined the army, and when he came back he married a Catholic girl in Somerset and worked in the grocery business with his brothers. The only ones we had at home then was Jennie and Tillie and Gwen—and it wasn't long until Jennie and Tillie went off and got married. Both of them came back and lived with us in the forties, though, so there was always a house full.

Every one of our children was married in the 1940s, but some of them got divorced. They were scattered out, and most of them had children—me and Addie must have had nearly a dozen grandchildren by the time the war was over. As quick as we got done raising one generation, we were helping to raise another one.

Bruce was the only one of my boys that had to fight in the war. Bill and Herbert got called to serve, but they didn't have to go overseas. Bruce had been in the army before the war, and after Pearl Harbor he joined the navy and went to the Pacific. He came back all right, but he had had some bad experiences, and they stayed with him. He got to drinking real bad, and finally him and his wife separated.

It seemed like the war changed a lot of things for the worse. So many boys lost their lives, so many families was torn apart. It was a terrible thing when we had to drop the atom bomb on Japan, but I didn't think about it that way at the time—all I could think about was getting the war over and bringing the boys back home. And then after they got home, it took a long time for things to settle down. I was very thankful that our family hadn't lost anybody, but some of our children had troubles in those years, and I always felt like it was the war and the unsettled times that caused it. Jennie's marriage broke up, and so did Tillie's, and both of them came back and stayed here with us quite a bit—Jennie and her three children, Tillie and her two. Carl never got called to the service, but he had some personal problems during and after the war. It just seemed like everybody was upset, and it was a common thing for families to break up. People had all sorts of problems. Life was just moving too fast.

I had been working for the Conn brothers in the hardware store for eighteen years when the war was over, and the Conns had troubles of their own, but the business was still in the family, and some of the sons had followed their fathers into it. In about 1945 or around in there, they sold out to Lucien Thompson and Paul Morrow, and I stayed on with them full-time for five more years. I kept on working part-time for a few more years, and finally I retired in 1953. Me and Addie had been married for fifty years then, and I was seventy-seven years old. If somebody had told me then that in another twenty-five years I would still be around here, me and Addie both, I wouldn't have believed it.

When I compare the first fifty years of my life to the last fifty, it's plain to me that the first half was a lot busier—that's when most of what all happened to me took place. Living in the mountains where people were so isolated, the pace was slower, but we had to work harder, had to make everything we used, from our hoes and our plows to our furniture and everything. Then we moved here to Garrard County, and we must have lived in a dozen houses before we got to this one. I had been a school teacher, a farmer, a salesman, and a storekeeper when I reached age fifty. I had grown up in a big family, then got married and had a bigger one of my own. I had been active in politics and the church and all sorts of community boards and such. By the time I was fifty in 1926, I had already done more living than a lot of people do in their whole lives—and of course the same was true for Addie.

Since then, our lives have slowed down a lot. I only had one job after I was fifty—clerk and manager of the hardware store. Once we got in this house, we stayed in it. Cars replaced mules and wagons, radio came, then TV. Our family grew up and moved out, and some of them came back, and we helped to raise some of their children—but compared to the way it had been before, it got to be pretty quiet at home. I was an election officer for fifty years, but finally I got to be too old to do that, and I went to church until I couldn't hear the preacher, so I gave that up too. I haven't traveled much in the last fifty years—especially the last twenty-five. I quit driving the car when my eyes got to bothering me. Look at everything I ever did in my life—and nearly all of it was in the first part. The times have changed, everything has changed. Life is faster and maybe even fuller than it used to be—but for me and Addie, life has gotten slower and emptier.

I wouldn't have you think I'm complaining, though. We've made out just fine. I had a good job in the hardware store for about twenty-five years. I knew how to take care of customers, and people depended on me. I was in complete charge of that store for Jim and John Conn, and I took a lot of responsibility for Thompson and Morrow too. In all that time, I never was late to work but once or twice. Generally I opened up no later than eight o'clock and stayed at least until six. People called me "Pappy" Ledford, and they depended on Pappy. I knew where everything was in that store, and I could sell things when nobody else could. One time after I retired, I happened to be in there when a woman I knew came in to look at some furniture. The other clerks had been trying to sell her a living room suite, but she wouldn't buy. I took her and showed her some new pieces that had just come in, talked to her about what she needed and all, and she ended up paying cash on the spot for a new living room suite—$169, I believe it was. When I was ringing up the sale, the other clerks said, "How'd you do it, Pappy?" I said, "I sold her something she needed and wanted. You've been trying to sell her something she didn't need or want."

Yeah, I did a good job of running that store. In the more than twenty years I worked there full-time, my salary only went up from twenty-five dollars a week to forty—but inflation wasn't high at all, and everything was inexpensive, and we got by on that.

I was superintendent of the Sunday school at the Lancaster Presbyterian Church for a good many years, and a deacon too, and I stayed active in the Republican Party until after I retired from the store. I went to Harlan almost every summer when my vacation came, and kept up with what few kinfolks I still had there, and I was always close to my brothers and my sister—Sarah and Jim lived here in Garrard County, and Speed moved to Ohio, and Ash to Florida.

I had a little tobacco allotment out back, and a corn patch, and me and Addie always had a big garden and kept a milk cow and some chickens. We had someone here with us most of the time, too, right up to when I retired, and even after that—our children, some of our grandchildren, even some others. So it wasn't like we was idle and didn't have anything to do. We stayed plenty busy right on through, right up to the last two or three years.

The first twenty-five years we was married, I worked for myself—farming, storekeeping. Then the next twenty-five, I worked as a salesman and storekeeper for somebody else. The last twenty-five I've been retired and working for myself again on this little farm, sort of like when I first started. But now I don't work at all. Those first years was the hardest and the busiest. Then it slacked off some, and then it got quieter still. I can remember some nice trips I had back in the thirties, and Addie made one or two good ones, but neither one of us has gone anywhere much at all in a long time.

I guess the biggest trip I was ever on was in about 1939. I went up to Dayton, Ohio, to see my brother Speed, and then went with him and his son out to North Dakota to look at some land Speed had bought with another fellow. Drove out there in a brand new car—Plymouth, I believe it was—and stayed a few days, and then me and Speed's son decided between ourselves that we would take us on down into Colorado to see my daughter Eloise and her husband. We left Minot, North Dakota, one morning headed for Bismarck, and below there we turned west toward Rapid City, South Dakota, and about a hundred miles out the road we had to stop and fix a flat tire. Speed was standing out beside the car, just thinking, and finally he figured out that we were headed toward the west. He had been sitting in the car talking, not paying any attention to where we were going, just assuming we were on our way home. "This ain't the way home, is it?" he said. We got a big laugh out of how we had fooled him.

We went on to Rapid City, because I wanted to see the Black Hills and the Mount Rushmore monument where Borglum, the famous sculptor, was carving the faces of four presidents. He died before he finished, not too long after we were there, but his son completed the work. You could make out the faces of Washington, Jefferson, Lincoln, and Teddy Roosevelt up there on the side of that mountain, and I was very impressed.

After we left there we drove through a very bad windstorm on our way to Fort Collins, Colorado, where Eloise and her husband lived. We stayed with them two or three days, and they took us to Denver and on up into the Rocky Mountains. It was in August, I remember, but there was snow up there, and at one place we stopped to make snowballs. We were throwing them at each other, and throwing them off the side of the cliff, watching them fall—seemed like they just kept falling forever. That was something that stuck in my mind, because I felt so good—felt like a little kid. I was over sixty then.

We were gone for a total of about two weeks on that trip. Came back across Kansas and Missouri to Illinois, visited Lincoln's tomb, then went on to Indianapolis. I got on the bus there and came to Louisville, spent the night with Dorothy and her husband, and came on home the next day. That was a fine trip, and I've never forgotten what a good time we had.

The only other long trip I took was in 1938, when Bruce took me to Harlan and then on down through Cumberland Gap and into North Carolina. One of the things I remember about that trip was finding an old beech tree on Crane Branch where we used to live. It was a thrill to find it, because there on that tree was my initials, mine and Sally Smith's—she was one of Creed's daughters. I had carved them there in 1888—fifty years before.

Carl took me to Cincinnati to see the Reds play one time after that—and that's the only other trip I can remember making away from Kentucky. Me and Addie used to drive to Louisville and Lexington to buy goods for the store, but we never did get to go on vacations together. One of us had to stay at home and look after the children, milk the cow, weed the garden, and such as that. She got to make a few trips, though.

Well, we made it through the Depression, through World War

II, through the Korean war, and I retired after that. It seemed like
Franklin Roosevelt was president forever, and then Truman got in
and beat Thomas Dewey, and we had to wait a while longer for a
Republican—had to wait twenty years, from the time Hoover went
out until Eisenhower came in.

Me and Addie left a busy time of change in our lives and came
into a quieter time of not much change—and all the while, the world
seemed to be moving faster and faster. I guess it was a good time
for me to retire. When we celebrated our fiftieth wedding anniversary in 1953, most of the children came home and brought their
children, and lots of our friends and neighbors and other relatives
came too. It was a very nice occasion. I remember thinking that a
lot had happened since we had our twenty-fifth anniversary. My
working days ended that same year, and I was seventy-seven years
old then. That's the time when most people just give up and die.
For some reason, that didn't happen to me. Me and Addie still had
a long way to go together.

*It was Addie's manner to suffer bad news with a stoic and un-
emotional calmness. Experience had developed that habit in her,
and it had become a predictable part of her character. Whatever
she might say to Burnam in private, to all others she said little and
showed less—no tears, no laments, nothing but a silent, determined,
rock-hard sense of endurance.*

*That had been her response to her father's passing, to her first
son's death, to her loss of two infant children, to her mother's mental illness. It had also been her reaction to the chain of events that
took away her family's home and livelihood in 1924 and forced
them to begin anew. That loss was especially bitter to Addie, for
she had begun to discover in the family store a promising outlet for
her energies and a showcase for her talent. Not since she had given
up schoolteaching had she known such an opportunity for accomplishment outside the home—and then, in one terrible season of
financial instability, the chance was gone. Privately, she may have
assessed the loss in the bleakest terms, but publicly, she held her
head high and said nothing.*

The move to Lancaster in 1925 and to their last homeplace three years later was a sharp change from the prosperous country life the Ledfords had known. Burnam was still a storekeeper and a farmer of sorts, but he was no longer his own boss, as he had been for so long. The children, too, felt their loss of status. And as for Addie, she was almost through having babies but not through rais-ing children, and that responsibility would continue throughout most of the second twenty-five years of her marriage.

Before she entered that phase of her life in 1928, she had been to the West Coast to visit her brother, and had given birth to an-other child (her twelfth), and seen him die, and given birth once more. She had also learned to face the harsh reality of daily life on an austere budget, and had accepted the family's reduced position and circumstances as irreversible, if not permanent. Years later, she would remember the difficult adjustment with great clarity—but with hardly more emotion than she had shown when the crisis was upon them:

When we broke up the business, Eloise wanted me to go back to teaching, but I knew I couldn't teach school with as many chil-dren as I had. Eloise got out of Berea and started teaching herself— she was only nineteen years old—and Bill and Carl got jobs after school, but I had too many little ones at home to even think about going to work.

Burnam started to work at the hardware store the same year we moved out here. He didn't make a big salary, but we got by— raised a lot of our food and made most of our clothes. I sewed some, but the customary way was to hire somebody to come in and stay a week and do the sewing. You could get dresses and things real cheap that way. We also sold a little cream and some eggs, and I even made a little bit of money hanging wallpaper. Some of the older girls helped me with that, and the boys helped with the farm-ing and gardening.

To tell you the truth, my children was all pretty free—they helped out some, but they was in a lot of things at school, and I let them go places when I could have used their help at home. I don't regret it, though. They all went to church with Burnam most of the time. I generally stayed home and cooked Sunday dinner.

So we got used to our new life here. I was disappointed at first. I liked living in the country, and I liked working in the store, and it would have suited me if we could have stayed there. But we lost out, and we just had to make the best of it. Burnam had been involved in so many activities before that—I always felt like that was one reason the business failed—but when we came to town he didn't do much besides work. Didn't have time for much else, and neither did I. I never did belong to any clubs or anything, and he wasn't a big joiner either. I just stayed at home and raised my children and looked after the place. And then later, when our children were grown, me and Burnam gave a hand to Jennie and Tillie with theirs.

We always spent a lot of time helping our children with their schooling. When Bill was little, he used to ask me hundreds of questions—he thought I was the bureau of information. I didn't know as much as he was asking me, but I told him what I thought. They all did pretty well in school, and I think all of them finished high school except Bruce and Tillie. Eloise was the only one to go through college. She was real smart—learned to read and write when she was just three or four years old. None of our children ever got in any bad trouble, as far as I know, and I'm thankful for that. They've all done right well—and a couple of them have made a lot of money. They know how to take care of it, too. That's the Skidmore in them, I guess.

When the Depression came, it was a hard blow for most people, but we had already learned to do without. The stock market crashed and a lot of the banks closed, but we didn't own any stocks and didn't have any money to speak of in the bank. I remember when we lived on Stanford Street—that's the main highway running north and south—we used to see lots of people going to Florida to get in on the big land boom down there, and then when the crash happened, we saw some of them passing through again, going back up north, and most of them was dead broke, just poor hoboes. We never took any chances like that. We stayed in one place, got our house and land paid for, and kept out of debt. I suppose that's why the Great Depression wasn't so hard on us.

Our oldest children went away to work in those years. Eloise ended up in Colorado. Carl went out to Washington where my brother was, but he came back. Lots of people went out west or up north then, looking for work. One that made it big—or thought she did—was Kate Conn. Her father was Jim Conn, one of the brothers that owned the hardware store where Burnam worked. Back before World War I, Kate went to New York to seek her fortune in show business—she was a singer. She met Adolphe Menjou, the movie star, and they got married, and I think Menjou adopted Kate's daughter by her first marriage. One time he came to Lancaster with her, but nobody paid any attention—they didn't know who Menjou was. They lived together for a few years and then got divorced.

I had a first cousin that went out west, and she had good luck—the man she married got to be a millionaire. Her name was Mildred Skidmore. She was from Harlan County, and she had a lot of get-up-and-go like most of the Skidmores. She never had been anywhere or seen anything, and she wanted to get out of the mountains, so she went to Denver, and there she met a man named Nelson—Chris Nelson, I believe. He was a soda fountain clerk in a drugstore. Well, one day he dropped some ice cream into a pan of hot chocolate by accident, and when he dipped it out, the chocolate got hard around the ice cream, and that gave him an idea. He started making what he called Eskimo Pies, got a patent for it, and pretty soon he was a wealthy man. Somebody asked Mildred how she caught this rich boy. She said, "Why, the other girls was chasing him, but I let him chase me—and he caught me."

None of my children had that kind of luck—didn't marry anybody rich or famous. Lucille married a Jewish man from Toledo who made a good bit of money. I didn't want her to marry him, but after she brought him to meet us, I liked him. He was a good man, and he knew how to make money. I went up there and visited with them once, and he was real nice to me. He gave me a ring and gave Burnam a watch, and he called us Mom and Dad.

Bill and Herbert have made a right smart as businessmen and

bankers. The others have done all right. But nobody in the family ever got big rich—and nobody ever got famous.

You remember Amelia Earhart, the woman pilot? She flew across the Atlantic right after Lindbergh, and then she tried to fly around the world. The papers was full of it. Well, our son Bruce was stationed in the Hawaiian Islands when she stopped there on that trip. He went down to the airfield and saw her, watched her take off, and right after that she crashed, and they never found her. For a long time, people thought she was on an island out there somewhere, maybe a prisoner of the Japs—but she was probably dead all the time.

I never did fly in a plane myself, me or Burnam either, but I did make two or three nice trips on the train. I told you about going out west to see my brother, and about going to Toledo to visit Lucille. Then in about 1938 I went to New Orleans to see my half-sister Delora, whose husband was in the navy down there. That was the most enjoyable trip I ever had. Delora had been here visiting, and I went back with her on the train. We got on at Danville one afternoon and got to New Orleans early the next morning. Delora and her husband were living in a big old house, a boarding house on St. Charles Avenue, the nicest street in town. We rode on the streetcar, went to the Roosevelt Hotel, went to all the very best places. We saw Ted Lewis, and heard him sing. I remember everybody was carrying big bouquets of flowers, and I asked why, and somebody told me it was Memorial Day, but it was in November. Must have been Confederate Memorial Day.

That must have been the only big trip I got to make in the 1930s. Me and Burnam never did have a vacation together. One of us always had to stay at home and look after things. We had children at home until Gwen got out of high school after the war—and by then, we usually had some of the grandchildren with us too. There was always somebody here.

It was in 1939 that my mother died in the hospital in Lexington, and we buried her in the cemetery at Manse. She had been sick for a long time—about twenty years—and we went to see her pretty regular, but she never got any better. From the time we had all those deaths in the family in 1918 until Bruce died in 1969, my mother was the only one in the family to die—her and those two babies I lost. We had other kinds of bad luck in those years, but we didn't have much sickness or death. This has always been a healthy family, healthier than most, and I consider us lucky that way.

Bruce lost his health in the navy in World War II, and he never was well after that. He was the only one of my boys that was in battle. Our children have had their problems, the way people do, but if any of them ever caused me any trouble, it didn't amount to much—and besides, I don't look back. I always told them what was right. Sometimes, you know, a person will think maybe it doesn't do much good, but if you'll be particular and tell them just exactly the truth, it's a lot of help. You might think I'm bragging, but I think our children have done better than the children in any neighborhood we've ever lived in. I feel good about the way they've turned out.

For about fifty years, starting when Ewell was born in 1905, the main job I had was raising children. I had thirteen of my own, and I helped to raise two of my half-sisters and three or four of my grandchildren. Two of Jennie's children, Bruce and Nancy, was born here in this bed, and their sister, Arletta, lived with us when she was in high school. Tillie's Bobbie Jo lived with us a lot, too. We didn't see as much of the others when they were growing up, and we don't see them very often now, except when they come for birthdays and holidays. They're all in school or working, and some of them have got real good jobs. We've got thirty-two grandchildren, and they're all doing well. Quite a few of them are married, too, and some of them have got teenage children now. Me and Burnam have got nearly forty great-grandchildren. If we live much longer, we'll start having great-great-grandchildren, I guess. They add up fast, don't they?

There were other things I wanted to do when I was younger, like teaching school and working in the store, but they didn't pan out. Burnam worked in town until he retired, and I stayed here at home, and we raised a big family. Sometimes it was rough. If I had it to do over, though, I guess I'd do the same thing again. I'd have to, if I wanted to raise my children. Maybe things work out for the best.

FOURTEEN

The Scattered Seed

Grands and Great-Grands

It was in the third generation, the generation of Burnam and Addie's grandchildren, that the family followed the American middle class into the modern age. Between 1936 and 1959, thirty-three children were born to the children of the elder Ledfords, and they were even healthier than their exceptionally healthy forebears: only one of them died in childhood. Their numbers and the times into which they were born determined their mobility and their diversity; however much they might resemble their parents and grandparents in particular ways, they were certain to be more different from them than alike. Technology and education and affluence and a dozen other forces would assure variety in every facet of their lives—their jobs, their homes, their lifestyles, their political and religious beliefs, their friends and associates and mates. They were the post-Depression generation, the war babies, the first children of the television era. Not by choice but by chance, they belonged to a new age, a contemporary society that was bound to move higher, farther, faster than its predecessors, and the pattern of accelerated change would continue into the next generation.

The Ledfords of the third generation ranged from early middle age to young adulthood when I met them. If it was difficult for me to establish a close acquaintance with all of their parents, it was virtually impossible for me to get to know each of them well enough to incorporate them fully into the Ledford chronicle. They were simply too numerous and too scattered for that—and their children, who ran the scale from the middle teens to early infancy, presented even more difficult problems. Nevertheless, I wanted to learn as much as I could about each of them, and I was reasonably successful. Of them all—thirty-two grandchildren and more than two dozen spouses in the third generation, close to forty great-grandchildren in the fourth—the only one I never saw was Eloise Ledford Beatty's daughter, Mary Ellen, who lived in Minnesota.

Between Eloise, the eldest surviving child of Burnam and Addie, and Dorothy, their fifth-eldest, who was childless, the offspring of Bill and Carl and Lucille totaled sixteen, and those children in turn were themselves the parents of twenty-three, of whom three were teenagers (see chart, page 354). In my interviews with one family after another, I was struck by how varied their experiences had been—and how much they departed from the hard and simple lives of their grandparents. Even in the briefest of profiles, the contrasts were apparent.

BILL AND JOAN LEDFORD'S four children included Burnam and Addie's eldest grandson and granddaughter—the only two members of the third generation to be born before 1940.

The senior grandchild was Billy Jack Ledford. Born in Somerset in 1936, he was eleven when the family moved to Mount Sterling. After graduating from high school in 1954 he went for a year and a half to Georgia Tech, but his efforts as a student and a football player there were unsuccessful. In the winter of 1956 he transferred to the University of Kentucky, where he joined a fraternity and ran on the track team, but he couldn't get serious about school, and the following year he dropped out.

For about a year, Billy was "on the road," hitchhiking through about forty states, "just messing around" in places as widely separated as New England and California and Florida. He was in Cuba a year before Castro overthrew Batista. Finally, in the spring of 1958, he joined the army and was sent as a technician to a security outpost on the Japanese island of Hokkaido.

In high school and later, Bill had dated a girl named Betty Von

Fuller, and when he returned from the service in 1961, she was working on her master's degree at the University of Kentucky. They were married that summer. Billy had intended to finish his degree, but when Betty got pregnant he decided to forget about school and go to work.

They built a house in a Mount Sterling subdivision in 1963. A dozen years and four children later, they bought and remodeled a roomy old house on the town's shady main street. Billy had developed a fifty-dollar-a-week job selling typewriter component parts into a lucrative position marketing special-order parts for business machines. He drove a thousand miles a week in Kentucky and Tennessee, and on the weekends he played golf and followed the high school athletic exploits of his teenage sons. Mark, sixteen, was the eldest great-grandchild of Burnam and Addie. He and his brother Richard were especially able golfers and football players.

Billy voted Republican, but he had little interest in politics. He went only occasionally to the Baptist Church with Betty and the children. Outside of his immediate family, he didn't have much contact with his Ledford relatives. He rarely saw his grandparents, and he had never been to Harlan. He showed some interest in the idea of making a trip there with them.

Polly Ledford Hawkins was three years younger than her brother Billy. She had graduated from the University of Kentucky in 1962 and was teaching school in Miamisburg, Ohio, when she met Robert Hawkins, a civil engineering graduate of Purdue University and a navy veteran who was nine years her senior. They were married in 1964, and Bob, who had shifted from engineering to sales, was transferred that summer to Birmingham, Alabama. They lived there through the remainder of the 1960s—the turbulent civil rights years—but in Polly's remembrance, "watching Huntley and Brinkley on television was about as involved as we ever got."

With her father's help, Polly and Bob returned to Kentucky and bought a 140-acre Bluegrass farm midway between Mount Sterling and Paris in 1970. Their first child, a son named Todd, was born in 1971, and Martha, their daughter, followed two years later. Without any prior experience in agriculture, Polly and Bob set about turning their small acreage into a profitable enterprise. Polly thought of them as "a fairly typical Kentucky farm family."

They voted Republican, and Polly and the children went to the Christian Church, and she and Bob worked long hours on the farm. She saw her parents and her brother Billy fairly often, her other brother and sister less frequently, and the rest of the Ledfords—her aunts and uncles and cousins—hardly at all, except at the family gathering in Lancaster each May. Once in the mid-1970s she was inspired by the Foxfire books to visit her grandparents several times and to tape-record eight hours of conversations with them. "I'll always be glad I did that," she said.

Polly characterized her family—both her immediate kin and the larger clan of her grandparents—as more different than alike: "We do different things, see things different ways. But there are similarities, too—we're all big talkers, but we're not huggers and kissers, not emotional people, not especially close. And Bob says Ledfords don't sweat—they're good traders, good businessmen, but not the type who love hard labor. I guess he's right. We do tend to stand back from deep and emotional involvement in things."

The third of Bill and Joan's children was Sally, who was five years younger than Polly. In her first year at the University of Kentucky in 1962, she roomed with Jane Ledford, one of her first cousins from Somerset, a daughter of her Uncle Herb. Two more of her first cousins—Carl's Richard and Eloise's Mary Ellen—were also freshmen there that year, but Sally didn't get to know them well.

Sally developed a career interest in medical technology. She also met Jerry Watkins, a graduate student in history, and in 1969 they were married. Soon thereafter they moved to Louisville and remained there, with Jerry teaching in a city high school and Sally working in a medical laboratory at nearby Fort Knox. Their sons, Brian and Greg, were born in the early 1970s.

Jerry was an active Democrat, but Sally, though she voted Republican, cared little about politics. They shared an interest in sports and in camping, taking their trailer on weekend outings and summer vacations. On an impulse in 1969, they rushed to Florida and waited through the night to see the Apollo XI astronauts blast off on their historic journey to the surface of the moon. But aside from such adventures, their lives revolved primarily around their work. Only occasionally did they visit Sally's closest kin, and only at the Memorial Day homecoming did she see her grandparents. "There never was a chance to get to know them at those reunions," she said. "With so many people there, you couldn't really sit down and talk to them. I remember them telling stories, but nothing registered. Now I wish that I could have spent more time with them."

In 1948, the fourth and last of Bill and Joan's children, John Garfield Ledford, was born in Mount Sterling. He followed his older brother and sisters to the University of Kentucky, and while he was still there he married Josie Carmichael of Atlanta. After graduating in 1971, John spent three years as an ensign in the navy. When he returned, he went to work in his father-in-law's tile business in Georgia. In suburban Stone Mountain, John and Josie raised their two children far from John's Kentucky origins, but life seemed much the same as always to him.

"In spite of all that's happened in this country," he said, "I don't think we've really changed all that much. Me, I'm still a hardcore Republican, a sports nut, a believer in the American system. We go to the Presbyterian Church, watch a lot of TV, like music and the movies. I live in an urban area instead of a small town now, and I commute to work on the freeway, and I don't have as much contact with my family in Kentucky as I used to, but I think of myself as still pretty much the same person I always was. In spite of inflation and all the signs that the good times may be over, I'm still optimistic. I still expect things to work out okay—for me, and for the country."

CARL AND GERRY LEDFORD had by far the largest family in the sprawling clan of Burnam and Addie: eight sons and three daughters, all born in Somerset in the 1940s and 1950s, who grew up together in a three-bedroom house. Their closeness bred a spirit of affection and loyalty to each other that was still strong and vibrant when the last of them went off to college. By then, seven of the children were married and had a dozen grandchildren among them. On Christmas and other holidays, the little house was, in the words of one son, "wall to wall with big and little Ledfords." The sons and daughters seemed very much alike, but their adult experiences had led them into a variety of locations and occupations.

The eldest was Edwin Earl Ledford, who reached the age of thirty-eight in December 1978. He was married to Jane Tibbals, a Somerset veterinarian's daughter. They and their two children—Joe, fourteen, and Debbie, eleven—lived in Middletown, a suburb of Louisville, and Eddie worked as a civil engineer in the city. At home and school and work, he had set the pattern for his younger brothers and sisters, and they had followed it. Eddie remembered growing up believing that "we could accomplish just about anything if we were willing to work for it," and he started early, getting his first job at the age of nine. Before he finished high school, he was an Eagle Scout and a member of the National Honor Society (as several of his siblings would also be), and after graduation he went with a scholarship to study civil engineering at the University of Kentucky.

After five years of summer jobs with the state highway department, Eddie joined the agency full-time in 1963, doing survey and inspection work on the interstate highway system. Then, after a year with a Somerset construction company, he joined a large engineering firm in Louisville. Ten years later, he and his family were "city people," urban dwellers—but in Eddie's view, they hadn't really wandered far from their small-town beginnings. He recalled his Somerset boyhood with pleasure, and attributed his adult achievements to the good start he had gotten there.

Summer visits to his grandparents' home in Lancaster were also an important part of his remembrance. He was amazed by their vitality and by their grasp of history, and when he was older he wished he had listened more attentively to their stories. Eddie was convinced that the Somerset-Lancaster background, the Ledford heritage, had given him something—habits, perhaps, or inherited traits—that made him who he was, made him work hard and love sports and stay healthy and vote Republican. He couldn't say exactly what it was, but he felt it in himself and saw it in his brothers and sisters. "We've got a lot in common," he said.

Fourteen months after Eddie came Sue Carolyn, and so many more followed that Sue found herself conscripted in later years to share the burden of child rearing with her mother. She grew to resent the heavy responsibility (she also worked at a drugstore after school and on Saturdays), and to resent as well the overcrowded house and the constant lack of material goods. She vowed to get away as soon as she could.

Her boyfriend was Joe Rudd. He was a couple of years ahead of her in school, and by the time she graduated, he had spent a year in college and another in the air force. They decided to elope. Sue packed a couple of suitcases, told her mother she was going to visit a friend she had met at camp, and walked to town to catch the bus. Years later, she still remembered:

"The bus came right by the house, and I had a window seat, and I looked out and saw Mother sitting on the porch with Steve and Bo, the two little babies, in her lap. She was very stoic, not crying or anything, but I started crying, and I thought at first that I would get off somewhere and turn back. But I also thought of Joe, who was riding a bus from Biloxi, Mississippi, to South Carolina—he would be waiting for me there. His parents were more opposed to our romance than mine were. We had made our plans, and I had to go through with them, even though I told myself that when I met Joe, I might tell him I had changed my mind."

But she didn't change her mind, and on a Sunday morning in June, 1960, they were married in a Methodist Church in Chester, South Carolina. A few days later, another bus stopped in front of the Ledford house in Somerset at seven o'clock in the morning, and the newlyweds walked into the chaos of a swarm of kids getting ready for school. Sue was convinced that her mother had known all along, but in both families there was shock at the news of the marriage, and it had not fully subsided when Carl Ledford drove his daughter and his new son-in-law to Selma, Alabama, where Joe had been transferred.

Many changes were ahead of them. Joe went from the air force to Auburn University to a traffic engineer's job with a Florida telephone company; Sue went from a radio station to secretarial work to motherhood; the young couple went from Selma to Auburn to St. Petersburg. They were in the midst of the tension and emotion and anger of the racially divided South, and they took first one side and then the other. Joe left the telephone company for graduate school in English literature, and then he and a friend started a cabinet-making business which was so successful that it became his principal occupation. Their only child, Andy, was born in 1967, and when he entered school in St. Petersburg he was bused to a formerly all-black school. For more than a decade, the Rudds faced one adjustment after another. "The changes were painful for us in many ways," Sue concluded later, "but I feel they were necessary changes. It's a growing process. I believe it has made us more patient and more tolerant." Along the way, Sue also reached a different feeling about her parents. She came to recognize that "they have devoted their entire lives to their children. It must have been terribly hard for them to overcome so many difficulties, but they did, and now they never talk about it. They have given so much, and asked so little in return."

Years after her "escape" from home to be married, Sue Ledford Rudd came back at least every year or two to be with her family. "It's been five or six years since we were all there together," she said, "but we go as often as we can, because it's just a nice feeling to stay close. I wouldn't like to live there any more—but I like to go back."

The third of Carl and Gerry's children was Richard Burnam Ledford, who was born in 1944. Like Eddie and Sue before him, he assumed responsibilities early, working first in the grocery and then, in his high school years, managing one of his father's laundromats. He also followed Eddie into civil engineering at the University of Kentucky, and then into a job with the state highway department.

But Richard wanted all along to return permanently to Somerset, and with that goal in mind he joined a large highway construction and paving firm in the area. Before he was thirty-five years old, he had moved out of engineering and into the firm's management and administration, and his continuing presence in the town of his birth seemed assured. Right out of college he had married Judy Warren of Owensboro, and she subsequently gave birth to a son and a daughter. In 1978, the family moved into a new house on the edge of Somerset—a house more than twice the size of the one his parents had raised their large family in. They were active in the Baptist Church—Richard as a Sunday school teacher and deacon, Judy as the church organist—and they spent summer weekends in their boat on the lake and a week or two each winter in Florida.

Richard saw it all as a natural progression, a case of working hard for what he wanted, and getting it. "I enjoy my work, my family, and this town," he said. "Even when I was working elsewhere, I knew this was where I wanted to live. My goal was to come back here, and everything just fell into my lap."

He saw his parents often, and his brothers and sisters whenever they were in town, and his grandparents on the Memorial Day weekend. That homecoming Sunday in Lancaster was also the only time he saw his aunts and uncles and cousins.

Jerry Allen Ledford followed Richard, and he too went to the University of Kentucky, but his hopes of becoming a pharmacist were thwarted. He transferred to a junior college, then married Brenda Kerr, his high school girlfriend, and in 1968 he completed a degree in chemistry at Eastern Kentucky State University in Richmond. From there he went to work for a chemical company in Louisville. Ten years later he was still with the firm, and he and Brenda and their three children were living in suburban Georgetown, Indiana.

A combination of urban worries prompted Jerry to move his family out of the city and into a small town. They liked the quieter atmosphere, the slower pace; Georgetown was more like Somerset than Louisville. They liked the little Baptist Church there, too, and Jerry had plenty of opportunities to play some team sports and to follow his favorite college and professional teams. He had a thirteen-mile drive to and from work every day, but he took that chore in stride.

Two or three times a year, Jerry's work took him to other plants in such places as Texas, California, and Canada. In 1977 he went to India to visit one of his firm's subsidiary companies. The poverty he saw there and the effects of the caste system made a deep impression on him, and he came home with a deeper appreciation for his own country's freedoms and its relative prosperity.

Like most of the others, Jerry voted Republican and went to church and thrived on sports and worked diligently at his job. He thought of himself and his brothers and sisters as being very much alike, and they were; it was their similarities that kept their family ties intact.

Perhaps the one whose life had changed the most was Judy Lynn Ledford. At age thirty-two, she was the office manager of a large stockbrokerage branch in the Los Angeles area. She was single, secure and happy with her work and in her circle of friends. She enjoyed sporting events and concerts and the theater, she liked to jog and take classes and travel, she did volunteer work for such agencies as the YMCA and the Foundation for the Blind. Ten years on the West Coast had completely converted her to a California lifestyle. "I'm a totally different person," she said, "but my values are basically the same."

Once a year, she went back to Somerset and slipped comfortably into a way of life she remembered fondly. On one such trip, she talked about what it was in the return that gave her pleasure:

"Maybe it's the security, the knowing who everyone is and what they're really like and how they all fit together. Whatever it is, I love it. I tell my friends in California they wouldn't believe the good times we have. And we always had them, the good times—if our house was crowded, if we were poor by today's standards, we never thought about it then. I can come back now, and within two minutes I feel right at home. I've even thought I might want to move back sometime—but not really seriously. I've made a new life in California. All in all, it's a very full life, but it's fairly low-keyed and uncomplicated, and I like that. I've had ten years of being very independent, and I wouldn't want to give that up."

Judy thought of herself as "a combination of the old and the new." She was a women's rights advocate, but "not an activist, not a banner-waving type." She was also a Democrat who voted for Richard Nixon and lived to regret it. She had departed in many ways from the patterns of her family—and yet, she said, "I care very much for them, and I know I'll always be close to them. In the bigger family of my father's brothers and sisters and my grandparents, there isn't much closeness, and that's something I've always regretted. I can't really say I ever got to know any of them very well, and now I doubt if I'd recognize any of my cousins if they were to walk in that door. If it weren't for my grandparents, I doubt if any of these families would ever be in touch. My grandparents are remarkable people, but I was never close to them. I don't feel that I have a clear picture of what their lives have been like. As I get older I think about that, and I wish I knew more—but now it's really too late. That's sad, isn't it?"

A year and a day after Judy's birth on January 1, 1947, Becky Anne Ledford became the sixth of Carl and Gerry's children. As soon as she had finished high school and a one-year secretarial course in a vocational school, she went to the state capital and got a job as a secretary in the Kentucky Department of Human Resources. A dozen years later she still held that position, but her circumstances were changed. In 1977, she had married Richard Eversman, who worked in the same department, and Becky had given birth to a daughter. She would have preferred to quit her job and stay with the baby, but she and Richard wanted to buy a house, and it took two salaries to do that.

"It's the typical American story," Becky said. "We've got a mortgage, two cars, payments to make on appliances and other items, and it takes two salaries—in our case, about $23,000—to make ends meet. We can't save much. We take our lunch to work, because the cafeteria is too expensive. Day care for Melissa is another big expense. We might have to sell one of our cars. We don't go out much—mostly we visit our friends who have children, and play cards, or listen to the stereo, or watch TV. Rich plays golf and belongs to the Jaycees, and we go to the Christian Church—same church I grew up in—and about once a month we drive to Somerset to visit my family or up to Fort Thomas to see Rich's. We don't go on any big vacation trips. We're fortunate to have excellent health, so that's not an expense. Still, the money doesn't go very far, and inflation is making it harder and harder to get by."

In spite of their preoccupation with living expenses, Becky and Richard liked their jobs and their friends and their house, and they planned to stay in Frankfort. They were making progress, moving up, getting established, and they were optimistic about the future. They could be close to their families and still have a life of their own, and that combination felt just right to them.

The only one of Carl Ledford's eight sons to enter military service was Michael Brent, who joined the air force in 1970 at the age of twenty-one and subsequently decided to make a career of it. The war in Southeast Asia was winding down, when he enlisted, and he never was sent abroad. Instead, he served in Texas, Illinois, South Carolina, and finally at Dover Air Force Base in Delaware, where he rose to the rank of staff sergeant and headed a crew of aircraft mechanics working on the massive C-5 transport plane. He had married Jenny Vanhook of Somerset in 1971, and they and their two sons had begun to think of the small city of Dover as a permanent home. Michael liked the air force and his job and the comfortable life they had built there.

He also liked to visit in Somerset, and they came back about once a year. "I wonder sometimes how we made it with thirteen people in that little house," he said, "but we always seemed to have a good time together. I think maybe the secret was that my folks didn't have favorites—everybody was always treated equal."

He remembered the Sunday afternoon trips to Lancaster as a treat. "I loved going," he said. "Grandpa and Grandma Ledford always were amazing people, full of all kinds of good stories. The last time I went, Grandma recognized me and called me by name— even with my beard, she knew who I was. Grandpa always tells me, 'If I live through March, I'll live another year,' and he just keeps on going."

Next after Michael was Charles Robert Ledford—Charlie Bob to his family and friends. Of all the children, he was the one most interested in politics. As a state park employee after high school and then as a community college student, he had made a name for himself as a young Republican leader, and he had ambitions to go farther, perhaps even to run for office himself. But in 1975, six years after his graduation from high school, Charlie Bob had given up college and politics and moved to Lexington, where he answered a newspaper ad and got a job as an apprentice surveyor. After a period of drifting from job to job, he was ready "to learn a trade or get started in something and settle down."

In Lexington, he had expected to have plenty of activities to choose from and to be busy every night. Instead, he found himself alone most evenings, watching television "until it was driving me up the wall," and he was going home to Somerset almost every weekend. His father, seeing how lonely he was, reminded him that he had some Ledford kinfolks there who might like to see him. After much hesitation, Charlie Bob finally decided to call his late Uncle Bruce's only son, John Bruce. It turned out to be a fortunate decision:

"Now John Bruce is one of my closest friends. He invited me to come out to see him at his liquor store, and we talked for two or three hours that night, talked about the family and all—he had sort of gotten away from that. I went back to see him several times, and when he saw that I was hunting friends, he invited me to eat with his family, and took me to Jaycees with him, and even offered me a job. He really befriended me. Life with Bruce and his family is about the only life I have here, outside of my work. When I really needed a friend, he turned out to be the one person who reached out to me."

On one of his trips from Lexington to Somerset, Charlie Bob stopped in Lancaster to see his grandparents. Being there alone with them was different from being there in the homecoming crowd, and he stayed for a long and enjoyable conversation. Later, when his job as a surveyor involved him in the laying out of a new subdivision in Lexington, he was flipping through a dictionary, searching for words to use as street names (Snaffle, Nevus, Bamboo, Parasol), when suddenly an inspiration struck him. Charlie Bob thought of his aged grandparents—and he named the next street Ledford Court. "Daddy told Grandpa I named it after him," he said with a smile. "He was real proud of that."

The ninth of Carl and Gerry's children was David Arnold, born in 1953. An Eagle Scout like his eldest brother Eddie (and as his

two younger brothers would be later), he went to a national jam-
boree in New Mexico when he was fifteen—and discovered that traveling and seeing the country was a pleasure. But when he married
Cathy Dye in 1976 and a son soon came along to join them, David
found that travel was a luxury he couldn't afford. After high school
he had studied accounting for a year at the local community college,
and he hoped eventually to go on and get a degree, but first there
was a car and a house trailer and a TV set to make payments on, and
his job with a stone company in Somerset was all he had time for.

"I'm looking to be out of debt in five years," David said, "if we
don't get any more big bills on us. We bought this trailer when we
got married so we wouldn't have to pay rent, and then our son was
born and we didn't have any insurance. Inflation is eating up everything we make. Sometimes I wonder how middle-class people are
going to survive in this country. I don't worry much about it, though.
That's something I've learned from my parents—if you've got a
roof over your head and food on the table, you've got a lot to be
thankful for."

With his brothers and sisters David shared pleasant memories
of growing up. "My parents were always willing to listen, to discuss things," he said. "I never had any bad arguments with them.
We all felt wanted, felt like we belonged—and we still do. I think
that's why we still like to go home. Everybody in the family is a
little different, but we did a lot of things together, and we have a lot
in common. Most of us are Republicans, and we're all big University of Kentucky Wildcat fans—so we agree on the big things, and
that doesn't leave much to fight about."

Five years after David was born, Stephen Mark Ledford arrived,
and he was followed eleven months later by the last child, James
Martin Ledford. After high school, Steve went to Henry Watterson
College, a two-year technical school in Louisville, to prepare to be a
laboratory technician. When his turn came, James enrolled at
Somerset Community College and then transferred to the University of Kentucky to pursue a degree in business administration.

In Louisville, Steve visited occasionally with the families of his
older brothers, Eddie and Jerry. He had been to Harlan, too, had

listened to the stories of his grandparents, and was beginning to develop an interest in family history.

"I wasn't named for anyone in particular," he said, "but I've learned that there was a Stephen Ledford in our family way back in the last century. Grandpa told me about him. I went to Harlan once with a cousin on my mother's side of the family, and it surprised me to see Ledford names on the mailboxes. And then when I was in high school we played football against some schools from the mountains, and they had some players named Ledford, and they were all black. I told Grandpa about that, and he explained to me how the former slave families took the Ledford name when they got their freedom. I really don't know much at all about the family's history in Harlan County, but I'm curious about it. It's very interesting to me. I'd like to know a lot more than I do."

As the last in a long line, James turned out to be something of a political maverick, at least among Carl and Gerry's sons and daughters who remained in Kentucky. "I'm a registered Democrat," he boasted, "and if I had been old enough to vote in 1976, I'd have voted for Jimmy Carter." He took some good-natured ribbing from the others for his defection, but they finally forgave him, acknowledging that he was, after all, a good Scout, a faithful churchgoer, and a rabid Wildcat fan—and nobody's perfect.

Following the pattern of bestowing a nickname on every family member (Jerry was "Pop," Richard was "Butch," David was "Tex," and so on), they gave James the name "Bo"—and "Bo" was the good-humored "baby" of the clan. As he put it, "I'm the last child, the last grandchild, the last everything." When he was born, his Grandpa Ledford was eighty-three years old.

LUCILLE LEDFORD SMITH, the fifth-born of Burnam and Addie, and Harry Smith, her husband, spent their married life in Toledo; their only child, David Michael Smith, was born there in 1948. Of all the life histories of Burnam and Addie's thirty-three grandchildren, his is by all odds the most unusual and the most absorbing.

In subtle and ironic ways that he could only regard with won-

der and a quiet pride, David Smith was a product of two immi-
grant minorities, two wandering tribes: the Jews of Eastern Europe
and the mountaineers of Appalachia. By the time he was thirty
years old, he had gained an understanding and an appreciation of
that double heritage, and he saw many of its manifestations in his
own life. With candor and humor and keen insight, he told me
about himself, about where he had come from and where he had
been and where he was going.

My father didn't talk much about his family background, and
he died when I was only thirteen years old, so I grew up without
knowing much about his past. I always thought he had been born
in New York City in about 1896, but in recent years I have learned
differently. What I've discovered may not be accurate, and it certainly isn't complete, but it's more than I knew before.

He was born, as I understand it now, in Austria, an Austrian
Jew by the name of Herschel Pasternak, and he immigrated to this
country in about 1910, when he was fourteen years old. He didn't
change his name to Harry Smith—it wasn't an assimilation thing at
all. He just came through the line at Ellis Island, couldn't spell his
name in English, and the immigration official wrote down "Harry
Smith" and passed his papers on, to keep the line moving.

Whether his parents were with him or not, I don't know. I have
the vaguest recollection of a story about him wandering through
the South as a young boy, but I'm not at all sure it's true. I think he
lived in New York most of the time, worked in open-air produce
markets, and in the early 1930s he headed out west. He had a brother
named Joe who supposedly lived in Chicago—could have been a
half-brother, I'm not sure—and my dad got as far as Toledo, and he
must have decided he'd been separated from his family so long it
didn't matter to him any more, because he stopped there.

Toledo was a rough town in the Prohibition and Depression
years, and my dad was there in the midst of it, a rough-and-tumble
character in his thirties. By the time he met my mom in about 1938,
he was pretty well set up in the produce business. He had a friend
in the Teamsters Union who was married to one of my mom's friends

from Lancaster, and that's how they met. They were introduced in the fall and got married the next spring, and they worked together in the business until I was born nine years later. World War II had come and gone by then, and my mom was about thirty-five years old, and my dad was over fifty.

I remember a lot about him when I was growing up. He was a big man—not tall, but barrel-chested—and he was tough and shrewd, a wheeler-dealer. He was a vulgar man, in the best sense of that word—course, blunt, direct, honest. He was no stuffed shirt, no pompous ass. There was no facade about him. I can remember as a kid of four or five playing gin rummy with him and listening to "Gang Busters" on the radio, and I can remember going down to the warehouse in the summers, watching the activity, being a pest. I called him Papa, and I loved being with him, loved to listen to him trade on the telephone, buying and selling peppers by the thousands of bushels, making clever deals.

We lived on Prescott Avenue, in what is now referred to as the inner city of Toledo. My father was making big bucks, and we could have lived out in the suburbs, but he wanted to be pretty close to the warehouse, so we lived there in the old Jewish section of the city, two blocks from the synagogue where I went to school—B'nai Jacob, Children of Jacob.

I never saw my father inside a synagogue, but he was an Orthodox Jew, and he made sure I was too. By definition, by Talmudic law, the religion of the mother is normally the religion of the child, but that wasn't true in my family; Papa was Jewish, so I was too. I don't mean Jewish in a gastronomic sense—you know, lox and bagels and cream cheese and kosher foods—but in an ethnic and religious sense. Unfortunately for a lot of Jews in America, synagogues are for the kids, and that's the way it was for me. My father didn't go to synagogue and my mother didn't go to church, but he was the dominant figure, so I was raised the way he had been raised. The only time I remember him giving in to her was when she insisted I join the nearest Boy Scout troop, which happened to be in a Baptist Church.

So I went to the synagogue school until it closed when I was in the third grade, and then I went to the neighborhood public school, which was still heavily Jewish. English was almost a second language there, as it was in the synagogue and the neighborhood. I grew up with Yiddish and Hebrew, with survivors of the Holocaust, with first-generation immigrant Jews—and more and more with blacks who were following the Jews in another migration, out of the inner city and toward the west end of Toledo. I learned to speak Hebrew, of course—but unfortunately, about all I retain now are what I thought of as the rote prayers, like the Hebrew version of "Hear, O Israel, the Lord is One, the Lord thy God is One." I'd be hard-pressed to read or extemporize in Hebrew any more.

I kept going to Hebrew school even after I entered public school, but as I got older, I felt a lot of confusion and conflict, and my own assimilation, like my father's, was fairly complex. The first time a Jewish boy finds out he's Jewish is when he encounters Gentiles in the shower room—that was a rather typical and visible distinction in the 1950s, anyway. It took me a while to figure that one out, but slowly I began to understand. Then when I was thirteen and into the whole puberty scene, my father was sick and dying, and I didn't have a Bar Mitzvah. He died in September of 1962 without ever making contact with his brother or anyone in his family, and for several years after he was gone, I had quite a bit of disaffection from Judaism.

During the years when I was learning through my father's influence to be a Jew, I was also learning that the only extended family I had was on my mother's side, and that was a very different heritage. Several of my aunts—Dorothy, Jennie, Tillie—came to stay with us, and my Uncle Bruce lived with us from about 1954 until my father's death, and we went to Lancaster to see my grandparents at least once a year. I had first cousins, too, a whole slew of them, but I probably couldn't name more than ten of them now, and I wouldn't recognize that many if I saw them. One thing I do remember: an old photograph of Mary Ellen Beatty and me sitting on Dixie, a horse that belonged to Grandpa.

I got to know my Aunt Dorothy and some of the others pretty well, and of course I knew Uncle Bruce very well. He wasn't what you'd call an ideal role model for a kid, but I liked him. But my grandparents I remember best of all. Grandpa was past seventy when I was born. That's the age when most people are quitting, but he was a very spry old gentleman until the last few years, still raising tobacco and working every day. His birthday and Thanksgiving were the big occasions when the family gathered, and we were usually there. Once when he was up in his eighties, all the sons were there except maybe Bruce, and they put bottles and cans up on the fence out in back of the house, and took turns shooting at them with a pistol; Grandpa did pretty well, as I remember it. Another time, when I was about ten, Grandma made a huge blackberry cobbler in what looked like about a ten-gallon pan, big as a piano. It was the best thing I ever tasted, and there was enough for everybody, even seconds. I can still see Grandma ladling it out.

Those were happy times for me, and I remember the warmth of that household, and what I recognize now as a sense of history in it. My grandfather always struck me as an oral-history treasure. He remembered what people said and how they felt and what they did. He was the Chicken George of Central Kentucky. By contrast, Grandma was more in possession of factual knowledge and formal history—she knew names and dates, facts. With the two of them, especially as they got older, there was a little bit of antipathy whenever the folk knowledge and the formal knowledge were in conflict. They have clashed, and it hasn't always been easy for them, but I think they've gotten along pretty well. Seventy-five years of living together has got to be more than just habit. Whatever their troubles may have been, they've given us all some pretty happy times, and some sterling examples of good, basic moral values that you don't see much any more. I don't guess you could say those values have been passed down to the next generations without modification, but I think we've all salvaged something from them. There may be skeletons rattling all over that old house of theirs, but to me, it's the source of some of my most pleasant memories.

I remember particularly the trip I made to Harlan with Grandpa in about 1965, after I was out of high school. I had never been there before, and all I knew about eastern Kentucky was what I had learned from reading Jesse Stuart. My mother and I drove to Lancaster, and several of her sisters were there, and we all decided to go to Harlan. There were too many of us for one car, so all of the women rode together and Grandpa and I went alone.

There were no freeways then, and all I had to guide me was a Standard Oil map and Grandpa, who steered by dead reckoning. He'd say, "Look for a dirt road off to the right just past the next store," and the store might be gone, but the road would be there, and we'd take it, and we never got lost once. He hadn't been there for years, but he knew, he recognized—he was nearly ninety years old, but he remembered. We had a lovely three days, went to a big reunion and a fiftieth wedding anniversary celebration for somebody named Ledford, and he was pleased that the folks were as he remembered them—the ones who were still alive—and the places looked the same. It was the first time I fully grasped that they had migrated out of the mountains the same way his great-grandfather had migrated in, riding mules and wagons on mud roads. I felt like we were in a Conestoga wagon instead of a Plymouth Valiant— and the dust and tobacco juice on the side of the car added to the feeling.

That trip showed me how old Grandpa was—but also how young he was. When we got to Harlan, we stopped at a hotel in town to wait for the women. I went to the restroom, and when I started back, I heard a funny little noise: *tap-shuffle-shuffle, tap-shuffle-shuffle.* I looked in the lobby, and there was Grandpa with this very gorgeous young hotel receptionist, showing her how to dance, turning on the charm. She was all smiles, and I smiled too, and thought to myself: *Heredity is on my side.*

I was just sixteen years old then, but I had started school young and skipped a year, so I was out of high school, and I was in the middle of some big changes in my life. It was hard for me to figure out what I was, or who I was. Was I strictly Jewish, the way my father had raised me, or informally Jewish according to certain moralistic teachings, the way he was, or not Jewish at all? I thought I was a political liberal, too—it was a very idealistic time in America, the Kennedy years—but then President Kennedy was killed, and that affected me very much. I went to Toledo University for a year and lived at home with my mother, but I was too young for college, and I got into academic difficulty. I transferred to Defiance College next—a small Protestant school where there were maybe thirty Jews on campus—and I got back into a heavy Jewish consciousness for a while, but that didn't work either, so finally I dropped out.

The Vietnam War was in full cry then, and I was going to be drafted, so I volunteered for the draft. At Fort Benning, Georgia, I tried to keep kosher. I was an oddity, a Jewish boy named Smith, and people would say to me, "You don't look Jewish." My stock answer was, "That's easy to explain: half those genes came from Harlan County, Kentucky." I had been in ROTC, and in the Pershing Rifles, a hawkish, right-wing kind of outfit, and my attitude about the war was, "better me than some guy with a wife and four kids." I may have had grave doubts about the validity of the war, but it was there, and people were going to fight it, so I went with them. It almost broke my mother's heart. She was against the war, not for political reasons but because it was hitting home. I was a small-arms rifleman with backup training as a finance clerk, and when I went to Vietnam with the Fifth Infantry Division, I didn't even tell my mom I was in the infantry. She didn't need that to worry about.

Vietnam was a strange war—no front lines, no real sanctuaries. It was a very insecure place. For about a month and a half I went out on patrols, and we got into fire fights, people were shooting at us and we were shooting at them—I guess that's combat. Then I spent some time in a field hospital with a kidney infection, and after that I was reassigned to a finance unit. But there were rocket attacks when I was in the hospital, and we got rocketed at the base camp where I was finance clerk, so you couldn't really say where the war was, or what combat was. It was everywhere. You can't talk about Vietnam like any other war. I don't like to talk about it at all.

When I got back to Defiance in 1970, all I wanted to do was get my degree in music. I had been interested in music since grade school—clarinet, then oboe. I wanted to be a symphonic musician with the oboe, and that's what I worked toward, and it was all I wanted to be involved in. I didn't want to talk about the war or religion or politics. Religiously, I was an agnostic; politically, I was apolitical, just barely interested enough to vote. I half-heartedly voted for McGovern in 1972 because he was running against Nixon, and that was enough for me. The big confrontation between students and National Guardsmen at Kent State happened the year I got back from Vietnam, and there was a memorial ceremony at Defiance, as there was on most campuses, but I wasn't interested. I watched the people march past, and then I just went on about my business—went to a piano lesson.

In 1971 I finished my degree and got a job teaching high school music. By then I had left Judaism behind me—it was part of my past, but not part of my future. When I was a senior I had met Mary Emmitt, a freshman. Her father was an elementary school principal in a little town just outside Akron. They belonged to the United Church of Christ, the church that Defiance was affiliated with, the church that had sponsored the missionary school my grandmother had gone to back in Harlan County. Mary was four years younger than me. Just the warmth, the tranquility, were what I wanted and needed. We got married in 1972, and had a little girl, Amanda, in 1975, and now we're expecting another baby.

The year we got married, I moved to another school in a small farming community south of Toledo, taught instrumental music in grades five through twelve. After three years of that, of working day and night, raising money for uniforms, giving speeches, promoting, dealing with parents, I decided that wasn't what I wanted to do. If I could get into the army music system, I could do all the good things in teaching and not have the bad things to deal with. You don't have to raise money for uniforms in the army—they've got lots of them.

So I went back in the service as a private, started over, and in three years I worked my way back up to staff sergeant. They sent me to Germany, where I worked in communications and training and got a short stint with the army band in Stuttgart. Now I've got a new assignment at the Naval School of Music in Norfolk, Virginia. I'm hoping to be put on instructor status or promoted to warrant officer and made a bandmaster. If it all works out, I'll stay until I can retire.

And now here I am, your average cocktail-circuit liberal. I voted for Jimmy Carter. I think the ideals of the civil rights movement are just grand, though I have to admit that sometimes the carrying out of those ideals bothers me. I guess I'm an optimist, a skeptical optimist. I'm like my father, trying to live by a set of moral values rather than by a formal creed. Maybe I haven't changed so much after all. I still like to see my mother, and to visit my grandparents, though I don't get to do that very often. I hope they can live out their lives the way they want to, and die peacefully at the old homestead. I don't know how practical that is, or how possible, but I know they'd be happiest that way, and that's what I wish for them.

Everybody should be lucky enough to have a heritage as rich as mine.

FIFTEEN

The Scattered Seed

More Grands and Great-Grands

Six of Burnam and Addie's ten adult children and two-thirds of their grandchildren had lived most of their lives in Kentucky, and in 1978 only two members of the second generation, nine in the third, and eight in the fourth were permanently settled away from the state. As it had been for nearly two centuries, Kentucky remained the dominant geographical influence on the family. But even among those who had never moved away, there were differences of education and occupation and income, differences of perception and belief, that made them stand out one from another. They may have been more like one another than like their out-of-state brothers and sisters and cousins, but geographical proximity by itself was not enough to make them seem all the same.

The youngest five of the Ledford children—Herb, Bruce, Jennie, Tillie, and Gwen—had given Burnam and Addie a total of fifteen grandchildren. All but three of them had married by 1978, and among them they had sixteen children, bringing the number of the elder Ledfords' great-grandchildren to thirty-nine (see chart, page 354). Only three of those grandchildren and only two of the great-grandchildren lived outside Kentucky, but where they lived seldom seemed to be a major factor in the shaping of their lives. As I interviewed them, I saw signs of diversity and variety and change that had somehow taken root and blossomed, even within the same household—and signs of similarity and continuity that transcended the miles and the years that separated them.

HERB AND HAZEL LEDFORD'S four daughters grew up right across the street from their high school in Somerset, and the Methodist Church was not far away. Those three places—home, school, church—were the reference points around which their lives turned. Jane and Alice were born about a year and a half apart in the mid-1940s, and they carried on a lively and sometimes abrasive competition throughout their teenage years. Then, in the mid-1950s, Emily and Sarah came along within a year and a half of each other, and the pattern of competitive involvement and conflict was repeated.

Jane was one of six Ledford grandchildren to be born in 1944. She knew some of her first cousins in high school and others at the University of Kentucky, where she entered in 1962, but no lifelong friendships developed from those associations. Before she transferred after two years to Union College in Barbourville, Kentucky, Jane had met Ronald Shelton, a senior in mechanical engineering; the following year, she quit college to marry him.

Over the next decade, they lived in Alabama, New York, Michigan, and Florida as Ron moved through a succession of jobs in the aerospace industry. His work in thermodynamics involved him in the space exploration program, and Ron and Jane were close enough to the Apollo moon missions to take a special pride in them. In 1974, when the space program had peaked, Ron entered graduate school at the University of Florida. Two years later, he and Jane settled in Oak Ridge, Tennessee, where his new work involved designing heating and air conditioning systems and making energy conservation studies.

At age thirty-four, Jane Ledford Shelton's life was pleasant and comfortable and relatively uncomplicated. With no children and no job outside her home, she had time to pursue her own interests—music, books, tennis, travel. After years of living in apartments they had bought their first house in Oak Ridge, and Jane had taken pleasure in decorating it. They had gone on vacation trips to Europe and the Caribbean. They drove to Kentucky occasionally to visit their parents, and every May they went to the Ledford homecoming in Lancaster, where Ron and Jane both enjoyed visiting with her relatives, particularly her grandparents. And when she and her sisters went back to Somerset to see her parents, it pleased her to find that "we get along a lot better now than we did when we were kids."

Alice King Ledford (the King in honor of her Grandma Ledford's maiden name) had given her older sister plenty of challenging competition; she was a versatile and talented musician, an excellent student, a band majorette in high school, president of her sorority in college. The year she got to the University of Kentucky, Jane transferred out, and it was not until they were both married and secure in their separate pursuits that they were able to enjoy each other's company.

Alice graduated from the university with a major in music in 1968, and a year later she married Robert Frields, whom she had met when he was a student in mechanical engineering. He was a Catholic, and their wedding in the Catholic Church in Somerset was unsettling to her parents, though they soon got over it. Alice and Bob moved to his hometown of Henderson in western Kentucky, where he went to work for an insulation company. Within a few years, he had started his own insulation business and designed and built a new home for them.

Their only child, Elaine—Herb and Hazel's only grandchild—was born in 1970. Alice had been teaching school before that, but then she started giving private piano lessons at home. She once had been a church organist, but she no longer went to church, though Bob and Elaine went regularly to Catholic mass. Her interest in Republican politics had also diminished. "We don't vote," she explained, "and we don't complain about the government." Their main activity outside of work was sports, particularly water sports; Bob had two speed boats, and he raced them competitively.

Except at the homecoming, Alice never saw her grandparents or any of her aunts and uncles and cousins.

Emily, the next sister, "joined everything" in her turn at the University of Kentucky, as Jane and Alice had, but instead of music she pursued a political science degree and went on into law school, graduating in 1977. She belonged to the conservative "new wave" that followed the protest era of the late 1960s, and she missed by a few votes being elected vice president of the university student government.

In the last semester of her senior year she met Thomas Lawrence, who was in business administration, and they went together while he worked for a group of Kentucky banks and she attended law school. They were married the summer before she graduated. Tom joined the First National Bank in Louisville; Emily took a job with a firm that operated a storefront law clinic in the heart of the city for low-income and working-class people.

She remained a Republican and a conservative, but her experiences as a woman and a lawyer made her a believer in the ideal of equality, and she took pride in her ability to work easily with all kinds of people. "I learned growing up that I was as good as anybody, that I ought to approach people as an equal," she said, "and that's what I do now—whether they're poor or rich, white or black."

Emily and Tom liked Louisville—it was, she said, "just a grown-up country town, just another Somerset on a bigger scale." Her parents came to visit them, but they went to Somerset only on special occasions, and to Lancaster only on homecoming day. Her grandparents had always seemed old to her. She remembered stopping to see them once on her way from Lexington to Lancaster. "I had my overalls on," Emily recalled, "and later, Grandma told Mother if I couldn't afford a dress or a skirt, she'd buy some for me."

Sarah Ledford, the last of Herb and Hazel's girls, followed along in the busy pattern of school and church activities set by her sisters. She even shared Jane's and Alice's interest in music. But by the time she was ready for college, it didn't suit her to follow them to the University of Kentucky; she wanted to go "someplace where I wouldn't have to be 'little sister' for a change."

At William Woods College in Fulton, Missouri, she joined a sorority, served as president of the campus Republican club, took an active part in music and theater groups, even got engaged—but when she graduated a semester early in December 1977, she had put aside all her interests, romantic and otherwise, in favor of her first love: horses.

She had studied to become an equestrian instructor, and directly from college she was hired by the Rock Creek Riding Club, a sixty-year-old private club on the edge of Seneca Park in Louisville. "The hours are long and the pay isn't very good," she said, "but I love it. I'd rather do this for fifteen hours a day than sit in an office for eight." She had a new romantic interest, too—Robert Byers, a fellow instructor at the club—but she no longer had time for music or politics.

Sarah's parents came to visit her often, and took an interest with her in horses and horse shows. She saw her sisters occasionally, and the other Ledfords once a year "or less." On the rare occasions when she saw her grandparents, "Grandpa always tells me about the horses he used to have, and I think somebody else way back—his grandfather, maybe—also raised horses. I enjoy listening to his stories."

BRUCE AND ANITA LEDFORD'S two children, John Bruce and Mary Helen, were seven and five years old when their parents divorced in 1949. They never had seen much of their father, and after that they saw him even less—so little that when he died in 1969, they hardly knew him at all. They lived in Somerset with their mother until 1958, when she and they moved to Lexington.

John Bruce graduated from a Catholic high school there and then went briefly to the University of Kentucky before he decided to become a mortician. After a period of training, he spent several years as a funeral director in four widely separated Kentucky towns. In 1963 he married Brenda Jane Brown of Lexington, and the first of their four children, John Bruce II, was born a year later.

In 1973, John Bruce and Brenda became the owners and managers of a liquor store on Limestone Street in inner-city Lexington. His father had died an alcoholic, but John Bruce was not like his father; he was, in fact, "more like Grandpa, who always said he never touched the stuff. I seldom take a drink—not even once a month." As a retail merchant, he was following in the tradition of his father and grandfather, but they had not taught him to be a storekeeper; he had learned that strictly on his own, working from the time he was eleven years old.

Growing up without his father, and without close ties to anyone else in the Ledford family, John Bruce thought of his recent friendship with Charlie Bob, one of Carl's sons, as his only Ledford association worth mentioning. "I don't feel any special attachment to the others," he said, "except my grandparents. I don't see them very much—not as much as I should—but I think they're fantastic old people, just full of love for everyone, and I admire them a great deal. They're understanding and forgiving people who don't hold grudges, and they're wonderful storytellers too. One of the things I admire so much about them is that they always seemed to accept their children and grandchildren for what they were, good or bad. They haven't favored some and rejected the rest. We're all very different, but I think they've tried very hard to treat us all the same."

Mary Helen—or Dolly, as everyone called John Bruce's sister—also graduated from a Catholic high school in Lexington, and then went to work as a secretary at the University of Kentucky. A few years later, she married Larry Casey of Lexington—not an Irish Catholic, but a Kentucky Baptist—and they had a son and a daughter in the late 1960s.

A little later, Dolly went back to work in the university's college of medicine, and then she became administrative assistant to the director of a demonstration project for health-care delivery in Appalachia. Then, in 1975, when she was thirty-one years old, she enrolled as a freshman at the university and put her energies into intensive pursuit of a degree in accounting.

"I guess the reason I did it goes back to growing up without a father," she said later, "and wondering what would happen if I had to take care of myself. I watched my mother support us on a very meager salary, and I'm not willing to be that vulnerable." Larry Casey worked for a greeting card company, and Dolly wanted to work too. "I like to work," she said. "I'm not your average Suzie Homemaker."

She could "count on one hand" the memories she had of her father, and she was not especially close to her mother or her brother. The other Ledfords were hardly known to her at all. She and her children were active parishioners in the Catholic Church, and Dolly

was a Democrat, one of the family's few. She thought of her grandparents often, and went to see them occasionally, because it gave
her a family relationship that had been missing from her life.
"They've always made me feel very welcome," she said. "They're
not overly affectionate, but that's nothing personal—this never was
a family of big touchers and huggers. I don't feel any strong need or
desire to be close to the rest of the family, but I do think it's important for me to have a good relationship with my grandparents, and
even though my children don't feel very close to them, I at least
want them to understand the connection."

JENNIE LEDFORD'S conflict-torn marriage to Revis Mills lasted for a
decade before it finally fell apart in 1951. She had spent a large
part of the time away from him, living at her parents' home in
Lancaster, and it was there in Burnam and Addie's antique Lincoln
bed that Jennie's first two children were born—Bruce Burnam in
1942 and Nancy in 1944. She had a third child, Arletta, in a Danville
hospital in 1945.

From infancy, Nancy lived with her father's parents in Danville,
but Bruce and Arletta and their mother remained in the Ledford
household until 1951, when they moved first to Toledo (where sister Lucille lived) and then to Indianapolis. When Jennie and Arletta
left there in 1959 to return to Lancaster, Bruce stayed behind, living with his Aunt Tillie and her family until he finished high school
a year later. Arletta lived with her grandparents until she graduated
from high school and got married in 1964.

Having spent the first nine years of his life in Lancaster—and
almost every summer after that until he was out of school and on
his own—Bruce Mills looked upon the elder Ledfords as "more
like parents than grandparents to me." They were the only island
of stability in his young life, and years later he retained a special
fondness for them.

Bruce worked for the post office and went to college in Indiana
after high school. He entered the army in 1964, serving as a medic
in Japan during the Vietnam War. When he returned to the United
States, he left the service on the West Coast and stayed there, mov-

ing through a variety of jobs to become a laboratory technician for the Shell Oil Company.

Over the years, Bruce managed to reestablish contact with his mother back in Kentucky and with his father, who had settled in California. With his grandparents in Lancaster, though, no renewal of ties was necessary; the mutual affection had always been there, and it remained. He didn't see them often, but he kept in touch through the mail and on the phone. They were the first and most important elders in his life.

Nancy Mills saw little of her mother or her brother and sister when she was growing up, except on occasional visits in Lancaster; she lived with her father's parents and then with one of his sisters, and it was they who provided the same sort of safe harbor that Bruce and Arletta found in Burnam and Addie.

Right after high school in 1962, Nancy married Larry Allen, a Danville automobile dealer's son who was three years older than she, and in a year she had given birth to a daughter, Kimberly. In 1967, after Larry had completed a degree in accounting, they moved into a northern Kentucky suburb of Cincinnati and Nancy began studying to become a registered nurse. Ten years later they were comfortably settled suburbanites in a big old house on a quiet and shady street. Larry had advanced steadily in business and had time to enjoy his interest in flying; Nancy, after working for a few years as a nurse at Jewish Hospital in Cincinnati, had quit in order to devote more time to her family and a variety of community interests; and Kim, the second-oldest of the Ledford great-grandchildren, was a typically active teenager.

In the late 1970s, Nancy made an effort to establish better ties with her mother, with Bruce and Arletta, and with her Ledford grandparents. When her father had a heart attack in California, she went to spend three weeks with him. As she grew older, family relationships seemed more important to her. She particularly wanted Kim to know Grandpa and Grandma, "because they're really what makes us a family." Once Kim had taken her tape recorder on a visit to them, and it pleased Nancy to see how interested she was in their stories.

"Then, just the other night," she said, "we watched *Little Big Man* on television, and it made us think about Grandpa and his storytelling. They're such great people, he and Grandma. I don't think any of us are as strong as they are."

Arletta, like Bruce, had always had a special closeness to her Ledford grandparents. She had lived with them until she was six, and again for five years when she was a teenager. She had married then, and eventually had followed her husband, a neighborhood farmer's son, to a new home in Colorado and a succession of upward moves with IBM. But almost every year they returned to Kentucky to see their families—including, of course, the elder Ledfords.

She called them Papa and Mama, "because they raised me." Their house, in her remembrance, seemed always to be full of people: "Besides Mother and Bruce and me, others lived there from time to time—Tillie and her children were there some, and Mama's half-sisters from California and Oregon came to visit in the summers, and so did Aunt Eloise and Aunt Lucille. Papa had a brother, Uncle Noble, who lived for several years in a trailer right out beside the driveway. And then there was Kelly Ledford. He just showed up at the door one day, convinced Papa they were some kind of kin, and kind-hearted Papa let him move in. He stayed for at least a year or two. Mama couldn't stand him, but Papa forgave him all his shortcomings—he had plenty—until Kelly got into so much trouble that Papa finally lost his patience and called the police to come and get him."

They helped Arletta with her school work, and she helped them around the house and in the garden. She went to the Presbyterian Church with her grandfather. When she started dating Donald Bourne, who lived on a farm just a mile or two away, they overlooked the fact that he was a Baptist and a Democrat and approved of him because they knew and liked his father and grandfather.

She and Don were married in 1964, and though neither of them went to college, they advanced steadily in their work, he in IBM's engineering division, she in management with the telephone company. They had a son in 1969, moved to Colorado four years later, then had a daughter in 1977, and by then Arletta had decided against continuing her outside job.

Through the years she had stayed on good terms with her mother, but it was her grandparents to whom she felt indebted. "I can look back on my life and be truly thankful for them," she said. "They steered me in the right direction, taught me right from wrong, taught me that material things are not as important as honesty and pride. They've always been there when we needed them, always welcomed us without question or criticism, never turned any of us away. They've meant the world to me, more than anybody. If I could do anything to help them, I wouldn't hesitate."

TILLIE LEDFORD'S two children—a son born in her first marriage and a daughter in her second—spent much of their early lives in Lancaster. Gary was born in Toledo in 1945. His parents separated soon after that, and he and his mother moved in with Burnam and Addie, joining Jennie and Bruce and Arletta there. Gary remained there most of the time until he was eleven. His mother was remarried and had another child by then—Barbara Jo, born in Danville in 1949—and even though Gary eventually finished high school in Indianapolis, he and Bobbie Jo lived much of the time in Lancaster.

Gary remembered his grandparents as busy and active people who seemed younger than they actually were. His grandfather worked in the hardware store and in the garden, and he read a great deal. Gary, who was nearsighted, developed his own thirst for books. "I took up reading with him," he recalled. "Maybe every kid should be nearsighted until about fourth grade, so he'll learn to read before anything else. It's a habit I've kept, and I owe that to Grandpa. I still love to read history."

After high school Gary returned to Kentucky. At the state university in Richmond he met Phyllis Ann Kash and married her in 1966. Their only child, Bryan, was born the following year, soon after Gary had quit school and moved back to Indianapolis to work for the Chrysler Corporation. Phyllis didn't like Indianapolis, and Gary lost the index finger of his left hand in a dye-press accident; in 1969, on the spur of the moment, they packed up and moved to Lexington. Ten years later they were still there, and Gary was doing well with his own business, a diesel truck repair shop.

His principal leisure-time activity was drag racing, and he often towed his souped-up 1969 Chevrolet Chevelle station wagon to the tracks in Atlanta and Darlington and Bristol. Occasionally he won a little purse money. Phyllis was a student at the University of Kentucky, preparing to teach elementary education. Bryan was a first-rate Little League baseball player. They stayed busy. Gary was aware that as the years had passed, he had drifted away from his grandparents. "I don't go to see them as often as I used to," he said. "It seems like I just don't take the time. I feel bad about it. I look up to them more than anyone I've ever known. I'm pretty close to my mother and my sister now—but I'll always feel something special for Grandpa and Grandma."

Bobbie Jo also felt a deep affection for Burnam and Addie, having spent her pre-school and high school years in their house. She finished high school in Lancaster in 1967 and went to work for the telephone company as an operator. She met Michael Bryant of Berea that year, and they got married in 1969. They lived in Virginia for a year while Mike was in the navy, and then they returned to live and work in central Kentucky. Their son, Casey, was born in 1975.

With Mike working as a lineman for the local electrical utility and Bobbie Jo getting regular raises at the telephone company, they were able to buy a comfortable brick home on the edge of Richmond. In the meantime, Tillie had divorced Bobbie Jo's father, returned to Indianapolis, and married and divorced the same man twice. It was Burnam and Addie's sanctuary for Gary and Bobbie Jo that made it possible for them to sustain a good relationship with their mother through all the turbulent years of her marriages. When Tillie finally returned in 1978 to live with and look after her parents, one of the benefits of that change was the opportunity it gave her to be closer to her children and grandchildren.

Bobbie Jo enjoyed that too; she and her mother got along well. But Bobbie Jo looked back on her childhood with particular appreciation for her grandparents, who had been "the same as parents" to her. She went to see them often, not out of a sense of duty but because she felt welcome there, felt at home and at ease and secure in their company.

GWEN AND RUSSELL GASTINEAU'S four children had all stayed close to their roots, like their parents and grandparents before them.

Carole, the oldest, was thirty in 1978. She had gone to the university in Richmond for a year after high school, hoping to become a nurse, but then she had settled for a job as a technician and aide at the hospital in Lancaster.

One day Paul Starnes, a high school classmate and casual acquaintance of Carole's, entered the hospital suffering from a severe viral infection. She helped to nurse him back to health and eventually she married him. Paul was from a farm family near Paint Lick; he was also a student at Eastern Kentucky University and a radio dispatcher for the Kentucky State Police. He went into the army in 1968, got engaged to Carole just before he left for Vietnam, and then married her three days after he came home in 1970.

They lived for a year in Carlisle, Pennsylvania, where Paul served out his last year of military duty. Then, returning to central Kentucky, they moved into an aged white frame house on the old road between Berea and Richmond, the narrow trail that once had been part of Boone's Wilderness Road. Paul landed a good job as a quality control specialist for a wire and cable company in Richmond, and they enjoyed being back in the same area as their parents.

In 1974, Carole gave birth to twin boys, but they had died hours before the delivery as a result of a sudden and unexpected medical problem that the doctors were at a loss to explain. Carole and Paul were deeply grieved by the loss. Two years later they had a son, Steven Paul, and his presence helped to fill the void.

David Gastineau, Carole's twenty-eight-year-old brother, was married to Brenda Renfro two years after he graduated from high school in Lancaster in 1968. He was called twice to be examined for military service, but failed the physical exam both times because of low blood pressure. "I wasn't a draft dodger in the sense that I did anything illegal," he said, "but if I had been called up, I think I might have gone to Canada. Some of the guys I worked with did—and stayed, even after they were given amnesty. One of my closest friends got killed in Vietnam. It was such a waste, so unnecessary. That war was a damn shame—all it did was thin out the population and keep the economy up. And we never tried to win the war anyway—it was just a circus we were holding over there."

In the first decade after high school, David was a farmer, a factory worker (Square D, Goodyear), a student, a musician, and a solitary tinkerer in his back-yard garage, where he often worked on an old school bus and dreamed of taking it on cross-country trips. He liked working alone, making things, "fooling around with ideas." He was fascinated by the space program, and fully expected to see people going to other planets to live during his lifetime; he even thought he'd like to go himself.

David and Brenda had two young sons. Their home "and an acre or two of land" was on the road between Paint Lick and Berea. He worked some crops with his father and brother and got along well enough with everyone in his family, but he was an individual. "It's hard to figure out what I am," he said. "I've just got different ideas. I hardly ever watch TV, not even football games. I love to be outdoors, but I don't like to hunt or fish. The only politician I ever worked to elect was Richard Nixon. I can't really say why I liked him—I just did. He'd probably think I was a long-haired hippie."

For as long as he could remember, his Ledford grandparents had seemed old but very active to David. He thought of his eighty-year-old Grandpa working his garden with an old-fashioned, long-handled hoe, and his Grandma keeping lush beds of flowers all along the driveway. David didn't see them much any more.

Richard, the third of the Gastineaus, was three years younger than David. He had gone to the University of Kentucky after high school to study dairy science, but had dropped out after a year because he thought "I'd have to leave this community to make a living, and I didn't want to live and work in Ohio or Pennsylvania or someplace away from here." In 1972 he married Adrienne Parson, whom he had known throughout his school years in Garrard County, and they had a daughter in 1974.

On his parents' farm north of Lancaster, Richard had built a brick home, and he helped his father with the tobacco crop. He also worked on the maintenance crew at a Danville factory that made conveyor belts for airports and warehouses. Like his father, he was a Baptist and a Democrat—but like his mother and his grand-parents, he had voted in 1972 for President Nixon. Richard, like David, seldom went to see his grandparents.

The last child was Rebecca Ann Gastineau; she was only a month older than Carl Ledford's son James, the youngest of Burnam and Addie's grandchildren. Becky was a freshman at Eastern Kentucky University in Richmond. Like her older sister, she wanted to be a registered nurse and work in a hospital somewhere in central Kentucky.

With her mother, Becky went often to the home of her grand-parents. She had an easy, comfortable manner with them, and they enjoyed her visits. Of all their grandchildren, Becky was the one they saw the most of in the last part of the 1970s. She was eighty-three years younger than her grandfather and seventy-five younger than her grandmother, but the years were no barrier between them.

Almost all of the adult members of the Ledford family had contributed to the twentieth-century continuation of Burnam and Addie's story. One by one, they had searched their recollections and told me as much as they cared to have known about themselves and their family. Some remembered more than others; some were more detailed or more descriptive in what they told; some were better storytellers, and some had more to tell. Collectively and selectively, they had recorded a lengthy account of one family's passage through a century of American life. It was not a complete record, not an exhaustive and comprehensive rendering; some memories were too personal, some thoughts too private, perhaps too painful. In that respect, the Ledfords were not unlike any other family. The most virtuous of people, or even the dullest, can rarely tell with complete candor all that they have known and experienced, not until time or distance or death allows the whole truth to emerge—and even then, some of the story may remain a secret. Those who are closest to any family, any group, invariably find yesterday's scandals and skeletons and tragedies easier to discuss than today's.

But in all that they had chosen to tell, the Ledfords had assembled a chronicle of personal joys and sorrows, of gains and losses, that could be read as a representative story of middle-class life in the United States. In the vast arena of the national society in which they held their small place, they seemed to me to be fairly characteristic of the majority of citizens—neither rich nor poor, powerful nor powerless, famous nor completely unknown. As a group, they tended to be observers rather than participants, spectators rather than players. The family's interest in politics and sports was intense, but no politician or athlete or entertainer or preacher or other public figure had risen from their midst. To the major events and issues of the mid-twentieth century—armed conflict, technological revolution, human rights movements—the Ledfords had responded with ambivalence. Some had gone willingly to war, others had not; some had identified with space exploration, others had ignored it; some had agreed with the efforts of various minority groups to attain equality in American society, others had been indifferent or hostile to those efforts; some had responded emotionally to political assassinations and presidential scandals and mass public protests, others had been unmoved by them. They were reactors to change, not generators of it, and in that fundamental way they were very much like the majority of us.

The story of the Ledfords had begun with the living, with Burnam and Addie. It had gone as far into the past as their memories could reach, and as far forward as their descendants could be counted. Raising a family, Burnam often said, was like farming—a process of preparation and planting and cultivating and harvesting. He and Addie had sown a lifetime of seeds, and they had taken root and spread and borne their fruit in abundance and variety, perpetuating themselves in new generations of birth and growth.

SIXTEEN

Harlan One More Time

"I haven't been to Harlan in ten or fifteen years," Burnam said. "I reckon the last time I went was when David Smith, one of my grandsons, took me. They had a big Ledford-Skidmore homecoming there—used to have it every year—and I wanted to go. David had just graduated from high school up in Toledo, and he drove down here in a new car to see us, and we decided to go to the reunion. He never had been to Harlan. We had a big time—stayed all night with a cousin of mine in Pennington Gap, then went to Cawood for preaching, then went to the homecoming in Harlan Town. There must have been three or four hundred people there, and I was the oldest one. We stayed all day, just made a big day of it. I introduced David to all his kinfolks."

His remembrance of the journey differed somewhat from David's, but no matter; Burnam blended more than one Harlan homecoming in his thoughts, and all of them gave him pleasure. He paused for a minute, turning the experiences over in his mind. Then he began to laugh.

"They gave a prize for the oldest person there," he went on, "and of course I got it—a big three-pound box of candy."

"Don't you tell that story, Burnam," Addie warned, frowning at the prospect.

"When I got home," he continued, "Addie asked me where the candy came from, and I told her, 'They gave it to me as a prize.' She asked what for, and I said, 'For being the best-looking man there.' And you know what she said? She said, 'Shit!'"

His laughter was so contagious that Addie finally caught it. She had been holding her hands over her face, waiting for the punch line. When it came, she peeked between her fingers and shyly chuckled.

"I could tell you a better one than that on him," she said, recovering quickly. "Burnam never would say a smutty word—nothing that was bad, you know—but one time I went out in the field where he was plowing, and he got mad at the mule, and pretty soon he commenced cussing the worst you ever heard. I've never seen Burnam so mad."

We shared the amusement. Then I said to Addie, "When was the last time you went to Harlan County?"

"I don't remember. I can't keep up with it."

"I'd like to go back one more time," Burnam said. "It had changed a lot the last time I saw it. I guess it's changed even more now."

"Well, maybe we can go pretty soon," I responded. "Now that fall's here and the weather's cooler, it would be a good time to go."

"I'd like to," Addie said. "I was kind of thinking about it when you said that. I'd like to go back to Kildav, just to see what's there. The worst thing I'd hate about it would be if you called a lot of people's names and they said they was all gone. For anybody who's been away as long as we have, you might just find that nobody you knew was still living."

"Yeah, most of the ones we knew are gone," Burnam added. "Everything has changed. All the coal mining in Harlan has taken place since we left. There wasn't any coal being mined to speak of when I lived there—not even when me and Addie got married. I went to the mouth of a coal mine once, but I never did go down inside one. The coal was always there, but it wasn't important until after we had moved away. When the big companies from the North came in there, commenced building the railroad and all, there wasn't even a sawmill in the county. The little people couldn't do nothing with the coal—they didn't have the money or the machinery. You couldn't even build a road except with a pick and shovel. People had pride, but not much money. Then the big companies came in, and pretty soon people had more money, but they didn't take as much pride in their surroundings. There's been a lot of trouble between the companies and the miners. The rich companies have taken a lot more out of the mountains than they've put back."

"Do you know anything about all the labor-management problems they had there in the 1930s?" I asked.

"No, not much," said Burnam. "I just know it got plenty rough. Harlan County was a dangerous place in the 1930s, maybe more dangerous than it was when all the feuding was going on. It was between the miners and the coal companies. I guess they was both wrong, in a way—both sides went to extremes. But I don't know much about it, because I had been living in Garrard County for forty years by then. I was busy trying to make a living in Lancaster. We had lost our farm at Manse, lost the store and moved to town, and we were trying to recover from our losses and get back on our feet. I didn't have time to think about Harlan County then. I had enough troubles of my own."

Addie's mind was still on the Harlan of old. "I can tell you all about what it was like growing up back there," she said. "It's still fresh in my mind. When my father bought that farm at Kildav, there was a one-room hewed log house on it. He built on a room in front, a kitchen and another room in the back, a front porch and a back porch, and he got a man to build three fireplaces and chimneys. Then the house was weatherboarded and sealed. There was three beds in one big bedroom where me and my three brothers slept, and my parents used the old log room for their bedroom. We had wide plank poplar floors, and we slept in feather beds and got our light from coal oil lamps. My mother cooked on an old-fashioned wood-burning step stove—two caps in front and two up higher in the back. We kept big fires in the winter, stayed real warm— burned wood and some coal. At night we'd sit by the big fireplace in the kitchen and play games like 'War of Words'—that was a card game—or read to one another, or tell stories. I could repeat some Longfellow poems, like 'I stood on the bridge at midnight,' and 'The day is cold and dark and dreary.'

"My father went to Cincinnati once and bought a pump organ for my mother, paid over a hundred dollars for it, and pretty soon she could play anything she had music for. My mother could weave and spin real good. She and an old woman she hired made our clothes, wove us linsey dresses and shirts and blankets. When we moved to Harlan Town from Kildav, I wore those home-woven linsey dresses to school, and when I found out most of the other children didn't wear them, I laid mine aside. We had a Bible and an atlas and a dictionary at home, and my father read newspapers and magazines—he subscribed to the *New York Tribune*—and I recall we had a picture of President Harrison and his vice president, Levi P. Morton, up on our wall. We had a nice place, and we lived well. We had an apple orchard and a patch of cane, and we had two mules, a horse, a milk cow, hogs and chickens, twenty geese and forty ducks. Yes, I remember well.

"And I'll tell you something else I remember: When I was about twelve years old, I went to a hanging in Harlan Town. Buford Overton, a boy from a prominent family, had killed two old peddlers passing through, and they tried him and convicted him, and thousands of people came to his hanging. It was in 1897, I believe, or maybe '96. Burnam was there too, but we didn't know each other then. We can sing you a song about that killing: 'A peddler and his wife were traveling, along their lonely way . . .'"

Burnam had been waiting for a chance to break into his wife's long narration. He joined her in singing a verse of the song, and then he turned the conversation in another direction:

"'. . . But as they came around the bend, shots rang upon the air, and as the echoes died away, those beings perished there.' It was in 1896. Grant Smith was the sheriff, and he let me and Wade Skidmore go up and talk to Overton before they hung him. That was the first year I was back in Harlan from Garrard County to teach school. I was twenty years old then, and I had been out of the mountains, and I thought I'd seen a lot. Until we moved away from there in 1889, I never had been anywhere except across the mountain to Hagan and Hubbard Springs, and to Harlan Town a time or two.

"Up there on the upper part of Martins Fork and Cranks Creek there was just a few families scattered about, farming and cutting timber, marrying off one another's children. The way of life changed very little from generation to generation. When we first moved onto Crane Branch in 1882, we had a one-room log house with a shed on the back for a kitchen—and that was the same kind of house my grandparents had lived in. My father built on an ell, and two big stone fireplaces, and he put in puncheon floors, and in the main room he hung a big picture of President Garfield and Vice President Chester A. Arthur. Our house was the last one at the back end of Crane Branch hollow. Before we moved out of there in 1889, there was six of us children with my father and mother in that small house, but I don't ever remember feeling too crowded. In fact, we thought we was pretty well fixed—had a smokehouse full of meat and a cellar full of vegetables. Seems strange to say it now, but those early years I spent in Harlan County was the time I think we lived better than ever, before or since. I wouldn't want you to think it was an easy life without any hardship or troubles, but it was a good life.

"When we left there to come up here, I thought we was going to another world, a level land full of sunshine and blue grass, but I was greatly disappointed when we got here. People in this part of Kentucky had a bad opinion of mountain people—thought they was all just rough and ignorant. They was greatly surprised to find out I could read and write and stay ahead in school. I was proud, too. I loved the mountains. They were pretty to me, and mountain people were friendly and peaceful and right smart, most of them. Outsiders didn't feel that way, but they just didn't know—they were ignorant themselves. They looked down on us—but to me, being a mountaineer from Harlan County never was something to be ashamed of, and I wasn't ashamed of it, not a bit."

Burnam paused to cut himself a chew of tobacco, and in the silence on the porch, we reflected on the image he had constructed of early Harlan County. Presently, Addie spoke:

"I could go. I could make the trip. There's some interesting places back there. I don't know if I want to go or not, but I'm able. What do you think, Burnam?"

"Well, I talked to Bill about it, and he seemed interested. He said something about Billy and his two boys going too. We could all go, I reckon. I'll think about it."

They were interested but noncommittal. "Maybe we could try it next weekend," I suggested. "Leave on Saturday morning, spend the night at a motel in Harlan, and come back home on Sunday afternoon. I talked to Bill about it too, and he's ready. He said he would drive."

Doubt crept into Burnam's voice. "Well, we'll see about it," he said. "I want to go, in a way—but I don't expect to find anybody much that I know, or anything that I recognize. It's changed so much, I'm sure of that—maybe it's better not to see it again. But I do want to. Let's just wait until Saturday and decide then."

By Friday afternoon, he seemed to have lost all interest in the trip. He was sitting alone in the bedroom when I arrived. Addie came out to meet me at the edge of the porch.

"He says he's not going," she whispered. "To tell you the truth, he doesn't want me to go along. He's always made ten trips to my one. Maybe he just doesn't feel like I'm able to make the trip. He's well enough to go, though, so I'll try to talk him into it. I'd like to go, but it doesn't matter that much to me. Just tell him you're ready to leave in the morning, and I'll help you out all I can."

When I went inside to see him, I told him I had talked to Bill.

"What did he say?"

"He said he'd like to go if you still want to—said he'd be here at ten in the morning."

He weighed that news for a moment, and then, turning to squint at his wife, he said, "Are you going, Addie?"

She chose her words carefully. "Not if it would keep anybody else from going," she said.

"Well," he replied, "I'll decide when Bill gets here."

"One time's as good as another," Addie said, "but it might be best to go now, while you're feeling well."

I added my own encouragement: "They're saying the weather is going to be real nice this weekend."

Burnam shook his head. "Paper says showers tomorrow. Forty percent chance."

"It won't be raining up there," Addie countered.

I sensed that it was time to change the subject. The afternoon passed pleasantly, and when the burnt-orange glow of sunset had faded from the sky, a harvest moon, yellow as butter, rose out of the east. It didn't rain that night, but the next morning was overcast and cool. I got to the house before Bill, and we were sitting on the porch when he drove up in his late-model sedan and parked on the grass.

"He's been waiting for you," Addie greeted him.

Bill Ledford was a short, compact man with brown eyes and an easy smile. There was a sprinkling of gray in his dark hair. His neat, casual clothes seemed to match his unhurried manner. He wore his narrow-brim hat at a jaunty angle. Puffing on his pipe, chatting amiably, he gave an appearance not of a man in his seventieth year, which he was, but of someone much younger.

After the brief greetings, he said, "Billy and his boys couldn't make it." Then he turned to Addie. "Are you going with us, Mama?" he asked.

"No, I'm staying here with Tillie. If I could go with you I could explain everything, but Burnam can do that. I'm happy for him to get to go."

There was nothing else to be said. Presently, she got up and went inside, saying she wanted to get her shawl, but she didn't come back. When we were ready to leave a few minutes later, I went to the door to tell her goodbye. "Enjoy the trip," she said. She made no move to return to the porch. "I'll wait here until you all are gone."

With the aid of his walker, Burnam had made his way slowly to the car and was settled in the front seat. He was neatly dressed in pressed trousers and a shirt and tie, and he had also put on a striped wool sports coat and a battered straw hat. Tillie brought him a plastic container about six inches in diameter to serve as his spittoon.

"Maybe I'd better take a little brandy with me, in case I get to smothering," he said with a trace of apprehension, but a hurried search through the house turned up none. The gray clouds hung low and heavy, but no rain had fallen. Bill slipped behind the wheel and I got in the backseat, and at ten-thirty we backed out of the drive and pulled away.

Down Danville Street past the post office and the Presbyterian Church to the stoplight in the middle of the town square, right on Stanford Street, past the courthouse and the Thompson and Morrow hardware store, then left at the stockyard and out into the countryside on the road to Crab Orchard—the journey to Harlan had begun at last.

Bill sat comfortably in control of the big car. "I've been to Harlan a few times," he said, "but not with Papa—never went there with him. Billy has never been, period. I wish him and his boys could have come along, but they had other plans."

Burnam looked small and frail hunched down in the seat. He gazed about at the passing landscape with unseeing eyes, and for a while he said nothing. But if he could not see his surroundings, he could at least sense them; he knew exactly where he was. As the country landmarks—the old houses and barns and bridges—appeared and disappeared outside the car windows, he felt himself among them, and he began to see in his mind's eye, and then to talk about his earlier journeys along the same road:

"Preacherville—isn't that where Carry Nation was born? We're getting out of the Bluegrass now, getting into the Knobs. I used to travel through here in a Model T, selling hay and corn for Hudson and Farnau. Farmers bought it to feed their stock, and in the mountains they bought hay for the mules that worked in the coal mines. I used to know where every good apple tree was, all along through here."

At Crab Orchard, Burnam recited the town's historical significance as a major station on the Wilderness Road, then as a renowned health spa and resort spring in the nineteenth century, and as a one-time racing center and fairground for Bluegrass horse lovers. "They had what they called the 'Little World's Fair' here," he said. "Arch Kavanaugh used to bring our black mare here to compete in the horse show."

We drove on through Brodhead and Mount Vernon ("Here's

where I came to have my teeth made when I was about eighty years old"), onto Interstate Highway 75, south along the modern equivalent of Boone's path, past the town of East Bernstadt ("I ran a sawmill here back before the turn of the century"), past London and Corbin, then east to Barbourville and on along the Cumberland River to Pineville. Sprinkling rain fell intermittently. "To the hills I lift up mine eyes," Burnam sang softly to himself as the road narrowed and the mountains began to take shape on the horizon. JESUS IS COMING SOON, read a roadside sign, its letters worn with age and waiting. Now and then the sun broke momentarily through the clouds.

It was half past twelve when we stopped in Pineville to eat lunch at Colonel Lew's House of Beef Restaurant, next door to the Chained Rock Motel. Just down the road was the bridge across the Cumberland to Wasioto and the road to Harlan, thirty-three miles away.

"I'm not tired," Burnam said, slumping down at the table after he had made an extended and laborious trip to the restroom. "We're almost to Harlan, less than an hour from here. Back when we was moving in 1889, it took us three days to get from Crane Branch to the train station at Wasioto. That's where I saw my first train." He ordered a filet of fish and mashed potatoes and coffee, and when it came he leaned low over his plate and consumed every bite. The waitress and some nearby patrons watched him with interest.

"I guess the last time I came this way was about fifteen years ago," he said when he had finished eating. "David Smith drove me to the Ledford-Skidmore homecoming at Harlan." The waitress brought the check, and Bill invited conversation from her with the proud comment that his father was 102 years old.

"Are you kidding me?" she said in astonishment. "He sure don't look like it. Lord, how old does that make you?"

Bill smiled shyly. "Almost seventy," he replied. The woman shook her head in wonder. "We're taking him back to Harlan," he went on, "back to see where he used to live in 1889." All of the restaurant's customers had turned to look and listen. Burnam saw and heard little of what was going on. He casually whittled a plug of Day's Work and placed it between his toothless gums.

Back in the car a few minutes later, we drove across the bridge and slowed to a crawl to look around. "We put our stock on the train at Wasioto and sent them up to the Bluegrass," Burnam said— but now, Wasioto seemed no longer to exist at all.

Heading on up the river valley, we passed verdant walls of kudzu and amber patches of goldenrod. The road was three-laned on the long inclines that departed occasionally from the riverside. Burnam was surprised and impressed. "This is a very good road," he said, as we passed a loaded coal truck. "Back when I was a boy, Harlan County was fifty years behind Garrard County—isolated, cut off. But not any more. This road is as good as any you'll find." Somehow, he seemed able to determine not only the condition of the highway but our location on it, and he waited in anticipation as the last miles fell away.

A new bypass diverted traffic from the narrow streets of downtown Harlan. We followed it to its terminus and then entered the town on the old road, and only then did Burnam get his bearings. The new Harlan, like the old, had a dusty, disheveled look about it. We circled the courthouse and then joined the slow procession of cars and trucks moving southward, following Martins Fork toward Cawood and Cranks and Pennington Gap. At Bays Motel on the south side of town, we got the last room, a large room with two double beds. And again, Burnam displayed an uncanny sense of place:

"Felix King used to live over there and Vinie Howard—I used to stop to see her. Right across the road from here was a big mound— they thought it was an Indian mound. And that homecoming I told you about, it was right here in this bottom, at Daniel Skidmore's place. I can't hardly recognize a thing, but I know where I'm at."

After we had checked in and left our bags at the motel, we set out on our first objective: to find Addie's old homeplace at Kildav on Clover Fork, and to search for familiar names and faces on the streets of Evarts. The eight-mile drive along the creek was quickly done, but Kildav almost passed unnoticed; it was nothing more than a narrow strip of bottomland across the creek from the road. A bridge led us into a tiny cluster of trailers and cottages and 1930s-era coal camp shacks. Several inquiries finally led us to a woman in her eighties. She had never heard of Ewell Van King, and had no idea that he had once been the Harlan County sheriff and had owned this slender strip of bottomland.

"When was that you said he lived here?" she asked.

"From about 1885 to 1895," I repeated.

"Too far back for me. Earliest I can remember is about 1910, and I'm the oldest person here."

In Evarts, the result was the same. Black Mountain Academy, where Addie had gone to school in the 1890s, was long since gone. We were told that the town's oldest resident was a ninety-five-year-old man, but we were unable to find him. We could find no one named King, either, and almost no one past the age of seventy-five.

"Most of them are not even as old as I am," Bill said with surprise. "They're younger than me, not to mention Papa." We stopped at a drive-in restaurant for soft drinks and then, not knowing what else to do, drove back along Clover Fork to Harlan.

"It's just as well Addie didn't come with us," Burnam said. "She'd have been mighty disappointed."

The houses lining Harlan's narrow streets were drawn snugly side by side and close to the curb, as if they had been shoehorned into place. Traffic clogged the streets circling the courthouse, and a good many people milled about on the corners and in the courthouse yard. Bill inched the car around the square, looking for a place to park. His father peered in the direction of the sixty-year-old building that housed the offices of county government, but it was not recognizable to him. He could not even see the bronze statue beside the steps that depicted a World War I doughboy holding a rifle and bayonet in one hand and a grenade in the other. As we passed the office of the *Harlan Enterprise,* the local newspaper, I could see that it was closed.

"Does this look like Harlan to you, Papa?" Bill asked.

"Nope. Not a bit. I can't recognize a thing."

It was past four o'clock when we got back to the motel. Burnam was a little frustrated, and restless. He picked up the telephone directory and began to read the names, holding the thin book close to his good eye. "I've got two cousins at Cawood," he said. "Ruth Hubbard and Ollie Delaney. I'd like to talk to them. See if you can get one of them on the phone." Bill dialed Ollie Delaney, and when he identified himself, she was astonished.

"You sound like you're sixteen years old!" she exclaimed.

Bill laughed. "That's how I feel," he said. "Here's Papa. He wants to talk to you."

Burnam took the phone. "How am I feeling?" he asked, repeating her question. "I'm all right, for a boy. Addie didn't feel like making the trip. She's 93, you know. I'm just 102, so I could make it." He made arrangements to meet Mrs. Delaney and Mrs. Hubbard outside the Presbyterian Church at Cawood the next day. When he hung up, he was chuckling.

"I finally found somebody to talk to," he said.

"Maybe if we called up the editor of the *Harlan Enterprise*, he would send somebody out here to interview you and take your picture," I suggested. The idea appealed to Burnam. I found the name of Everett E. Davis Jr. on the paper's masthead and then found his number in the phone book and dialed it. His wife answered; he was out. When I explained the reason for my call, she said she would try to get a reporter to call us back.

Burnam, meanwhile, had turned his mind toward home. "I want to call Addie and see how she's feeling," he said. Bill dialed this time, and Tillie answered. When Addie got on the line, Burnam took over, shouting his account of the day's activities.

"What did she say?" Bill asked, when his father had hung up.

"She said she misses me. I don't know why, but she does. After seventy-five years of being together, I guess it makes a difference when you're gone. She said they've made out fine, though."

It was getting to be time for supper. We had already decided to go out and get Burnam's food for him, but Bill had another mission first. "I wouldn't mind having a little drink," he said, "and I didn't bring anything with me. Wonder if we could find anything in a dry town like this?" We discussed the prospects for a minute or two, and Bill finally decided to go and see what he could turn up.

Thirty minutes later he returned with a half-pint of brandy.

"Every town's got its bootleggers," he explained with a smile, "but most of them can come up with something better than this." We poured small shots into three of the motel's plastic glasses. Burnam touched the liquid to his lips and then handed the glass back. "That's awful stuff," he shuddered. "I don't see how anyone could like it."

Bill and I went out together in a little while, leaving the old man to rest. We picked up seafood dinners at a Long John Silver's outlet. "Look at this," Bill said. "Little mountain gals decked out as pirates, passing out fish and chips in Harlan. If you didn't know better, you'd think you was in Lexington, or Miami."

Back at the motel, Burnam ate sparingly of the greasy food. He was more interested in the evening newspaper's account of the previous night's heavyweight boxing title fight between Muhammad Ali and Leon Spinks. Ali had won a unanimous decision.

"I watched part of that, but I fell asleep before it was over," he said. "I'm glad he won. His people were slaves of Cassius Clay, I think. I suppose that's where he got his fighting ability. Somebody asked me, 'Why are you for that big-mouth nigger?' I said, 'We're kind of kinfolks. I'm kin to old Cash myself.'"

A little later, Bill turned on the television set and picked up a football game. "Hot dog!" he exclaimed. "Kentucky and South Carolina! I was hoping we could get it. Color, too." He settled down to watch, and his father soon joined him in a chair close to the screen. "We're all UK sports fanatics," Bill said over his shoulder. "Papa too. He's the biggest fan of us all."

We watched as Kentucky moved ninety-nine yards for a score and a 7-6 lead, but the game ended in a 14-14 tie, and we concluded in our own post-game assessment that it did not bode well for Kentucky's dreams of a superlative season. At nine-thirty, Burnam made his way to the bathroom. When he returned, he brought his carefully cleaned plastic spittoon with him to be used if needed as a chamber pot.

"Where's my handkerchief?" he asked, after he had settled into one of the double beds. "I'm like a little kid—I've got to keep my handkerchief wadded up in my hand all night." Soon he was curled up and ready for sleep. "We'll have a big day tomorrow," he reflected. "I want to be rested up for it." In a few minutes, he was sleeping soundly.

There being no roll-away, Bill and I had to share the other bed. It was earlier than I was accustomed to turning in, but there was nothing else of interest on television and I hadn't thought to bring reading material. Soon Bill went on to bed, and I followed. We lay there chatting for a few minutes, and then I heard him snoring softly.

A light from the parking lot filtered through the drawn curtains, lifting the room above the level of total darkness. I could make out the shape of the dresser and the television set on the opposite wall, and in the mirror I could barely see the image of a picture hanging just above my head. A car with a broken muffler roared past on the highway. I stared at the ceiling. Sleep would not come. Bill turned heavily in his slumber, and the bed sagged and bounced under our weight. It had been a long day, an interesting day. My thoughts were a jumble of yesterday's expectations, today's activities, tomorrow's plans. In my mind I wandered randomly over the road we had traveled, the long and ancient road to Harlan.

Aley, old Aley, the patriarch, the guiding spirit of Burnam, the founding father of several thousand Ledfords, most of whom may never have heard of him. He was barely thirteen when he came into this mountain wilderness. With a handful of others, he walked the last few miles through virgin forest from Cumberland Gap to the valley of Martins Fork and Cranks Creek, crossing from the known to the unknown, 175 years ago. Was he frightened? Could he imagine what lay ahead for them? And Betsy, even younger, a little girl of eleven or twelve, facing privation and hardship unlike any her descendants would ever know. Aley and Betsy, and then thirteen children, and every one, miraculously, surviving to maturity. Aley, born in the spring of George Washington's inauguration, lived until the administration of Ulysses S. Grant, and Betsy lived from Washington's time to Benjamin Harrison's. For the better part of a century they made their home here in these mountains, where presidents seemed as distant as European kings and the nation's growth and prosperity were neither seen nor felt.

And Aley and Betsy's James, their eleventh-born child—a log-
ger, a farmer, a mountain man all his life, his world defined by the
forested wall of rock that surrounded him. And James's Jesse, who
left the mountains for the Bluegrass in 1889, taking with him his
family, one among them being Curtis Burnam Ledford, a thirteen-
year-old boy then—and now a 102-year-old man sleeping peace-
fully in the bed next to me. Burnam and his bride-to-be, a pretty
teenage girl named Addie King, riding on horseback along Martins
Fork to Harlan, on the road right outside this motel, to get married
on a December day in 1903, the day after Orville and Wilbur Wright
cleared the sands of Kitty Hawk with their flying machine. Burnam,
who has memories of the past all the way back to forever, and
visions of the future all the way to infinity—and yet he thrives on
the present, on ball games and prize fights and presidential elec-
tions, on the Kentucky Wildcats and Muhammad Ali and Republi-
cans of all stripes. Burnam is a marvel. He is a living, breathing
volume of American history.

We have come in search of his family taproot, of some faint
sign of Aley's former presence, and Betsy's, and James's, and Jesse's.
We want to find the place where Burnam was born, and where he
lived before Jesse led them north to Garrard County. We are seek-
ers, hopeful, but also doubtful. Addie's homeplace has already eluded
us. Burnam left Coon Branch and Crane Branch and the long, wind-
ing, high-mountain valleys of Martins Fork and Cranks Creek
eighty-nine years ago. It has been so long, so very long—maybe it
has been too long. Maybe we shouldn't have come. Maybe the last
traces of Burnam's origin are gone too. What do you say to a man
who lives to see every familiar sign erased from the place of his
own beginning?

An hour had passed, maybe two hours, and I was no nearer
sleep. Bill mumbled incoherently and turned again. Finally I got up
with my pillow, found a couple of blankets in the dresser, and made
a pallet on the floor. After what seemed like another hour, drowsi-
ness slowly led me into a fitful nap.

Sometime later I awoke abruptly, aware of movement in the

room. In the semidarkness I could see Burnam sitting on the edge of the bed, groping blindly for the plastic container at his feet. Finally he found it. Weaving precariously, he emptied his bladder. Then he returned the pot to the floor and curled up again beneath the covers. Relieved but fully awake once more, I lay back on my pallet.

But I must have dozed off. When I sat up suddenly the second time, I could see Burnam reaching for the pot again. It was almost full. If he dropped it, if he fell. . . .

He was hunched at the very edge of the mattress when I walked over and stood beside him. There seemed to be no way he could maintain his balance and hold the container in his shaky hands. After a moment's hesitation, I reached down and took the pot from him.

"Unh?" He looked up, startled, seeing nothing in the darkness. Quickly, I ran to the bathroom and emptied the pot, and then rushed back and put it in his hands.

"Unh?" he grunted again. Then he realized that the pot was empty. He could not understand how his problem had been solved, but slowly he comprehended that it was solved. With the intuition of the blind, the faith of a child, he accepted a reality that his mind and his senses could not interpret or explain.

Looking down, he emptied his bladder again. When he had finished, I took the pot from him once more. By the time I had brought it back from the bathroom and set it down beside the bed, Burnam was resting quietly. He was still sleeping soundly when I got up to shower at half past six.

Sunday morning at Danny Ray's Drive-In Restaurant. Outside, a still, cool fog lay about the hills, but it was comfortable and pleasant in the diner, and an aroma of fresh coffee and frying bacon floated above our table. Burnam ordered a poached egg and toast, coffee and orange juice; Bill and I addressed heartier appetites.

A customer at a nearby table listened to our conversation with growing interest. Finally, he got up and walked over to us.

"I heard you say something about Ledfords and Skidmores," he began, looking down at Burnam. "My name's Howard Skidmore."

I recognized him from one of my earlier visits to Harlan County; seeking directions, I had stopped at his mobile home near the last turnoff to the head of Cranks Creek. Burnam leaned forward and squinted at him now, trying to get his face into focus. "Who was your mother and father?" he asked.

"Burnam Skidmore and Lizzie Browning," Howard answered.

"Lizzie? That was one of Lydia's daughters, wasn't it? Lydia was my aunt, my mother's sister. I'm kin to you on both sides of your family, Howard. Me and your father was cousins—and we was both named for the same man." Burnam pushed his plate back and warmed to the subject as Howard Skidmore sat down to listen and to answer the old man's questions. Bill and I followed the exchange as best we could.

Howard had heard stories about Aley and Betsy—he had, in fact, been born in the old log house on Cranks Creek that they had built early in the nineteenth century—but he didn't know where either of them was buried. The log house, he said, was gone, burned down at Halloween just a few years earlier. Howard was able to answer many of Burnam's questions about past and present kinfolks, but his store of knowledge was no match for the centenarian's. The people of Burnam's remembrance were like the creeks of Harlan County, numberless and interconnected and continuous. He recalled them in precise detail—the names, the characteristics, the intricate and complex matchings and couplings. Howard sat in awe of the performance, and when the conversation was over, Burnam himself seemed inspired and primed for the day's activities.

His mind was far ahead of his body. Walking back to the car, he wobbled to a pause and leaned unsteadily on his walker. "My legs are like rubber," he said. "I can't tell where they're going."

"You sure you feel okay, Papa?" Bill asked.

"Yeah, I'm all right. It just takes me a while to get started."

The fog was lifting and a sunny autumn day was in prospect. We drove slowly along the highway flanking Martins Fork, and Burnam let his instincts be his guide. He gave us a running commentary:

"Turtle Creek—that's where me and Addie first went together, a mile above here, and that's where old man Snodgrass gave me to Addie, said he'd promised her one of his boys and I was the best. And I taught school over there across the ridge, on Bobs Creek. Back then, Martins Fork ran a lot fuller than this. Is it almost dry now? We're getting close to Cawood—that's where I kept store in 1898."

At Cawood we turned south toward Cumberland Mountain, toward the village of Smith. We were still following Martins Fork, climbing toward its source. The road was narrow and crooked, bordered closely by sycamore and hickory and poplar. "There was a grist mill along in here," Burnam said, but we couldn't find it. "I can't see nothing," he muttered. "Where's Coon Branch? It ought to come into Martins Fork along in here somewhere."

Five miles above Cawood, we came upon a structure so massive that Burnam had no trouble seeing it. A sign identified it as Martins Fork Dam, a project of the U.S. Army Corps of Engineers.

"Well, here it is, Papa—this is that dam they've built to flood the valley." Bill turned up a side road and drove to the top edge of the concrete wall. He took binoculars from the glove compartment. Through them, we could see Martins Fork meandering through a stretch of bottomland that had been cleared. "They haven't shut the gates yet," Bill concluded. "It's just an empty valley, waiting for the water to fill it up."

The old road to Smith was in the valley, no longer accessible; it too would be flooded. A new road at a higher elevation skirted the hillsides. We followed it, picking up a man and a woman walking along the way, but their guidance proved not to be helpful. Finally we reached Smith, or what was left of it: a small wooden building with a post office sign on it. The valley was like an empty bowl, scraped bare. Farther along, we saw a man working on his car in the yard of his house. "If you had a four-wheel drive, you could follow this road on over to Cumberland Gap," he said, "but you'd never make it in that car. There used to be another road that went from here over to Hagan on the Virginia side of the mountain, but it's closed. Ain't much left up here now, buddy. What the coal trucks haven't tore up, the Corps of Engineers got."

"Where's Cranks Creek?" Burnam called to him. "Where's Coon Branch? I can't figure out where I'm at."

The man directed us to the point where Cranks Creek enters Martins Fork, close by the road in the bowl of the valley. Once we found that spot, Burnam concluded that the mouth of Crane Branch was only a short distance downstream. "First comes Board Branch," he said, "then Crane Branch. It's less than a mile from here." We turned onto a one-lane gravel road, thinking it might lead us to the mouth of Crane Branch hollow, but Burnam could not get his bearings, and Bill and I were unable to help him.

"These people are like me," Burnam sighed as we turned around. "They don't know nothing. The settlers have all moved out. Everything's gone—houses, stores, roads, trees, creeks, everything."

We returned to the new road on the ridge that encircled the valley. When we reached the closest point to the confluence of Cranks Creek and Martins Fork, Bill pulled over and stopped, parking in such a way that his father could stand at the open door and study the full sweep of the valley through the binoculars.

Burnam tried for a long time to get his bearings, but the effort was futile. "I kept thinking if I could just look up at the outline of the mountains, I would know where I was," he said at last, "but it's no use. Everything has changed so much. It's all very confusing. I know Crane Branch is across yonder somewhere, but I can't make it out. If we could drive up that hollow somehow, I know I'd recognize it, even though the house is gone. But we can't even find the right hollow, much less the road to it. And when they close the dam, it'll all be under water. Then nobody can find it."

He stood there for several minutes, leaning on the car door. I could hear grasshoppers in the weeds around us and crows calling in the gentle breeze, but as far as the eye could see, nothing moved. The golden fringes of fall had tipped the leaves of the tulip poplars and the air smelled sweet and fresh. After the fog had come a china-blue sky.

Burnam was as close as he would ever again be to the main stage of his history. If he could have climbed to the top of Cumberland Mountain, looming to our left along the south wall of the valley, he could have paused at the summit between Smith and Hagan and seen everything, imagined it all, from Aley Ledford's exodus across Carolina to his own place in the Garrard County Bluegrass. Seven generations—three before Burnam and three after him—were balanced there on that mountain crest. But he could not get there, could not find the peak or the hollow. Bill and I stood and waited. Burnam made one more effort with the binoculars, and then turned back to the car. When he was seated again and we had started back to Cawood, he spoke the epitaph of Crane Branch and its sister streams and the fertile bottomlands they once watered:

"I couldn't find it," he said. "It's gone, disappeared. All that's left is what I carry in my head."

At a few minutes past twelve o'clock, we pulled into the gravel driveway of the Presbyterian Church at Cawood and parked in the shade. The front door of the white frame church was standing open, and the sound of the preacher's voice could be heard in a sonorous recitation of scripture:

"Come unto me all ye who labor and are heavy laden, and I will give ye rest. . . . Be obedient unto the Lord. . . ."

About a dozen cars and trucks were in the parking area. The sun had brightened and warmed the day. We opened the car doors and rolled down the windows.

"Been a long time since I was here," Burnam said, regaining his sense of location. "One winter after I had taught in Harlan County, I ran the store at Cawood and served as assistant postmaster. I was twenty-two years old."

We were waiting for church to end. "Ollie said she'd be here," Burnam reassured us. "Her and Ruth Hubbard. And Wash Ledford also goes to this church. You know Cawood Ledford, that broadcasts all the Kentucky Wildcat games—well, Wash is Cawood's father. Wash is a grandson of Aley Ledford II, so his grandfather and my grandfather James Ledford were brothers. That makes me and Wash second cousins."

The church piano sounded, and we could hear the congregation singing the closing hymn: ". . . to be trusting in Jesus, for there's no other way."

Ollie Delaney and Ruth Hubbard came quickly out the door and looked around the shady lot. When they spied us, they hurried over, two warm and pleasant middle-aged women eager to see a venerable relative. Burnam greeted them with his usual humorous and light-hearted banter. Bill stood to one side smiling, saying little. Then Wash Ledford walked over, a tall and erect white-haired man of eighty. As the voices rose in number and volume, Burnam sat on the edge of the car seat, his head cocked quizzically to one side, trying to take everything in. The little knot of Harlan County kinfolks lingered there under the arching oaks after everyone else had gone, savoring their brief moment of mutual remembrance.

When it was over and we were back on the road, Burnam was curiously quiet. We followed the highway east out of Cawood, twisted across a high ridge, passed the dusty black entrance of a mountainside coal mine, and came down into the upper valley of Cranks Creek, the last valley before Kentucky met Virginia at the crest of the next ridge. As we approached level ground in the Cranks valley, we spotted the Wash Smith Cemetery on a knoll to the right of the highway. Bill turned in and drove as close as he could to the cluster of old and recent graves.

Burnam was not able to walk with Bill and me among the hillside stones, but he was certain of where we were. "This valley is where Aley and Betsy spent all their married life," he said. "Their house was near the head of Cranks Creek, a mile or two on up the road. Then after Aley died, Betsy came and lived with her youngest son, Stephen, in a log house right near here, almost in sight of this place where we're standing. That was Blind Granny. I saw her when I was a boy. She was over a hundred when she died, and I was always told she was buried right here in this cemetery."

Bill and I found the graves of Stephen Ledford and his sister Nancy, the first wife of Noble Smith, obscured in the thicket of honeysuckle vines, but no stone bore Betsy Ledford's name. I had made the search before, but we looked again for new evidence before we returned to the car. Burnam was sitting at the open door waiting for us, facing the valley and the long mountain ridge beyond. The scene was rich with color: the green valley meadow, the intrusion of vivid reds and greens on the forested slope, the bright blue sky above.

"When Aley and them came here," the old man said to us, "this was as good as the Bluegrass, so instead of going on up there, they stayed here. I imagine it must have looked like a haven to them—a new country full of virgin timber and game and clear streams. It still looked a lot like that when I lived around here. I've walked across this mountain many a time, and ridden it on a mule. If you turn down there below the cemetery, that road follows Cranks Creek towards Martins Fork, over to that valley where we were this morning. These creek bottoms and the hills between them and the little villages—Smith, Cawood, Cranks—these was the places where we grew up and lived. The creeks was our roads, and I knew every one that emptied into Martins Fork, from Cranks and Crane and Coon clear on down into Harlan Town. When I lived in these mountains, it couldn't have been much different for us than it was for my father and grandfather and great-grandfather. It's different now, though—a whole lot different."

We had one more stop to make, in the last hollow of Cranks Creek. If there was a single place in Harlan County that could be said to be the original domain of the Kentucky Ledfords, the last hollow of Cranks Creek was that place. Aley and Betsy had built their first and only house there, and in it they had given life and love to their thirteen children. They had cleared ground for farming, cut timber and floated it to market, hunted and fished and kept bees and raised horses in that hollow. Aley had freed his slaves there, and given then a generous portion of the creekside land and the high slopes, and they had stayed and built a life of independence and dignity for themselves. Burnam knew all those stories, and more. In his remembrance, the head of Cranks Creek was a familiar and important place, even a hallowed place.

But in his vision and his senses on this day, the scene was another cause for disappointment, and he took it in with a look of sadness and dismay. Even on a quiet Sunday afternoon, the intrusive presence of strip-mining was everywhere in evidence. Huge chug-holes were gouged in the dusty road. Tumbled spills of sheared timber and blasted rock were scattered below the flattened ridgetops where the coal had been laid bare. All along the creekbed were strewn the pieces of evidence that gave mute testimony to the earlier ravages of floodtide. The last hollow of Cranks Creek once had typified the forested beauty of the mountains; now it represented the worst of mining's devastating consequences. More than half of Harlan County's 300,000 acres were owned by absentee corporations whose primary interest was mineral extraction. After more than a century, the largest such landowner was still the Kentenia Corporation, through which the antecedents of Franklin D. Roosevelt had purchased thousands of acres and millions of tons of coal from the antecedents of Burnam Ledford. The corporations paid only a few pennies per acre in property taxes to the county, but their profits ran into the tens of millions of dollars. They left behind land too eroded to farm, water too poisoned to drink, air too polluted to breathe. In Appalachia, in Harlan County, in the last hollow of Cranks Creek, the ultimate price was being paid for the land's underground riches.

"It's nothing but coal mines now," Burnam lamented. "It's a sad thing to see, when you know what it used to be like. Where do you reckon Aley's house was? I have no idea. He's buried up in here somewhere, too, but you'd never find his grave now. It's all so growed up in weeds, so covered up with coal dust and dirt, you'd never find anything in here."

He was ready to go, and Bill, sensing it, chose not to follow the broken road to the end of the hollow. Instead, we turned around and went back to the highway, and continued out of the valley and over the mountain into Virginia. Near Pennington Gap, we stopped for gas and a country-store snack of soft drinks and cheese crackers. Burnam munched his mid-afternoon lunch without saying much. He was beginning to feel the physical and emotional effects of our two-day adventure.

At Pennington we turned toward the southwest, passing through Jonesville and Rose Hill on Boone's Wilderness Trail to Cumberland Gap. We paused in the gap, and Burnam spoke once more of Aley and Betsy's childhood experience there, and then we drove on to

Pineville, where the circle we had begun the previous day was completed. The rest of the way home, Burnam was alone in subdued reflection. Occasionally he made some comment, but his thoughts were turning away from Harlan County, turning gradually back to the only place he had left to call his own.

"I never did like to get in home after dark," he said late in the afternoon, as Lancaster neared. "Addie would always stay later if she could—she liked to stay out whenever we was away visiting—but I knew we had to milk when we got home, so I always wanted to leave in time. Home is the place to be when night comes. Looks like we're going to get there before dark today, and I'm glad of it."

Addie and Tillie were sitting on the porch when we drove up. Bill pulled the car to within a few feet of them, and Burnam, leaning on his walker, made the transfer from the car seat to his rocking chair. As soon as he was seated and had a chew of tobacco in his mouth, he and Addie began to talk about the journey.

"What kind of time did you have?" she asked.

"It was tiresome. Just about everybody is dead. I'm wore out— I'm just about done for."

"Did they say everybody had died?"

"The younger ones have moved out, the old ones are dead, and new people have all come in there. Miners, people to work on the dam, things of that kind, you know—people from all different parts of the country. You couldn't tell nothing about the place. Nobody knows anything about the old people, or anything of the sort. There's just nobody left."

"Are you glad you went?"

"Yeah, yeah—although in a way it was a disappointment. We couldn't recognize anything. Up on Crane Branch, on the upper part of Martins Fork around Smith, everything has been moved out. There's not a single house up either side of those creeks. When they fill up the dam, the water will reach to the head of each one of them branches. I kept looking for the houses and all, but then I realized the government had condemned them, tore them all down. It was sad."

"I'm kind of glad I didn't go," Addie said.

"I thought about that too. You wouldn't have enjoyed it at all. After I got there, I was glad you didn't make the trip."

Addie reflected on her husband's descriptions for a minute. "Well," she said, "people got tired of the country, you know, when it wasn't fixed up. And we've been gone from there so long, I was afraid you wouldn't find anybody familiar to talk to. Tell me about going to Evarts."

"It looked sort of run-down. Harlan too. When I was a boy, Harlan County was a real pretty place, and the people were proud. You'd see log cabins with their yards fenced in, and they'd have stile blocks for the women to get on and off their horses, and on each side of the walk that went through the yard to the house, you'd see flowers growing. Now you see some better houses, but you don't see people taking as much pride as they used to. We went to Kildav, too, but didn't find anybody who knew anything about the old settlers. Then the last place we went was up on Cranks Creek. Couldn't find Blind Granny's grave in the Wash Smith Cemetery, or Aley's up at the head of Cranks, and their log house burned down. Cranks is a mess, all tore up with strip mines. We saw Wash Ledford and Ollie Delaney and Ruth Hubbard at the Presbyterian Church in Cawood, and they was the only people we talked to that knew anything at all about the families—them and Howard Skidmore, Burnam Skidmore's boy."

"Well, does it feel good to be home?" Addie asked him.

"Yes indeed. I'm glad I went, though. I wanted to see it one more time before I die, and now I've seen it, and I don't care to go back any more. It's kind of like we used to be. We'd go off someplace and come back, and when we got in sight of home, we'd say home looked better than any place we'd been. That's about how I feel now."

SEVENTEEN

A Safe Harbor

Burnam and Addie, 1953–1978

The leaves had turned and fallen and scattered in the wind. From a distance, the square frame house on the Old Highway 52 seemed to blend into the wall of gray clouds that hung low around it. Another winter was at hand, announced by a swirl of snowflakes around the corners of the abandoned porch. In the cozy warmth of the bedroom, Burnam and Addie were adjusting to another season of protective hibernation. Harlan had departed from their conversations, if not from their thoughts. They faced the approaching months of confinement and inactivity not with dread but with resignation, knowing that boredom and loneliness were an inescapable part of every winter. Tillie was with them, making her own adjustment with quiet determination and a saving sense of humor. It was humor, in fact, that kept boredom at bay for all of them.

Burnam had made one last trip to town for a haircut before the cold weather set in, and the silky fringe of white hair that lapped over his collar was now as close-cropped as a choirboy's. He had swapped jokes with the barbers: "When I went to pay for the haircut, they wouldn't take my money. The man said, 'We won't charge you nothing this century, but we'll charge you double next century.' So I thanked them, and then I told them the story about the man who went in the barbershop with just one dime in his pocket. He ordered the works—haircut, shave, shampoo, shoeshine, even got his nose hairs clipped. When it come time for him to pay, he handed over the dime and said that was all he had, so they kicked him out the door. There was a bunch of men standing out there watching. The fellow got up, brushed himself off, and commenced to laugh. One of the men asked him what was so funny. He said, 'I got myself a real bargain in there. Got a haircut, shave, shampoo, shoeshine, my nose picked, and my ass kicked, all for a dime.'"

He chuckled at his own humor. Addie put her face in her hands and pretended not to hear. Burnam spat in the cuspidor at his feet and wiped his chin with the handkerchief he kept wadded in one hand. He was still thinking about the barbershop:

"I didn't see a single soul I knew up there. I used to know every person in this town, but I've lived so long that practically all of them have died. Now I don't hardly know anybody."

"Martha Conn comes to see us pretty often," Addie said. "We've known her for a long time—she's about ninety years old. She was a Noe before she married—came from Harlan County. Her grand-mother was Susan Skidmore, the one we called Aunt Sook. Me and Burnam are both kin to her. Martha married Bris Conn, one of Jim Conn's children—Burnam used to work for Jim in the hardware store. And Bris's sister, Kate, is the one I told you about that mar-ried Adolphe Menjou. Martha's right spry—you'd never know she's as old as she is. She still drives her own car."

"Yeah," Burnam said, "there's still a few people around that was living in Lancaster when we first moved to town, but there's not many. And there's none that was here when we came to Garrard County from Harlan in 1889. I walked behind our livestock up Stanford Street, and it was dirt—all the roads was dirt. Nobody is left who remembers that but me. I've seen a lot of people come and go past the hardware store and the courthouse. I had already seen a bunch of them pass when I retired from the store—and that was twenty-five years ago."

He had retired with Addie to the little farm at the edge of town, and with the predictable regularity of the seasons they had settled into a relatively quiet and uneventful pattern of living. The garden and the tobacco patch had to be tilled and planted and harvested, the dependable Jersey cow had to be milked morning and evening,

the chickens had to be nourished for their yield of eggs and meat.
Addie had her flowers to tend and her canning and preserving to
do; Burnam continued for a while to take part in church and politi-
cal activities as well as to handle his domestic chores.

They continued to rely on the natural air conditioning of sum-
mer evening breezes, and to draw their warmth from coal fires in
the open grates, and their principal liquid was rainwater from the
backyard cistern; not until late, and with reluctance, did they ac-
cept the modern conveniences of gas heating and indoor plumbing.
In the slow but certain turning of the years they lived a simple
country life, and their children and grandchildren and finally their
great-grandchildren, caught up in the accelerating pace of modern
life, could look to them as a fixed and dependable beacon on the
ever-changing horizon. There might be war in Korea or an obses-
sion with the threat of communism in Washington or racial strife
in the South or a Russian Sputnik blinking across the night sky, but
at the tiny farm on the outskirts of Lancaster, life turned on a few
simple and reassuring certainties—biscuits for breakfast, dinner at
high noon, milking every evening, company on Sunday, and Waite
Hoyt presenting Cincinnati Reds baseball through the tinny static
of the bedroom radio.

Change was almost imperceptible on the surface of Burnam
and Addie's lives. And yet, they kept up with the state and national
and world news in the pages of the Courier-Journal *and* Time *maga-*
zine and the Reader's Digest, *and they heard—and eventually*
watched—the blend of fact and fancy that radio and television pre-
sented. And perhaps most important of all, they maintained a con-
temporary outlook on life by welcoming, as they always had, a
constant stream of kin and acquaintances and even strangers to
take bed and board with them.

Most of the sons and daughters and grandchildren came occa-
sionally for brief visits, and so did Addie's half-sisters and some of
Burnam's close relatives. For a few people, however, the Ledford
household in the 1950s and 1960s was more than a place to visit; it
was a permanent shelter, a safe harbor in times of need. Four of the
grandchildren—Bruce Mills and his sister Arletta, Bobbie Jo

Hammon and her brother Gary—lived there for extended periods and looked to Burnam and Addie as the principal figures of authority in their lives. There was also Burnam's brother, Noble Ledford, who took up permanent residence in a house trailer beside the driveway, and Kelly Ledford, a friendly stranger of distant kinship who showed up at the door one day and managed to stretch his "visit" from a few minutes to a few years.

The elder Ledfords seemed always to be available when someone needed help. Without complaint or judgment or thought of reward, they made themselves useful to kin and friends—and in so doing, they extended their own independence and perhaps even lengthened their lives. Burnam thought of the years following his retirement as a time of uneventful quiet, and compared to their earlier lives, it was—but he and Addie could not fully grasp what an influence they had had on the lives of those who were closest to them. Even though he was almost eighty years old when he retired, Burnam had too much energy to fall into a pattern of inactivity. He managed to keep himself occupied, but he also noted with some regret the shift of his life into slow motion:

From about 1953 on, not much happened around here. We generally had somebody visiting or living with us, but we'd always had that, so it wasn't anything new. I didn't go to Harlan any more the way I used to—in fact, I hardly ever got out of town, me or Addie either. I think I went to the Keeneland racetrack in Lexington once or twice, and to see the Cincinnati Reds play, and that was about it. I never did go to see the Kentucky Derby. I've lived to see little airplanes get to be big jets, and jets turn to moon rockets, but I never have left the ground myself—and I don't want to now. Here in town, I went to see some high school football games and a few picture shows, but mostly, we have just stayed at home. I kept going to church every Sunday up until about ten years ago, but finally I got to where I couldn't hear the preacher, so I quit. I guess the one thing I have kept doing the same as always is reading—that's a habit I've never changed.

After I left the hardware store for good, the Social Security man came to see me and signed me up. Addie was already on it, I think. Anyway, I was about seventy-seven years old then, and we commenced drawing a check together. It's gone up some, and now it amounts to about $265 a month. Me and Addie never was rich or poor—just medium—but we've got a little bit saved away, and it don't take much for us to live on, so I don't worry about us running out. From the time I was ten years old I've always managed to have my own money to spend, always been prepared to pay my part. My children have done the same thing. We taught them that—and they've prospered.

I can remember some big things that happened in the last twenty-five years, but none of them happened to me. Politics has always been one of my main interests, you know—I've always kept up— but by the time President Eisenhower put the Republicans back in power, I was too old to do anything more than vote. I remember when Alaska and Hawaii became states, and when old Khrushchev came over here and visited a farm out in Iowa or somewhere, and I remember how everybody was talking about things like communism and outer space and integration. When John F. Kennedy beat Richard Nixon for president in 1960, I voted for Nixon because he was the Republican—but I liked Kennedy right much, and I liked his brother Robert even better. Those assassinations made me real sad—it was a shock, a shock to the whole world, when President Kennedy got killed. I can remember when McKinley was assassinated, and even President Garfield—I was five years old when he got shot—but the assassination of President Kennedy and the killing of his brother was very upsetting to me, even though I wasn't on their side politically.

Same thing with Martin Luther King—I thought it was mighty bad that someone shot him, and I was sad about it. I never have believed in killing, or even in hurting anybody. I've always been a compromiser and a peacemaker. To me, Martin Luther King was that way too—a peaceable man, never raised his hand against anybody, as far as I could see. In most of what he did I thought he was right—I thought he was a good man doing good work. A lot of people hated him, said he was just a nigger, but I liked his ideas, and felt like he did a lot for his people—in fact, for all of us, and for peace between the two races. Seems like things have got worse since he died. I thought more of King than I did of George Wallace, who seemed like a selfish man to me, greedy for power. I didn't hate him, and I was very sorry he got shot, but I never did think Wallace was a real good man.

Lyndon Johnson was a powerful man in a lot of ways, but he just wasn't big enough to handle the job of being president. He got all messed up in that Vietnam affair, and it ruined him. I thought we had no business in that mess. I never was a pacifist or an isolationist, exactly, but I always believed in keeping out of entanglements with foreign countries as far as possible. Johnson fell into that trap, and he was just like Herbert Hoover or Grover Cleveland—when hard times hit, everybody blamed him for it because he was the man on top. Johnson, though, made his own trouble.

Then it was Nixon, and I voted for him twice more, and I'm not sorry of it. I still think he was basically a good man and a good president, especially on foreign policy. I've been reading *All the President's Men* lately, and I'm convinced it was the men around Nixon that broke him—and they came mighty near breaking the nation when they did it. I've seen lots of crookedness in politics, some of it just as bad as what happened in the Nixon administration, and nothing was said or done about it. It was not Nixon but the men he had under him that started the crookedness—and some of them was Democrats.

I liked Jerry Ford, too, and he did a lot to bring the country back together. And now Carter seems like a good man to me, an honest man trying to do his best. But all I can do is read and watch TV now—I can't get involved like I used to years ago. I served as an election officer for over fifty years, and campaigned for William O. Bradley for governor over eighty years ago, and I ran for county clerk nearly fifty years ago. But since I retired, I don't do nothing in politics except try to keep informed.

Yeah, I've seen a right smart happen in the past twenty-five years, but most of it happened to somebody else. What happened to me was mostly right here around this house. I had a small to-

bacco allotment up until I was about ninety, and that plus the garden and the cows and our family has been the main things me and
Addie have stayed busy with. Before I started using this walker a
few years ago, I carried a long walking stick, and I had a dog,
too—Blackie, an English sheep dog, the most devoted dog you ever
saw. He went everywhere with me. Addie despised him, because he
was always killing her chickens. He killed just about every cat,
every polecat, every groundhog, every possum in this neighborhood.
Blackie would go to the barn with me, and drive the cows up from
the pasture. He was a real fine dog. Once in the wintertime I got
over by the barn and fell flat on my face. It was a cold day, snow on
the ground, and I thought I wasn't going to be able to get up. Blackie
commenced barking, and directly Noble came over and helped me
up. No telling how long I might have laid there if it hadn't been for
Blackie. I never thought I'd ever shed a tear over a dog, but when
he got run over and killed by a car about eight years ago, I cried. I
never have wanted another dog since then.

I always kept a pistol, too, just in case I needed it, but that was
back when I was still working at the store. They had a big joke on
me about that pistol. One morning I saw an old hen pecking off my
beans down in the garden. I shooed her off a couple of times, but
she kept coming back. I went in the house to eat dinner, and then
I looked down there and saw her again, so I got my pistol and
fired it to scare her off—and I hit that hen right between the eyes,
killed her. I went in the kitchen and told Addie, "You've got a
dead hen down there in the garden," and then I went on back to
work. When I came home that evening, she had cleaned that chicken
up and served it for supper. She kidded me a lot about that. I decided I'd better get rid of that gun before I accidentally shot somebody.

Nobe was living out here in a trailer back then, and Kelly
Ledford lived upstairs, and they helped me some. Nobe came sometime back in the sixties, and later on he moved to an apartment up
in town. He had been married, but he didn't have a wife then, or
any children. He was nearly twenty years younger than me. He
was the one, you know, that was driving when that train hit the car

and killed my mother and father. Nobe died in about 1975. He's buried beside our parents out at the Paint Lick cemetery.

Kelly came about the same time Nobe moved to town, as I remember. He just appeared at the door one day, said his name was Ledford, he wanted to meet me. His grandfather was a cousin to my father. I never had seen him before, but I took pity on him—he was down and out, had nowhere to go, just drifting. He ate supper with us, and afterwards I told him he could find a bed upstairs, and he ended up staying about four years, just took up with us like a stray dog. Kelly was good to me—he worked in the garden, mowed the yard, did whatever I asked him to do. He wasn't a bit lazy. But he couldn't handle whiskey. He'd get his Social Security check and go to town, and I'd warn him not to come around me drunk, so he'd stay gone until he sobered up, and then he'd slip in, and the next morning he'd have breakfast all cooked and waiting, and I couldn't fuss at him too much. Addie couldn't stand him—said he talked nasty to her. We also found out he'd had his troubles with the law. But the only complaint I had against him was his drinking.

Finally, though, it got so bad that I couldn't put up with it any more, and I told Kelly he had to leave. I said to him, "I've done everything I could for you—took you in when you didn't have a change of clothes, gave you a home—and the more I try to help you, the worse you get. I don't want to see you any more."

He called me later on the phone, wanted to know if I was still mad at him. I told him I wasn't, but I still didn't want him to come back, and he never did. He left town after that, and I don't know what ever became of him.

Since Nobe died and Kelly left, me and Addie have lived here alone. Gwen used to come by and see us every few days, and she did our grocery shopping and all, but it was just the two of us living here until Tillie moved in back in the summer. These last few years have been very quiet. We always have the big gatherings around my birthday in May, and when we have our seventy-fifth anniversary pretty soon I expect a lot of the children and grand-children will come—but other than that, we don't do much.

But we've made out pretty well. Addie can't see to read any

more, and neither one of us can hear as well as we used to, but we get by. We've had plenty of time to think and talk about the old days—and one September morning about five years ago, I had an experience that gave me a look ahead into the future.

It was a warm day, and I was sitting out on the porch by my-self. I guess Addie was in the house. Suddenly, I was just wafted into Heaven, transported instantly. I passed through the gate and into the temple, and stood right in front of the throne. I was look-ing for God and Christ to be sitting up there, but the light was so bright, brighter than the noonday sun, that I couldn't even squint my eyes and look at it. Down at the foot of the throne an old man was standing—it was Abraham or Moses, I suppose—and he had the prettiest beard I ever saw. It was whiter than snow, fine as silk, and it came all the way down to his waist. I thought about shaking hands with him, but I didn't—didn't touch him.

All around the temple, angels were moving so gently and smoothly, just floating in the air, they made me think of snowflakes coming down, and they were so numerous that it would have been as impossible to count them as to count the number of flakes in a snowstorm. I was standing under the tree of life, the tree that bears all manner of fruit in all seasons of the year, and all I could think of was a question we ask on earth but cannot answer: Will we know one another when we get to Heaven?

About that time, a little baby angel floated right in front of my face. I wanted to take it in my arms so badly, but I couldn't. And I thought to myself: That must be our little baby that died in 1921, the one we tried so hard to save after the doctors had given up. And then I looked down among the thousands of angels and I saw one looking right straight at me, and I knew that must be Ewell, our thirteen-year-old boy that died in 1918. He meant so much to me. I had wanted to educate him, prepare him to do the things I had always wanted to do but never had the opportunity, but then he had died. When I looked at that angel, I was so thrilled I couldn't move. I said, "God was and is and ever shall be. He made man in his own image. How great he is."

The angels were coming and going around the throne so thick

they were like bees swarming around a hive. They were like God's messengers, and the message they carried was this: God so loves his people that he has made this lovely home for them, a place where there is no more death, sorrow, pain, or trouble—all is peace, joy, happiness, and praise forever. And I thought to myself. Why have I been spared through all these years, and why am I permitted to see all of this? And the answer came to me: "You are my witness."

And suddenly, I was back in my body here on earth, on my own front porch, switched back just as quick as a picture changes on television. I told Addie about it, and told one of my neighbors, but they didn't take it seriously. They said I probably just fell asleep and dreamed it. But I know better—I know I had a vision. I don't know why or how, but I know it happened. And it made me realize that when we get to Heaven we'll all be pure, washed in the blood of the lamb, and we'll be one big family, and we'll love one another, and there'll be no divisions, no sects or clans or tribes or anything of the kind, and our bodies will be perfect, without scars or blemishes, and no one will be blind or deaf or lame, and no one will grow old. We'll be not flesh and bone but spiritual bodies, made for eternity, and we'll never remember anything that happened in this life. And we'll all be the same, all united. Whites, blacks, Chinese, Indians, everybody—we'll all be alike, all be equal in the family of God the father.

I think God has a purpose in keeping me alive on earth as long as I've been here. God has a purpose for everyone, and we stay here until we've had an opportunity to fulfill it. It's up to each one of us whether we fulfill our purpose or not. For me, I think my purpose is to help others see the light—and I also think it's my purpose to tell the story of my life. Me and Addie come from the mountains of Appalachia, where lots of people have passed on their history through their families, from one generation to another. Used to be, people could tell you a lot more about their families than they can now. People live faster now—they don't have time to think about all that went before them. But me and Addie belong to the old way. We've always thought about our families, talked about them, tried to remember about the old ones. I'll keep on telling the story until I die—and I figure I'll die before Addie does, so she can keep on telling it after I'm gone.

Sometimes it's hard to be old, but in a way I think it's a blessing to live as long as I have. I think maybe my last days have been my best days—at least I look on life in a different way than I used to, and I look forward to the future life more than I did when I was younger. I don't want to live a lot longer now, and I'm not expecting to. I think I've about lived my time out. Not many people have had as full a life as I've had. Addie and I have been married for a long time, and we've got a lot to be thankful for. When I see all my children, my grandchildren, my great-grandchildren, see how well their lives have turned out, I know I haven't lived in vain. My life didn't turn out the way I hoped it would back when I was a boy, but I'm satisfied with it—and when it comes time for me to move on, I'll be ready to go.

Sunday, December 17, 1978: One day in advance of their seventy-fifth wedding anniversary, Burnam and Addie sat side by side near the corner stairway in the living room and received a steady flow of family and friends who came throughout the afternoon to share in their celebration. The room was usually closed and empty during the winter, but on this day it was warmed by the gas furnace in front of the fireplace and filled with a humming murmur of voices. Outside, the air was still and crisp and bell-clear under a cloudless sky.

Christmas and anniversary cards lined the mantel, framing tightly clustered photographs of brides and babies and graduates, and the familiar portrait of Burnam and Addie as a young married couple was carefully placed in the center of the display. Cut flowers and potted plants were placed about on the tables. On the wall above Burnam's head was a small, brightly colored painting of Jesus on the cross. On the opposite wall, a Ledford coat of arms was hung beside a citation designating Curtis Burnam Ledford as a Kentucky Colonel.

Addie wore a pink dress and a strand of pearls; Burnam was dressed in a dark blue suit, a white shirt, and a blue tie. A television cameraman and a newspaper photographer came to record them on film, and numerous members of their family took turns being photographed with them, and through it all, the venerable couple responded with patience and good humor.

"My children kind of fuss at me for not having more nice clothes," Addie said to one of her guests. "But I can beat them all saving money." She and Burnam each wore a diamond pin. "Bill and Joan gave them to us," she explained. "This is our diamond anniversary, you know."

All of the children were present except Eloise and Lucille, and more than a dozen grandchildren and their families were also there. One of the grandsons squatted in front of Burnam and spoke above the buzz of voices in the crowded room. "You and Grandma look real good, Grandpa," he said. "You look young for your age."

"We're getting along pretty well," he replied. "We're not suffering or anything. It helps to have good health. I expect one reason we've lasted this long is that we try not to worry about anything. We just go ahead about our business, and try to stay out of other people's. It don't pay to worry. It's better to look on the bright side as much as possible."

"Well, I want to wish you a happy anniversary—and I hope you have seventy-five more," the grandson said.

Burnam laughed. "No, thanks. We wouldn't want to stretch our luck. I expect this will be our last one."

"I guess we're the oldest married couple in this county," Addie interjected, "and one of the oldest in the country. Burnam read about a couple in Illinois and one in Oregon that married the same year we did, but they weren't as old as we are. I've never been acquainted with anyone who was married this long. It's kind of special, I guess. We've been feeling pretty good so far this winter, so maybe we'll last a while longer. The only problem I've got is my knee. It hurts to walk—and if I fall, I can't get up. I've never really thought much about getting old until now. I used to think a person who was 85 was real old, but I'll soon be 94, and Burnam is going on 103."

All afternoon the visitors came and went, and the old house

echoed with conversation and laughter. It was a scene that had been repeated many times over the years, but this occasion was special; the elders had reached a seldom attained pinnacle of endurance and longevity. They were like the winners and only finishers of a great marathon, and they accepted congratulations and praise for their achievement with grace and humor and quiet modesty.

They sat through the entire afternoon, and when dusk came and the crowd had diminished and the house was almost empty again, they showed no sign of weariness. "It's been a good day, a happy day," Burnam said, as Tillie served supper at the kitchen table. "I never thought I'd live to see it." He returned thanks, and then he and Addie, absorbed in the day's fresh memories, ate lightly without saying much. The red afterglow of sunset filled the room.

"I've had a good time today," Addie said before she retired. "I enjoyed it. It was easier on us than I thought it would be."

A warming southern wind brought rain in the night, and the morning of the eighteenth was cloaked in a gray drizzle. After breakfast, while Burnam was bathing, Addie sat alone on the edge of the Lincoln bed and gazed impassively through the rain-streaked window.

"The day we got married was a better day than this," she remarked. "The sun was shining, I remember. It was a day more like yesterday, only not as cold. I was wearing a long blue wool dress, and Burnam had on a new suit. We rode on horseback into Harlan."

The deep lines in her face were accentuated by the glare of the uncovered ceiling light bulb. Her watery gray eyes seemed to reflect the somber day. "I miss not getting outdoors in the wintertime," she said. "I can't go, though. If I tried to walk in weather like this, I'd probably fall."

In a sense, it was a day like any other winter day for Addie— but it was also a singular day of remembrance, an occasion to recall times past, to remember how things were and to wonder how they might have been:

We've been in this house for fifty years—and when we moved here, every one of our children had already been born. Gwen was just a baby, but Eloise had graduated from college and started teaching school. Bill was out on his own, too. Thirteen children, and ten of them got to be grown. You couldn't support a big family like that now—it'd take too much money. Back then, a little money went a long way. We'd had a little, too, until we lost the farm and the store at Manse. Burnam was a good worker, the best—he got along good working for somebody else—but when he had his own store, he gave out too much credit. He made good money, but he let people fool him out of it. If he had it to do over, I don't think he'd let just anybody buy from him on credit. I've heard him say that, anyway.

I liked that store, liked to work in it, and I've always wished I could have kept on doing it. Our boys were practically raised in a store. They caught on fast, too—they learned how to manage, how to treat people, and every one of them made good storekeepers when they got grown.

I never got to work any more after we moved to town. I couldn't—I had too much to do at home. Maybe it was for the best. Anyway, I've made the best of it. I've had a pretty happy life, everything considered. For an old broke-up woman, I've done pretty good. I learned early to take care of myself, and I still know how. You have to be careful, and look after your money, because you never know what might happen to you in the oldest part of your life. I've always wanted to have something, to get ahead. Burnam appreciates it, in a way, but sometimes he says I've been too cautious about spending money. He can't criticize me too much, though. For my age, I guess I've had about as much education and experience as any woman.

When Burnam was working at the store up in town, I stayed at home and looked after the children, and I've stayed here ever since. We had the garden and our flowers to look after, and I did a lot of canning, and I did most of the milking. That's how I hurt my knee— the old cow pushed me over once when I was milking her. Every doctor that's ever examined me said my knee was out of place, but I just got used to it. Up until the last year or two, it never bothered me much.

After Burnam retired, practically all of our activities was here in the home, and we seldom left the place. Our children were gone, of course, but we were helping to raise some of the grandchildren. Seemed like there was always somebody here with us, either visiting or living in. And then every May we'd have the coming-together for Burnam's birthday. We've been doing that almost ever since we moved into this house, but it's been years since all of the children were here at the same time. I can't even remember when the last time was, but it's probably been twenty or twenty-five years. Maybe they all came when Bruce died, but I don't think so. That was in 1969.

I've only been back to the Paint Lick Cemetery a time or two since then. I don't like to go to cemeteries—they're full of sad memories about people who are gone. It's not that I dread dying or anything—everybody has to die, and it doesn't bother me at all to think about it. I've always tried to live right and be respectable, and I'm not worried about dying. I try not to worry about anything, and I don't cry about what's past. I never was one to cry much—not enough to hurt.

It's not easy to stay married seventy-five years. You have to have extra good health, and you have to get along. We've had some hard times, but we've lived through them, and now we just want to stay together the rest of the way. When I went to the hospital last summer, they wanted to keep me there—and they would have, if I had been willing to stay. If you'd let them, they'd harness you up and take you right on to the nursing home—especially if they knew you had the money to pay for it.

I'm not ready for that, though. If something was to happen to Burnam, I don't know what I'd do, but I wouldn't want to leave here. I'd rather be here than anywhere else, even if I had to be alone. Maybe Tillie would stay on. Burnam's always said I'll outlive him, just so I can catch up to be his age. But you never can tell what will happen.

When both of us are gone, I guess the children will sell this place. It's an old house, not in the best of condition, and I don't imagine any of them would want to live in it. Tillie will probably go back to Indianapolis, and Gwen's got her own home, and I don't reckon Dorothy or Jennie would want it.

I doubt if the family will still come together much after we're gone. They're all scattered out, and they've got their own lives to live. If they weren't coming here to see me and Burnam, they probably wouldn't have much reason to keep holding a homecoming every year.

EIGHTEEN

Waiting for April

Burnam and Addie, 1979–1982

Christmas passed, and through the short days and long nights of January, Burnam and Addie waited patiently in their warm cocoon for the signs of reassurance that another season of new beginnings was approaching. The first such sign was January 1, the start of the new calendar year of 1979. It came riding on frigid gusts of arctic wind, and the siege of ice and snow that followed seemed almost interminable. Then came January 25, Addie's personal new year, the beginning of her ninety-fifth year of life.

"I never was this old before," she said with a smile, "and I never thought of getting to be this old." She got several cards in the mail, and some phone calls, and she had a few visitors, but in the main it was a quiet day like most others, and in her tranquil countenance she seemed content with that.

Burnam's anniversary of birth was May 26, four months after Addie's, and he looked forward with some enthusiasm to reaching the age of 103. But before that day came, there would be another day of new beginning for him: April 1. It was his annual symbol of safe passage, a vital transition from the dark death of winter to the healing warmth of spring.

"If I live through March, I'll live the rest of the year," he liked to say, and he had been saying it for a quarter of a century or more. Winter, he reasoned, was the time to die, when nature itself was either dead or sleeping and the frozen landscape seemed to offer no hope of resurrection. Every year between December 19 and March

31, Burnam pronounced himself ready and willing to go at any moment, but he disliked the thought of dying between April 1 and December 18. In his mind, that would be like walking out on unfinished business, almost like leaving in the middle of things, and he had always dismissed the very idea of such a waste. He realized, of course, as he moved on into his second century, that he had no more unfinished business left, and his rational side fully accepted the prospect of death, even welcomed it. Even so, his optimistic nature and sheer force of habit seemed to focus his winter thoughts in the direction of April 1.

February was the worst month—the shortest, but the hardest. Winter's novelty had long since worn thin, and the muffled beauty of the first snowfall had faded from memory, giving way to the dingy gray ugliness and discomfort of endless weeks of ice and slush and bitter cold. The worst of that never touched Burnam and Addie directly, but almost as bad as the weather was the waiting, and it could not be avoided; they got around it simply by accepting it, and by making the most of every diversion.

Company was one such pastime and television another, and perhaps best of all was remembrance. Burnam spent much of each day reading, but they also talked a lot to each other, to Tillie, to visitors, and even to themselves. Better by far than any soap opera, talk was a nourishing and stimulating part of their diet, as vital as daily bread. Talk took them back to Harlan, to Paint Lick and Manse; it took them from women's suffrage to the Equal Rights Amendment, from covered wagons to space exploration, from Grover Cleveland to Jimmy Carter.

"I feel for Carter," Addie said one day. "He's in a tight spot. I sympathize with him." Burnam readily agreed.

"Would you vote for him next time?" I asked.

"I might," Addie replied. "It all depends on who the Republicans put up. I liked President Ford, and I like Senator Dirksen's son-in-law, that young fellow from Tennessee, but I like Carter too. He's an honest man. That's hard to find in a politician."

One of Burnam's principal winter interests was basketball, and in particular the fortunes of the University of Kentucky Wildcats.

He watched them avidly on a nineteen-inch portable black and white television set, and on the wall above it hung an autographed picture of the previous year's team, which had won the national collegiate championship. Coach Joe B. Hall and the team members and their play-by-play broadcaster, Burnam's distant cousin Cawood Ledford, were all aware of his support, and Cawood had been known to refer to Burnam on the air, though they had never met. Burnam reveled in his growing renown as "the oldest Wildcat fan."

When the 1979 tournament began, he wore his Wildcat cap and socks for good luck and sat close to the TV screen, his expression a blend of joy and expectation. Later, when the last hope of a second successive Wildcat championship had flickered and died, he was momentarily a picture of dejection, but it didn't take him long to recover. There was always next year—and better yet, almost immediately, there was baseball.

This year, though, there was another disturbing development: Pete Rose had deserted Burnam's beloved Cincinnati Reds and joined their hated rivals, the Philadelphia Phillies. When he allowed himself to dwell on the defeat of the Wildcats and the prospect of the Reds without Rose, it was only a short distance to the conclusion that serious problems in the world of sports were a portent and a symbol of deeper ills in the world at large.

"Ever since Rose hit safely in forty-four straight games last summer, he's been a changed man," Burnam said sadly. "Greed ruined him, and it's ruining baseball and all other sports. The big stars get too much money and too much praise, and it's gone to their heads. They think they're so important that they can get away with anything. Pride goeth before a fall. People are like nations—they get too big, too rich, too self-centered, and sooner or later they're bound to fall."

"People aren't as honest now as they were back when I was small," said Addie. "Growing up in the mountains, I don't remember knowing a single dishonest person where we lived. There was plenty of rough ones, but they weren't dishonest. A man's word was his bond. And people don't work as hard now, either. They get more money for less work."

"They don't have to work as hard," Burnam responded. "Nobody has to make do the way we did. Compared to when I was a boy, it's different now, altogether different. It's better in some ways—people are broader minded, better educated, they have more opportunities, they can dream bigger dreams and have more hope of making them come true. They know a lot of things we didn't know. But they don't know the right things. They're not any smarter. They have more information, but they don't know as much about living as we did. I think I'd rather grow up back then than now. It was a slower way of living, and it didn't change much, and you knew what to expect. It wasn't an easy life, not nearly as comfortable as now, but I thought of it then as a good life—and I still do."

"Politics is not as bad now as it used to be," Addie said. "People seem like they're more divided, though, don't you think? But you can't have your pick of times to live in."

Burnam was silent for a moment; then he said, "You can take history clear back to the beginning, and you'll see the same story repeated over and over. When people get prosperous and self-dependent they forget about God, and then trouble comes, and they have to fall all the way to the bottom before they can start back up again. This world is in a terrible mix-up right now because so many people and nations are acting that way, and there'll be a showdown one of these days. Everywhere you look there's dissatisfaction, there's wars and rumors of wars. We're falling down to the bottom, and we've got to get on our knees before we'll ever come back up. I don't know how long it'll be before the world hits bottom, but it's coming. I'm not worried about it for myself, because I'll be gone soon—but I worry about it for the people of the future."

Burnam could not have imagined, in the spring of 1979, that he would still be alive and alert past the age of 106 in 1983, or that Addie would still be with him, as serene as ever on her ninety-eighth birthday in January 1983. Their combined age of 204 might have made them the oldest living couple in the nation, had there been reliable records of such longevity, and their seventy-nine-year marriage also must have ranked among the longest. Their status as minor celebrities grew with each passing year, not only in Garrard County and central Kentucky but beyond; newspaper and television reporters recorded each new milestone, and the mail brought congratulations and good wishes from kin and friends and even strangers. Radio commentator Paul Harvey, the National Broadcasting Company's *Today* show, and three presidents of the United States sent post-centennial birthday greetings to Burnam.

"The Lord works in mysterious ways," he concluded, shaking his head. "He must want to keep us here for some reason, so we'll just have to be content to stay and wait." Thus, in the rhythmic turning of the seasons, with resignation and some impatience, Burnam and Addie waited.

In the first year of my acquaintance with them and their extended family, I had recorded nearly a hundred hours of taped conversations and converted the tapes to more than 600 pages of typed transcription. In addition, I had accumulated hundreds of pages of handwritten notes and a bulky assortment of maps, clippings, letters, charts, and photographs. As I worked periodically during the next three and a half years on the mammoth task of turning the material into a single narrative, I continued to make regular trips to Lancaster, adding all the while to my store of genealogical and historical information.

Since I already had virtually all of the material I needed in order to complete the book, the visits I made to Burnam and Addie and other members of the family between the spring of 1979 and the summer of 1982 were more for social than informational purposes. Nevertheless, I rarely came away without some new fact or quote or acquaintance to strengthen the story, and I kept adding notes to my collection as I went along. In my notebooks, numerous entries over those years attested to the magnetism of the elder Ledfords, and to their seemingly unquenchable vitality.

July 1979: A few weeks past his 103rd birthday, Burnam seemed to be rapidly losing his ability to walk, even with the aid of his aluminum walker. Tillie got a wheelchair to move him from the bedroom to the kitchen and the front porch, but that, too, proved to be hazardous.

On the 26th of June, Addie had decided to go out behind the
house to pick some blackberries. "I tried to talk her out of it,"
Burnam explained later, "but she wouldn't listen. Directly, she fell
down out there in the weeds and commenced hollering for somebody to come and help her. Tillie ran and got two of the neighbors,
and they went down there to get Addie up on her feet. I backed my
wheelchair off the porch and over to the driveway so I could see
what was happening, but I must have hit a bump or something,
because I turned over—just went over backwards out of the chair."
Tillie rushed him to the doctor, where he was found to have a
sprained shoulder and cuts on his forehead and one arm, but no
broken bones. When they were finally back at home and the excitement had passed, Burnam found humor in the incident. "I fall some,"
he admitted, laughing, "but I generally find a soft spot to land.
This time I didn't."

He was feeling well enough when I visited a few days later for
us to take a drive, so with Addie and Tillie we made a tour of some
of their former homeplaces in Garrard County—the Sugar Creek
farm on the Buckeye Pike, the farm on Doty Lane, and their last
country place across the road from the store at Manse. There was
nothing left to see except empty land, a few young trees grown old,
and the Manse store, which still dispensed country wares and yielded
up to us some soft drinks for our refreshment. At the old cemetery
nearby, we stopped briefly to see the graves of Ewell and Bruce, of
Burnam's parents and Addie's mother, and of other family members. "I don't like to visit cemeteries," Addie remarked as we drove
away. Burnam laughed. "The next time I come," he said, "I'll be
staying."

October 1979: Early in the month, Addie became suddenly and
quite seriously ill. Bloated, gray, gasping—but unexcitable, as always—she was taken by ambulance to a hospital in Danville. The
doctor diagnosed her ailment as a life-threatening accumulation of
fluid around her heart. She responded quickly to treatment, and
ten days later she was back at home, showing hardly a trace of the
trauma she had suffered. "I thought I had asthma," she explained.
"I couldn't get a good breath, and I had a strange noise in my chest.

Then my arms began to swell and turn hard as a rock, and I got a little scared. Everything's all right now, though—and I'm mighty glad to be back home."

As the Kentucky gubernatorial campaign drew to a close, Addie called it "the dullest election I can remember." She and Burnam both decided to vote Republican, as usual, rejecting the appeals of Democratic candidate John Young Brown Jr., whose father's mid-century political career they had admired but never supported.

Their ninety-one-year-old friend and neighbor, Martha Noe Conn, came frequently for visits, and her cheerful good humor always lifted their spirits. Eloise Beatty came from Colorado for a week's visit, and so did Martha Napier Nolan, Addie's half-sister. In 1925, she and her sister Delora had gone to the state of Washington on the train, taking Addie with them to see their brother George. Addie came back, of course, and Delora eventually went on to live elsewhere, but Martha now looked back on fifty-four years of life in the Northwest. For fifty of those years, she had been married to George Nolan, another expatriate from the hills of Harlan County. "Addie and Burnam helped to raise Delora and me when we were young," Martha said, recalling her childhood. "We've always loved them just like parents."

Helen and Henry Pope, two more native Harlan Countians— and kinfolks—also came to see the elder Ledfords and Eloise and Martha. The Popes were self-made experts on the history of Harlan County and the genealogy of many of its families. Their wealth of facts and lore and stories from the past made them especially welcome to Burnam and Addie. With them and Martha Conn and Martha Nolan present, the old house reverberated with mountain reminiscences.

February 1980: Burnam and Addie's seventy-sixth anniversary and Addie's ninety-fifth birthday passed without much fanfare. In a dark blue dress with white polka dots, Addie had looked her best—looked, said Burnam, "like a seventeen-year-old girl." Then the winter snows had come, in the midst of which Tillie had gone to Richmond to help her daughter Bobbie Jo, who had just given birth to a baby girl. Gwen came by daily, but Burnam and Addie were alone most of the time—somewhat handicapped, but uncomplaining. "Looks like we're up against it," he said, when I happened by to see them. With a three-day growth of white whiskers he looked weary, but he insisted that he had been eating and sleeping well. He was reading John Fetterman's *Stinking Creek,* a penetrating portrait of mountain life. "It's good," he said, "it's true." His grandson Gary Hammon, Tillie's son, had just brought them a big-screen color television set "just in time for the basketball tournaments," Burnam exclaimed. Even so, the snow was deep and the weather was bitterly cold, and they were indeed at a disadvantage.

Addie seemed completely unaffected by the turn of events. "No use to get nerves," she said casually. "We'll make out all right. I've seen better days, far better—but I've seen worse, too. I've seen it all. I understand it all. Don't worry. We'll get by." And they did.

July 1980: Having "made it through March by the skin of my teeth"—and made it cheerfully through his 104th birthday celebration—Burnam found himself in mid-summer facing "spells where I can't get my breath, and I feel like I'm choking, or smothering to death." But he had a new doctor and a new friend in George Noe, a thirty-two-year-old physician and kinsman whose grandfather had been a turn-of-the-century student of Burnam's at a school near Paint Lick. The quick rapport that developed between Dr. Noe and his elderly patient was readily apparent. "I'm not too anxious to stay around much longer," Burnam said, "but while I'm still here, Dr. Noe is taking good care of me."

His recovery may have been hastened by the advent of the political season. The new TV set stayed on throughout the conventions. "Reagan is a stranger to me," Addie said. "I'm not acquainted with him." For his part, Burnam was paying close attention, and not much of significance escaped him.

"Jerry Ford made the speech of his life last night," he told me one morning, after he had stayed up past midnight with the Republicans. "Betty looked good, too—better than she used to. Reagan is going to beat Carter, no question about it. I feel sorry for Carter. He's an honest man with good intentions, but he just can't handle the job."

November 1980: They cast their presidential ballots for Ronald Reagan. "Somebody's got to lose," Burnam said philosophically. "To tell you the truth, I feel sorry for whichever one wins. In this case, the winner might turn out to be the loser. This Iran situation worries me. Looks like we're in bad shape. The world's in bad shape, pitiful shape."

Addie, too, was melancholy. "You know," she said one day, "old age slips up on you. I hadn't realized I was old until just lately." She had experienced no more heart problems, but was recovering slowly from a heavy case of flu.

Their solemn mood may have been a carryover from the shock of Becky Ledford Eversman's death in September. The thirty-two-year-old daughter of Carl and Geraldine Ledford had been stricken with a rare form of encephalitis. She was the first of Burnam and Addie's thirty-two adult grandchildren to die.

May 1981: On the occasion of his 105th birthday, Burnam seemed to have found an untapped reserve of strength: Throughout a long and strenuous day, he sat uncomplainingly in his wheelchair on the front porch, welcoming all of his nine children and most of his grandchildren and great-grandchildren, along with scores of other well-wishers. In addition, he and Addie were the star performers in a thirty-minute television documentary being videotaped by Randy Smith, a talented young camera artist from Arkansas. From early morning until sundown, the aged couple performed like seasoned troupers. They were constantly on camera, but they never flagged—and they seemed to enjoy every minute of the day.

July 1981: Burnam spent ten days in the Garrard County Hospital for treatment of pneumonia, fluid around his heart, and other complications. "His mind is as good as ever," Tillie said, "but his body is just about shot, just worn out." He had been home from the hospital several days when I went to see him. "They just made a guinea pig out of me," he complained. "Filled me full of pills and stuck me with needles until finally I told Tillie to get me out of there and let me die at home. I'm pretty helpless now. Tillie has to bathe me and shave me, and I have to be lifted in and out of bed. I couldn't have made it this far without Tillie. She's been wonderful. She's made a big sacrifice to stay at home and look after us."

A hospital bed had to be crowded into the Ledford bedroom to accommodate Burnam when he returned home. Propped up there, he looked smaller somehow, as if he had been physically diminished by his ordeal. His untrimmed fringe of white hair was spiderweb fine and curling over the collar of his pajama shirt. He spat tobacco juice into a stainless steel hospital pan. In spite of his frailness, he managed to talk and smile and laugh the same as always.

"Addie thinks I ought to get over there and sleep in the bed with her, but I can't," he said. "I have to have these railings to hold on to." Later, when I told him goodbye, he grinned and said, "I'll try my best to wait around here until you come back. I couldn't get into any meanness if I wanted to."

February 1982: They had celebrated yet another anniversary in December, and Addie had quietly observed another birthday in January, but February was a bad-luck month: Tillie developed congestion and a heart problem, Burnam suffered from a badly infected toe, and both of them ended up in the hospital at the same time. I went to visit them at the first opportunity, and found Tillie already at home and making a rapid recovery. "The medicine did wonders for me," she said. "I definitely feel a lot better. The doctor says I might even get stronger than I was before I got sick—if I can quit smoking."

But Burnam remained in the hospital, and poor circulation eventually led to the amputation of his infected toe. He came through the operation with no complications, but he was fussy and in low spirits when I went in to see him. "The Lord spent 105 years building me up, and now these doctors are trying to drug me to death in a few days," he complained. "I'll be glad when I die and go to heaven, so I can get away from doctors and drugs."

"What if there's doctors and drugs in heaven?" I responded.

"Can't be. If there was, everybody'd be going the other way."

At the house, I had visited with Addie and Tillie and sister Jennie McLendon, who had come from Lexington to take over Tillie's chores. "Addie seems to be getting along all right," I reported to

Burnam, "but she misses you. She told me, 'I'm so lonesome I don't know what to do.'"

"She's been up here to see me several times," Burnam said, "and when she comes, she wants to kiss me. I guess that's a sign she misses me, all right."

The television documentary about the Ledford family home-coming was shown for the first time on the Kentucky Educational Television Network late in February. I couldn't be present to watch it at the hospital with Burnam, but Gwen was there, and she told me about it later. "Everybody was gathered around the TV set in the big public room," she said, "and Papa was right up front. He sang a hymn at the end of the movie, you know—and when it came on the screen, he just sang right along with himself. It was really something. There wasn't a dry eye in that room."

May 1982: In Burnam's absence, Addie seemed vulnerable and dispirited. "She's pretty hard to get along with sometimes," said Tillie, whose own illness had kept her down only briefly. "Papa's well enough to come home, but he has to be lifted in and out of bed, and I can't do that. We'll bring him home for his birthday, of course, but unless we can figure out a better arrangement, he may never get out to stay. He gets more attention from the nurses than I can give him, and he has more company there too. I hate to say it, but in some ways he's better off in the hospital than he would be at home."

When the first of April had come, Burnam had felt both better and worse—better because April was his sign of survival, and worse because he remained confined away from home. Addie, after suffering two serious cases of winter flu, was hospitalized with pneumonia in May, and for a time it appeared that neither of them might make it home for Burnam's birthday. But by Memorial Day, May 30, Addie had been released—and when Burnam was driven into the front yard in a rescue squad ambulance, he emerged on a stretcher singing hymns of praise.

"Hallelujah!" he shouted. "I never thought I'd live to see this day!" Settled in his wheelchair, he was taken to meet Addie on the porch, and then they were relocated on the shady lawn, where they exchanged a kiss as cameras clicked.

The family was there in large numbers for the occasion: nine children, twenty-two grandchildren, forty great-grandchildren, eighteen spouses. Scores of in-laws, cousins, neighbors, and friends swelled the crowd to about two hundred. It was a changed family since I had first met them in 1978. One grandchild had died and seven great-grandchildren had been born; four grandchildren had married, but the marriages of four others had ended in separation or divorce. There were forty-six living great-grandchildren. At one time or another 142 individuals had belonged by birth or marriage to the four-generation family of Burnam and Addie; death or divorce had removed 22 of them, but 120 remained, and 82 of them were present on the day their patriarch celebrated the attainment of his 106th birthday.

There were larger and older families in America, closer ones, richer and more accomplished ones. The Ledfords belonged to the uncelebrated center, the middle mass of citizens about whom history customarily is not written. Yet they and other families strikingly similar to them had always been the nation's majority, the followers without whom there could have been no leaders. If they had not made history, they had at least made it possible.

Nine generations and two and a half centuries after three young men named Ledford left England—quite possibly from the vicinity of a place called Lancaster—in search of a new life beyond the Atlantic, one of their descendants reached the age of 106 in a place called Lancaster, Kentucky. Between the former and the latter, countless thousands of Americans had come and gone in the burgeoning clan of Ledfords. Thousands still remained, more often than not without any knowledge of those who had borne their name and prepared the way for them.

With their keen sense of history, Burnam and Addie understood this lesson of continuity as few could. For a century, they had lived and listened and remembered; it was all in their thoughts, kept there for any who would pay heed.

As his birthday drew to a close, Burnam was quietly reflective. "I haven't allowed myself to think much past today," he said. "I've just been thanking God for letting me live this long. I've been wonderfully blessed to be able to keep my mind, so I can think and talk and read, and so I can enjoy all the people who come to see me. This day was worth waiting for. Me and Addie are thankful for this family, and mighty proud of them, every one of them. When we started out together in Harlan County seventy-eight years ago, we never could have dreamed it would come to this."

In the healing days of a benevolent Bluegrass summer, Burnam was to make a remarkable comeback. In July, he would leave the hospital for home and for a resumption of life with Addie and Tillie in the weathered old farmhouse on the edge of Lancaster. In August, their neighbors and the public officials of Garrard County would change the name of the road in front of the house from Old Kentucky Route 52 to Ledford Lane, and Burnam, wearing his blue and white Kentucky Wildcat cap, would say at the ceremony of dedication that he was touched by the honor, and express the hope that all who entered the street would think of it as "a road of love." And in September, as Garrard Countians celebrated the harvest of their number one cash crop, tobacco, their number one citizen, Curtis Burnam Ledford, a tobacco chewer for almost a century, would serve as grand marshal of the local tobacco festival parade. With Addie and Tillie, he would ride in an open convertible through the streets of Lancaster, not seeing the smiling faces or hearing the cheers of his fellow townspeople but sensing the praise, and receiving it with gratitude and humility.

After a separation of nearly six months, Burnam and Addie were together again in the old house. Through the rest of the summer of 1982, they were back in their familiar place on the front porch, and I and others who went to visit became accustomed again to finding them there, still remembering and repeating the stories of continuity and change that had shaped their lives, their history. For nearly five years, they had been telling those stories to me. Together we had looked backward across the generations and the centuries, assembling a scattered and largely unrecorded account of one anonymous family's endurance. Burnam and Addie, the principal narrators, had given the story color and vibrancy and meaning; they had made it real. I in turn had written it down, not as a literal and mechanical transcription of our recorded conversations or as a studiously detached and objective rendering of their lives, but as an interpretation drawn from all the Ledfords and sifted through the filter of my own imperfect understanding. Now it was almost finished. Burnam had already studied most of the manuscript, and he had read portions of it aloud to Addie. We shared a sense of completion in it, a sense of accomplishment; along with that, we also shared the rare pleasure of an intimate friendship.

Summer faded, and another autumn splashed the leaves with crimson and amber and then swept them away in waves of wind and rain. Winter emerged again in the relentless cycle, advertised by every approaching line of dark and heavy storm clouds. Slowly, the land was drained of its color, reduced to dull, flat shades of brown and gray. There was something about the somber landscape, something both sad and comforting, that reminded Burnam of Harlan, of home. The scenes and the sounds always came back to his mind in the fall and winter—mellowed now, no doubt, by his distance from them in space and time. He remembered Harlan County once again, remembered vividly and with pleasure the adventures of his boyhood and youth in the mountains.

"I memorized dozens of hymns and songs when I was a boy," he said one afternoon. "I can still remember a lot of them. Me and Addie sing them together sometimes."

His voice was high-pitched and a little shaky, but it was loud, and it conveyed deep feeling. When he had finished one verse, Addie joined in on the next, singing deeper and softer than he but with the same feeling, and their duet reverberated against the thin bedroom walls that sheltered them from the cold, wet, winter wind:

I'm thinking tonight of my old cabin home,
That stands on the brow of the hill,
Where in life's early morning, I once loved to roam,
But now all is quiet and still.

Another verse followed. They sat close together in the middle of the room. Their aged and lovely faces were a study, a picture of remembrance and forgiveness and endurance beyond imagining. They sang the last verse:

One by one they have gone from that old cabin home,
On earth we shall see them no more,
But soon we will meet in that heavenly home,
Where parting will be never more.

Peacefully, patiently, they waited together for the end of winter—and for the first day of April.

Homecoming, 1983

Sunday, February 13: Burnam was propped up in a chair beside the window in Room A-4 of the Garrard County Memorial Hospital. He had been a patient there for almost a week, suffering from shingles, flu, and pneumonia. At one point he was in critical condition, struggling for his life under an oxygen tent, but now his amazing recuperative powers seemed to be working once again.

"Is that you, John?" he asked, squinting to bring my face into focus. "I've been looking for you, hoping you'd get here." Dorothy was sitting with him, and Jennie and Herb and Carl were coming later. Addie and Tillie were at home in bed with the flu; Owen was looking after them. Bill and Eloise and Lucille were also preparing to come. The concerned family was drawing closer.

"I've always told you I'd try to wait around until you come back," Burnam said, "but this time I just barely made it." The effects of his ordeal were etched in the lines on his thin face.

"Everyone has told me how sick you've been," I said to him. "I'm glad you're better. It's a good sign that you're able to sit up."

He shook his head. "Uh-uhm. I'm not going to get well. It's time for me to go home now, John. I'm ready to go. I feel like I've done all I can do in this world. I thank God for letting me keep my mind right up to the end, but I don't want to stay any longer. I'm getting out of life now, before I get old and lose my mind."

There was nothing I could say in response to that. I tried to change the subject: "I brought you something, Burnam. Here's our book at last, all set in type, ready to be printed. It's finally finished. You need to get well now, so we can go around and show it off together." I placed the sheaf of page proofs in his lap.

339

He picked them up, weighed them in his gnarled hands, held them up close to his face. For several minutes, he read silently from the paragraphs on the top page. Then he put the pages down again.

"I'm glad you're through," he said. "Some people will get a lot out of reading that book. I'd like to read it again myself, but I won't be able to. It doesn't matter, though—I know what's in it. I'm just glad I could wait this long, so I could see it. But I don't want to wait any longer. I'm tired now. I'm ready to go on."

Once more I tried to redirect his thoughts. Some funny stories he had told me came to mind, and when I awakened his memory to them, he dutifully told them again. Slowly, his mood changed; in a few minutes he was smiling, and then, between deep coughs, laughing.

". . . and Hardin kept unwrapping and unwrapping that package, and finally he held up a bottle of whiskey, and Bradley said to him, 'Wat, that's the first good thing I ever saw come out of the *Courier-Journal* in my entire life.'" Burnam coughed again, and then went on:

"There's one thing in my life I'm proudest of: I've heard Republicans and Democrats both say I was the one person in Garrard County they could count on to be fair and honest to everybody, no matter what politics or color or religion they was. I always was a peacemaker. Now that I've come to the end of my life, I can truthfully say that I love everybody. I have absolutely no hatred in my heart for anybody in this world."

A nurse entered, smiling, and gently tried to win his acceptance of the pill she had brought him, but Burnam adamantly refused. "No more medicine!" he exclaimed. "I won't take any more! No more pills! I'm done with pills! They've been a curse to me! I'm trying to die and go home! You tell that doctor not to send me any more medicine!" Then, reaching back into some long-shuttered repository of lyrical and poetic expression, he sang, "This world is not my home. This world's a wilderness of woe."

His voice was hoarse and strained. Fierce defiance flashed in his blue eyes. His facial features seemed accentuated by his thinness. Wispy strands of snow-white hair curled softly against his ears and the back of his neck. I listened to him and looked at him in wonder. He was a hawk, a great bald eagle, ancient and indomitable.

The nurse retreated. We sat in silence for a few moments. "I'm not going to wish you to live as long as I have," Burnam said at length. "It's pitiful to get to be helpless. I've tried my best to die. I guess I just don't know how."

I groped for a response. Nothing came. Finally, I told him I had been to see Addie and Tillie, and they were better, recovering from their siege of flu.

"They brought Addie up here to X-ray her," Burnam said, "to make sure she didn't have pneumonia. They let her come in here to see me. I said to her, 'Addie, I'm ready to go home, ready to die. Are you ready to go with me?' She said she wasn't. So I asked her, 'If I go on ahead and then call you to join me, will you come?' And she told me she would. That put my mind at ease. I feel a lot better now, just knowing that she would come if I sent for her."

I remembered a story that Tillie had told me earlier in the winter. She was in the living room one evening after Burnam and Addie had gone to bed, and she heard this exchange:

"Burnam, are you awake? I love you."

There was no answer. Addie spoke louder: "Burnam? I said I love you."

"Huh? What'd you say?"

"You can't hear thunder! I SAID I LOVE YOU! I never did love anyone but you."

After a pause, Burnam replied, "I love you too, Addie. I must have loved you right from the first. You're the only one I ever did ask to marry me."

Now their seventy-nine-year union was almost over. Burnam sat like a traveler with his bags packed, waiting for the train. He had made his preparations; now he was impatient to leave.

We clasped hands, embraced, said our goodbyes. "I'm not going to promise you any more that I'll try to wait for you to come back," he said. "This is the last time I'll see you."

When I reached the door and looked back, he waved to me.

There was the faintest trace of a smile on his face. Then he looked away. Deep in the mountain valley of his mind, the train's whistle was sounding, coming closer.

Sunday, February 20, 1983: The last homecoming for Curtis Burnam Ledford brought the generations together one more time. They followed him across the pastoral Bluegrass landscape from Lancaster to the old Paint Lick Cemetery at Manse, and there they stood in a circle around him for a few last words of parting. It was a glorious late-winter day, warmed and brightened with a promise of the April he could not wait for.

Afterword, 2003

The publication of *Generations* in the fall of 1983 was a bitter-sweet occasion for me. After six years of searching and research-ing, writing and rewriting, I was finally finished with the book that had come to dominate my working life, and its completion was certainly a cause for celebration. But the leading man, Burnam Ledford, was not around to take his bows, and without him, the story he had longed to see in print could only have a wistful ending.

After Burnam was laid to rest at Paint Lick, no one in the fam-ily could muster the spirit to organize another Memorial Day home-coming at the old house in Lancaster, and so the occasion of his 107th birthday on May 26, 1983, passed quietly without a formal observance. A few months later, as his beloved Addie seemed to be slipping toward physical infirmity, their nine remaining children decided to move her into a nursing home in Stanford, ten miles away. Tillie King, the daughter who had come down from India-napolis five years earlier to assume primary responsibility for her parents' care, was beginning to develop health problems of her own; she could take a small apartment in Lancaster, they all agreed, and the house would be sold.

The first time Addie had found herself facing this prospect, in 1978, she had talked her way to freedom—but this time there would be no escape, and she knew it. Whatever else Addie was, she was a realist; she had learned from long and sometimes bitter experience when to keep fighting and when to give up. The last place on earth she wanted to die was in a nursing home, but that was the unavoid-able destination she saw in front of her. So when they took her there, she held her head high and fixed her eyes forward and sat ramrod-straight in her wheelchair. You would have thought the queen of England was coming to live in that cheerless place.

The children and grandchildren divided up the family belongings. (Carl got the Lincoln bed that he and Bill had bought at auction for their parents in the mid-1920s.) By December 18, the date of Burnam and Addie's eightieth wedding anniversary, the weatherworn homeplace on Ledford Lane stood dark and empty, awaiting eventual sale and renovation by new owners. Addie, the stoic heroine of *Generations,* never saw the house again. She remained in the Stanford nursing home for four more years. Finally, on December 12, 1987, six weeks shy of her 103rd birthday, she died peacefully in her sleep.

She was alert and inquisitive all the way to the end, intently practicing her history and striving to keep it straight in her mind. Almost a century after she had started first grade in a tiny one-room schoolhouse in Harlan County, she still took innocent delight in learning and remembering. Through eight decades of married life, Addie and Burnam had fashioned a simple but sturdy framework for their intertwined historical narrative, and it unfailingly sustained an engaging dialogue of adventure, drama, mystery, and humor interspersed with poetry and song. Addie was always more reserved than Burnam, but she had every bit as good a grasp of their family's cast of characters as he.

Even in the nursing home, she retained an air of quiet dignity. The last time I visited with her there, she seemed weaker than ever before, unable to move about independently or to perform the simplest functions without assistance. Her long, silver hair was combed out straight, not piled and clasped at the crown of her head as she had customarily worn it, and the effect was to diminish her somehow, to make her appear even more fragile. But she sat erect with her hands folded in her lap, and her voice was strong and steady. As we talked, her mind floated in and out of reality, from vivid daydreams through blank spaces to the solid ground of minutely detailed recollections.

"Who'd you say you were?" she asked, holding her fingers to

her lips in a familiar pose of reflection. "Where did I know you? Your name sounds familiar. I remember somebody named John, but now I don't know who it was." She paused, searching her mind for the connection. After a minute, she said, "Old John Skidmore was my great-grandfather. He came with Aley Ledford and their families through the Cumberland Gap. He and Aley were the same age, born in 1789. Old John married a nineteen-year-old girl when he was seventy, after his first wife died, and they had several children. Four, I believe it was."

Suddenly her expression shifted and her eyes brightened, as if it was all becoming clear to her. "Listen!" she hissed, in a conspiratorial whisper. "Everything I've told you is the truth, honey, and that's a fact—at least I'm trying to tell you the truth the best I can, but sometimes I forget. Did you know I'm over a hundred years old? I was born in 1885. What year is this? Actually, I think I'm a hundred and two. I don't feel real old, though. I can't get around as good as I used to, but I do pretty well for an old lady." She chuckled softly. "Fact is, I'm a very able-bodied woman for somebody my age."

I asked her if she felt any discomfort. She shook her head and replied, "I'm not in any misery. I've got some kind of disease, but the doctor hasn't told me what it is. My father died of tuberculosis when I was ten. He was a hard worker, but he drank pretty heavy. He was still young when he died—in his thirties. That was in 1903, I believe—no, 1903 was the year I married Burnam. I was almost nineteen and he was twenty-seven. He was a self-made boy, a school teacher. He was born and raised in Harlan County, and moved away, and then he came back to teach. That's when I met him. I was starting out to be a teacher too."

"Tell me about the day you got married." I wanted to hear the story one more time.

"It was a pretty day, but cold, the 18th of December. Me and Burnam met up at my Uncle Curl Pope's house at Cawood. We borrowed horses from Uncle Curl and rode the seven miles into Harlan Town. George Pope, my first cousin, went with us to be our witness. A Baptist preacher named Randall Browning married us at his house. We ate dinner in town and rode back out to Uncle

Curl and Aunt Jerusha's house before dark. Then pretty soon—the next day, I believe it was—we walked across the mountain to catch the train, and moved up here to Garrard County. Paint Lick. Burnam kept store, and I had children—thirteen of them. Let's see: Ewell, Eloise, Bill, Carl . . . I know all of them, if I could just think. You see, I'm getting pretty old. Somebody tried to tell me that I was just 101, but I knew better. I think I'm 102."

"You're right," I assured her.

"I am? You know, Burnam lived to be 106. I might live to be that old myself." She gazed out the window. "How long have I been in this asylum?"

"This is not an asylum, Addie. It's a nursing home."

"What's the difference?" Nothing in her manner made me think she meant the question as a judgment, but still I squirmed under her unblinking stare. She looked away momentarily and then, abruptly, turned back to me with a smile of recognition.

"Did you say your name was John? Are you still writing books? Do you have good luck with them? I bet if you'd leave some of them with me, I could sell them to these old people around here. You could keep all the money. I'd be glad to help you any way I can. I'd like to see you make enough to justify you in fooling with it."

This was familiar ground for both of us. I pulled out the book and showed it to her again, and she examined it as if for the first time. As I read a couple of passages to her, she nodded in affirmation without speaking. When I finished, we sat for a few moments in silence. After a while she said, "So you've got it all written down, have you?"

"Yes, just like you and Burnam told it to me."

"Well, I told you the truth. Everything I told you is the honest truth, and that's a fact." She looked serene and at peace, very much the same as she had the first time I ever saw her. She was confident in her truth, and it had set her free.

A few weeks later, the far-flung Ledford family was summoned once more to Lancaster for Addie's funeral. When the service was over, we lined up behind the hearse for one more caravan to Manse, and there, in the ancient Paint Lick Cemetery, we left her to rest again and forevermore at Burnam's side.

The surviving siblings had asked me to say a few words of parting and remembrance at the funeral home, and I readily agreed, but to my surprise—and theirs—I became choked with emotion in the middle of the eulogy and struggled clumsily to regain control. There was so much that I had wanted to say about Addie and Burnam, but I fell far short of recounting the lives of such remarkable and valiant people.

When it was over, most of the family graciously overlooked my less-than-eloquent performance. Then, to my relief, Tillie came up and hugged me and said—with a mischievous chuckle that could have been her mother's—"We had wanted you to speak at Papa's funeral too, but we didn't think you were ready."

Truth be told, I hadn't been ready for Burnam's passing, and I was just as unprepared for Addie's. It was certainly not that they hadn't lived long enough—almost 210 years between them, and eight decades in the bond of marriage. Rather, it was their stories that I hated to lose, the history that they had kept intact and ongoing. Much of it was passed on orally at first, and then there were tape recordings, and now some of it is even written down, but nothing could ever replace their tandem voices in harmony, spinning by turns the saga of Aley and Betsy and all the Kentucky Ledfords who followed in their wake.

Burnam's death in 1983 and Addie's in 1987 finally halted their narration of a family saga spanning almost two centuries. It had begun with a gripping tale of the death of Aley Ledford's parents at Cumberland Gap on a stormy night in 1802—and it had ended 185 years later in the stillness of a rural Kentucky graveyard just seventy-five miles or so northwest of the gap. But that doesn't begin to measure the distance covered, for in a figurative and representative sense, their journey ranged as far and wide as the history of the American nation itself. Even now, a generation after the passing of Burnam and Addie, the chronicle of the Ledfords invites us all to contemplate a realistic picture of how—family by family, homestead by village by city—our multifaceted country came to be.

At the time of Addie's passing, five of their thirteen children had died previously: two in childbirth, one (Ewell) from an accident at age 13, and another (Bruce) of disease at age 50; the fifth, Jennie Ledford McLendon, was 62 when she died of illness in 1984.

The eight who survived were still going strong a decade after their mother's passing—living proof of the potency of their Ledford longevity genes. But then, beginning in 1999, five of them were gone within the span of just two years. Lucille Smith at age 87, Dorothy Jackson at 86, Tillie King at 77, and Carl Ledford at 91, died in succession, of natural causes; Bill Ledford, who was 92, and Joan, his wife of sixty-seven years, both succumbed to the trauma of an automobile accident near their home in Mt. Sterling in August of 2001. (This was a stunning repeat of history: the third time a senior male Ledford and his wife had died together in an accident. Aley's parents were crushed to death when a tree fell on their wagon, and in 1918, Burnam's parents died when a train struck their car at a railroad crossing near Paint Lick.)

Still surviving in the spring of 2003 were Eloise Beatty, the eldest at 96, living in Colorado; Herbert Ledford, 86, at home in Somerset with his wife, Hazel; and Gwendolyn Gastineau, 75 and the youngest of the original thirteen, living near Lancaster with her husband, Russell. Though all of Burnam and Addie's children had been born in Garrard County, Gwen was the only one to remain there.

The Memorial Day homecomings that had kept the family connected for so many years were never resumed after Burnam's death; by that time, the extended family spanned four generations and included almost 150 people. After the last big event in 1982, the one family splintered into several, and these in turn have tried, with varying degrees of success, to keep intact some semblance of their Ledford heritage. The largest by far is the Somerset-based clan of Carl and Geraldine Ledford, sixty strong and still growing in the new century. They gather in full force for ceremonial occasions, and when Carl passed away in May 2001 (dying in his sleep in the antique Lincoln bed that had belonged to his parents), all of them came together around their matriarch, Gerry, who had assured the great size of their branch of the family tree by bearing eleven healthy children in the 1940s and 1950s.

The sons and daughters of Burnam and Addie did occasionally gather in clusters of two or three or more after their parents died, but by 2001, the only interfamily meetings were at funerals. By then, the original total of ten senior siblings had fallen to only three, and the family focus had already shifted to the next generation.

The children of Burnam and Addie's children collectively carried some readily identifiable Ledford traits. For example, they were remarkably healthy; all but one of the thirty-three had reached adulthood without a life-threatening illness or accident. One of these, Becky Eversman (daughter of Carl), died at age thirty-two of encephalitis, and another, Carole Starnes (daughter of Gwen), was killed in a car accident when she was forty. With few exceptions, the other thirty, who ranged in age from the mid-forties to the mid-sixties, had no life-altering health problems as of 2003.

They were lifetime Kentuckians, by and large. All but four of them had been born in the state, and two-thirds lived within its borders as the new century began. Most of them by far were college graduates (unlike their parents, only one of whom had earned a degree), but in several other dimensions—religion, politics, occupation—their profile tended to resemble that of their elders: nominally Protestant, habitually Republican, primarily engaged in business. Woven into that familiar fabric were a few different threads—Catholic and Jew and agnostic; Democrat and independent and nonvoter; teacher, lawyer, farmer, broker, mechanic. As a group, they were about as disposed as their parents to marry and have children (but, curiously, only half as inclined to divorce).

In general, the Ledford grandchildren had fulfilled the dream of their forebears that their generation would share more fully in the fruits of an affluent society. The thirty of them could fairly be said to symbolize and personify the upwardly mobile American middle class. Indeed, their material possessions and modern lifestyles far exceeded anything their grandparents could have imagined when they married in Harlan County in 1903. Back then, even the most prosperous families in Harlan lived by lantern light, spring water, wood heat, and mule power; in contrast, these urbanized descendants had the world at their fingertips—and credit cards to pay the fare. It is hard for anyone who has grown up in the contemporary electronic age, with its myriad choices and instant gratifications, to fully grasp the pervasive isolation and hardship that characterized life in the Kentucky mountains a hundred years ago, or fifty, or even more recently.

In the next generation of Ledfords—the great-grandchildren of Burnam and Addie—changes came at an even swifter pace. Starting in 1962, a total of fifty-eight babies were born into this wave of the extended family, and by the time the last of them came along in 1997, a dozen of the older ones were already having children of their own. Fifty-five of the great-grandchildren entered the twenty-first century in good health. (Carole Gastineau Starnes gave birth in 1974 to twin sons that were stillborn, and sixteen-year-old Mark Ledford, one of Carl's grandsons, died in a car wreck in 2000.)

The first two to reach the age of forty, in 2002, were Bill Ledford's grandson Mark, who was serving as president of a bank in Mt. Sterling, and Jenny Ledford's granddaughter Kimberly Allen, who was a commodities trader specializing in corn futures at the Chicago Board of Trade. The youngest at that time was Becky Gastineau Hacker's five-year-old son, William Russell Hacker. All but seven of the fifty-five were in their twenties or thirties. Some of them were still pursuing higher education, but for the most part they already had college degrees, the most advanced being the Ph.D. in neurobiology earned at Yale University by another of Jenny's granddaughters, Jennifer Bourne.

About half of the great-grandchildren lived in Kentucky, but the rest were scattered across more than a dozen other states. Though they were different in many ways from their predecessors, this generation also exhibited some typical Ledford qualities, such as remarkably good health, easygoing dispositions, and a general inclination to avoid life's spotlights in favor of a comfortable seat in the audience. There were exceptions, of course; some of Bill's grandsons played college football (one of them at West Point), Herb

Ledford had granddaughters who exhibited show horses in competitions, a granddaughter of Lucille Ledford was an actress in New York, and Eagle Scouts seemed to pop up in every generation. But the great-grands were not performers, by and large, any more than their grandparents and parents had been—not professional artists or musicians, not courtroom orators, not politicians or preachers. Their more frequent roles after finishing school were as business managers or employees, consumers, and parents. In that last capacity, they were especially prolific.

By the end of 2002, the fourth generation of Ledfords descended from Burnam and Addie already numbered forty, and most of the mothers were still well within their child-bearing prime. The first forty, all healthy except one who died of complications at birth, were about evenly divided between school-age children and preschoolers. The eldest, at fifteen, was Erin Melton, a great-granddaughter of Carl Ledford; she was born in the same year that her great-great-grandmother Addie died.

In sum, what Curtis Burnam Ledford and Addie King started when they were married on December 18, 1903, was a nuclear family that in ninety-nine years would produce 13 children, 33 grandchildren, 58 great-grandchildren, and 40 great-great-grandchildren—altogether, 144 direct descendants. If all the living members of that select group were to gather in, say, Lexington or Lancaster or Harlan in December 2003 to celebrate the centennial of their progenitors' wedding, and if all of their current spouses came along with them, their number would approach 200.

But it is a long way from here to Lancaster, to Harlan—a long way from the contemporary lives of this recognizably if not typically American family to the times and places and circumstances of their forebears. Fewer than half of the living brothers, sisters, aunts, uncles, nieces, nephews, and cousins have any recollection of the Memorial Day homecomings on Ledford Lane in Garrard County that ended in 1982—and only a handful of them have ever set foot in the winding valleys carved by Cranks Creek and Martins Fork in Harlan County, where the Ledford clan spent all of the nineteenth century, from Aley and Betsy's arrival to Burnam and Addie's departure.

It seems highly unlikely that there will ever be another intergenerational homecoming of Ledfords in Harlan, or even in Lancaster. Had it not been for the tradition of oral history, preserved with such diligence by their elders, the descendants of Aley and Betsy today would not have much of a link to their past. The "Harlan century" lost its last eyewitnesses with the departure of Burnam and Addie, and in Lancaster, only the family of Gwen Gastineau carries over from the Ledfords' "Garrard century."

Physical evidence to certify and affirm the Ledfords' Harlan County saga of the 1800s is thin and fragmented—census data, property records, a few wills, a scattering of tombstones. Most of what is now known about the family's long tenure in Appalachia came from the stories told by Aley and Betsy to their children and grandchildren, stories finally entrusted to their great-grandson Burnam, who with Addie became the steward of the family narrative.

The history that is recorded in books, letters, and photographs—or captured with even newer technology, such as video, compact disc, and e-mail—is the conventional and primary source of our remembrance of things past, the record that authenticates our passage into the present. By most assessments, this documentary evidence is more reliable and complete than the oral histories passed along from one generation to the next. Verbally transmitted stories are an inevitable blend of fact and fiction, truth and legend—or so we are inclined to assume.

But history is more than the sum of what has been preserved in physical or electronic form. History is also memory—the past as recalled by those who lived it—and what people remember, whether accurate or not, is as real to them as if it were chiseled in stone. "Everything I've told you is the honest truth," Addie was fond of saying, "and that's a fact." What made her truth and Burnam's so remarkable was the meticulous care with which they gathered information, sifted the wheat from the chaff, and committed to memory the essence of events. Oral history is certainly not foolproof, not universally reliable—but neither are written records. Recorded history is not a neat compilation of everything that has happened but rather a subjective selection of representative happenings interpreted by the recorder. Its effectiveness depends in large measure on who selects the events and how they are reconstructed. When it comes to the telling, the historian using conventional methods and the chronicler of a carefully preserved oral history may stand side by side on a level stage, each armed with the "facts," the "truth." The question is not whether one is better than the other but whether history can ever be fully revealed without the contributions of both.

When the past is presented to us by such memorists as Burnam and Addie Ledford, with their orderly and capacious recollections, it is almost as vivid as if it were still happening and we were living it. Burnam was not born until three years after Aley had passed away, but by the time Betsy died he was sixteen and curious, intrigued by the familial ties that bind—and that personal experience, a direct physical bond across four generations, was something he never forgot. As Burnam and Addie gradually came to understand that they were the designated keepers of the family's history, they took the responsibility to heart and carried it forward for the better part of another century, by which time four more generations had been added to the continuum.

Standing at the graves of the Ledfords in the Paint Lick Cemetery on February 20, 2003, the twentieth anniversary of Burnam's burial there, I knew that their long and winding story had finally reached an end, and it would not be revived and continued as a narrative unless a young listener in the family came forth to pick it up. That could always happen—it happened, after all, to Burnam and Addie—but it seemed unlikely.

Every family has a story to tell, but only the most fortunate have resident storytellers to nourish the roots and keep the chronicle alive. Without them—without people such as Burnam and Addie to breathe air and light into the murky past—we are like miners without lamps, digging in the dark.

The Family of
Curtis Burnam Ledford (1876–1983)
and Addie King Ledford (1885–1987)
as of June 2003

JESSE EWELL LEDFORD, 1905–1918

MARIAN ELOISE LEDFORD, 1907 (m. Fred Beatty, 1938)
  Mary Ellen Beatty, 1944 (m. Hobart M. Corning III, 1967)
  James Burnam Beatty, 1954–1957

CURTIS BURNAM LEDFORD JR. (Bill), 1909–2001
        (m. Joan Enoch, 1934)
  Billy Jack Ledford, 1936 (m. Betty Von Fuller, 1961)
    Mark Bradley Ledford, 1962 (m. Christy Calvert, 1985)
      Micah Bradley Ledford, 2000
    Richard Alan Ledford, 1963 (m. Tarrie Roberts, 1989)
      Bradley Alan Ledford, 1993
      Annie Elizabeth Ledford, 1994
      Sadie Mitchell Ledford, 1995
      Holly Katherine Ledford, 1996
    Sarah Enoch Ledford, 1966 (m. Mike Curtis, 1997)
      Kylie Jo Curtis, 2002
    Jon Scott Ledford, 1970 (m. Ellen Whitley Jones, 1998)
      Ellen Scott Ledford, 2001
  Polly Ann Ledford, 1939 (m. Robert P. Hawkins, 1964)
    Todd Curtis Hawkins, 1971 (m. Amie Newell, 1998)
      Meghan Ann Hawkins, 2000
    Martha Ann Hawkins, 1973 (m. Bryan Manley, 1998)
  Sally Ray Ledford, 1944 (m. Jerry Scott Watkins, 1969)
    Brian Scott Watkins, 1971 (m. Tanya Marie Coleman, 1997)
      Nathan Scott Watkins, 1998

Isabelle Rose Watkins, 2002
Greg Thomas Watkins, 1972 (m. Angela Gayle Barrett, 2001)
John Garfield Ledford, 1948 (m. Josie Carmichael, 1970;
    m. Janet Marcusson, 1989)
John Garfield Ledford Jr., 1971 (m. Samantha Burney, 1997)
Davis Grey Ledford, 2000
Jessica Reeves Ledford, 1974 (m. Brian O'Neil, 2000)

EDWIN CARL LEDFORD, 1910–2001 (m. Geraldine Dutton, 1940)
Edwin Earl Ledford, 1940 (m. Jane Tibbals, 1962)
Joseph Allen Ledford, 1964 (m. Alanna Taulbee, 1990)
Katherine Elizabeth Ledford, 1990
Emily Anne Ledford, 1994
Deborah Kaye Ledford, 1967 (m. James Melton, 1986)
Erin Alexandria Melton, 1987
Sue Carolyn Ledford, 1942 (m. Joe B. Rudd, 1960)
Joseph Andrew Rudd, 1967
Richard Burnam Ledford, 1944 (m. Judy Warren, 1967)
Richard Bryan Ledford, 1968 (m. Cindy Jones, 1989)
Carl Richard Ledford, 1992
Anna Elizabeth Ledford, 1993
Laura Elizabeth Ledford, 1971 (m. David Dees, 1992;
    m. Darren Carpenter, 1997)
Logan Bruce Carpenter, 1999
Jerry Allen Ledford, 1945 (m. Brenda Kerr, 1966)
Lori Lynn Ledford, 1968 (m. George Savage, 1995)
Garrett William Savage, 1998
Tammy Sue Ledford, 1972 (m. C.J. Jackson, 2000)
Clay Charles Jackson, 2003
Greg Allen Ledford, 1975
Judy Lynn Ledford, 1947 (m. Owen Jones, 1983)
Becky Anne Ledford, 1948–1980 (m. Richard Eversman, 1977)
Melissa Anne Eversman, 1977
Michael Brent Ledford, 1949 (m. Jenny Lou Vanhook, 1971)
Michael Brent Ledford Jr., 1973
James David Ledford, 1976
Jennifer Suzanne Ledford, 1983
Charles Robert Ledford, 1951

David Arnold Ledford, 1953 (m. Cathy Dye, 1976;
    m. Nancy Combs, 1987)
  David Lawrence Ledford, 1976 (m. Laura Story, 1993;
    m. Melanie Hinkebein, 2000)
    Austin Tyler Ledford, 1993
    Jacob Aaron Ledford, 1994
    Jessica Nicole Ledford, 1996
  Latrisha Ellen Ledford, 1981 (m. Billy Knight, 2000)
    Kaley Madison Knight, 2000
    Joseph Lee Knapps, 2002–2002
Stephen Mark Ledford, 1958 (m. Patricia Moss, 1979)
  Jamie Renee Ledford, 1981 (m. Mark Holzheimer, 2002)
  Mark Edwin Ledford, 1984–2000
James Martin Ledford, 1959 (m. Robyn Burkett, 1980;
    m. Lisa Stamper, 1995)
  James Carl Ledford, 1981
  Christopher William Ledford, 1988

VESTA LUCILLE LEDFORD, 1912–1999 (m. Lee Bell, 1931;
    m. Harry Smith, 1939)
David Michael Smith, 1948 (m. Mary Emmitt, 1973)
  Amanda Emmitt Smith, 1975 (m. Matthew Ball, 1995)
    Hannah Christine Ball, 1998
    Elizabeth Anne Ball, 2000
  Sarah Ledford Smith, 1979

DOROTHY ELEANOR LEDFORD, 1914–2000 (m. Ed Siegel, 1939;
    m. Henry Jackson, 1962)

HERBERT RAYMOND LEDFORD, 1917 (m. Hazel Perkins, 1943)
  Jane Perkins Ledford, 1944 (m. Ronald L. Shelton, 1965)
  Alice King Ledford, 1946 (m. Robert S. Frields, 1969)
    Elaine Lynn Frields, 1970 (m. Kenneth Thomas, 1994)
      Grantham Alan Thomas, 1995
      Emma Katherine Thomas, 1998
    Stephen Matthew Frields, 1983
  Emily Ray Ledford, 1953 (m. Thomas B. Lawrence, 1977)
    Elizabeth Hensley Lawrence, 1984

Margaret Lee Lawrence, 1988
Sarah Robert Ledford, 1955 (m. Robert C. Byers, 1981)

BRUCE BARTON LEDFORD, 1919–1969 (m. Anita Wahle, 1939)
John Bruce Ledford, 1942 (m. Brenda Jane Brown, 1963)
John Bruce Ledford II, 1964 (m. Cheryl Henage, 1988)
John Eric Ledford, 1994
Leigh Ann Ledford, 1967 (m. William Collins, 1991)
Anna Nicole Collins, 1993
Rachel Britton Collins, 1998
Leah Grigsby Collins, 2000
Stephen Harold Ledford, 1969
Malinda Jane Ledford, 1971
Jessica Haley Ledford, 1996
Mary Helen Ledford, 1944 (m. Larry D. Casey, 1965)
Larry Dean Casey, 1967 (m. Delia Dodd, 1988)
Michael Shawn Casey, 1989
Karen Lynn Casey, 1968
Conlon Fitzgerald, 1995

MYRTLE LEDFORD, 1921–1921

JENNIE SLAVEN LEDFORD, 1922–1984 (m. Revis Mills, 1941;
m. Charles Thornberry, 1951; m. Morris Toomey, 1961;
m. Alexander McLendon Jr., 1972)
Bruce Burnam Mills, 1942
Nancy Mills, 1944 (m. Larry Allen, 1962)
Kimberly Lynn Allen, 1962
Arletta Mills, 1945 (m. Donald Bourne, 1964)
John Russell Bourne, 1969
Jennifer Bourne, 1977

MATILDA ELIZABETH LEDFORD, 1924–2001
(m. Lawrence Woods, 1943; m. Robert Hammon, 1948;
m. Charles King, 1970 and 1974)
Gary Allen Hammon [born Woods], 1945 (m. Phyllis Ann Kash, 1966)
Bryan Allen Hammon, 1967 (m. Tricia Alyse Teipel, 1994)
Josie Alyse Hammon, 1996

Lincoln Paul Hammon, 2000
Elizabeth Ann Hammon, 1981
Barbara Jo Hammon, 1949 (m. Michael Bryant, 1969;
        m. Jim Bombard, 1990)
Casey Bryant, 1975
Brandy Nicole Bryant, 1980
Tanner Ray Redmon, 2003

GEORGE KING LEDFORD, 1925–1925

GWENDOLYN LEDFORD, 1928 (m. Russell Gastineau, 1947)
  Carole King Gastineau, 1948–1988 (m. Paul W. Starnes, 1970)
    Benny Starnes, 1974–1974
    Denny Starnes, 1974–1974
    Steven Paul Starnes, 1976 (m. Ammie Anderson, 2002)
      Chalder Andrew Starnes, 2002
    Charles Russell Starnes, 1981
  David Allen Gastineau, 1950 (m. Brenda Renfro, 1970;
        m. Marilyn Neely, 1992)
    David Scott Gastineau, 1971 (m. Melissa Laxton, 1996;
        m. Gale Ingersoll, 2000)
      Lacy Nicole Gastineau, 1997
    Jason Keith Gastineau, 1974 (m. Melissa Whitlock, 1996)
      Haley Elizabeth Gastineau, 2000
  Richard Lynn Gastineau, 1953 (m. Adrienne Parson, 1972)
    Elizabeth Nicole Gastineau, 1974 (m. Larry Branch, 1996)
    Richard Micah Gastineau, 1981
  Rebecca Ann Gastineau, 1959 (m. David S. Hacker, 1980)
    Stephen Hacker, 1984
    Robert Hacker, 1989
    William Russell Hacker, 1997

DATE DUE
